Contents

Introduction	4
Safety	10
Grades	14
Tides	16
DWS Tactics	18
Glossary of Terms	22
The Flying Fish Top Ten	24
The Evolution of DWS	28
Advertiser Directory	30
Acknowledgments	31
Symbol and Topo Key	32
Venue Guide	33
Swanage	34
Lulworth	54
Portland	68
Devon	94
Cornwall	134
Pembroke	146
Scotland	188
Rest of the UK	202
Portugal	210
Costa Blanca	232
Mallorca	252
Rest of Europe	282
Australia	294
Rest of the World	306
Route Index	316
General Index	320

Gavin Symonds swinging out across the roof of *Cod Tympani* (7a+) - *page 107* - above Rainbow Bridge at Berry Head, Devon. Photo: Mike Robertson.

Introduction

Conner Cove, 1992: what a place! I had the audacity - me, an E2 climber - to attempt the glorious E4 line of *Freeborn Man*, today perhaps one of the best-known solos in the deep water solo world. I battled up that steep, pocketed mid-section, got through that stretchy crux undercut move by sheer good fortune and willpower, did that funky wild traverse left, dead pumped now, then promptly got shut down on that funny little rock-over move, to gain the upper slab. Damn it! And as I plummeted towards the sea, I thought of the folk who'd been there before me, all falling in much the same way. Because that's the thing, once off the rock, we're all the same, and grades are irrelevant, we're merely airborne, we're adrift and heading down towards the subterranean green room, the place of bubbles, and of silence. And we all get wet in much the same way.

Time marches on. It's now 2007, and this guide is so very close to being finished. I went back to do *Freeborn Man* after that first fall, and I've now done it more times than I can admit to. But it's still the same, every time, that vital stretch for the open undercut, the

Maximum effort!
Jason Porter at Cave Hole, Portland.
Photo: Mike Robertson

gripping span left for the big pocket, the final wild step-up to gain the easy top slab. It's just divine, and those moves still inspire me to travel the world in search of more, and more. Since then, deep water soloing (DWS) has taken me to every corner of the UK, to the islands and obscure coastlines of Europe; even to Asia and Tasmania. It's been a journey of unimaginable contrast and beauty, and this guide is a product of that experience.

You have in your hands the ticket to so many places I didn't have when I began: the historical DWS crags of Dorset, the wild traverses of Devon, the craglets of Cornwall, the crazy, mammoth tidal venue of Pembroke. Even North Wales and Scotland are introduced here - madcap places indeed! In the rest of Europe we have the stunning cliffs of Mallorca, the absolute serenity of Portugal's Sagres, and the sunny stretches of the Costa Blanca. Add to this Asia and Australia, and all those endless possibilities; barely-developed islands, projects and suchlike ... and, quite frankly, I really do think you need to get out more ... and so do I.

So here it is: Deep Water. DWS, as it stands right now. The shifting currents of life are ever-changing, and who knows where we'll end up tomorrow: I can only hope that this guide will inspire you to go and find more, and to never stop exploring. DWS is the purest form of climbing known to man: take a hold and see if it grabs you. And let me know how you get on.

Mike Robertson, Wareham, Dorset, April 2007
www.wildartproductions.com

Leah Crane on the finishing moves of the classic *Freeborn Man* (6c) - *page 49* - at Conner Cove, Swanage. Photo: Mike Robertson.

Introduction

The Guidebook

Rockfax publish full colour guidebooks to UK and international climbing areas. This is our 25th guidebook and the first that covers deep water soloing venues in the UK and beyond. Rockfax utilise state of the art publishing techniques and are dedicated to presenting essential climbing information in a clear, easily understood and attractive format, that both informs and inspires.

This book presented a unique set of challenges, not least the immense task of collecting sea cliff photographs. Usually crag shots are relatively straightforward to take. As you can imagine, a salty, wet and sometimes stormy approach is not straightforward. The author Mike Robertson is not only a world authority on DWS but is an enthusiastic sea kayaker and with his highly sensitive and expensive camera equipment in a dry bag, he had many adventures taking the crag shots that illustrate this book.

Watch it! Mad Max on *Reel 'Em In* (6b+) - *page 85* - Cave Hole, Portland. Photo: Mike Robertson

There is one new Rockfax symbol, Atlantis man, you'll have to follow him after your spashdown to regain terra firma. Another first for this guidebook is the sport grade combined with the DWS adjectival grade: *S0, S1, S2, S3*.

As is now standard in all Rockfax guidebooks, great care and effort is taken in selecting inspiring action photographs. We hope you enjoy them.

Web Sites

For further information on DWS exploration worldwide, go to **www.DWSworld.com** (see page 15). Daimon Beail, who's been spending time off Mallorca's south-east coastline, has been branching out and giving his website a global spread, so expect a lot of worldwide projects and information, as well as a kind of DWS hang, where folk can drop tips and pick up a little guidance and knowledge. There are future plans for information on Croatia, Summersville Lake - USA, Squamish - Canada, and Malta. The Rockfax website too will have a section dedicated to deep water soloing information - **www.rockfax.com**.

Klem Loskot on *In The Night, Every Cat Is Black* (8a) - page 264 - Cova del Diablo, Mallorca. Photo: Mike Robertson

This is the hardest of the lot. Mallorca's Es Pontas arch: the scene of Chris Sharma's mega-route, which took the U.S. strong-man a total of four visits and some 80 attempts. The crux is an overhanging 2.2m dyno, and this desperate move alone saw 50 splash-downs. This lower crux, coupled with the difficulty of the upper section, gives the line first prize in the 'most-fallen-from new DWS route! Sharma has declined to grade it, but, in view of his similar efforts on Realization in France, the grade appears to be around 9a/9a+. Sharma is a true convert: "Since I started deep-water soloing," Sharma said, "I've wanted to find something that's at my limit - that's really a project ... I wanted to find something comparable to Realization, taking it to the highest level possible."
Photo: Corey Rich/Aurora Photos

Safety

Like all forms of climbing, there are general guidelines for deep water soloists that govern how you go about things when at the crag. The following pointers are advice/good practice - adherence to these ought to keep you safe and sound, but always use your own judgement!

Tides
WARNING: checking tides and depths is the most important safety aspect of DWS. Crag tide requirements are covered extensively on page 16 and are a factor that should never be ignored. Realising this fact will also save you time, petrol and much angst.
Make a point of getting the tides on your side, especially at venues such as Pembroke, Cave Hole and Devon. Remember at these venues that the S grades will tie into the correct tide levels, and ignoring this WILL leave you short of water.

Height and Depth
The higher you get, the more risk you'll be taking; and the shallower the water, the more risk you'll be taking. So get used to DWS by way of S0, and not S2 or S3! Get your solo head on by doing plenty of mileage on the classic S0 and S1 routes, and do a little jumping practice, too. Check page 14 for more about S grades.

Currents and Rough Seas
The ideal soloist's day will include a calm sea, with no currents or swells. But life's not that straightforward, and you will find yourself climbing above a bit of roughness from time to time. So, to increase your safety, stay within sight of your pals, remember your own swimming limitations, and ALWAYS plan your exit in advance. Bear in mind that exiting onto boulder beaches or reefs can be much more difficult in heavy seas, and always take into account the possibility of currents, particularly around headlands and promontories. Remember that a hanging rope can be a life saver, as can a pal who can throw one.

Reefs and Boulders
Sub-surface boulders and reefs are never an exact science (they've been known to shift around in the winter) and my efforts to reveal them in this guide are bound to be flawed, despite my best attempts. So know your depth before you set off, and always swim your landing zone if you are unsure.

Water Temperature
Here's a working example: the sea temperature in Dorset is around 9°C in early April, thereafter building through the summer to around 19°C in early September. So it doesn't take a genius to work out that late season is going be the best time to work that project ground-up. The same annual temperature change timing applies to the Mediterranean, albeit with slightly higher temperatures overall. Remember that cold water saps your strength very quickly, as well as interfering with your breathing.

Guidebook Footnote
The inclusion of a climbing area in this guidebook does not mean that you have a right of access or the right to climb upon it. The descriptions of routes within this guide are recorded for historical reasons only and no reliance should be placed on the accuracy of the description. The grades set in this guide are a fair assessment of the difficulty of the climbs. Climbers who attempt a route of a particular standard should use their own judgment as to whether they are proficient enough to tackle that route. This book is not a substitute for experience and proper judgment. The authors, publisher and distributors of this book do not recognise any liability for injury or damage caused to, or by, climbers, third parties, or property arising from such persons seeking reliance on this guidebook as an assurance for their own safety.

Cheap and portable 'kiddy boats' also help you get to the base of the routes in many venues. Photo: Mike Robertson

Swimming Ability
Deep water soloists who are strong swimmers tend to be the most confident with falls and exits. So hone your swimming skills if you fall into the category of 'nervous around water'.

Floats and Boats
These can be utilised for situations where you may be unsure about currents, or maybe your (or someone else's) swimming strength. Manned boat use is self-explanatory - less obvious is the concept of a rope dangling down into the water, with an inflatable boat or a rubber ring attached to it. This could also be thrown with a rope, in the same manner as the classic seaside rescue rings.

Abseiling into the Route
This generally presents a relatively safe situation - you'll usually be above water (see page 18 for info on the quick-release tape harness arrangement). It's also worth remembering that jumars are regularly used by deep water soloists - it's a great way to clean and investigate routes, and will give you the option of climbing back up the rope if you have a change of heart, or if you find the sea state to be too spicy. But always remember that it is worth practising the art before you need to do it! Also bear in mind that on steep crags, clipping bolts or threads or runners will often facilitate reaching that start ledge!

Topping Out
Top-outs can vary from a solid crag top at 10m, to a pre-placed rope finish on looser ground, to a 'climb to a small cave and jump' scenario. The best advice is to know exactly what you're getting into before you set off and make adequate preparation if it is needed.

Don't go Solo!
This is important. Although many confident soloists do solo 'solo' (as it were) from time to time, I'd recommend that you stay within earshot or sight of a mate. If you did pull a hold and fall badly, the sight of your pal jumping in to sort you out would be a very welcome one indeed.

Safety

Splashdowns

Regular - A normal splashdown into deep water is well-illustrated in the sequence to the right. The climber stays loose just about all the way down, then assumes a good entry position in the last few metres of the fall (or jump). This initial 'looseness' of the body is important, as it prevents that 'tightening' of the body, which so often results in an off-kilter landing. So stay relaxed and wriggling almost all the way to the water! It's also worth remembering that 'wheeling' your outstretched arms in small circles provides a way of rotating the body forwards or backwards whilst in the air (just try it whilst sitting down).

Upon entry, keep your arms tightly in, and your head upright (don't look down during entry, you'll get a face-full). And don't forget to shut your legs! Enemas are unpleasant and rather messy.

Tim Emmett demonstrates the art of the entry, on *For Those About To Rock* (6c+) Spiderman Wall, Thailand. Photo: Grant Farquhar

Armchair landing

- An armchair landing is used to limit deep entry, and is used solely for a shallow splashdown - it's not suitable for long and much faster falls. In the water, your body position assumes the posture of someone sitting in an armchair, but this position is ONLY assumed on point of first contact with the water's surface; a backwards-revolving motion at the very last moment. 'Feet in, lean back'. This revolving motion will allow falls into 1.5m of water from 9m up - I've done this in the past without injury. When you perform this landing, bear in mind that, unlike the normal entry, you'll use your arms. Stick them out: they will further decrease your velocity towards the sea floor.

When it goes slightly awry! Matt Ward off the same route. Photo: Grant Farquhar

'S' Grades

Devised over one (or three) pints of Ringwood Best by the Dorset crew in 1995, and (considering its beginnings) has stood the test of time admirably. The simple S Grade consists of a 0, 1, 2 or 3. S0 gives relative safety, with S3 offering considerable possibility of injury in the event of a fall.

S0	Safe at most tides, not particularly high crux moves. Avoid bottling out of an S0 if possible. These are essentially safe, so climb until you fall. Commitment normally pays off!
S1	Care required; either the tide or the water depth needs checking, or maybe there is a high-ish crux on the route. Remember that, in big tide venues, a huge tide and good timing can turn an S1 into an S0.
S2	A little more care than S1 required. Possibly spring-tide only (higher water levels). Check your tide timetable carefully. 'Landings' can be more significant - maybe a crash landing into shallow-ish water required, or a slight 'push' to clear rock or a slight slab/reef below. Likely to have a high crux.
S3	Expect the water to be either too shallow, or too far away! You can't really afford to fall off an S3 without a large measure of control or timing. Failure on the route might require a full body length crash landing into the deepest water available, or a long and scary downward flight. If you're operating in a tidal venue, wait for the biggest high tide possible.

Sport Grades - why?

The mixing of various grades in the UK has always caused a high level of confusion, and with good reason. The Brits seem obsessed with making things as complicated as possible! This is especially true in the game of deep water soloing, where historically we've used a combination of three grading systems. These are:

Extremely Severe 'XS' grades - These were often used for deep water solos with many references in the 1996 Climbers' Club Dorset DWS Guide. The XS grade prefixed the hardest English technical move. The problem with the XS grade is that it doesn't tell you how sustained the climbing is; it only tells of how hard the hardest move is.

English grades - (As in E4 6a). These weren't so bad for DWS, but the problem was the 'E' bit of the grade, which all too often denoted the danger element, due to the lack of available wire protection. A further difficulty was that you don't drag a full climbing rack up a deep water solo! A deep water solo just doesn't need this 'E' grade (we thankfully don't have to fumble endlessly with wires), which was why more and more new routes were being put up using the Sport, or 'French' grade.

Sport/French grades - Adopted wholeheartedly for this guide, and universally understood - the World's favourite grade. The sport grade was initially used in DWS for areas such as Dorset's Stair Hole, where the routes were put up as sport routes, then later soloed. The grade quickly picked up momentum within the grading of new DWS routes, especially at venues such as Mallorca's pumpy Diablo. This grade gives an overall impression of difficulty, and fits the DWS genre almost perfectly, although it's not quite as fitting for boulder-problem solos.

For more on grading systems - **www.rockfax.com**

Tides

Picnic under the Big Easy Face, Cave Hole, Portland. This picture was taken at the lowest tide level of 2006. See page 85 for more 'normal' conditions!

Throughout one lunar month there are two spring or high range tides, and two neap or low range tides. Spring tides occur during the 'full' and 'new' moons, when the sun and the moon are in line and the combined gravitational pull causes the highest tides, which then ebb to the lowest level. During the first and third quarters of the moon (found in most diaries), when the sun's and moon's attractional forces are at right angles, we experience the lower neap high tides, along with the higher low tide levels.

Here's how it all relates to the deep water soloist:

> The majority of the routes in this guide are best enjoyed at high tide, but it's important to understand the tide levels concerned. Sometimes too much water can affect your approach to the route, especially if the sea is a little rough. The lower sections of traverses can particularly be affected by water levels.

> Venues with big tide variations, or 'swings' (such as Pembroke) will need extra savvy and knowledge, so always buy a tide timetable before you visit. Areas in the rest of Europe and the Mediterranean are almost unaffected by tides.

> The high spring tides ALWAYS fall early or late in the day (don't ask me why!) So, if you need a decent spring tide, you'll be climbing your chosen route before 10am, or after 6.00pm. To clarify this: you will get high tides at midday, but they'll ALWAYS be the smaller, neap high tides.

> If that neap tide is sufficient for you (ie. at Conner Cove, or Lulworth Cove), that's a HUGE bonus - this means you can climb at a more civilised, midday hour!

Tides

Swanage	The tides are usually unimportant here. Dorset's average tidal swing is about 1.7m, and the water is so silly-deep that an average neap tide is probably your best bet. An afternoon high tide would be about ideal.
Lulworth	Absolute neap tide territory. Neap tides will give plenty of water to climb just about all the routes, and all of the time. The extra bonus: all those low-level traverses at Lulworth are accessible with neaps: most definitely not with springs.
Portland	Big swingers required! Portland has the same average Dorset swing of 1.7m or so, but you'll need to pick some hefty spring tides to tackle most of the routes safely, as the water depth is crucial here. This means climbing early and late. A morning spring tide gives you the best conditions for the east-facing Cave Hole.
Devon	Devon's 'swings' can be as big as 5m, so if your priority is climbing those lengthy traverses, a neap tide will suit you better, giving an even spread of water. For the up-routes, you'd be better timing a spring-like tide with sunshine on the crag. Now that's a challenge.
Cornwall	Nare Head has plenty of water, so don't worry too much about your precise timing, although a high-ish tide would be ideal. Access is generally pretty much the same whatever the level. Take a good high tide for all routes on the Lizard.
Pembroke	A tough one. Pembroke's tidal swings are vast (up to 8m) so timing is EVERYTHING! A high-ish tide is a good idea for a lot of Pembroke, but remember that lower access ledges during massive tides can be greatly restrictive, especially at venues in the Penally region. For the taller venues, such as Stennis Ford and Blind Bay, take a big spring tide. North Pembroke's Barrel Zawn is a perfect neap tide venue, so you can loiter there all day with your sandwiches.
Vivian Quarry	Consider this venue fully tide-free! The only UK fresh water venue.
Mediterranean	The Med's tide swings are usually less than 0.5m, and Portugal's aren't much bigger. Consider these venues as pretty much non-tidal.
South-East Asia	The Andaman and South China seas have a tide much like Dorset's in size.
Tasmania	Considering Tasmania's global position on the very edge of everything, the tides are amazingly minuscule; expect a maximum of less than 1m, much like Portugal.

> Don't assume that big tides are always good news. BIG ALSO MEANS LOW! Let me reiterate: big tides swing very low! For example, a high spring tide in Dorset will mean insufficient water to climb at Lulworth Cove at midday.

> Remember that spring tides always generate stronger ocean currents.

> If you arrive at your chosen venue and find yourself unsure as to which way the tide is going, choose a 'marker', such as a horizontal crack. 20 minutes later, the tide's progress should become obvious. This method is also used when you've made a decision about the minimum level for that venue - simply choose a 'marker' that reflects this ideal minimum level, and refer to it on future visits.

> High tides, regardless of their actual level, occur roughly every 12 hours and 20 minutes. This means that an 8am high tide on a Saturday morning will give approximately a 8.40am high tide on the Sunday morning etc, etc.

> Tide times for all UK coastal areas are available on **www.bbc.co.uk/coast/tides/**. Tide timetables are often available close to your chosen crag - check out Post Offices, fishing tackle shops and diving centres.

DWS Tactics

Tape Harness Arrangement

Highly useful on abseil-in routes, it's both light and quick, and with a little practise, it'll be possible to arrive at any decent hold, even a small crimp, and get off the rope quickly. Use a 2.4m (8ft) sling to give you the (very) basic harness (see photo right) and arrange a big pear karabiner/grigri so that it's possible to lose 2 loops of the 'harness' swiftly. After abseiling, simply pop those loops (it can be set up to favour a start hold for either hand, if required) and let the whole thing go. Use of a 'clean nose' notch-less karabiner will greatly facilitate detachment of the tape itself, which is by necessity a one-handed task. If possible, abseil into your chosen route slightly 'off line', which means that you can throw the rope away from the route once you've let it go (or ask your mate to do that job for you).

Tape harness

Photos: Mike Robertson

Bench Seat Arrangement

A belay seat/chill-out zone, from where you might contemplate your fate ... especially useful for times when you are pushing your limit, and feel the need for a little comfort prior to your ascent. Take a plank of wood (or plastic), drilled both ends, and fit a triangular rope cradle. Make it wide enough to get comfortable on, and use double holes at either end - this makes it more stable. The rope cradle should be tall enough to allow you room to sit 'within' it. Simply abseil down to the seat, get your harness off, and chill on the seat before departure. It's a bonus to have someone to pull the seat up when you've got on the rock - it's not a good thing to hit, should you take a fall! The down-side is that the seat arrangement, whilst great in actual use, is quite bulky to lug around.

Wet Suits

The use of wetsuits in DWS is still not especially widespread, and for good reason - it does tend to inhibit your movement, and also smacks of non-commitment! The real bonus in wearing a suit is probably that, when you are climbing something highball, you are less likely to be injured in the event of a fall. A wet suit can also be useful when you're taking repeated falls in early season off a

Bench seat

project. The knowledge on wet suits is that you'll need a full-stretch version for climbing. Salomon make exceptionally elastic wet suits in 2mm, and these (or something similar - 3mm maximum) are the business, allowing good limb movement and not 'cooking' you prior to your ascent!

Chalk Bag Elastic

A simple idea, but an improvement over the usual chalk bag string. To replace your normal chalkbag waist cord, buy a length of 6mm shock cord from a boat suppliers' (chandlery) and tie it permanently into your chalkbag. This makes taking your chalk bag on and off much easier, and avoids that maddening moment on a dry-bag ledge, when you find yourself dropping your chalkbag into a puddle whilst tying your knot.

Ken Palmer making full use of the good holds on *Octopuss Weed* (6c) - *page 92* - at Cave Hole, Portland. Photo: Mike Robertson.

Chalk Bag and Boots Advice

As a general rule, you need to carry enough boots and chalk bags for your day's climbing, and in the event of all your gear getting doused at some point, you need to consider a means of getting it all dry enough for the next day! Hot summer days present less of a problem (set up a clothes line!) but extra chalk bags are always recommended, as these, unlike boots, really do have to be completely dry before further use. Bear in mind that, after a dousing, chalk bags should be completely flushed through BEFORE exiting the water! This clears the bag of all chalk residue, as this wet chalk will never dry off properly, and makes your chalk bag somewhat slimy and uninviting for its next excursion.

Further tips include tying your gear to the car when travelling between venues (or trap it in the window) and remember to climb with less than a full bag of chalk, especially if you're expecting to fall in!

For a trip to Portugal, I took 3 pairs of boots and 5 chalk bags - this amount, combined with good sunny weather, meant I never ran out of usable gear.

Dry-baggin' at Ponta Garcia: Neil Gresham in action. Photo: Mike Robertson

Dry-bags

A dry bag is a fold-top waterproof bag that can be used to keep your gear dry. Here's a run-down on dry-bag uses and possibilities:

> **Fold-top dry-bags** are available in both lightweight and heavyweight options. Use the heavy-duty ones for multiple excursions and boat trips, and use the lighter variety for climbing with (avoid barnacles with this type). For the lightest dry-bags on the market, try the super-light products made by Swiss manufacturers Exped - www.exped.com - will give the relevant details on where they're available. Try the 8 or 13 litre variety for clipping to your chalk bag elastic.

> **Dry-bag rucksacks** are a brilliant idea and these lend themselves beautifully to the intrepid soloist, especially when embarking on boat jaunts and getting dropped off in outlandish places - you'll be able to swim around/in with your day's requirements on your back!

> **Lightweight dry-bags** are useful for the growing number of routes which terminate on ledges and terraces, and are finished off with a jump into the water. This can now be achieved without soaking your boots and chalkbag (and even your clothes). Climb with your dry-bag clipped around your chalk bag elastic, and when the route is over, pack your boots/chalkbag/clothes into it. Throw it into the water and jump in after it!

There is only one...

Awesome Walls Climbing Centre
Liverpool

www.awesomewalls.co.uk

St Albans Church, Athol Street, Liverpool, L5 9XT. Tel 0151 298 2422

Glossary of Terms

Armchair landing (page 12) - A controlled landing used to limit deep entry, and used solely for a shallow splashdown.

Barnacle line - That crunchy, barnacle-built piece of crag that is sometimes encountered on low-level traverses, especially in big tide areas such as Devon and Pembroke. Weight your feet gently!

Bench seat arrangement (page 18) - A hanging wooden seat, from which your chosen route is tackled. Most often replaced with the excellent tape harness arrangement these days, but still useful, esp. in-situations when you feel the need to chill and get your thoughts together.

Chalking stick - Not often used: a long stick with a sponge or similar on the tip, which is used to chalk holds prior to your attempt. Stair Hole's diminutive inner West Cave is a good example of a venue where this is handy.

Diablo - A fabled place: a close-to-perfect crag. Rumoured to already exist in Mallorca; some folk believe there might be another 'Diablo' out there.

Dry-bag (page 20) - A dry-bag is a lightweight fold-top bag that keeps your gear dry during a swim, or when kicking about in the bottom of your boat. The expression 'swim in with your dry-bag' denotes taking along your boots, chalkbag, clothes and a small towel.

Dry-bag ledge - A start ledge for your chosen route, gained by swimming in with your dry-bag. This ledge might be affected by the tide level or rough seas.

Early breakfast venue - Cave Hole is a prime example; morning sun, and with a good early spring tide a necessity. You'll need to get some early grub down ya' and get on with the climbing.

Exit - Your method of escaping the water after a fall. Mostly refers to a swim to an easy exit, but can sometimes be an escape by way of a pre-placed rope on steeper ground (often knotted).

High water mark - Usually abbreviated to 'HWM'. This is the usual scoured mark on the cliff that indicates the approximate level/height of the average high tide at that crag.

Kiddy boat (page 11) - Any small inflatable craft that will suffice for fun/viewing/your journey to the route of your choice. Usually less than £30 including paddles, and most often bought by a team upon arrival at their chosen foreign destination. Usually quite useless, and regularly overmanned/half-sunk/thoroughly wet inside.

Piscodbloc - The original Welsh term for deep water soloing; sometimes misspelt as 'Psicobloc'.

Tape harness setup (page 18) - This is an arrangement that gives you the chance to abseil in on a rope and get off it very quickly and easily, and all without using to a climbing harness.

'S' Grade system (page 14) - This was devised in a Dorset pub in 1995, and has stood the test of time admirably! A grading system of 0, 1, 2, 3: S0 provides the soloist relative safety, with S3 offering considerable possibility of injury in the event of a fall.

Splashdown (page 12) - This is what happens when you fail to reach the top! Seen by some as failure, and others as fun.

Steep and juggy. Silvia Fitzpatrick on the brilliant *Circus Dog* (6b) - *page 246* - Cave of Pets, Cala del Moraig. Photo: Mike Robertson

The Flying Fish Top Ten

Bit of fun this, so don't take it too seriously (especially if you didn't quite make it onto the list). With much heart-searching and thought, I've come up with a top ten listing of deep water soloists. The list takes into account these three basic qualifications:
> Long-term DWS track record, including foreign trips.
> Numerous splashdowns mandatory.
> Enthusiasm for DWS surpasses all other forms of climbing.

So - do you qualify? The track record takes some time, the often-burly grades mean a certain strength, but bear in mind: it's not just the grade and the history - it's the getting wet that counts, as well. Without literally dozens of arse-to-the-wind, on-sight splashdowns, you're just not on the list. Do you get the picture? Ok, so here we go:

1. The Wadfather

Once referred to in the British climbing press as one of the UK's great visionaries, the highly adventurous, often madcap **Crispin Waddy** has a DWS history no other mortal can equal. From his early first ascents at Conner Cove in the mid-eighties to his wanderings all over the south-west, Wales and Europe. There's been many a globe-trotting soloist who's climbed a new route - to be later told "ah, yeah, I think Crispin's probably done that one already". Never the outspoken self-publicist, the legendary, quietly-spoken Waddy paved the way for the rest of us loud, crowing types! His new routes are many and diverse; particular mention is due to the brilliant *Fathoms* (6b) at Conner Cove (way back in 1986), the incredible *One-Eyed Man* (7a), at Pembroke's Blind Bay, and the first solo ascent of Devon's stunning 12-pitch *Rainbow Bridge* (7a+).

2. The Linesman

International off-shore rigger **Julian Lines** is a veritable seal. He's almost at home in the water as he is on land. Veteran of hundreds of new and established DWS's both here and abroad, he's the textbook deep water soloist - steely, handsome, and full of boisterous charm (women have been known to fall softly at his feet). After some crazy years soloing the Aberdeen sea cliffs above chilling, glacial seas, he's recently put highball DWS's at Pembroke to the top of his substantial list. Hits include the first ascent of the amazing *Abyss* (7b) at Mother Carey's. After numerous trips to the DWS hotspots of Europe and beyond, his plans for the future include the 'Linesman Manual' - the working title of his forthcoming book on solos around the world. Just don't ask him about walking around Rio De Janeiro with 25 thousand dollars in cash in his back pocket - that's a secret.

3. Those Cook Bros

Now these guys have been around since way back, before it got really notorious. Witness the **Cook brothers'** explosion onto the DWS scene back in 1992, when they both shaped the genre and kicked it into the next generation's laps. Tall man **Joff** gave us *Captain Blood's Cavern* (6c+) at Conner Cove and first solo ascents of sport routes such as the brilliant *Gates of Greyskull* (7b+) down at Stair Hole. The slightly younger **Damian** provided us with classics such as *Octopussweed* (6c) at Portland's emerging Cave Hole, and *Leap of Faith* (6b+) at Conner. The third of the brothers (there were actually eight) even jumped the Swanage cliffs with a car-cover parachute - that'd be **Dominic**, the wackiest of the lot. Between 'em, they've fallen in zillions of times - and that's what counts; commitment at its best. They are the original water babies!

4. Kenny Palmer

Ah, that cuddly Devonian **Ken Palmer**. What a chap! Acres of new solos all over Devon, more falls into the sea than hot dinners, and with a mad hairdo to match. Most often seen cruisin' along the brilliant traverse of *Rainbow Bridge*, and usually before breakfast. His harder DWS ascents include *Christine* (8a) down at Devon's Long Quarry Point, the ultra-steep *Hairbear* (7c) in Mallorca - and 'that' *Barrel Traverse* extension of *Rainbow Bridge*'s crux pitch, which has yet to receive an on-sight; what grade is that, really?!

5. The Muppet Show

Oft-described as a walking one-man show, boy **Timmy Emmett** generally has his fingers in at least one pie too many - although, for this man, the concept of a 'pie too many' could be lost. He's been responsible for audacious solos all over the UK, including Pembroke's mean *Hunter Killer* (7b) and the first ascent of *Jaws* (8a). As well as scores of DWS's all over the world, he's proved adept at the great game of base jumping, clocking up 50 jumps in his first year (that's about 5 lifetimes' of adrenalin, to us mere mortals). The curly hair has now been updated, the venues never stay the same, but for this tinker, the stakes are always gonna be raised. He's the ultimate junkie, and the prize is sweet life itself.

6. Gav Symonds

Local legend tells of a blowhole-dwelling, be-muscled beast that inhabits the remote edges of the craglets of the southern shoreline. There are some that have witnessed it and lived to tell the tale, and they speak of devilish screams and mind-bending powers of levitation. Whatever the truth about the legend, it's worth noting that Dorsetian **Gavin Symonds** is more often than not in the vicinity during sightings of said beast. Cool-as-you-like ascents of classics such as *Mark of the Beast* (7c) and new grabs such as the desperate *Thieving Gypsy* (7b+) at Stair Hole pay credence to the fellow, but don't ask him about that day he 'touched down' on the *Hermann Borg* slab at Conner Cove … oops!

7. Neil Gresham

Globe-trotter **Neil Gresham** is one of those rare commodities - described once by a fledgling journalist as the 'complete man', he's gotta be close to that. Winter stuff, hard trad ascents, sport routes and bouldering. But what concerns us here is DWS, and he's right on the money, with the first ground-up ascent of a new 8a solo *The Wizard* in Pembroke and numerous new lines all over the world, including Spain, Portugal and Vietnam. He's even turned into a fine DWS cataloguer and photographer! From his first splashdown at Conner Cove in the summer of 1997, he's come a long way - and shows no sign of hanging up his chalk bags yet.

8. Ladies from up North

All those DWS trips to venues as far away as Mallorca and Portugal have shown who really cares about the genre, and the ever-cheerful team of **Ruth Taylor** and **Elinor Currey** have shown their considerable mettle, with a concerted effort to travel and to repeat the test-pieces of the south coast and beyond. They are the ready smile at the crag, they often carry out the wettest clothing (yep, proper committed water babies) and they even manage to keep a steady check on the dubious, hideously unfashionable outfits of the Linesman and the author (no mean feat). We luv 'em!

9. The Pickford Files

A first meeting with **Dave Pickford** leaves you gasping for brain cells, as he both educates and baffles with his all-encompassing knowledge (I once became convinced he had a babel fish in both ears). But under that scholarly exterior lies a DWS heart of gold, and a generous nature to boot. Dave's exploits in the world of DWS are manifest, with 'nipping in' repeats of hundreds of routes all over the south coast and beyond. Last seen looking for his glasses somewhere underneath *Mark of the Beast*.

10. World Class

DWS has officially taken off. Witness the participation of some of the world's best, including our very own **Steve McClure**, and U.S. convert **Chris Sharma**. Steve has been rapidly turning into a mean repeat machine, with fast ascents of just about every classic solo in the southwest, and has even been spotted falling off a project in Pembroke's Breakfast Zawn - watch this space! Whilst Chris spent a few months in 2006 trying a radical new line at Mallorca's amazing outcrop of Es Pontas, finally succeeding after a zillion or so splashdowns. The grade? Don't ask, as he's neglected to grade it - but expect something around the 9a+ mark (see photo on page 8). As for Austrian **Klem Loskot** - you'd think a man once known for the world's first V14 might lack stamina - but you'd better think again. That boy has both the guns and the desire, with first ascents of such test-pieces as *Loskot and Two Smoking Barrels* (8a+) in Mallorca.

... and last but not least ...

There was once this scruffy bloke that used to cycle and play table tennis. Then, one day in 1990, he watched a documentary of Catherine Destivelle soloing, high up on the sandstone cliffs in Mali. The scruffy bloke was inspired, and decided to give it a bash. His name was **Mikey Robertson**, and little did he know that what he was about to try would change his life for ever. He's still scruffy, he does a bit of writing and photography these days, and he asked me to tell you that his favourite new route is *Crab Party* (6c), at Cave Hole.

Climbing, Walking and Camping Equipment.

Joff Cook on Water Wings (7a+). Photo: Mike Robertson.
See page 71 to discover what happened next

**01929 550882
outdoorsl.co.uk**

North Street, Wareham, Dorset, BH20 4AB

The Evolution of DWS

The evolution of DWS, or, simply, how it all started. Make no mistake: this great game came to be for a reason, and it wasn't because of lack of equipment or money, nor was it because of some sort of lofty moral high ground. I'll stick my neck out here: DWS came to be because it's the purest form of climbing. Let me clarify this: I mean climbing as in fingertips-on-rock, as in aesthetics of movement, as in un-encumbered, as in FREE.

You won't get the same feeling from dragging a full rack and two ropes up a classic trad pitch, and you won't find the same experience on a hard sport route, with a harness and rope always to hand. Even conventional free soloing, with all its thrilling but ultimately too-serious dangers, must play second best to the sheer joy of hanging above the ocean on a glorious summers' day.

So now we've established why we do it. Next is the when, that crazy slice of history, the gradual creeping and intermingling of disciplines. Short trad routes are perfect for DWS, and so are small, steep sport routes.

Once a sport route... Damian Cook ignoring the bolts on the brilliant *Mark of the Beast* (7c) - *page 67* - Lulworth Cove. Photo: Joff Cook

Take a look at the history of Lulworth Cove in Dorset - from a steep sport crag in the early nineties, to one of the UK's top DWS crags - and all in the space of some eight years. These days, a rope in sight is an exception! And you need look no further than Dorset's Conner Cove to see the absolute invasion of DWS on some of the UK's traditional sea cliffs. There's natural protection in good supply on Conner Cove's routes, but we made a simple choice back in the late eighties, and finally left our ropes in the car.

The final touch is the development of DWS cliffs all over the UK and Europe, and rope-free from the very start. This is the future for DWS - take a look at this guide's section on Mallorca's stunning Diablo to see the genre at its cutting-edge finest. 2001 saw climbers working projects at Diablo ground-up, content to fall, drying off, and going again. This is the last word on the development of DWS, and what makes this great game so very special.

The S3 game

Final mention here must go to the S3 grade. This constitutes the deep water soloist's upper limit, that grey area. S3 is the very edge of the S grade scale, and takes us gradually closer to other places, those more serious disciplines. S3 is most often too shallow or too tall, and provides the dedicated DWS addict with something just a little more heady. The picture opposite shows the author on *Rocket USA*, down at Swanage's Smokey Hole. The route was originally an E6 6b trad route, and it constitutes around E8 6b for the solo: yet another crazy twist on the DWS theme.

Neil Gresham on Pembroke's *The Wizard* (8a) - *page 186*. The route was first climbed ground-up, with some 10 splashdowns before success – this makes it the UK's first 8a done ground-up as a new DWS route. Photo: Mike Robertson

The biggest fright of the lot: Mike Robertson on the big *Rocket USA* (E8 6b) - *page 41* - Smokey Hole, Swanage. Photo: Steve Taylor

Advertiser Directory

Rockfax is very grateful to the following companies who have supported this guidebook.

Accommodation

Vernon Lodge - Page 39
Swanage
Tel/Fax: 01929 423880
www.vernon-lodge.co.uk

Tom's Field Road - Page 39
Langton Matravers, Swanage
Tel: 01929 427110
www.tomsfieldcamping.co.uk

Weymouth Campsites - Page 59
Sea Barn Campsite. Tel: 01305 782218
www.seabarnfarm.co.uk
West Fleet Holiday Farm. Tel: 01305 782218
www.westfleetholidays.co.uk
Bagwell Farm Touring Park. Tel: 01305 782575
www.bagwellfarm.co.uk

Accommodation and Courses

Orange House - Page 235
Tel: 00 34 965 87 82 51
www.theorangehouse.net

Hort de Gloria (Aqua Ventura) - Page 235
Tel: 00 34 965 87 90 00
www.aqua-ventura.com

Gear Shops

Rock On - Page 2
Mile End and Craggy Island - in London
Tel: (ME) 0208 981 5066 (CI) 01483 565635
www.rockonclimbing.co.uk

PlanetFear - Inside Front Cover
John Street, Sheffield
Tel: 0114 276 3944
www.planetfear.com

Outdoor SL - Page 27
Wareham, Dorset
Tel: 01929 550882
www.outdoorsl.co.uk

Foracorda - Page 257
Palma, Mallorca
Tel: +34 971 463 004
www.foracorda.com

A right spectacle: Patch Hammond "off" *Mark of the Beast* (7c) - page 67 - at Lulworth Cove. Photo: Grant Farquhar

Courses and Instructors

Dorset Climbing Activities - Page 73
Tel/Fax: 07747533507
www.dorsetclimbingactivities.co.uk

Serac Outdoor Sports - Page 257
East Boldon, Tyne and Wear
Tel: 0191 519 4495
www.seracoutdoorsports.co.uk

Climbing Walls

Awesome Walls - Page 21
St. Alban's Church, Athol Street, Liverpool.
Tel/Fax: 0151 298 2422
www.awesomewalls.co.uk

Outdoor Gear

Berghaus - Inside Back Cover
Extreme Centre, Sunderland.
Tel: 0191 5165600 Fax: 0191 5165601
www.berghaus.com

Black Diamond - Outside Back Cover
Tel: 0162 958 0484
www.blackdiamondequipment.com

Acknowledgments

Where do I start... Firstly, I owe the biggest thanks to all the people with whom I've shared the great game of climbing over the years since 1990. A huge thanks to my early mentor John Sharratt, who somehow taught me how to climb on Swanage's big sea cliffs; to Joff and Damian Cook, who've given me both inspiration and smiles in equal measures; Mark Williams, Steve Taylor, Dave Pickford and Gavin Symonds, who've provided me with unfailing friendship over the years; and to local legend Pete Oxley - bound for New Zealand as I write - best wishes, Pete. Thanks to the Climbers' Club for their support with the original 1996 Dorset DWS guide - *Into The Blue*. And to all the other local dudes, surfers and friends: Barry Clarke, Ju Walker, Neal Heanes, Danie Rushmer, Jon Biddle, Libby Peter, Robbie Dixon, Amy Colson, Charlie Woodburn, Meilee Rafe, Ben Stokes, Zoe Lee, and that rascal of a sea dog, Scott Titt.

For DWS elsewhere in the UK and the world, I owe a massive thanks to that true solo master Julian Lines, who has been a source of constant inspiration, a partner in crime, and has supplied me with endless information - thanks Ju! To Crispin Waddy, that man who was there right from the start - a big thanks for all your help and advice. And to Neil Gresham and Seb Grieve, who took me on those 'team boiling' trips as photographer all those years ago...huge thanks to you guys for being such pals. As for all those other DWS crazy-types such as Ken Palmer, Nick Hancock, Timmy Emmett, Ruth Taylor, Elinor Currey, Johnny Woods, Jason Porter, Klem Loskot, Miquel Riera, Adam Wainwright, Martin Crocker, Mike Weeks, Anthony Alexander and Matt Maddaloni - what an amazing bunch of folk; please keep up the good work!

There have been a number of photographers who've added flavour to this guide; thanks to all of you, with special gratitude due to Joff Cook, Grant Farquhar, Dave 'Cubby' Cuthbertson, Dave Pickford, Julian Lines and Simon Carter.

This guide wouldn't have been possible without the valued and capable support of Alan James at Rockfax - Alan, a big thanks for your faith in me to come up with the goods. And it's been a sheer pleasure to work with Mark Glaister on the many intricacies of the guidebook's layout - many thanks, Markie. A big tata to Daimon Beail for his great work with the Mallorca section, thanks to Chris Craggs and Graham Hoey for their proof reading, and tata to Sam and Rich at the Blanca's Orange House, who showed us all where the treasures were hidden in Spain. Lastly, a really huge debt of thanks to Bernard and the team at Climber magazine, who've unflinchingly taken and dealt with my pictures and words for almost a full decade now - thank you!

But, quite frankly, none of these DWS antics would ever have happened to me without my Mum and Dad. It's a fundamental thing. Dad nearly despatched my Mum and himself on Porlock Hill in the west country in 1956, whilst on a motorbike journey; brake fade on a grand scale. They survived the event, sold the bike, and promptly dropped three mischievous kids; I was the middle one, and I owe them the gift of life itself. Thank you.

I must save a few moments silence here for the memory of my pals Damian Cook and Brian Tilley, who are still very sorely missed in our small Dorset climbing scene. This guide is dedicated to them, and to the memory of my older sis Christine, who left us all far too soon. But I'm going to be indulgent here and pay heed to young blood: this book is also dedicated to my very young and noisy niece Amelie, daughter of my sis Caz and her partner Ken. Amelie, you are the future, and one day soon we're going to show you the sea and the sun.

Mike Robertson, April 2007

Symbol and Topo Key

Atlantis Man - Swim Outs

Each topo has a yellow 'Atlantis Man' who indicates the best place to swim out to should you happen to fall. This is not necessarily the only place to regain solid ground, but is generally the easiest exit. In some cases the swim out is quite long, and this is indicated on the topo with a swim distance. Also pay careful attention to the text on the topos, and in the introductions, which indicate certain special considerations when planning your exits.

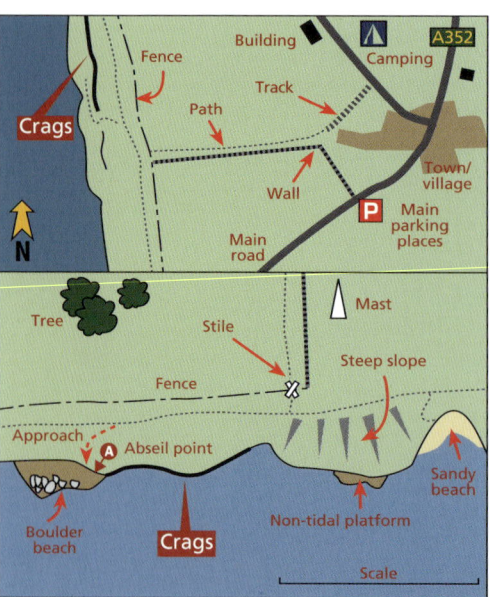

Route Symbols

☆1	A good solo which is well worth climbing.
☆2	A very good solo, one of the best on the crag.
☆3	A brilliant solo, one of the best!
	Technical climbing requiring good balance and technique, or complex and tricky moves.
	Powerful climbing; roofs, steep rock or long moves off small holds.
	Sustained climbing; either lots of hard moves or steep rock giving pumpy climbing.
	Fingery climbing with significant small holds on the hard sections.
	Fluttery climbing with big fall potential; S2 or S3 climbing and/or a high finish.
	A long reach is helpful or even essential for one or more of the moves.
	Some loose rock may be encountered.

Crag Symbols

 Angle of the approach walk to the crag with approximate time.

 Approximate time that the crag is in the direct sun (when it is shining!)

 An abseil rope is required to get to the starts of some or all of the routes.

 An access restriction because of nesting birds is sometimes in place; check crag introduction.

Crag Popularity

 Deserted - Currently under-used and usually quiet. A long walk-in and/or less good routes.

Quiet - Less popular sections on major crags, or good routes but hard to get to.

Busy - Places you will seldom be alone, especially at weekends. Good routes and easy access.

 Crowded - The most popular sections which are always busy.

Venue Guide

Venue	Routes	up to 4+	5 to 6a+	6b to 7a	7a+ and up	Significant tides	Summary	Page
Swanage	75	5	19 ✓✓	33 ✓✓✓	18 ✓✓✓	Tidal	Where it all started. The marvellous Conner Cove heads the line-up, with some smaller venues waiting in the wings.	34
Lulworth	41	1	5 ✓	12 ✓✓	23 ✓✓✓	Tidal	Steep, solid, and brilliant. Mostly tough grades, but on rock crammed full of pockets and jugs.	54
Portland	97	6 ✓	28 ✓✓	38 ✓✓✓	25 ✓✓	Tidal	Mostly short, always good, and lots of fun! A terrific spread of routes, and at all grades.	68
Devon	115	11 ✓	28 ✓✓	51 ✓✓✓	25 ✓✓✓	Tidal	Long traverses on excellent rock, and on great, multi-coloured limestone. There are plenty of 'up' routes, too.	94
Cornwall	25	3 ✓	7 ✓	13 ✓✓	2	Tidal	A little serenity guaranteed. Some great lines, especially in the mid grades.	134
Pembroke	159	6 ✓	41 ✓✓	79 ✓✓✓	33 ✓✓✓	Tidal	The UK's most tidal venue, but with a massive and varied spread of great routes.	146
Scotland	36	1	3 ✓	25 ✓✓	7 ✓✓	Tidal	Get exploring; more diversity than you can imagine. Cool water and utter calm.	188
Rest of the UK	Detailed information on the Bathtime wall in the Vivian Quarry, North Wales. Other limited information for more sections of the Devon and Cornwall Coastline, the Scilly Isles, more in North Pembroke.							202
Portugal	74	4 ✓	15 ✓	42 ✓✓✓	13 ✓✓✓		Sun, sea and brilliant soloing. Great rock, and an amazing place to hang out in late season!	210
Costa Blanca	42	2	17 ✓✓	18 ✓✓	5 ✓		Warm water, a great climate and ace soloing make the Blanca a terrific visit.	232
Mallorca	88	1 ✓	18 ✓✓	31 ✓✓✓	38 ✓✓✓		A stunning island, and with routes of all shapes and sizes. Cova del Diablo is utterly extraordinary.	252
Rest of Europe	How many possibilities can you fit into Europe? Snippets of information on the West Coast of Ireland, Sardinia and Croatia, along with ideas on venues such as Malta, Italy and Bulgaria.							282
Australia	15			6 ✓✓	9 ✓✓		Crafty's is the ultimate fresh-water venue, and Tasmania provides more exploring than you can fit into a lifetime.	294
Rest of the World	The remainder. This final chapter of Deep Water provides the ideas; it's up to you to go out there and obtain the goods! Info includes Bermuda, North America, Oman, and the amazing South East Asia with its stunning rock formations rising from the Andaman Sea.							306

Quality and range of routes in different grade bands: ✓✓✓ - Excellent, ✓✓ - Good, ✓ - Okay, NO STAR - Not worth a visit

Swanage

Danie Rushmer on the popular *Troubled Waters* (5) - *page 49* - at Conner Cove, Swanage. Photo: Mike Robertson.

Swanage

Welcome to Swanage, arguably the birthplace of UK deep water soloing as we now know it. Situated on Dorset's stunning world heritage coastline, the Swanage region is well-known for its diverse collection of deep water solos, and has a history that dates back to the mid-eighties. Here lurks the mighty *Conger* (6b), an atmospheric and committing line that breaches the very edge of one of Swanage's biggest sea caves. It was at Conner Cove (part of the Fisherman's Ledge area) that the first ever DWS festival was located in 1998, and it's likely that many climbers will have experienced their own introductions to DWS on the crisp, south-facing architecture of the Cove's shapely limestone walls.

It's true to say that Conner Cove represents the very best of what Swanage has to offer, but let's not forget the development of smaller crags, such as Tilly Whim, Hidden Quarry and the Lighthouse Cliffs. Whilst the well-regarded Conner Cove is a sheer delight, some of its less vertically-challenging neighbours promise a steadier and more digestible introduction to the genre.

Conditions and Tides

Swanage's tides rarely present much of a problem since most of the venues have plenty of water depth. This makes the region a neap tide/midday high tide venue - ideal for those long and lazy days spent lounging about at Conner Cove!

Most of Swanage's solos are on less steep rock than the neighbouring Stair Hole, so summer condensation is less of a problem. Always important is the sea state, so check forecasts and the sea state upon arrival. Any good summer's day should have you on the rock.

Accommodation

There's a ready supply of hotels in the region, as well as numerous B&B's - check the internet for these; one possibility is **www.vernon-lodge.co.uk** (see page 39). For a more affordable bed, try the Swanage Auberge bunkhouse, run by climbers, and in Swanage town itself - **www.swanageauberge.co.uk**. There are a number of campsites in the Swanage area, including the popular Tom's Field at Langton Matravers - **www.tomsfieldcamping.co.uk** (see page 39), which is within walking distance of the crags. Also nearby is the Woody Hyde campsite, just back up on the A351.

Food and Booze

Swanage is a tourist destination, and has a comprehensive supply of food and drink establishments, along with the usual facilities, including banks. There are plenty of pubs in town, whilst out of town you'll find the brilliant Square and Compass along at Worth Matravers - long regarded as one of the best pubs on the south coast, and a must for cider enthusiasts! Breakfast meets are perhaps best arranged in Swanage town, either in Harman's Cafe, or the Italian-run Cafe Tratt, along towards the pier.

For further entertainment check out the chalk stacks of Old Harry - they're one of the most stunning bits of architecture in the UK. Just along to the west, the big headland of St. Aldhelm's Head offers some breathtaking views, with the added attraction of one of the oldest chapels in the country. The beaches of Studland are beautiful, and also well worth a visit for some exercise is the bizarre Agglestone - a huge, remote sandstone boulder overlooking Poole harbour.

Jane Weir shows the way on *Fathoms* (6b) - *page 47* on the Funky Wall, Swanage. Photo: Mike Robertson.

Swanage

Approach

Swanage is situated on the rounded peninsula that is known as the Isle of Purbeck, and is found on the south coast just west of Poole. Whether you're approaching from Poole or from Dorchester, you're going to be on the coastal road - the A35. Follow the signs off the A35 to Wareham, and then strike out south from that town on the A351. This takes you through Corfe Castle and on to Swanage town, found some 9 miles south of Wareham. Following the brown signs to the pay and display parking of the Durlston Country Park is your best option for accessing Tilly Whim, the Lighthouse Cliffs and Fisherman's Ledge for Conner Cove; a right turn a mile or so outside town will guide you westwards towards Langton Matravers, and the best parking for Dancing Ledge, Hidden Quarry and Smokey Hole. To get to Seacombe and the Aquanaut Buttress, drive along to Worth Matravers, and park in the car park there - a signposted path will guide you down the fields to the Seacombe quarries.

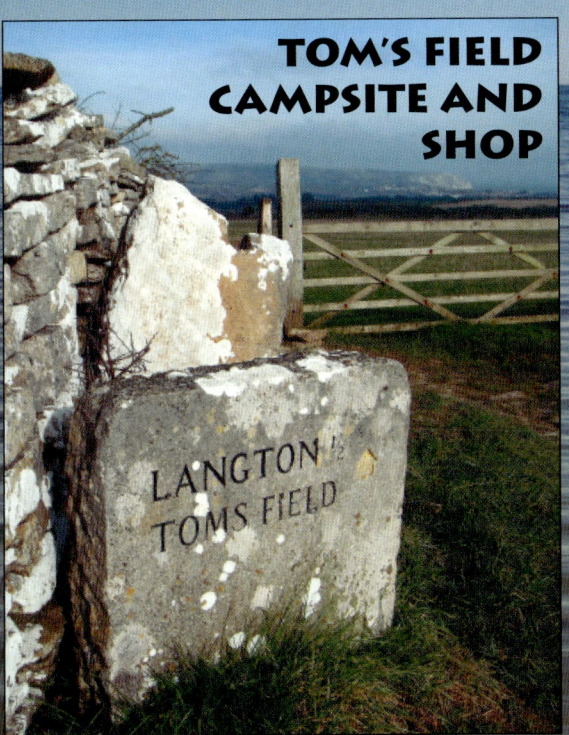

TOM'S FIELD CAMPSITE AND SHOP

Tom's Field Road
Langton Matravers
Swanage, Dorset BH19 3HN
(see map opposite)
Tel: 01929 427110
email: tomsfield@hotmail.com
web: www.tomsfieldcamping.co.uk

Our peaceful site is close to the Jurassic and Heritage Coastal Path, just 20 mins walk away. Ideal base for climbing, walking and family holidays. Dancing Ledge is within easy walk.

Our shop has general and camp supplies. Tom's Field has a strong commitment to re-cycling.

The campsite is mostly on a first come first served basis. Reservations may be taken in the Whit Week and the school summer holidays for a minimum of 5 nights.

Walker's Barn available all year, limited space and advance booking necessary. Not available Christmas or New Year's Eve.

VERNON LODGE

Beautiful Bed & Breakfast in Swanage

Large twin/double ensuites from £50
(20% discount for Rockfax readers)

Jurassic Coast just 10 minutes away
Complimentary pick-ups and drop-offs to choice climbing locations

Climbing instruction and rope courses also available on request. Drying room for equipment.

Call Joe and Sarah on
01929 423880

www.vernon-lodge.co.uk

Swanage — Seacombe - Aquanaut Buttress

Seacombe - Aquanaut Buttress

The low walls of Seacombe's eastern reaches are home to some fine little propositions which are almost all very safe. The rock is excellent and the routes never more than 8m high.

Approach - From the parking at Worth Matravers, follow the signed path down through the fields to reach the Seacombe quarries. Once there, walk the coast path eastwards for about 200m, until you reach a dry stone wall with a stile. Hop over this and abseil off the second fence post east of the stile. This will take you down a wide grassy gully and then an easy, east-facing ramp (located slightly to the left, looking out). The easy ramp is solid and around grade 3. The rope is for the earthy finish, which is not recommended. A 30m rope gets you to the top of the Aquanaut Buttress where you have ready access to almost all the routes and plenty of room for hanging out and gearing up. To do the routes, you'll need to down-climb something or make a short abseil.

Conditions and Tides - The buttress is fast-drying and the routes get plenty of sun. You'll need a good cool wind and calm seas to dry the cave interior and have a go at any projects here. There's a lot of water around this buttress, so any high-ish tide will be quite adequate. Many of the routes can be climbed at lower tides.

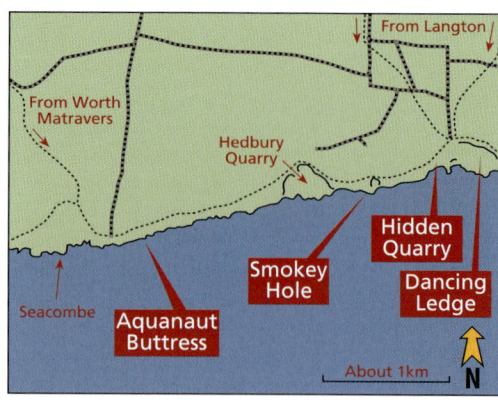

❶ The Aquanaut.......... 3+ S0
8m. The west-facing wall. From the base of the wall, climb on good jugs all the way to the top.
FSA. Scott Titt 31.8.2003

❷ The Lens.............. 4 S0
8m. The compact wall right of the south-west arete. From small foot-ledges at the base, climb up the wall right of the arete, on excellent rock, back to the main ledge. *See photo on page 53.*
FSA. Scott Titt 17.9.2003

❸ Summer's Dying Days..... 3+ S0
8m. This line finds steady climbing on a good collection of holds, just right of the centre of the wall.
FSA. Scott Titt 31.8.2003

❹ Lost in Time............ 4+ S0
7m. A beautifully positioned gem. From the base of the wall, climb the excellent wall, just left of the south-east arete, all the way back to the main ledge above.
FSA. Scott Titt 31.8.2003

❺ Barkin' Mad...... 7a S0
7m. Dead small holds and great moves. From the good resting foot ledge on Lost in Time, swing around the mid-arete to crimps, and slap yourself up these to the top.
FSA. Mike Robertson 27.8.2006

❻ The Pony......... 6c S0
7m. The face left of *Codfish* is fun. Find a handful of small crimps and use these to lock for a hold in the upper break.
FSA. Mike Robertson 27.8.2006

❼ Codfish............ 5 S1
8m. The distinctive corner. Traverse in from *Lost in Time* on the lowest break, to gain a ledge at the base of the corner. Ascend the corner on finger jams and laybacks to reach the top.
FSA. Scott Titt 17.9.2003

❽ The Howling... 7b S0
7m. This ultra-steep line offers a short but highly aerobic struggle. From the base of *Codfish*, use undercuts to pull out into the hanging roof/groove on the right. A highly improbable bridge (be warned) gains side-pulls, heel-hooks and a sloping undercut. A final dyno gains a flat jug and then the top.
FSA. Mike Robertson 27.8.2006

❾ Diana................. 6b S2
7m. This line is reached by traversing the fault-line above the right cave, to gain the next sea level ledge to the right. The line throws itself across the hanging wall to the left of the lower right ledge. Pull up to reasonable holds, and make moves up and left, to finally reach the main ledge above.
FSA. Mike Robertson 27.8.2006

Smokey Hole — Swanage

Smokey Hole

Smokey Hole is a terrific, tucked-away venue, home to Swanage's most feared DWS to date. The main attraction, however, is the excellent lower buttress - a fine, south-facing area, offering a number of safe, quality solos on good rock, which finish 12m above the sea.

Access - This area forms part of Swanage's seasonal bird restrictions, and is off-limits between March 1st and July 31st inclusive.

Approach - From Dancing Ledge (see page 44), follow the path past the Hidden Quarry and the grey box. At around 100m or so west of the grey box, Topmast Quarry comes into view on your left. Walk around it and down its central grassy ridge to the quarry floor. A few more metres will find you at the quarry's western edge, where a look down will reveal the large ledge below, which is formed by the top of the Zircon Buttress, 12m or so above the sea. The down-climb/abseil into the Zircon Buttress is here. To reach the start of *Rocket USA*, use *Aquamarine*.

After gaining the spacious top of the buttress by a down-climb or an abseil, you'll need to either continue the abseil to sea level, or just down-climb the easy 3+ groove on the east edge of the buttress. The traverse of the crag to gain the lines is actually some 5m up.

Conditions and Tides - The crag is fast-drying and faces both south and west, and is usually in good condition. You'll need a high-ish tide, although water depth is rarely a problem here, and a high neap tide should suffice for most routes.

⑩ Rocket USA 7b S3
28m. This monster solo barely squeezes into the S grade bracket, and is the south coast's most intimidating DWS to date. The route's start is gained by way of *Aquamarine*, and rises from the eastern edge of Smokey Hole and climbs the towering upper groove. The hard, steep climbing itself tops out at around 24m, the rock's imperfect, and the water's depth is a little in question, due to an invasive boulder. That said, the line is utterly inspiring but... "I wouldn't do it again for a thousand pounds."
See photo on page 29.
FSA. Mike Robertson (with fixed exit rope for loose top) 8.2001

⑪ Aquamarine 5 S2
16m. This amazing bit of architecture is thoroughly absorbing. It is most usually climbed both ways, and often reversed to gain the leaning west face to reach any one of the following routes, such as *Zircon*. The given S grade denotes the slightly bold moves stepping across the narrowing of the low zawn - don't do this if you're unsure.
FSA. Crispin Waddy 1986

⑫ Marvellous Maggs . . . .  6a+ S1
15m. The full-length line on the buttress is a tasty one. From the easy way down, follow *Zircon* leftwards to the arete, and then continue the traverse into the shade of the leaning west face. Fire up the steep and juggy face above, finishing right out on its juggy and wild left edge. Crazy positions!
FSA. Mike Robertson 8.2001

⑬ Zircon . . . . 6a+ S1
14m. The buttress's left arete is startlingly good. Traverse the excellent break leftwards along the lip of the long overhang. At the arete, climb straight up (sometimes quite blind) to finish on a series of huge jugs.
FSA. Crispin Waddy 1986

⑭ Gemzone . . . . 6b+ S0
11m. By way of contrast to the juggy passage of the last three routes, this one gives a fingery crux on the smooth face. Follow *Zircon* almost to its niche, and climb up over the bulge to a small projecting hold in the break. Finish up the slabby face directly and more easily.
FSA. Martin Crocker 24.8.1999

⑮ Jargoniser . . . . 6a+ S1
10m. From the left-hand end of the start ledge, climb up and head onto the technical slab above, moving gradually leftwards. Some baffling moves (hint: undercut) take you up and left to an enormous projecting spike. Finish easily to the top.
FSA. Martin Crocker 24.8.1999

Swanage Hidden Quarry

Hidden Quarry

This delightful area is a recently appraised addition, and, despite an approach that requires a little knowledge, is a terrific venue, and with a grade spread that should appeal to the mid-grade soloist. The bonus is the very deep water giving a full spread of S0s.

Full FSA details were not made available to the author during the writing of this guide, but all routes here have been climbed by either Martin Crocker or Mike Robertson during the period 1997-2006.

Approach - From Dancing Ledge (see page 44) walk west towards Hedbury (on the cliff side of the coastal path fence) for about 150m, to within 20m of a big grey box on the cliff side of the fence. Walk towards the cliff edge and drop back left - to find a hitherto hidden quarry; the South Face is right below this quarry. From the western edge of the quarry, either abseil off the thread to gain the lower fault line ledge, or simply down-climb at grade 3 (start by the small, square cut-out on the very edge) to gain the spacious ledge system below.

Access - Please note this area forms part of Swanage's seasonal bird restriction, and is off-limits between March 1st and July 31st inclusive.

Conditions and Tides - Hidden Quarry's East Face gets a full hit of morning sun, followed by sun for most of the day on the south face. A calm sea is ideal here. The amount of water, combined with the short, compact nature of the routes, means the tide is not so important - a high midday neap will be fine.

South Face

The first routes are reached by down-climbing a 3+ corner, just to the right of the routes themselves.

❶ Cryptoclidus **6b** *S0*
9m. From the base of the 3+ corner, traverse the obvious break leftwards for about 6m, towards a looming, jutting roof. Just before that roof, pull up to pockets and rock-over to side-pulls. Continue to the top more easily.

❷ Icthyosaurus . . . . **6a+** *S0*
9m. From the 3+ corner, traverse leftwards for 3m, and climb the shallow groove, moving slightly left to gain the top.

The next batch of routes are gained by down-climbing the grade 3+ wall just left of the routes themselves.

❸ Stegasaurus **5** *S0*
8m. The hanging arete is both shapely and safe. From the base of the wall, climb up the left side of the arete, to find yourself right 'on it', in a truly sweet position. Move slightly right, to finish on great holds.

❹ Allosaurus **6b** *S0*
9m. The front face of the buttress, slightly left of middle. From the base of the previous route, traverse right, to gain some amazing chicken heads. Pull up powerfully to a horizontal break, then stretch for an obvious (and excellent) pocket. A rock-over gains better holds, and finally the top.

❺ Seismosaurus **6b** *S0*
9m. The wall right of the last route gives this tight line. Gain it from either side; safer is the low traverse in from the left. Crimp across to the right edge of the buttress and pull up to good 'chicken heads'. Make a long reach for a flat hold, and step up to gain better holds, move left to a good slot and the top.

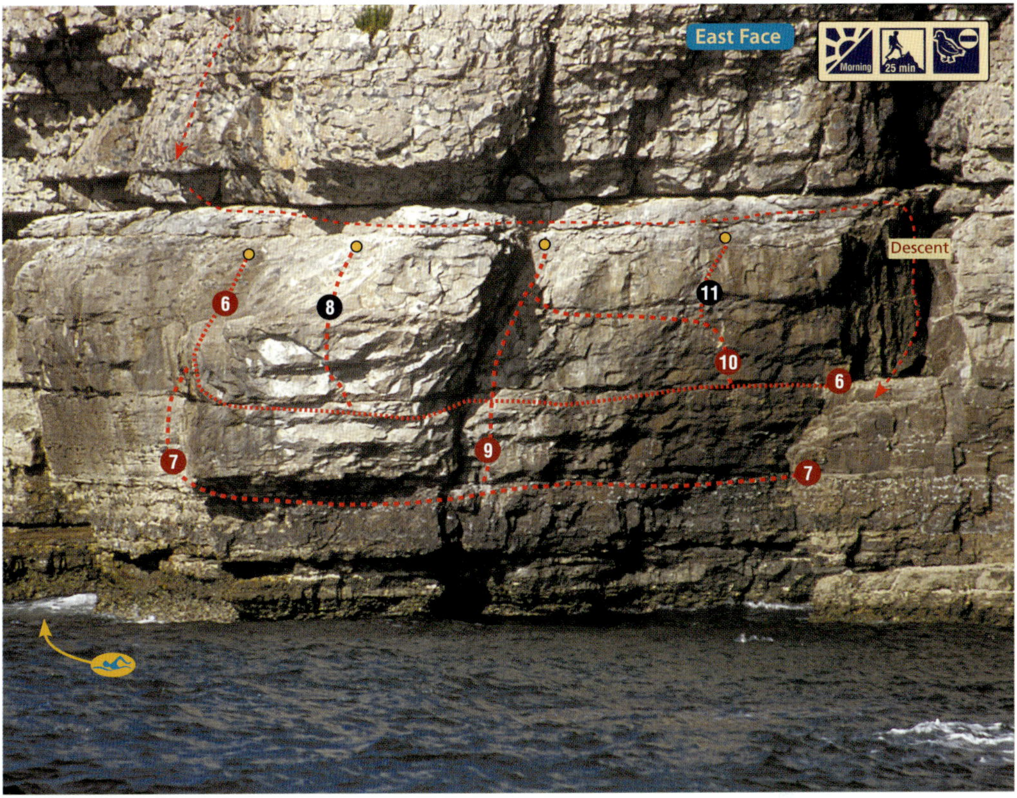

Hidden Quarry Swanage 43

East Face
Hidden Quarry's steep East Face, although not visible from the approach, is easy to recce in advance from the neighbouring Dancing Ledge - from where this crag shot was taken.
Approach - *From the base of the abseil/down-climb, follow the ledge eastwards around the arete and descend a groove to ledges.*

❻ Ultrasaurus 6c *S0*
16m. This brilliant traverse is probably the best route in the area; terrific climbing, and in amazing positions. Top of the grade. From the gully at the north end, drop across the gap and sprint across the higher traverse, to gain a rest near the hanging groove of *Triceratops*. A further series of extending and beautifully-positioned moves gain the left prow - continue around this to join and finish as for *Supersaurus*.

❼ Supersaurus 6c *S0*
17m. This fantastic traverse is both appealing and on terrific rock; it's almost as good as *Ultrasaurus*. It tackles the lower of the two horizontal break-lines. From the access gully, swing left onto the lower face, moving down to gain the lower break proper. Follow the breaks all the way across the crag and continue around the arete, to make good moves to gain the prow above - a fitting finale.

❽ Brachiosaurus . . . . 7b+ *S0*
9m. Yet another of those *S0's*, but the deep, inviting water won't help you much here since the moves are desperate. Reverse the last section of *Ultrasaurus* to gain the big jug rail; from here, contemplate the bulge above.

❾ Triceratops . . . . 6b+ *S0*
14m. A gem. The central, steep juggy groove can be accessed by way of either *Ultrasaurus* or *Supersaurus* (the latter provides the slightly more sustained variation). Traverse the break-line of your choice, and power up the central groove to the break.

❿ Gryposaurus 7a *S0*
9m. This tricky and sustained route takes in the steep and crimpy territory on the upper face of the buttress. Yard your way across the upper break of *Ultrasaurus*, and crank for a tiny spike in the face above; use this marginal hold to gain the slight, highest break and follow this on improving holds to a junction with *Triceratops*.

⓫ Oviraptor . . . . 7a+ *S0*
7m. The direct finish to *Gryposaurus* adds a grade. From the slight upper break, make a further hard move straight up to better finishing holds.

Swanage — Dancing Ledge

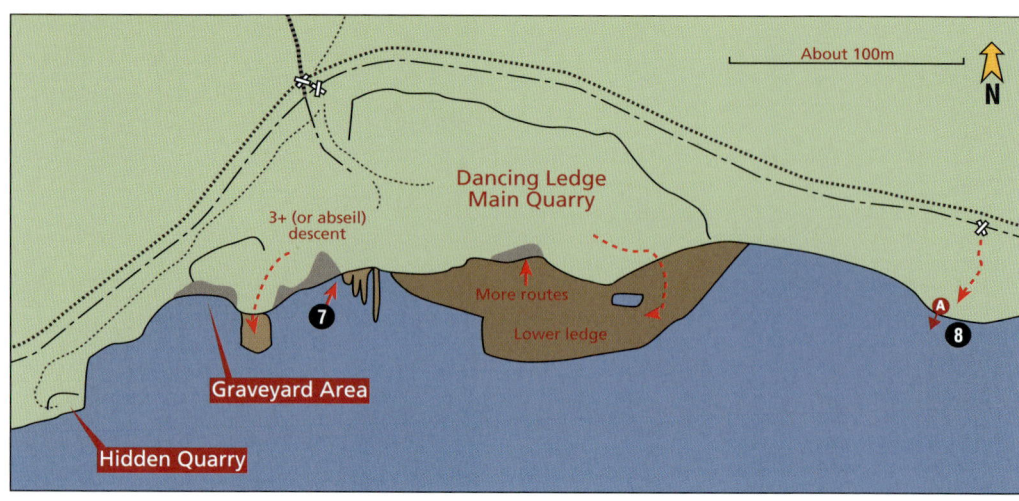

Dancing Ledge

A cunningly crafted little venue, with the most substantial area being neatly packed into the far west cave, below Dancing Ledge's main sport climbing walls. It has to be said that the venue is something of a high S grade spot, so keep away if you're looking for S0's and S1's. Most of the routes are fully bolted here, which can help a bit when you're trying to work out where everything goes.

Approach - Dancing Ledge is best approached from Langton Matravers. Once in the village, go past the post office and turn left into Durnford Drove. The free car park is 300m down here, just beyond Langton House. From the parking, walk south on a good path past four fields and Spyway Barn. After the 4th field, head down a big hill towards Dancing Ledge which lies directly below the coast path. From here steps lead down into the quarry. The best way to access the Graveyard Area is to set up a short abseil rope, although most locals warm up by down-climbing *Mr. Fantastic* (4+).

Conditions and Tides - The cave gets sunshine from mid-afternoon on, which often helps dispel the morning damp. The best conditions are often late in summer, when the sun is a little lower. The rock is good, although an inspection of all the big S grade routes here is highly recommended. Your best tide for a visit is a big one; a late afternoon spring tide would be excellent timing.

Graveyard Area

Dancing Ledge Swanage

Graveyard Area

❶ Mariner's Graveyard
7a+ S3

18m (First pitch only). Brilliant; a scary but superb pitch. It's very, very sustained, and also a little shallow, so find a huge tide if you can. As a solo, it'll need to be climbed in reverse (ie. left to right) for the safest tick, and you'll need to have some thoughts about your landing zones. Access by abseiling down the second pitch to arrive at the sport route's original half-way belay ledge. Climb rightwards along the break (crux) to better holds and a rest (of sorts). Bash on for a flying, safer finish above deep water.
FSA. Mike Robertson 10.8.2005

❷ The Pump Will Tear Us Apart
7a+ S3

16m. A wicked, ballsy frightener with barely adequate water and fine positions. Arm yourself with a good spring tide and check the depth carefully first. Monkey leftwards, reversing *Mariner's Graveyard*, along the enticing horizontal break (under *Lucretia*) to a cunning little rest, and yard through the overhead bulge on slopers (crux) to gain easier ground and a flake-line. Follow this to the top.
FSA. Mike Robertson 29.9.1995

❸ Lucretia, My Reflection
6c S1

13m. A hanging line of great quality which is almost designed for short folk; the hanging slab is generally celebrated with all manner of scrunging oddness! Brilliant rock and good water. Start from the ledge. Dangle across the void on jugs to arrive at the well-constructed slab, and squeeze along this to reach steeper ground. Venture on through the tricky upper section to reach the top shelf.
FSA. Mike Robertson 24.9.1995

❹ F.Y.B.
6c S1

10m. This little beauty shares a start with *Lucretia*, thereafter moving off rightwards. Start as for the mother route, swing leftwards onto the short, hanging slab, and make strenuous moves up and right to gain the steep wall above. Follow this to the top.
FSA. Mike Robertson 7.10.1995

❺ Here Comes the Hizbollah
6b+ S2

10m. A terrific little dash up the right-most line of bolts. Climb up to a deep (left hand) side-pull, and power quickly and confidently up to the safer roofs above. A few stiff locks will see you to further jugs, and the top.
FSA. Mike Robertson 24.9.1995

❻ Mr. Fantastic
4+ S2/3

9m. An overhanging groove well-blessed with jugs, above a ledge that's just a tad too large. Climb easily up the steepening groove to big side-pulls. Use these to swing left to easier ground, and the top.
PFSA. Mike Robertson 1990's

A further line exists in the Dancing Ledge area for the devotee. It's alone, and found at the right end of a wide cave, about 40m or so from the West Cave. It is easily reached by a down-climb (2+) down the rib on the right (looking in) of the cave.

❼ Mucho Gusto!
7b+ S2

10m. This wildly overhanging solo takes on the challenge of the rock at the right end of the long set of overhangs, down in the lower reaches of Dancing Ledge. A damn good blast! Climb up and left to gain the handrail (spotter definitely required for this start), and launch out across the roofs (crux; no surprise there…). Continue slightly more easily to the top.
FSA. Pete Oxley 8.1998

White Rave

The last line on the list in the Dancing Ledge area is the stunning line of *White Rave*. To find it, walk east from Dancing Ledge, and drop down the hill some 20m before the stile. An abseil from the fence (70m rope, or tie two together) will get you to the edge proper, where an odd limestone 'sofa' can be found set just above a line of bolts. This is the line; take your jumars with you if you're uncertain about your way down.

❽ White Rave
7a+ S3

20m. An isolated, dazzling test of nerve, taking a bulging line of pockets on a perfect white prow. This immaculate line overlooks the very western edge of Guillemot, some 25m to the west of the classic Swanage trad route *Tudor Rose*. Please note the presence of an intrusive boulder in the water, which pushes the grade up to S3. From the lower bolt belay, follow the strenuous line of pockets up the hanging prow; a final wilting rock-over gains the easier top slab. Arrive back at terra firma by scrambling up and over the short outcrop above - an in-situ rope is desirable, although not used on the FSA.
FSA. Mike Robertson 8.2001

Swanage   Conner Cove - The Funky Wall

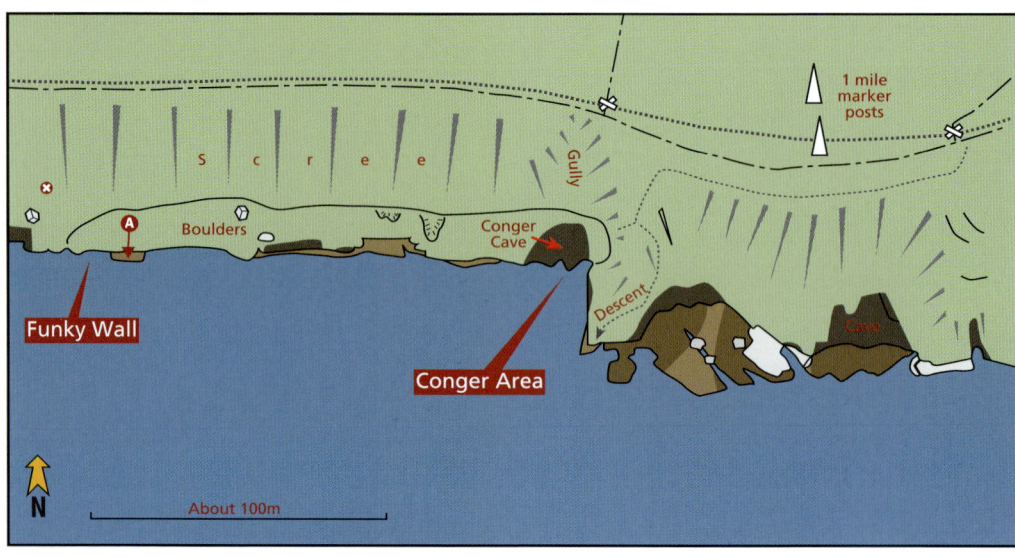

Conner Cove - The Funky Wall

This amazing region of deep water solos comprises the 'other bit' of Conner Cove, where the rock is equally good, comprising of strong lines on perfect, often grit-like rock. The sector is often eerily quiet, even on gorgeous summer days, and contains many routes that remain un-ticked in folk's climbing guides. This is undoubtedly due in part to the fact that the wall is completely hidden from view! So take an abseil rope and take a peek over the edge, where an obvious big ledge can be seen jutting below. This is referred to as the Funky Ledge, and life as we know it starts from here. A lengthy break-line close to sea level forges its way westwards to give access to some of the best solos in Dorset.

Approach - From Durston Country Park parking and the lighthouse, walk along the coast path to the stile before the mile marker pylon. Cross the fence and continue along its seaward side for 300m, to where a slight ridge descends to the cliff-top above the Conner Cove. Locate the abseil stake, set back from the cliff edge, some 150m further west and use a 25m rope to get down to the spacious Funky Ledge.

Escape - Recommended is a set of jumars, or even just a grigri: with these plus your harness waiting on your abseil rope, you'll have no problem exiting the area - it's the quickest, easiest and safest way out, and the locals have been using this method for years. The alternative is to swim over to *Helix* (150m - see Conger Area), or solo up *Funky Nomadic Tribes* - something else the locals have been doing for years, but NOT a deep water solo.

Conditions/Tides - You won't have any problems with tide levels, excepting the fact that a spring low will give you a much longer fall. So climb on neap days (high tides around midday), when the tidal swing is minimal. The rock is generally dry here, but the streaked areas can be greasy; also worth remembering is that *Captain Blood's* and *Fathoms* suffer from early season drainage, so leave these until they're well chalked up! (Is that cheating?)

❶ Davy Jones' Lock-off
.... 6c+ *S1*

35m. A brilliant and lengthy expedition, which is essentially an extension to *Captain Blood's*. Beautiful climbing, with no hard moves above 10m. The total route length of 35m represents the entire expedition from the Funky Ledge. Follow *Captain Blood's* to arrive at the rest prior to the final bulge. Drop down slightly and teeter across the very lip of the cave (the edge of nowhere) to find yourself faced with a series of undercut moves. Commit to these to arrive at jugs, and continue to the top.
FSA. Crispin Waddy 8.1994

The following route lengths represent the vertical route distance from the prominent traverse break-line to the top.

❷ ...And Captain Blood's Cavern
.... 6c *S1*

18m. An arching groove of superlative quality. One of the area's best giggles, featuring pumpy undercut moves, a fair dash of technical footwork, and stunning positions. Discovered by a young and fresh-faced Joff Cook, and almost certainly his greatest find! Traverse the break leftwards for miles, continuing past *Fathoms* to the second arching groove; this is the line. Battle it out with a technical and powerful sequence (crux) to gain the arch, and follow it on tricky undercuts to finally find solace on better footholds. Swing left under the roof section above, and blast through the final bulge on flatties to gain easier ground.
FSA. Joff Cook 8.8.1990

❸ Privateer .... 7b+ *S1*

16m. This brilliant proposition ascends the hanging finger crack in the headwall above the arch of *Captain Blood's*, on perfect rock throughout. Follow the mother route until beneath the crack, and reach for good finger locks in the crack. Either continue on to the top (very blind side-pull moves) or fumble around for a while, get pumped, and eventually jump into the sea.
FSA. Pete Oxley 23.5.1998

Conner Cove - The Funky Wall Swanage

4 For Whom the Swell Tolls
.... 7b+ *S1*
16m. A big and daunting line on immaculate rock, with two separate cruxes found en-route, and including some very steep territory in the upper section. The route bisects the wide bulging face between *Captain Blood's* and *Fathoms*, and there are no recorded on-sight ascents to date. From the break, climb up and then leftwards, to gain a huge undercut. Continue on up through very steep ground, to a mantelshelf exit.
FSA. Pete Oxley 23.5.1998

5 In Too Deep 6c *S1*
16m. This route was soloed before *For Whom the Swell Tolls* was climbed, and is thus included here, as the grade is somewhat more useful for most people! Climb the face a little right of *Captain Blood's* groove, then move rightwards to finish up *Fathoms*.
FSA. Pete Oxley 8.1997

6 Fathoms 6b *S1*
16m. A truly natural gem, and in a glorious architectural setting. From the Funky Ledge, traverse the break until the first arch is encountered. This is *Fathoms*, and a small, square ledge above the break allows you to stop and marvel at your destiny. Follow the stunning undercut arch to the apex, where a really huge jug is encountered, and then prevaricate on it for a couple of minutes before committing to a move that guides you quickly to the top.
See photo on page 37.
FSA. Crispin Waddy 8.9.86

7 Feeding Neptune .. 7b+ *S1*
16m. A good line, but with some hard and not-so-obvious moves. From the small standing ledge, climb up and then gradually leftwards, to layback the almost holdless rib. Continue slightly leftwards to gain the easier top section.
FSA. Pete Oxley 24.7.1999

8 Donald, Where's Your Trousers?
.... 6a+ *S1*
16m. Brilliant climbing; this is probably your first choice as an introduction to the area, climbing up a series of easy-to-follow finger-jugs and flakes. It's also easy to find, has an ace traverse in, and shares that very convenient small square ledge at the break with *Fathoms* (chilled contemplation is never a bad thing). Climb up and slightly right on beautiful rough rock, aiming for an undercut feature. Continue fairly direct, on good and usually accommodating holds, to the top.
FSA. Crispin Waddy 8.9.86

9 Amazonia . 6c *S2*
16m. This tough little cookie is very sustained for the grade, and features an endless series of testing, fingery moves on perfect rock. It traces a roughly diagonal line across the face left of *Funky Nomadic Tribes*. The route doesn't always give its secrets away easily. Check out water depth above the shelf for the first few moves, thereafter it's a nice clean drop into acres of water. Climb up and then gradually left, pushing slowly for the small breaks and pockets under the upper capping roofs (don't stay lower, on the central face; it'll prove harder). Continue leftwards and up, to finally dive for a good flake. Finish more easily.
FSA. Joff Cook 4.6.1993

Swanage — Conner Cove - Conger Area

Conner Cove - Conger Area
A superb and testing arena; considered the birthplace of deep water soloing as we know it, and rightly so. The quality of the routes is exemplary, the water is very deep (about 9m), and the viewing galleries are legendary!

Approach - The first six routes are all best started from ledges at the base of *A Bridge Too Far*. To reach the base, set up a rope 7m west of the *Conger's* finish, from a small blade stake 2m back from the edge (back it up with thin tapes/small wires). Abseil down, gently swinging to stay in contact with the rock, until it's easily possible to gain a big jug at the base of *Tsunami*. Once in the groove, slip your harness off (easy) and let it go.

Conditions and Tides - Climb on crisp days, especially in the shadowed regions of the cave, which can be damp. The tide levels aren't especially important, but don't climb on a spring low unless you want to fall a lot further!

❶ Leap of Faith ..... 6b+ S2
16m. A challenging escapade, which will require a steady head to avoid thought of the slight ledge protruding at the base. Climb the front face of the arete on good, deep pockets, eventually trending leftwards to a decent protruding foothold. The finish is slightly disjointed, moving awkwardly rightwards to easier ground.
FSA. Damian Cook 6.1993

❷ Tsunami .... 6c+ S1
16m. This daunting but safe line is unfortunately often wet, in which case it is best left for another day. Climb the left arete of *A Bridge Too Far*, then swing leftwards around the arete to a crux finish up the face on the left.
FSA. Damian Cook 6.1993

❸ A Bridge Too Far 6a S1
16m. A terrific piece of climbing at a sensible grade; avoid it in damp conditions. Climb the airy, wide groove until a committing rightwards move across a bottomless chasm takes you to one of those airy, Conner-stylee snappy-fin finishes. Ah, the joy!
FSA. unknown

The next three routes all start by way of a traverse across the lower face. This traverse has been known as the John Williams Traverse, but is not separated as an individual route here, as it's now just used as an obvious approach to gain the three routes below.

❹ Crime Wave 6b S1
16m. The face to the left of *Furious Pig*; fine climbing on good face holds makes this a terrific route. Traverse rightwards to a long, flat hold beneath a small pink prow, then climb the face above direct to join *A Bridge Too Far*. Finish rightwards more easily.
FSA. Damian Cook 6.1993

❺ Furious Pig .... 6b+ S1
16m. A solid and well-positioned arete, and poised right above the briny. Traverse the lower face all the way across to the arete, give a brief, balancy throw for a big jug, and follow the arete with gradually easing difficulty to the top.
FSA. Crispin Waddy 3.1989

❻ The Great Shark Hunt
.... 7a S1
16m. Excellent climbing up the steep groove system to the right of the *Furious Pig* arete. Follow *Furious Pig* to the base of the arete, and then swing blindly off rightwards into an excellent, very bottomless groove system. Follow this, with plenty of interest, to finish as for *The Conger*.
FSA. Pete Oxley 1994

Conner Cove - Conger Area — Swanage

The next two routes are variations on the theme of The Vanishing, and are excellent in their own right, but bear in mind you'll need a decent boat to stand in to reach the start holds.

❼ The Appearing .   **7a+** *S1*
24m. From the boat, stretch for a hand jam, and pull into the chimney. Follow cracks up into the roof, to join *The Vanishing* at its high point.
FSA. Adam Wainwright 31.8.2002

❽ Red Bully . . . .   **7a+** *S1*
24m. Start as for *The Appearing*. Break out of that route, and cross a slab and a bulge to join *The Vanishing* just before it reaches daylight.
FSA. Adam Wainwright 31.8.2002

❾ The Vanishing .   **7a+** *S1*
27m. A thrilling and energetic blast from the bowels of *The Conger* Cave. This mini-expedition takes on the full challenge of the cave, forcing a passage all the way out to the jugs in *The Conger* finishing chimney. Approach either via a condition-dependent traverse in (around 6c - and only possible with low swell and low tide); an easy swim-in with dry-bag setup; or cadge a ride on a boat. Leave the back right ledge via a gripping rock-over. Continue rightwards to the arete and climb this past a massive pocket to an overhang, above which there's a huge, lie-down rest (hint: seats at least three). Look to the south and head off towards the smooth walls of the inner *Conger* chimney (sustained and absorbingly technical). Now you're smiling!
FSA. Mike Robertson 16.8.2001

Approach (Routes 10 to 18) - *Reverse down the easy route Helix (3) or abseil, to reach a sea level ledge at the base.*

❿ The Conger **6b** *S1*
22m. Just stupendous. An inspiring route of quality and excellence, and one of the best DWS's in the UK. Traverse the base of the *Freeborn Man* wall to gain a chimney (often wet out of season). Squeeze in, and then bridge leftwards onto a slab. Continue across the slabs to arrive at an arete, where two tricky sequences finally get you to big jugs within the infamous *Conger* chimney. From there it's plain sailing; take care with those 'fins'.
FSA. Nick Buckley 26.6.83

⓫ Snap, Crackle and Plop   **6b+** *S2*
18m. A committing direct finish to *The Conger*, unfortunately marred by the quality of some of the resident 'fins'. From the Conger chimney, dive out and up, to arrive at the top.
FSA. Dominic Cook 11.9.1990

⓬ Jellied . . . .   **6b+** *S1*
17m. An excellent right-hand finish to *The Conger*. Climb *The Conger* to the chimney and break out rightwards to gain a slim hanging ramp. With hands on the ramp, continue to arrive at the finishing ledge, pumpy. Stepping onto the ramp and using the skinny 'fins' above gives a worrying and 'starless' 6b!
FSA. Jon Biddle 3.8.1990

⓭ The Drowning Pool
. . . .   **7b+** *S2*
16m. A tough challenge. From *The Conger* slab, make some tricky moves up through a bulge, to gain holds under the huge roof. From here, a very technical leftwards sequence should get you to the finishing jugs.
FSA. Pete Oxley 27.3.1989

⓮ Swordfish Trombones
. . . .   **7a+** *S2/3*
17m. One of the finest propositions Conner Cove has to offer, with incredible positions throughout. In the event of a fall, there is a small possibility of hitting the reef below *Musharagi Tree*; - be warned; folk have been close, yet the route has seen dozens of falls. Break out of *The Conger's* slab to find yourself adrift in a very technical groove. Continue to a roof and perform some fairly gymnastic shenanigans through the roof (body bridge no-hands rest, if you dare) to finally gain the upper hanging slab.
FSA. Andy Donson Summer 1995

⓯ Musharagi Tree . . .   **6b** *S1/2*
16m. The rightwards-trending groove is solid and entertaining throughout. The drop zone feels slightly narrow. Start either for *The Conger* (6b) or, more sustained, climb up and leftwards through the lower bulge (6b+). Gain the groove, and follow it all the way to the top.
FSA. Jon Biddle, Jon Williams 1.8.88

⓰ Herman Borg's Basic Pulley Slippage
. . . .   **7b+** *S2*
17m. A trial of escalating difficulty to the left of *Freeborn Man*. The S grade reflects the slight possibility of touching the lower slab if a swing inwards from the crux is taken. Climb the lower slab, and make long reaches between pockets to finally snatch for the slight rib/side-pull. Swing immediately right and charge for the top pockets of *Freeborn Man*.
FSA. Pete Oxley 23.5.1998

⓱ Freeborn Man **6c** *S1*
14m. A line of pure brilliance and on fantastic rock throughout. From the lower slab, move up into a slight groove on the left. Dive up rightwards into the rising line of pockets, make a hard reach for the undercut, then move leftwards from the undercut to gain a big thread in the lip; the final rock-over awaits.
Variations - A right-hand finish through the top roof is the same grade. The direct line, avoiding the undercut entirely, is hard 7a.
See photos on page 2 and page 5.
FSA. Nick Buckley 1980's

⓲ Troubled Waters . . .   **5** *S1*
14m. Possibly the most frequented and best 'starter' DWS at Swanage - reasonably safe, steady, and very accessible. Climb leftwards onto the steep slab, continue to the concavity, and then barrel on up the steep upper wall, on the biggest holds you can imagine. *See photo on page 34*.
FSA. Pete Oxley 15.7.85

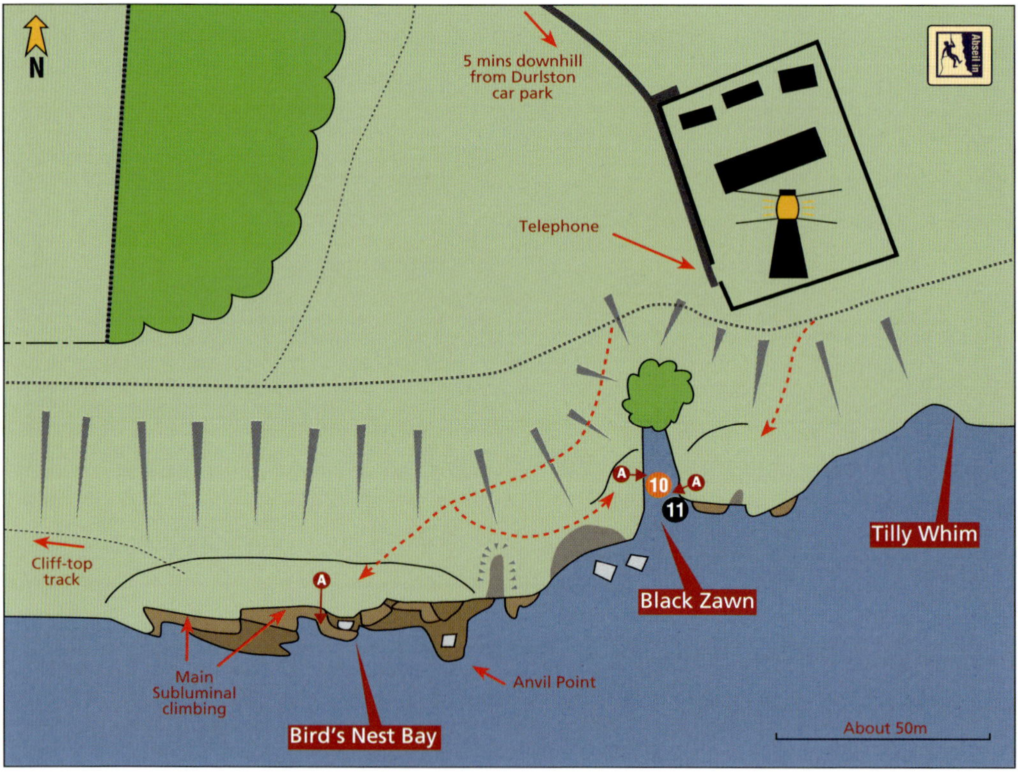

Swanage — Subluminal - Bird's Nest Bay

Subluminal - Bird's Nest Bay

Bird's Nest Bay is a small but inherently safe DWS zone, found in two small bays under the route *Bird's Nest* at Subluminal. Mid to high tide is best for access, the rock is excellent, and all the routes are short and sweet. The water is rarely that deep (around 2-3m at best) but as the routes are so short, water depth is not really an issue. The routes average around 6m high, they're on good quality crinkly rock throughout, and often quite sustained for their length. Combine this sector with the neighbouring Tilly Whim, and you'll have some fine, short pieces of rock to play on.

Approach - From the Durlston Country Park car park (pay and display) walk along the narrow tarmac road, following it all the way down to the lighthouse. Walk down and rightwards to gain Subluminal's very popular top ledges, where you'll find plenty of gearing-up space. A 13m abseil will gain the lower ledges, where the solos are found - or warm up by down-climbing *Pedestal Crack* (3), which is down a corner-chimney on the west side of Subluminal's prominent pedestal feature. From these main ledges, the three short descents shown on the topo will get you down to the starts of the routes themselves.

Conditions and Tides - The rock here is usually dry, but avoid choppy seas and late afternoon dampness, as the routes can be wet in these conditions. Visit on a big morning tide, when the sea will provide an adequate cushion. Avoid heavy swells, as these might affect access across the bottom of the walls.

❶ **Stir Crazy**............ **6a+** *S1*
6m. From the ledge on the left, traverse into the base of the line; climb straight up the left edge of the tight chimney recess on crimpy edges.
FSA. Mike Robertson 9.9.2005

❷ **The Puzzle**....... **6c+** *S0/1*
6m. The left arete of the face gives a fine (and puzzling!) escapade; the hardest route here. Traverse leftwards across the face to gently layback the rounded arete. Use the small flared pockets to finally gain the top. The crux features a short, stubby arete coming in from the left face; use this in any way you can.
FSA. Mike Robertson 29.4.2006

❸ **Bathtubb**........ **6b** *S1/2*
6m. The terrific, black face gives a technical sequence on very small edges and side-pulls. Traverse leftwards and tackle the wall directly above the right side of the trench. Don't fall off rightwards.
FSA. Steve Taylor 1990's

❹ **Bird's Nest Arete**..... **5+** *S0*
6m. A fine and very amenable little route. Climb the arete (the grade will depend on how far left (easier 4+) on the arete you venture), finishing on the main ledge.
FSA. Scott Titt 1980's

Subluminal - Bird's Nest Bay Swanage

❺ Sweet Surrender... 6b S0
6m. Safe as houses and with great moves. Swing rightwards and climb the excellent, crinkly face direct, a couple of metres right of *Bird's Nest Arete*.
FSA. Mike Robertson 1990's

❻ Project 7c? S1
6m. The tight wall right of *Sweet Surrender* is very thin indeed.

❼ White Flag 5+ S1
6m. This line climbs the crinkly wall left of the flake-line. Traverse leftwards at sea level to gain the base of the wall; a tricky rock-over gives way to bigger holds.
FSA. Mike Robertson 1990's

❽ Gid's Landing 5 S1/2
6m. This short flake-line is found almost directly under the trad route *Philatus*. Approach from the right/east, and climb the face on the left of the crack thingy (just about above the safe trench) to emerge on the main ledge.
FSA. Scott Titt 1980's

❾ The Scotty Dog Traverse 6a+ S1
25m. This little low-level mini-expedition gives some welcome fun and frolics, but hasn't been repeated in a good number of years. So you're on your own with this one - choose your tide to suit. Tactics of the day included nails in boots, flagons of local ale, and a complete disregard for human life as we know it. Drawbacks included zero chalk and woolly jumpers renowned for catching on things.
FSA. Scott Titt 1970's

Black Zawn
The atmospheric Black Zawn sees regular solo action, but most of these lines are a little off the 'S' scale. Mammoth spring tides, however, bring these next two routes into S3 condition:

❿ Astrid 5+ S3
25m. The deep cracks of the zawn's west face are an absolute delight. From the lower pedestal (gained by abseil), tackle the steep corner to resting jugs, then continue up the flakes above to a gradually easing exit.
FSA. Unknown

⓫ Last Great Innocent 7b S2/3
20m. The gritstone-like prow on the eastern edge of the Black Zawn features exceptional climbing on minuscule slopers, and is a DWS classic in its own right. Gain the base by way of a straightforward abseil from the twin stakes at the top of the zawn. You'll need a decent spring tide for your ascent, as the water depth rarely creeps above 2m. The hard climbing is all over at 11m; thereafter juggy 4+ to the top.
FSA. Mike Robertson 3.5.1997

Swanage Tilly Whim

Tilly Whim

The diminutive caves of Tilly Whim are short, on good rock, and are mostly set above good water. The region is more famous for the now-banned Tilly Whim quarried caves, found over the big brick wall immediately to the east, and the two venues are often confused. Also notable are the natural sea walls found below the upper brick wall; these offer good bouldering and a perfect warm-up.

Access - The solo area itself is not part of the year-round ban on the quarry, but it carries a seasonal bird restriction, which operates March 1 to July 31 inclusive.

Approach - From Subliminal, walk east along the coast path. Walk down the slope beyond the lighthouse and drop down again rightwards, to gain lower ledges. This is the gearing-up spot for all routes here.

Conditions and Tides - You'll need calm seas and a mid to high tide here, although *Camel Filter* and *Llama Roundabout* will need a calmer sea than their neighbours, as the bridging 'entrance' into the tunnel is very close to the sea. Looking down into the finishing blowhole of *Camel Filter* or the finishing cleft of *Slap ya' Dromedary* will confirm whether the routes are dry.

❶ Numb Bum/Turkish Delight

. . . . **6b+** *S2*

12m. Excellent climbing and with a very pumpy finale. You'll need a good high tide for this one; check the depth carefully, as the level beneath this bit is not so deep. Follow *Slap ya' Dromedary* across the square zawn, and traverse to the arete; continue boldly across the wildly leaning wall, and finish up the ultra-steep crack in the centre of the wall.
FSA. Jon Williams 1988 and Andy Donson 1989. Please excuse the duo for the first ascent; it's still unclear as to the exact line of the first-claimed Numb Bum.

❷ Slap ya' Dromedary . . . **6a** *S0*

9m. A popular and fine little dash across the square-cut zawn. Start on the main ledge, as for *Camel Filter*. Traverse the break, to forge left off slopers to gain the corner. Bridge into this, and continue 'into' the looming rift to a fine bridging finish.
FSA. Jon Williams 8.88

❸ The Hump **7b** *S0*

4m. For years it's been uncertain just which finger holds this boulder problem route actually uses, and it still is. It's essentially an eliminate above the traverse of *Slap ya' Dromedary*, with a savage crux tackling the enticing, short leaning wall. The line wants to go slightly right or a little to the left; the super-direct is very hard indeed. There's no evidence of a direct ascent to date, and the last move is a balls-out dyno.
PFSA. Jon Williams 6.88

❹ Camel Filter . . . . **6a+** *S1*

12m. Tilly Whim's finest route takes low-level traversing to new levels (of depravity), tackling the problem of how to enter the tunnel cave below the edge of the platform. A damn good probe! Climb down along the zawn wall, enter the narrow cave/tunnel with some proper legwork (crux), and continue in the same line to a blowhole exit. The *S1* is for the exit, although the moves are easy.
FSA. Jon Williams 28.4.88

❺ Llama Roundabout . . . . **6a+** *S2*

18m. This little voyage is an extension of the previous route, performing a circuit of the cave beyond *Camel Filter's* blowhole. Very subterranean indeed. Follow the mother route to the blow-hole, and continue around the inner cave, anti-clockwise (and with a brief boulder-jump) to arrive back at the same blowhole. Exit as for *Camel Filter*.
FSA. Mike Robertson, Mark Williams, Mark Arnall 14.8.1994

Scott Titt on the short but sweet *The Lens* (4) - *page 40* - on the Aquanaut Buttress, Seacombe, Swanage. Photo: Mike Robertson

Lulworth

Charlie Woodburn on the Lulworth classic. *Gates of Greyskull* (7b+) - *page 63*. Photo: Keith Sharples.

Lulworth

The main attraction at Lulworth is the superb Stair Hole, a significant landmark on the map of UK deep water soloing venues. The impact it has had on the UK deep water solo scene cannot ever be over-estimated. Stair Hole's short leaning walls, amazing pocketed rock, deep water and huge collection of well-catalogued routes have to be seen to be believed: it's a hell of a way to spend a day! Added here is the famous and photogenic archway of Durdle Door - one of Britain's most-loved coastal features, and home to a few high quality and very bold solos.

The deep water soloing in the area is extensively developed, with numerous link-ups and route variations - the lower arch in the East Cave even has one or two 'named' holds! The routes are mostly located on the grossly-steep, reverse side of Stair Hole's big slabs, with further routes and traverses found within the crazy architecture of the well-constructed West Cave. Possibly the best single feature of Stair Hole, especially in the impressive East Cave region, is the abundance of 'tree holes' - big, accommodating pockets, which offer themselves up just when you want them most.

Access

The Lulworth area is owned by the Weld Estate, who do not wish climbing to take place on their land. Officially climbing is not allowed, and the descriptions are included here for completeness.

Approach

All approaches to the area are likely to bring you to either Dorchester or Poole. The road that sweeps the coast between these two towns is the A352; find your way to Wool, a small village some 12 miles east of Dorchester. At the railway level-crossing in Wool, take the smaller B3071 down to the village of West Lulworth, where the road's end brings you to the Pay and Display car park (recommended is the free parking by the church, back up the road a little). Walk out of the car park past the Lulworth Cove Centre, and take the small track up onto a wide ridge, from where you'll get your first view of Stair Hole, seen down to the right. A short walk down the steep hill leads you to the boulder and pebble beach, which is the best gearing-up spot. Durdle Door is found just a little west of Stair Hole - for the approach, see page 60.

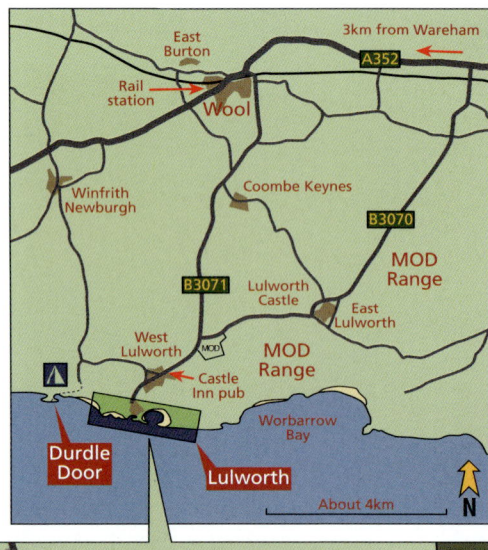

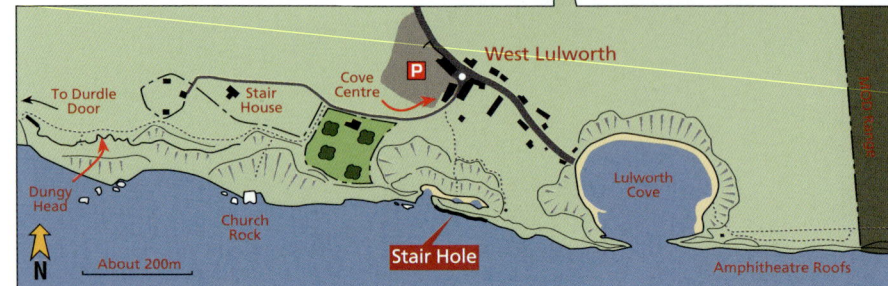

Danie Rushmer enjoying the sunlit prow of *Cheddar Direct* (4+) - *page 62* - Stair Hole. Photo: Mike Robertson.

Conditions and Tides

Although Durdle Door is by necessity a spring tide venue, the more popular Stair Hole is perfect for neap/smaller tide days, with plenty of water in the middle of the day, when you need it. Note that bigger tides make some of the traverses a little more problematical, especially with a little swell thrown into the equation - *The Maypole* is an example of this.

Although conditions here are usually fine for a visit, it's hard to predict the arrival of condensation on some of the steeper routes. This is partly due to the canted angle of the cliff - the height of the sun in the summer denies many of the routes a full hit of sun, despite the south-facing aspect of most of the routes.

One further point: new for 2007 is the re-vamped local sewage system for West Lulworth - never again will we have to share the ocean with floating 'undesirables'!

Stair Hole Approaches

The West and East Caves of Stair Hole have various approaches and traverse pitches:

West Cave Approach 1 - *The Maypole* provides the approach into the cave, coming in from the west/seaward side. The climbing is about grade 3 until you reach the cave entrance, and this approach takes you past routes from *Cheddar Direct* through to *Animal Magnetism*. To reach the start of *'Skeletor* and *Herbert'*, you will need to embark upon some of the harder moves on *The Maypole*, to get inside the cave proper.

West Cave Approach 2 - To gain the ledges below *Gates of Greyskull*, your preferred method is to scramble up to the ridge and drop down into the Grotto Ledge. From here, the traverse line of *Last Season's Loozas* will take you all the way along to the eastern/seaward edge of the West Cave.

East Cave Approach 1 - As with West Cave Approach 2, the ridge scramble gets you along and down into the Grotto Ledge. *Stage Divin'* starts directly from this ledge. From here, an easy down-climb drops you to sea level to gain routes from *Captain Bastard* through to *Window of Opportunity*.

East Cave Approach 2 - To reach the short slab below the start of *Horny 'Lil Devil* and *Mark of the Beast*, continue along that top ridge (gearing spot), and along the continuation upper faultline, then drop down a short groove to gain the slab. Scramble back westwards towards the cave to reach the routes.

Three Great Parks
One Superb Destination

3 Great Parks
Situated Nr Weymouth only 5 miles from Portland

Sea Barn Farm • www.seabarnfarm.co.uk
Probably the most beautiful park in Dorset. Quiet family run park with fabulous views over coast and Dorset countryside.
Email: enquiries@seabarnfarm.co.uk • Tel: 01305 782218
Open March 15 - 31 October.

West Fleet Holiday Farm • www.westfleetholidays.co.uk
Kids love camping at West Fleet with its family clubhouse and outdoor pool.
Email: enquiries@westfleet.co.uk • Tel: 01305 782218
Open Easter – September

Bagwell Farm Touring Park • www.bagwellfarm.co.uk
Family Park open all year for caravans, tents and motor homes. Overlooking the Chesil Beach. Bar on site in main season. Short walk to pub.
Email: enquiries@bagwellfarm.co.uk • Tel: 01305 782575

All 3 parks all have great views and are ideally situated for discovering Dorset.

Welcome to Dorset

Lulworth — Durdle Door

Durdle Door

Durdle Door's routes are legendary and often discussed in the DWS world (mainly in the pub), but they're rarely climbed. The arch's seaward face is canted at an alarming 35°, and both the height and the depth need a proper appraisal before your ascent. The lines here are absolutely inspiring - and the very top of the crag has been dived (Nigel Rendell, circa 1990). Recommended is an abseil inspection and recce, and an off-season timetable which avoids any damage to water-borne holiday-makers!

Approach - The best way to reach Durdle Door is to drive west out of the village from the church (towards Winfrith), and up the long hill to the very top, where a bend to the right provides verges and free parking. Walk down the tarmac road into the Durdle Door Caravan Park, and follow your nose. The path takes you through the site, and all the way down to Durdle Door itself. Take the slight path/scramble along the top ridge above the beach, which brings you out to the top of the arch.

Conditions and Tides - The rock on the arch is predominantly good, but expect to clean and inspect your line as a necessary part of your ascent. The arch is steep: the high summer sun, much like Stair Hole, will give shade on most of the walls here, so check for condensation and dampness before your ascent, especially in the evenings. A VERY big tide would be desirable - recommended is an early evening spring tide.

The first line is reached by abseiling from a block/thread on the ridge. The slabby/landward side is easier to arrange; but abseiling down the rear/left side will keep those tourist's photos uncluttered!

❶ Arcwelder 7b S3
28m. A huge and enticing challenge. It's effectively a counter line to *Riding to Babylon*, finishing in almost the same place. Climb the hard lower arete to better holds, and confidently commit yourself to a long and lonely wander, not all on jugs, all the way up the leaning face to the ridge above.
NYS

❷ Arch Enemy ... 7? S2
20m. This punchy, unrealised link-up constitutes the lower crux of *Arcwelder* with brilliant positions crossing the lower section of the arch. It thereafter crosses *Riding to Babylon*, finishing as for *Sardine Liberation Front*.
NYS

The next two routes are reached either by a down-climb at grade 3, or an abseil down the shorter buttress just right of the arch.

❸ Riding to Babylon 7a+ S3
28m. A stunning line. Mind-blowing positions on a sustained 35° overhanging face, with both a mid-height crux and a top one. Climb the lower arete direct up to the niche, thereafter eschewing the slab and heading leftwards up the hideously steep wall to (hopefully) pass a series of slopers just below the top. Walk the ridge with wobbly legs and retire for ice cream or beer.
FSA. Mike Robertson 1.9.2001

❹ Sardine Liberation Front 6c+ S2
20m. The original route here. A well-positioned line, venturing up the 'Door's perfect eastern arete. The arete can be viewed (as can the climber) from the main shingle beach. Follow *Riding to Babylon* to the accommodating resting niche. Pull strenuously rightwards out of this to a ledge system, and head off rightwards up the slab to the top ridge.
FSA. Andy Donson 2.7.1989

The Laws Traverse Wall — Stair Hole

The Laws Traverse Wall
The first area to be described is the Laws Traverse Wall, found on the far right as you walk down.
Approach - From the end of the beach, you'll need to scramble/paddle over to the fisherman's slab. At high tides, a little additional climbing will be required.
Conditions and Tides - The rock here gets a full hit of morning sun, and is normally dry. A high tide affects the approach, and also the brilliant low 'fin' variation. For the usual line of the route, a good tide and a calm sea will see you on your way.

❺ Trashy's Arete 5 S2
12m. Approach via *The Laws Traverse* (6b+!). The line of the left arete is taken to a finishing ledge. Once at the final, big standing ledge, your options are, ranging from safe-ish to scary; down-climb the route, down-climb *The Walking Dude* or jump!
FSA. Mike Robertson 7.9.2005

❻ The Walking Dude
.... 6b+ S3
13m. This shapely and very steep crack sees few ascents; it feels somewhat bold at anything other than huge spring tides. Swing across *The Laws Traverse* initial roof to the first rest, then climb the very steep diagonal crack up the buttress. Descend as for *Trashy's*.
FSA. Mike Robertson 26.6.1993

❼ The Laws Traverse . 6b+ S1
20m. The first ascent of this route involved a team of four; that's just how it should be enjoyed. Consider it generally around S1, although the roof crux is very depth-dependent. Swing powerfully below the first roof (crux) to gain a spacious sit-down rest (room for four). Traverse steeply leftwards to a rest in the second, smaller cave (beware flapping, restless pigeons), and continue to the far arete to finish. You'll now need to reverse the route to get out. At mid-tide there's a brilliant and pumpy low 'fin' variation; there's also a 6c variation at the end, possible at low tide only.
FSA. Pete Oxley, Steve Taylor, Mike Robertson, Gideon Fitch 29.5.1993

❽ Laws Direct Start 7b S1
6m. Outright burliness, but VERY close to the water indeed. This direct start swings through the prominent hole on big slopers to arrive at *The Laws Traverse* little sit-down slab in the first cave. Choose about 1m of water for a leg-wetting splashdown above shingle.
FSA. Mike Robertson 5.7.1995

Stair Hole — West Cave

Last Seasons Loozas
To beach

West Cave

The West Cave is an architectural delight, with pockets, grooves and roofs galore. It's actually steeper than the East Cave. The rock is usually impeccable, but take care with the exits up the easy upper slab.

Approach (see page 58) - *The Maypole* gets you to routes from *Cheddar Direct* through to *Herbert the Turbot*. For *Gates of Greyskull* through to *Hairy Clamber*, you'll need to traverse in along the line of *Last Season's Loozas*, described on page 64.

Conditions and Tides - Any midday neap tide will be just perfect. You can get to these routes at high spring tides, but only with a calm sea. A day with low humidity and a fresh breeze will give best conditions.

The Maypole can be performed either way, but recommended here is the anti-clockwise version. This is also your approach to the left side of the West Cave.

❶ The Maypole 6a *S0*
65m. A brilliant and popular traverse through Stair Hole's magical West Cave. The grade will depend on whether you use the higher slab variation to cross the inner cave, and also on the tide level of the moment. It can be very hard to keep your feet dry at higher tides, especially when climbing the low variation which feels more like 6b+ at higher tides. From the beach, traverse easily out into the bay, and continue on the sunny side all the way to the outer West Cave entrance. An involved and sustained section (the higher slab provides the 6a option) finally brings you back out to the beach.
FSA. Jon Williams 23.5.1990

❷ Cheddar Direct . . . . 4+ *S1*
12m. A steady route, taking the perfectly-positioned low arete on its nose, with plenty of water below. Care is required with the upper slab, which constitutes much easier climbing.
See photo on page 57.
FSA. unknown

❸ Truth, Justice and the Ragamuffin Way
. . . . 6a+ *S1*
12m. A beautiful line. Less visited than it ought to be; is it really that intimidating? Climb the lower face to a good rest, and pull steeply rightwards on jams and slots to stretch for the elusive upper groove. Finish much more easily, heading gradually up and right on the upper slab.
FSA. Jon Biddle 20.7.1991

❹ Crazy Notion . . . . . 7a+ *S0*
12m. A good direct version of *Animal Magnetism*, and a tricky on-sight proposition. Climb *Animal Magnetism* to the third hidden pocket, and continue direct up the very steep wall and groove to the top slab.
FSA. Mike Robertson 22.8.1995

❺ Animal Magnetism . . . 7a＋ *S0*
12m. A staggeringly good pocket-pull! Steep and powerful, and one of Stair Hole's finest. Climb the easy groove (big undercut), locate the sequential hidden pockets on the steep section, and swing up and rightwards to gain the jutting prow. Grasp for a 'pint glass handle' hold, and finish up the short but very punchy top groove.
FSA. Joff Cook 7.1994

West Cave **Stair Hole** 63

⑥ Never Kneel to Skeletor
.... 7c+ *S0*
13m. A maniacal blast up a wildly overhanging groove. One of the steepest lines in Dorset! Safe as houses and far more out than up. From the inner cave bolt belay above *The Maypole*, lunge outwards on an endless series of side-pulls, to arrive at a brief shake on a jug. Continue through the desperate, technical crux to gain the finishing groove of *Animal Magnetism*.
NYS

⑦ Herbert the Turbot
.... 7a+ *S0*
8m. A small route with a BIG reputation; superb! Start as for *Never Kneel to Skeletor*, but fall across the cave into a body bridge. Now you're committed! Grasp for good holds on the far side, then swing across with sweet abandon (you now have no choice in the matter…), and forge rightwards with sustained interest to arrive at the start ledge of *The Gates of Greyskull*.
FSA. Jon Biddle 22.7.1991

⑧ The Gates of Greyskull
.... 7b+ *S0/1*
11m. An exhilarating blast, and one of the best routes of its grade in the world. The line takes the hanging right prow of the west cave, and is witheringly steep. Head off from the lower shelf, and climb up a selection of jugs, to arrive at a series of flat side-pulls just below the top. Take a deep breath and slap your way up to a hidden slot just over the top; the last rock-over move is a breeze. *See photo on page 54.*
FSA. Joff Cook 14.8.1995

⑨ Magnetic Gates
7c *S0*
12m. A superb link-up, joining the lower juggy wall of *The Gates of Greyskull* with the top groove of *Animal Magnetism*. Climb the lower section of jugs, then make desperate moves leftwards across a slight hand ramp, to finish in the big V-groove.
FSA. Damian Cook 20.7.00

⑩ The Honorary Society of Self-Publicising Water Rats
.... 6c+ *S2*
10m. Negotiates the roof section to the right of *The Gates of Greyskull*. Climb the initial wall (keep a watchful eye on the jutting lower reef), then attack the bulges on a combination of slopers and big pockets. An under-rated line, although not without some danger and a few creaky finishing holds.
FSA. Damian Cook 6.1996

⑪ Hairy Clamber ....
5 *S1/2*
10m. A nice little delve into Lulworth culture. From the lower reef, climb up and then rightwards, to follow the weakness all the way to a final move onto the top slab. Finish much more easily.
FSA. Damian Cook 7.2000

Stair Hole — Inner West Cave

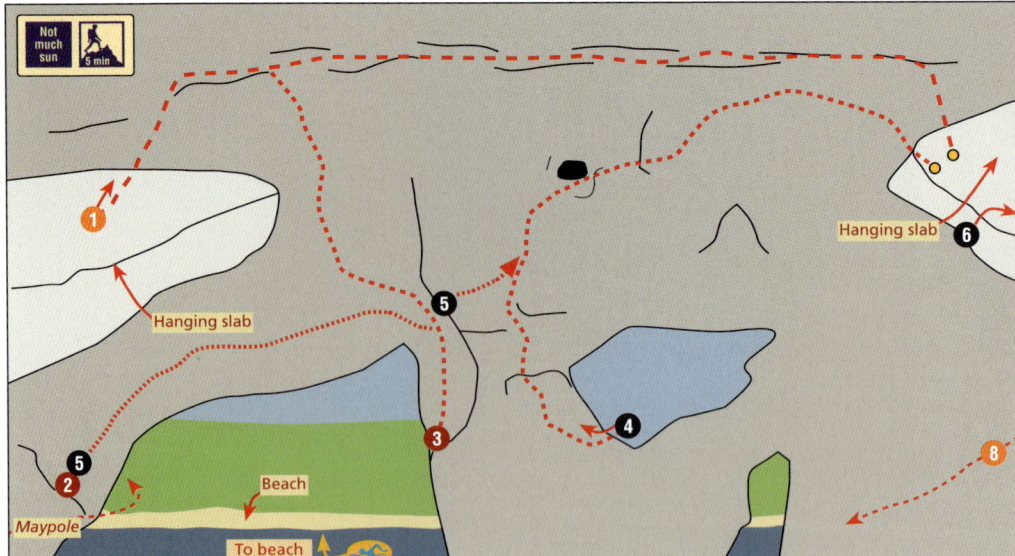

① Route 66 .... 6a S1
9m. This line is almost DWS caving, up high in the roof of the West Cave. From the hanging slab in the cave, make a bold move (spotter required) to gain the big, hanging roof 'tunnel'. Follow the tunnel all the way to the finishing ledge.
FSA. Mike Robertson 30.7.1994

② Escobar 7a S0
5m. Small and fun, but steep; expect a struggle. From *The Maypole* resting niche, crank rightwards across the inside of the arch (hidden pocket) and drop down slightly to gain the small, lower ledge inside the pillar. Traverse out and drop down to the window feature.
FSA. Joff Cook 1.8.1995

③ Contortions 7a S1
5m. Another micro-gem. Take a spotter (at *S1*) for the finishing moves, where the finish slab is close to your head. From the West Cave's 'window', traverse in and climb the overhang, with some wild moves to gain the central hanging slab.
FSA. Mike Robertson 1.8.1995

④ El Guapo .... 7b+ S0
9m. "The Beautiful". An excellent and bouldery test-piece requiring good conditions. From the window, attack the pockets on the grossly overhanging wall above with verve. Continue across and rightwards on progressively larger pockets, to the small finishing ledge high on the east side of the cave.
FSA. Joff Cook 19.9.1995

⑤ El Diablo Suelto 7c S1
14m. The hardest route inside the West Cave, linking just about every hard move on offer between *The Maypole* and the small finishing slab high on the east side. Start as for *Escobar*, but stay high for brief involvement with *Contortions*, before taking on the ferocious *El Guapo* all the way to its finish.
FSA. Dave Pickford 8.1998

Inner West Cave
The inner cave can be hard to find in good condition, but is a great venue when it dries out, usually in late season. Take a spotter in with you for the upper slab.
Approach - *Route 66*, *Escobar* and *El Diablo Suelto* are reached by way of *The Maypole* traverse. Reverse this route from the beach to gain an inner ledge system just inside the West Cave, which accommodates 2 or 3 folk. To reach *Contortions* and *El Guapo*, cross the beach and climb into the 'window'. The routes start inside the window's pillar.
Conditions and Tides - A calm sea and dry conditions are required here; a dry southerly breeze would be perfect. Any neap mid-high tide will provide enough water.

⑥ Old Timer's Club... 7b+ S1
10m. Starting from the finishing ledge of *El Guapo*, swing rightwards across the steep, slotted wall, until a full body-drop to the lip takes you rightwards to all the hard stuff on *Herbert the Turbot's* finish (page 63). Finish as for that route.
FSA. Mike Robertson 8.2003

⑦ Lower than Whale Shit . 6c+ S0
10m. This line traverses the east side of the cave at low tide only, and features some hard, technical moves. From the start ledge of *The Gates of Greyskull*, traverse all the way into the cave, finally gaining the 'window' at the landward entrance.
FSA. Damian Cook, Gideon Fitch 8.1995

⑧ Last Season's Loozas 5 S1
60m. A terrific little escapade, traversing all the territory between the East and West Caves, thereafter continuing through the West Cave and back to the beach. Best tackled at about mid-tide, especially for the entry into the West Cave. Start on the Grotto Ledge and wander off westward, with a circular deviation beneath a bizarre, overhead through-cave, to finally arrive in the West Cave. Continue into the cave, and climb diagonally upwards, then drop down a slabby chimney to reach the exit 'window'.
FSA. Cook Brothers 21.7.91

Sheffield strongman Neil Bentley on the crux of *Horny Lil' Devil* (7a) - *page 67* - at Stair Hole, Dorset. Photo: Mike Robertson.

Stair Hole — East Cave

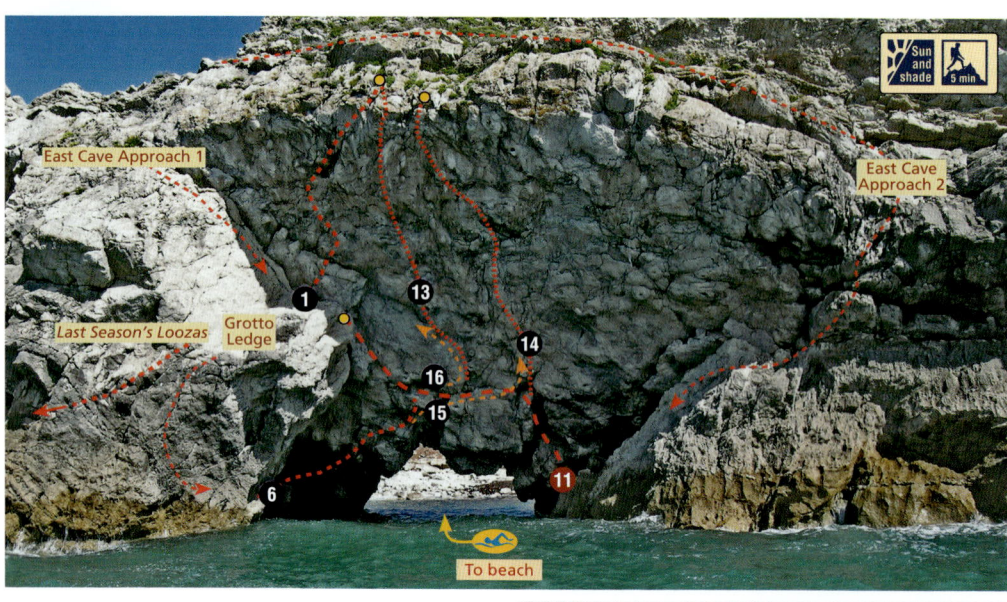

❶ Stage Divin'... 7a+ S2
9m. Use a spotter for the start moves. From the Grotto Ledge, make a desperate move to the right, and climb confidently up towards the diagonal niche above. Exit this rightwards, where some thought-provoking moves lead rightwards across the lip.
FSA. Pete Oxley 1993

The following routes are reached by down-climbing from the Grotto Ledge, via a steady line of jugs.

❷ Captain Bastard Got There First 6a+ S0
6m. The short, solid groove in the left side of the steep face. The climbing in the groove gets progressively harder, and the crux move is exiting the very top of the groove.
FSA. Joff Cook 21.7.1991

❸ Despicable Terrier 7a S0
7m. The right arete of *Captain Bastard*. Swing across the base of the very leaning wall, and make moves to gain the arete; a hard sequence on small holds gains the top.
FSA. Mark Williams 7.2004

❹ Anarchy Stampede 7a S0
8m. Steep as...! This oft-fallen-from line takes the grossly leaning face directly to the Grotto Ledge. The climbing is blind, and an on-sight attempt will rarely be static.
FSA. Jon Biddle 6.9.88

The following three routes will need a mid-tide or less.

❺ I Love Eszter 6b S0
10m. Sentimental old fool! The leaning corner/chimney to the left of *Windows of Opportunity*. Take it on when it's dry. From the groove of *Captain Bastard*, tiptoe rightwards along the low foot-ledge. Gain the challenging chimney line, and follow it past a big, jammed feature, to finally arrive back on the Grotto Ledge.
FSA. Damian Cook 10.7.1997

East Cave
Stair Hole's magnificent East Cave is a leaning wall slightly higher than the West Cave, and littered with tree-hole pockets of unimaginable size and depth. The rock is bullet-proof, the water mostly just where you want it, and the climbing exceptional.

Approach (see page 58) - The leftmost routes, from *Stage Divin'* through to *Window of Opportunity* are all initially approached by way of the top ridge, dropping down to reach the well-positioned Grotto Ledge. This ledge is also the best way to find the start of the 60m traverse of *Last Season's Loozas* (page 64).

The right-most routes, which all share the *Horny Lil' Devil* start, are gained by walking across the ledges at the top of the wall, then dropping down a groove to gain the lower slabby section of the crag.

Conditions and Tides - As with the West Cave, a neap high tide gives plenty of water. *I Love Eszter* through to *Window of Opportunity* as well *Sliding Down the Banister* need a lower tide to approach.

❻ Window of Opportunity 7b S0
12m. Entertaining and very pumpy. From the ledge at the base of *I Love Esther*, climb up and rightwards on side-pulls, jugs and pockets, to finally gain the double knee-bar on *Horny Lil' Devil*. Finish leftwards, as for that route.
FSA. Mike Robertson 8.98

The start of the next route is reached from the central beach.

❼ Thieving Gypsy 7b+ S0
12m. A very low tide and dry conditions will be required for success. Start from the beach slabs, and traverse in underneath the arch, heading towards the start of *I Love Esther*. The crux is on small holds and undercuts. Continue all the way across to the groove of *Captain Bastard*.
FSA. Gavin Symonds 9.2003

East Cave **Stair Hole** 67

8 Imp of the Perverse 7b+ S0
12m. Steep and fun. From the start of *Thieving Gypsy*, climb across the slab to gain the landward apex of the arch. Drop down and climb all the way around the underside of the lower arch, to finally reach the porthole hold on *Horny'*. Finish as for *Horny'*.
FSA. Gavin Symonds 6.2006

9 Hornier than Thou.. 7b+ S0
11m. A terrific route, and never very far from the ocean. From the start slab, drop across onto the lower face and flap wildly on slopers and side-pulls, to gain the wide niche on *Window of Opportunity*. Reverse that route to the other side.
FSA. Joff Cook summer 1999

10 Z Cars 7b S0
11m. This line is a powerful variation linking *Hornier than Thou* to *Horny Lil' Devil* by way of a rightwards move up into the deep pocket (the 'porthole' hold on *Horny Lil' Devil*).
FSA. Joff Cook summer 2001

11 Horny Lil' Devil 7a S0
11m. Brilliant and pumpy. An arm-shattering pump without the height. The footwork proves surprisingly technical. From the entry slab, climb up into the start niche (spotter advised for this sequence), and pop across the steep juggy break to a comfortable, hands-off double knee bar. After a breather, dive leftwards to finish at the Grotto Ledge. *See photo on page 65*.
FSA. Pete Oxley 1993

12 Sliding Down the Banister 6c S0
11m. A low-slung traverse, linking the wall with the slabs facing the beach. From the start of *Horny Lil' Devil*, drop down and climb past the roof of the through-cave until it's possible to gain the hanging slabs on the other side. A scramble across the slab to the central beach area gets you home.
FSA. Pete Oxley 23.5.1992

13 Adrenochrome . 8a+ S1
13m. A dynamic route of the highest calibre. The line of pockets up the very centre of the East Cave's leaning face is a gem. Start as for *Horny Lil' Devil* and continue directly up from its break on pockets, with a number of dynos in the central section.
FSA. Rich Bingham 8.1999

14 Mark of the Beast .. 7c S2
13m. This amazing, well-catalogued classic has seen more splashdowns than a public swimming pool. Take a large tide, as the lower slab is below you for the first third of the route. From the start of *Horny Lil' Devil*, glide up the juggy, leaning wall above, with the moves getting progressively harder. The crux is right at the very top, of course. *See photo on page 28*.
FSA. Pete Oxley 1994

There are two big and powerful link-ups that need a mention.

15 Pump up the Beast 8a S1
17m. The main event! A brilliant, very lengthy link-up of *Window of Opportunity*, *Horny Lil' Devil* and *Mark of the Beast*, providing the pumpiest solo at Stair Hole. Safe, hard and superb.
FSA. Rob Sutton 16.8.2003

16 Windows / Adrenochrome 8b S1
16m. This incredible link-up will one day be the hardest DWS in the UK. Take *Window of Opportunity* to the double knee-bar rest, then reverse the crux of *Horny Lil' Devil*, thereafter diving straight up the spaced jugs of *Adrenochrome*.
NYS

Portland

Steep and Juggy: Hazel 'Hammy' Findlay on the last hard move of the spectacular *Crab Party* (6c) - *page 89* - Cave Hole, Portland. Photo: Mike Robertson.

Portland

Dorset's Isle of Portland is one of the prime spots in the UK for deep water soloing, attracting a large number of visitors during the summer months. The Isle is the true home of *DWS before breakfast* due to large tides that only swamp the isle early and late in the day, on the bi-monthly spring tides. This gives the soloist an early start at the ultra-steep, morning sun venue of Cave Hole, which can be supplemented by an early evening dash to the western side of the Isle for a stab at some of White Hole's many face routes. If your idea of climbing utopia relies on a lengthy sunbathing session in the midday sun, regular visits here should prove to be right up your street! Portland's DWS history stretches back to 1989 when the first solo forays were recorded at Cave Hole and, since then, the solo scene has gone from strength to strength. Whatever your grade, and whatever your choice of angle, the Isle of Portland has plenty to offer.

Approach
Portland is just south of the coastal town of Weymouth on the south coast. An approach from the north, west or east will ultimately get you to the big town of Dorchester, where the A354 is taken, bringing you to the harbour in Weymouth. Follow the A354 signs to Portland, passing through the last mainland town of Wyke Regis. The drive across the unique Chesil Beach road follows, finally landing you on the Isle in the rather quaint 'outpost' of Fortuneswell.

Conditions and Tides
As hinted as above, the island is well known for its tidal quirks and the importance of your timing cannot be over-emphasised. The water is generally not very deep and some of the routes can even be walked under at a spring low tide (see picnic picture, page 16). For successful visits you will need to master the tide tables and visit at, or around, the twice-monthly spring tides which should give you ideal water levels before 11am and after 5pm. This timing NEVER changes! Put another way, you'll always have deeper water at high tides that occur early and late in the day, with your typical midday high tides offering much less water to climb above.

Conditions on the Isle vary considerably. Expect rock at sea level to suffer condensation in the shade, and always aim for a little sunshine, combined with a cool breeze. Cave Hole receives most hits in the morning, when the sun comes out to play; White Hole and the west coast see more attention late in the day.

Accommodation - www.rockfax.com/areas/dorset/accommodation.html
There are endless possibilities in the region for hotels and B&B accommodation. Any search on the internet will drum up some ideas, or try calling Portland Tourist Information (01305 861233) or Weymouth Tourist Information (01305 785747) - **www.weymouth.gov.uk/visitors/**. There's still no official camping on the Isle, but there are two campsites over on the mainland, off the B3157 near Fleet - 01305 782218 gets you through to both of these. For caravan parks, try the one near Easton, on the Isle's east coast - 01305 823548.

Food and Booze
Portland has a host of supermarkets, restaurants, pubs and take-aways. For breakfast, you will almost certainly end up in either the long-standing Sugar Loaf Cafe at Easton, or at the more recent and very popular Bluefish Cafe, in Fortuneswell. There's a good Chinese take-away close to the Bluefish, an Indian hotspot up the road, and, for sunsets from heaven, you'll always find the regular DWSers down at the Cove House pub on Chesil Beach - that is, when you can prise them away from the evening spring tides at White Hole!

All part of the fun! Local legend Joff Cook 'off' the test-piece *Water Wings* (7a+) - *page 89* - Cave Hole, Portland. Photo: Mike Robertson.

Portland

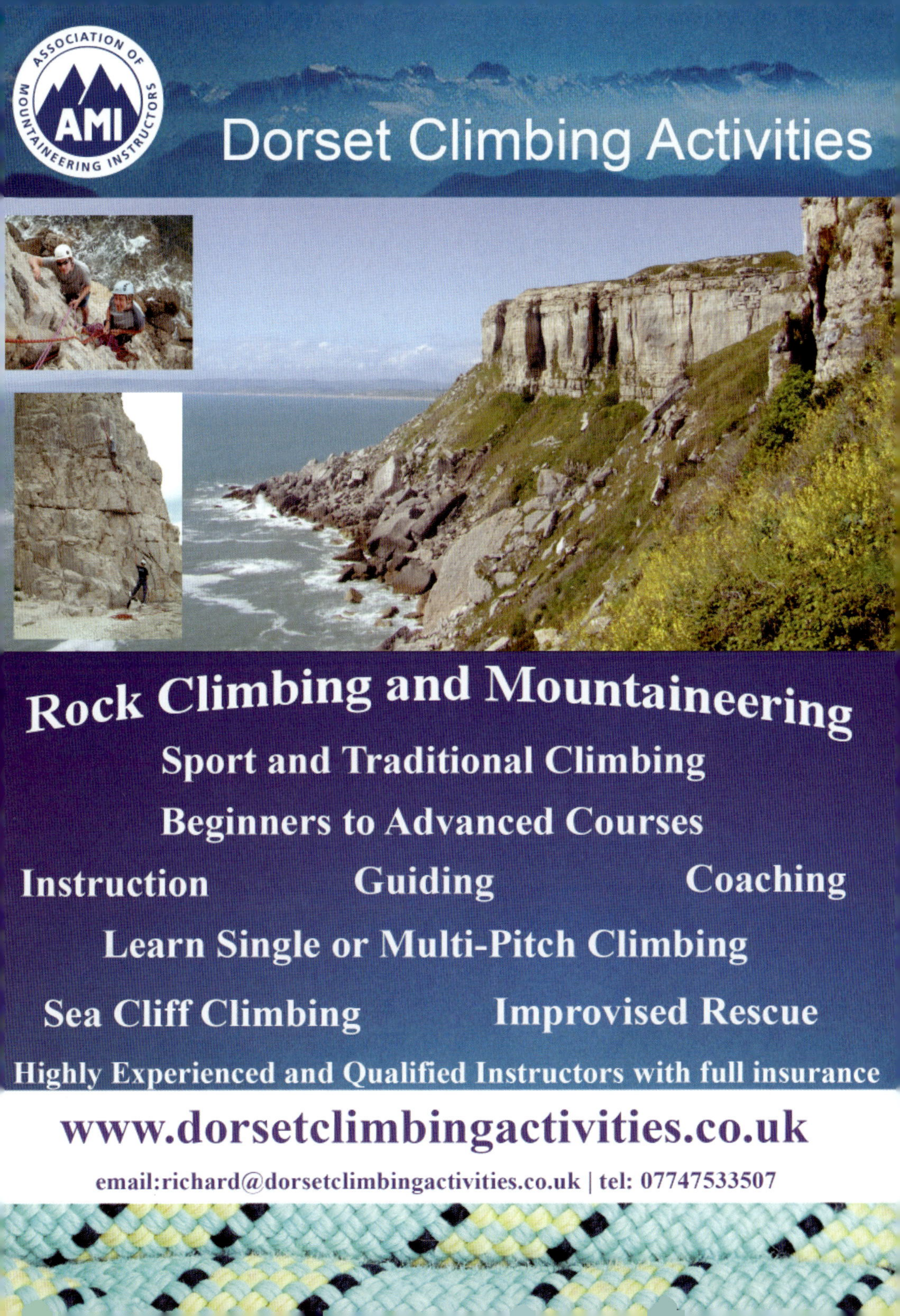

Dorset Climbing Activities

Rock Climbing and Mountaineering

Sport and Traditional Climbing

Beginners to Advanced Courses

Instruction   Guiding   Coaching

Learn Single or Multi-Pitch Climbing

Sea Cliff Climbing   Improvised Rescue

Highly Experienced and Qualified Instructors with full insurance

www.dorsetclimbingactivities.co.uk

email: richard@dorsetclimbingactivities.co.uk | tel: 07747533507

White Hole

White Hole is an essential part of the Portland DWS hit-list and has two main areas offering some amazing climbing which is more technical than steep. The rock is rough, the holds are often very small, and the climbing feels committing on your first visit (it won't later on, you'll be in love by then). Most of the routes are about 13m high and usually somewhere close to vertical, although there are a few lines here that steepen up a little more.

Approach
The crags are found behind the fence of the MOD establishment at Portland Bill. From the Pay and Display car park, walk past the toilets and keep close to the MOD fence, which is on your right. When the fence swings right at the sea level ledges, keep following it along to the final section of the zawn down and below to your left (this is Mirthmaid Zawn). You'll see a high, barbed-wire fence that seeks to prevent you taking the high path into the area (and a number of wild disclaimer notices!). Your choice here is to either; negotiate the left edge of this high fence past the barbed wire - VERY exposed - and the wire seems to get up-rated every so often, or; hop over the final narrow bit of the lower gully, scramble up the lower gully/zawn, and carefully climb up and leftwards to follow a shelf along to the main ledge at the top, to gain the big platform at the top of the Mirthmaid Wall.

Conditions
Humidity and damp weather will affect the routes at White Hole and, unless there is a cool breeze whistling through the zawns, the routes might feel a little stiff. The sea can get rough, so take care when selecting a time to visit, check the tides carefully, and scope your swim-out point in advance. If you can, stick to well-endowed spring tides, and pay the usual attention to currents. If in doubt, don't climb here!

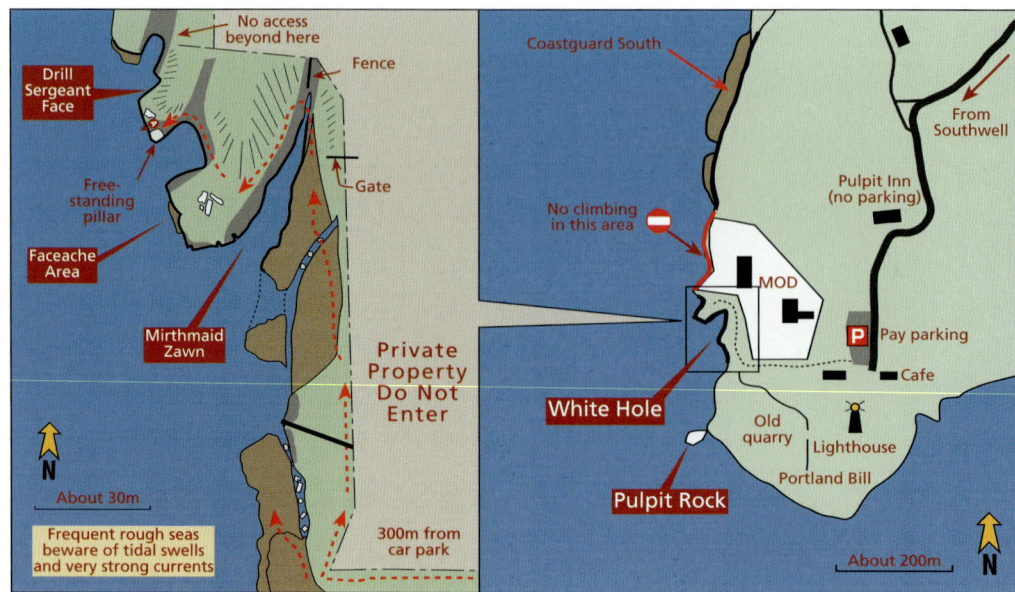

Drill Sergeant Face — White Hole

Drill Sergeant Face

A bizarre little inlet, tucked away below the barbed wire of the establishment above. One of those *it-could-only-be-Portland* scenarios! The few routes here are excellent and, with any decent high spring tide, you will have some gems to throw yourself at. *The Drill Sergeant* is one of the best in the area.

Approach - Access is by trotting around the 'narrow' top ledge from the main *Mirthmaid* platform (don't go too high, up by the upper fence - that's a dead end). Follow the top edge of the 13m cliff below you to reach a perched boulder at the top of *The Drill Sergeant*. This is your abseil point for all routes in the zawn. Take a Rock 3, a sling and a 15m rope for the abseil belay.

Conditions and Tides - A massive tide is required for *Until the End of Man*. For the rest, any reasonably high tide will do. The zawn gets evening sun in the summer and it is well worth planning your visit to coincide with a late afternoon tide.

❶ Hung, Swung and Zawned Out 6a+ *S1*
18m. A wandering line on the inlet's south side which has plenty of water on a good spring tide. Start at the high tide belay ledge on the front edge of the zawn. Climb leftwards into the zawn for about 10m, on the excellent horizontal jug rail, all the way to a bulge. Tackle this and follow a line of big flake features up rightwards, and then up to the top.
FSA. Pete Oxley 10.1.1999

❷ Paraphilias 6c *S1*
16m. Follow *Hung, Swung...* until it's possible to move up to the rounded arete feature. Climb this on the left to finish up a slightly easier groove.
FSA. Chris Weedon 2.2.2000

❸ The Drill Sergeant. 6c+ *S1*
14m. An absorbing and well-positioned line; excellent and technical climbing. From the start ledge, traverse leftwards and then up and right, to a hands-off rest. Contemplate the crack above and go for it! The last hard move is just below the final bolt.
FSA. Martin Crocker 5.5.2001

❹ Until the End of Man 7a+ *S2*
13m. A brilliant route, venturing up the hanging arete, with wild exposure throughout. From the start ledge, climb directly up to a beak of rock, then make hard moves to pull onto the face above. Continue, on sustained and technical ground, to finally gain easier climbing up the last slice of the arete.
FSA. Martin Crocker 5.5.2001

White Hole — Faceache Face

Photo labels: Faceache Face; Mirthmaid Zawn; Until the End of Man; Drill Sergeant Face; 1, 2, 3

Faceache Face and Mirthmaid Zawn

A cracking venue, previously (and collectively) referred to as White Hole North. The routes are brilliant and very memorable, usually featuring smallish holds and pockets. You will need your best slippers here; leave your old boots in the car!

The routes are all on the huge jutting block with its south face 'creating' the Mirthmaid Zawn. Routes from *One Life* to *The Skin Trade* are on the west face of the block, and routes from *Sad Young Biscuits* to *Sister of Night* are on the east-facing side, in the big Mirthmaid inlet itself. The traverse into the Mirthmaid face is around 5+, and is a fine introduction in its own right.

Most of the routes here have now been fallen from on numerous occasions.

Approach - For all routes except *Sister of Night*, abseil down the west face to a good ledge system, where it's very easy to get rid of your harness. From here, either move leftwards for *One Life* and *Faceache*, or climb rightwards around the whole crag to gain access to all routes from *The Skin Trade* to *Nightmirth*. For the separate *Sister of Night*, abseil to a starting ledge at the back of the Mirthmaid Zawn. An alternative form of access here is the tape harness arrangement to gain the 'sitting' belay ledge found below *Splendid Isolation*.

Conditions and Tides - A substantial high tide is required to feel comfortable here, although many of the routes have their crux low down. Visit on dry, breezy days for best results, as the edges and crimps can feel very small on hot or damp days.

Exit - The swim-out, should you need it (most folk do here - eventually..!) is 15m or less.

❶ One Life ... 7b S3
14m. A gorgeous, hanging arete, and White Hole's only three star route. Check the water depth very carefully. From the west face's lower ledge system, traverse around leftwards and climb up the face left of the arete, gradually moving right to the top arete; finish on the arete direct.
FSA. Gavin Symonds 11.7.2006

❷ Faceache 7b S3
13m. A classic fingery face climb. Wait for a good spring tide. From the west face ledges, swing leftwards and climb the technical face right of the arete on edges and pockets.
FSA. Mike Robertson 11.7.2006

❸ The Skin Trade .... 6c+ S1
14m. The well-positioned arete is a cool line, with the added bonus of the deepest water on this section of rock. From the lower ledges, climb rightwards to teeter onto a good foot-ledge on the arete itself; then climb the very technical slab just left of the bolt line.
FSA. Steve Taylor 15.8.1994

❹ Sad Young Biscuits . 7a+ S1
11m. The slight groove in the right-hand side of the arete, starting in the lower sentry box. This line is usually approached by abseiling into the sentry box itself. Pull out of the low hard crux section, moving slightly leftwards on small holds; this takes you into a technical groove and an easier top-out.
FSA. Joff Cook 28.6.1997

❺ Dead In Europe. 7b S1
13m. Fun-lovin' slap territory; a cracker. An on-sight is both hard to read and usually dynamic. From the jugs at the base of *Splendid Isolation*, swing left along the slight break, then yard your way up the open side-pulls, dive for a tiny side-pull and leap for a big jug. More tricky stuff up a crack gains the top.
FSA. Mike Robertson 15.8.1994

Mirthmaid Zawn — White Hole

Mirthmaid Zawn

Start by traversing around from West Face

❻ Spitting Bullets.... 7b S1
13m. Excellent face climbing and a hard crux give a route that is at the top of the grade. The six or so resident 'pock-mark' holds are, in fact, bullet hits and two of the bullets are still in place! From the first moves of *Splendid Isolation*, make hard moves on a side-pull to head leftwards on small holds, briefly gaining the flat hold on *Dead in Europe*. From here, make thin moves up and right to gain the selection of shot-holes. A final tricky sequence up the steepening face gains the top.
FSA. Mike Robertson 15.7.2006

❼ Splendid Isolation.. 6c S1/2
13m. Just superb! The steady classic of the crag; a perfect crack, which is followed (but not always used) to an absorbing, airy crux. The route's first solo ascent was actually a down-climb to get to *Mirthmaid*; the boy did well! From the lower belay sit-down, grab the jugs and head, not without interest, to the soaring crack in the headwall. Follow this all way to the top, with a final crux move at the very top (hint: don't go left). *See photo on page 78.*
FSA. Damian Cook 1996

❽ Just for a Day..... 6c+ S1/2
13m. This unbolted line follows the vague rib right of (and parallel to) *Splendid Isolation*. From *Splendid Isolaton's* start moves, swing right and follow the rib, on mainly small holds and pockets, to the top (avoiding the easy moves rightwards to gain the upper crack of *Mirthmaid*).
FSA. Pete Oxley 15.5.2000

❾ Mirthmaid.......... 7a+ S0/1
13m. The low roof right of *Splendid Isolation* provides a tasty and safe boulder problem. From the lower traverse, swing out to the low roof, gain a deep pocket, and tackle a couple of poor slopers to gain a big side-pull system. Build up your feet, stretch for the break above, and saunter to the top with a smile on your face.
FSA. Damian Cook 28.6.1997

❿ Nightmirth....... 7c S1
14m. This route gives some very different climbing to the usual White Hole fare. From the start of *Mirthmaid*, continue rightwards along the lower break on small slots, catch a reasonable finger hold and use it to extend dynamically to the break above. Finish much more easily up the crack above.
FSA. Dave Pickford 7.2000

Approach (Route 11) - *Abseil to a starting ledge at the back of the Mirthmaid Zawn.*

⓫ Sister of Night 7b S1/2
14m. The prow/banana-shaped groove is a gem. Probably a V5 boulder problem between the two breaks. Check the depth carefully on this one, even though the top section is easy. Traverse leftwards from the biggest foot ledge to gain a jug at the base of the groove. Swing slightly leftwards and dash up the slopers to the next break. Finish on steady ground.
FSA. Pete Oxley 24.6.2000

⓬ Gav's Long Link-up. 6b S1
22m. This lengthy and enjoyable link-up provides the first-timer with a more amenable introduction to the brilliant face climbing found on the Mirthmaid Wall. The 22m length is from the abseil ledge at the rear - this link-up gives the longest and most consistent outing at White Hole. All the hard moves are dispensed with by mid-height and the rock is excellent throughout. From the lower traverse in, start up *Splendid Isolation* and then break out rightwards to finish up the steady crack of *Mirthmaid*.
FSA. Gav Symonds 14.7.2006

The established routes to the right of Sister of Night are not considered DWS's on account of the big protruding slabs found at their bases.

Gavin Symonds lay-backing the crack of *Splendid Isolation* (6c) - *page 77* Mirthmaid Zawn, White Hole, Portland. Photo: Mike Robertson.

Lighthouse Area

Portland Bill lighthouse and the wide blue yonder.
Photo: Mike Robertson

The much-photographed Pulpit Rock, probably Portland's most notable landmark, is a excellent crag, with a smorgasbord of six routes to choose from. Avoid the attendance of the local tombstonin' crew if possible - there are a LOT of airborne bodies here when they turn up! ('tombstoners' = mad locals who hurl themselves off the cliffs in wet suits).

Its sidekick, the Pulpit Overhang, adds a small collection of S0's to the list. Further to the north-east, you will find the friendly Deep Zawn with its appealing short walls and boulder-problem routes situated above perfect water.

Approach
This area is probably best approached from the Portland Bill Pay and Display car park. Pulpit Rock is signposted and is found on the west side of the headland, Deep Zawn is found in the other direction, underneath a rather rusty crane.

Conditions and Tides
A visit to Pulpit Rock, and the Pulpit Overhang, is rather dependent on the currents. The two metre gap between the Pulpit and the mainland tends to generate some very fast currents so ensure you only climb here when they are weak. A breeze will help conditions, especially if your mission is the brilliant *Tombstonin'* (6b+).

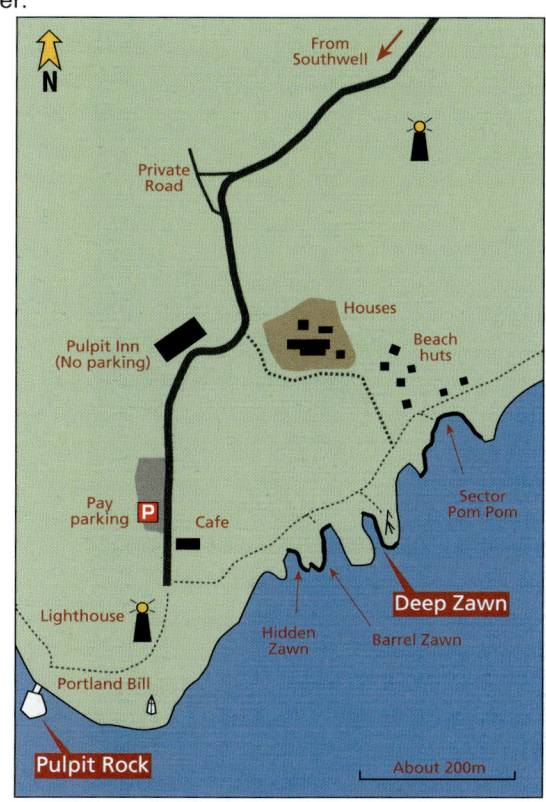

Lighthouse Area — Pulpit Overhang and Rock

Pulpit Overhang

An excellent, short, steep wall lying immediately north of the Pulpit. One of those perfect S0 scenarios: steep, never high and fully over the water.

Approach - Walk northwards from the Pulpit to an easy scramble down to the sea level ledges. Walk back along the bottom (towards the Pulpit) to reach the Pulpit Overhang. The access around the lower reef/ledges is easy, especially in calm seas.

Conditions and Tides - A weak current between the overhang and the Pulpit is essential - if in doubt, don't climb! On the plus side, the crag is about as S0 as it's possible to be, with deep water and routes never higher than 7m.

Pulpit Overhang

① Bent Pigeon 6c *S0*
6m. Short, punchy and fun. From the lower ledge, climb up and then right to an odd little 'sitting' rest; then climb through the roof and hanging wall above, on side-pulls and slopers, to gain the top.
FSA. Mike Robertson 27.6.2006

② Clarence 6c *S0*
11m. A very pumpy traverse of this steep wall. From the same start as *Bent Pigeon*, continue traversing across the steep wall, moving up a level after 5m, to finally finish under the big block that leans against the Pulpit.
FSA. Mike Robertson 27.6.2006

③ Project .... 7b? *S0*
7m. This possibility takes on the side-pulls over to the right of *Bent Pigeon*. From either side, traverse in to gain a small beak. From this, make hard moves to get established on the top wall, and throw for the top.

Pulpit Rock

Historically, the Pulpit hasn't featured on Portland's regular DWS circuit. This is due in part to voracious currents that occasionally sweep past the feature on falling and building tides. DON'T CLIMB HERE UNLESS YOU'RE SURE YOU CAN SAFELY SWIM OUT AFTER A FALL. That said, it's very obvious if there's a current running, as the sea looks like a river. Check this carefully before climbing here. The swim-out is short, except for *End of the Land*, which is more like 15m.

Approach - The routes on the Pulpit can be accessed by way of a tricky little 'drop' across the gap between the mainland and the block - this little escapade is on jugs, but feels a little committing when you first do it. This gives you the east face directly; for the other two routes, simply continue clockwise until you arrive at your chosen destination.

Conditions and Tides - Wait until there is a fresh breeze for the classic *Tombstonin'*; for the rest, a little morning sun comes in handy. A decent tide helps, but remember that possible current - it's more significant than the tide.

Pulpit Rock

④ Edge of Beyond 5 *S1/2*
10m. The flaked groove feature just right of the left arete offers some good moves, although the large flake at half-height moves slightly when prompted - so take care! The S grade caters for both this and the slight jutting ledge below.
FSA. Mick Ward 16.5.2004

⑤ Bleating Nincompoops .... 4+ *S1*
10m. The amenable groove to the right offers good climbing, and on excellent rock.
FSA. Mike Robertson 27.6.2006

⑥ Rapture of the Deep ... 6a *S0*
10m. This superb little route tackles the lower overlap, slab and a short finishing groove. Good positions, and safe as houses.
FSA. Mick Ward 17.5.2004

⑦ Swirling Pool 6a *S2/3*
10m. The crack in the right side of the face is great - but the landing 'trench' here is narrow. Take care.
FSA. Mick Ward 19.5.2004

⑧ End of the Land ... 6b+ *S2*
9m. The south-west arete is way out there! The lower reef is initially in attendance, but the first move of the route, heading leftwards towards the arete, puts you nicely above the drink, where you'll find a short section of balancy climbing. Start from the 1/3 height ledge at the back of the Pulpit. Climb leftwards from the ledge on small pockets, and embark on a series of excellent but technical moves up the right side of the arete itself.
FSA. Pete Oxley 25.6.2000

⑨ Tombstonin' .... 6b+ *S1*
11m. A divine feature: the dark north-west arete of the Pulpit offers superb climbing. A miniature classic. Ideally needs a stiff breeze to gain the right conditions for an ascent. A tricky traverse rightwards from the regular zawn crossing gains the low (the lowest) start ledge, or traverse the entire Pulpit clockwise to reach the same place. Pull through a steep start (start ledge initially slightly below you), moving leftwards on jugs to a tricky but safe rock-over and a rest. Move back right, then climb the cracked left side of the sharp arete to the top.
FSA. Pete Oxley 25.6.2000

Deep Zawn Lighthouse Area

Pulpit Rock

Deep Zawn

10 Project .... ? *SO*
8m. The striking crack feature will have a crux traverse to get to it. It looks hard and fingery.

11 Project .... ? *SO*
7m. The slanted groove to the right looks terrific. Any takers?

12 Sugar Daddy ..... 7a+ *SO*
7m. A brilliant and technical line. Descend the rusty chain. Traverse left around the prow on the vague foot break to gain the inviting tenuous layback; climb the wall on small side-pulls and pinches.
FSA. Ben Stokes 25.6.2000

13 All Things Being Relative
.... 6a+ *SO*
5m. A saner version of *Sugar Daddy*. Using the same start, swing around the prow; thereafter climbing the face to the left.
FSA. Matt Stammers 25.6.2000

14 Relativity.............. 6a+ *SO*
4m. The tight line of holds just to the right of *All Things Being Relative*. Climb the left side of the hanging prow directly.
FSA. unknown

15 The Red Crane Traverse ... 5 *SO*
18m. A superb introduction to the delights of the east coast, and on immaculate rock throughout. From the bottom of the chain, traverse rightwards along the break, all the way around the pointed headland, to finish on a ledge just above sea level.
FSA. Ben Stokes, Matt Stammers 25.6.2000

16 Wall of Squares .... 6a *SO*
4m. The face between the square quarried cut-outs. Start as for the *Red Crane Traverse*, then climb up the compact wall on pockets and edges.
FSA. Katie Dominey 2000

17 Red Crane Wall .... 6a *SO*
4m. The face right of the right-hand quarried cut-out. From the *Red Crane Traverse*, make tricky moves up and left, to gain the lower right edge of the square cut-out.
FSA. Phil Harris 2000

Deep Zawn
Great swimming and diving, excellent deep water, and nowhere too high: paradise! The venue is ideal for those getting acquainted with DWS for the first time.
Approach - From Portland Bill Lighthouse, walk along the coast until you reach the big rusty crane situated above a water-filled inlet. This is Deep Zawn. Descend via the rusty chain or ladder.
Conditions and Tides - Deep Zawn is entirely sheltered from south-westerlies, so any clear, sunny day should give optimum conditions. You'll find a mid-tide is easily enough water to climb above.

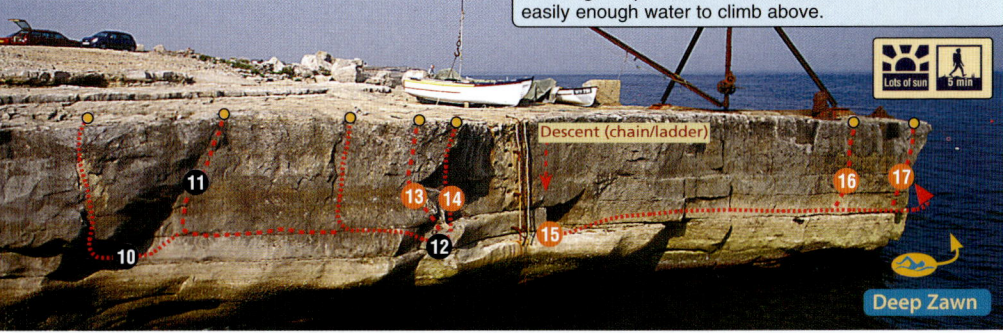

Deep Zawn

Cave Hole

Cave Hole consists of an amazing spread of caves, zawns and walls, all found on Portland's south-east coastline. This area is a mecca for the deep water soloist and offers everything from vertical walls to fully horizontal roofs; from sea level traverses to powerful boulder-problem routes. Here you'll find such classics as *Temporary Lifestyle* (4+), *Ixtlan* (6a), *Octopuss Weed* (6c), and *Crab Party* (6c), to name just a few.

The cliffs are rarely higher than 9m high, and this gives the area a generally comfortable feel - it's not unusual to find yourself immersed in a mob of climbers numbering at least 20, such is the pull of Cave Hole on balmy summer days.

The swimming, snorkelling and cliff jumping at Cave Hole are legendary - indeed, this latter pastime is de rigueur on the Isle, with youngsters (aka. *Tombstoners*) of every age turning up in their wet suits to have a bash.

Approach

Follow the coast path north from the main car park down at Portland Bill (Pay and Display). You'll walk past Deep Zawn, and continue walking past the biggest group of huts, until you find yourself looking down on a shingle beach in an inlet. This is Too Funky Beach, and everything north of here for about 300m constitutes Cave Hole. It takes a few visits to get properly acquainted with the area, as it's pretty sizeable; once you've got a few routes under your belt, you'll start to feel at home.

Conditions and Tides

The limestone is generally similar to the rough-textured west coast variety, although its situation in the many deep-set caves sometimes requires good dry conditions for the optimum climbing experience. As you'd expect on Portland, the tide and sea conditions have a great affect on the climbing here. Added to the difficulties of finding tides that are big enough, you'll also sometimes experience the frustration of the rather narrow tide 'window', which is usually limited to about 4 hours. The rock doesn't suffer much from seepage in the DWS season, the more usual problem is condensation, especially in the afternoon.

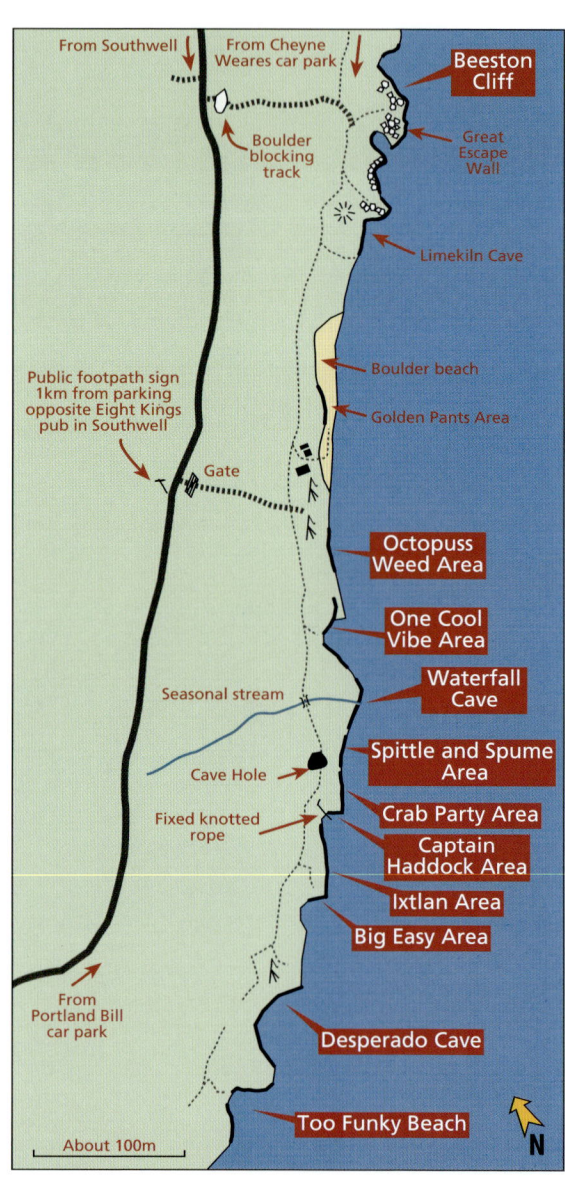

Too Funky Beach Cave Hole

Too Funky Beach

Trashy's Traverse

Too Funky Beach

Too Funky Beach is a great little cliff, although it is one of Cave Hole's most tidal venues. The routes are short and sweet, and pack in some great moves.

Approach - Walk along the top of the wall and down-climb an easy corner to sea level. This leaves you next to the arete of *Makin' Bacon* and from here all routes are reached by traversing leftwards across the wall's lower break-line.

Conditions and Tides - The Too Funky Beach is a spring tide venue. An early evening spring tide will do nicely, which gives the wall a chance for a full hit of sun before you arrive.

❶ Memory Lane 6a *S1*
30m. Not pictured. This fun traverse takes you southwards out of the Too Funky Beach. A high tide is recommended. Traverse out of the beach and continue past one hard bit to arrive at the finishing promontory.
FSA. Mark Williams, Mike Robertson 6.8.1994

❷ Penny Lane .... 6a+ *S1*
10m. A good traverse which can be performed in either direction (or, commonly, probably both). If the tide is up, start from the seaward end. Traverse the distinct hand break across the wall.
FSA. Mark Williams 6.8.1994

The steep Too Funky Wall is excellent, but only holds the DWS tag for as long as the water is up; catch a 2.1m tide or greater, for best conditions. The flat shingle below can offer some comfort where the water is shallower. Bear in mind that at a spring tide, the mid-height cruxes will drop you a mere 2-3m into the briny (it's not far!).

❸ Too Funky (For Me) . 6c+ *S3*
7m. A little gem, above shingle and just enough water. Climb up and right to a hard move (hint: get your right toe VERY high...) and continue on better holds to the top.
FSA. Mike Robertson 11.8.1995

❹ Big Boss 7a *S3*
7m. A narrow line between *Marine Boy* and *Too Funky*, with some very powerful moves above just about adequate water. Crank up to the roof and cross it, finishing direct.
FSA. Paul Savage 8.1998

❺ Marine Boy .... 6b+ *S2*
7m. Good climbing on this one. Originally soloed at high tide; the bolts were erroneously added later. Tackle the roof stack, on good but spaced holds.
FSA. Mike Robertson 10.6.1995

❻ Godzuki .... 6a+ *S1*
6m. The left-hand side of the arete. Similar climbing to *Marine Boy*, but a little less sustained.
FSA. Damian Cook 9.6.1995

❼ Makin' Bacon 6a *S1*
5m. After a hard start, launch your way up the arete direct to the top shelf.
FSA. Mike Robertson 5.8.1995. Named after a pair of socks.

Trashy's Traverse

The next two routes are found in the continuation cave just to the right of the Too Funky Face. You'll need a mega-tide for these.

❽ Trashy's Traverse .. 6b *S3*
12m. An atmospheric traverse-line on big, hanging flakes. From the left side of the cave (looking in), swing up and in to gain a very prominent sticking-out flake. Test your weight and continue, reaching easier ground for the second half of the traverse. Finish around the arete, where you might be tempted by the next route.
FSA. Mike Robertson 11.8.1995

❾ Eight Inches 7a *S1*
8m. This powerful route is poised over the high tide pool on the right side of *Trashy's* cave. Start on the right and traverse into the cave by way of a hard (and irreversible!) move, to find yourself committed to the route's finish. Make hard moves through the roof off an undercut/side-pull to gain the rail above.
FSA. Johnny Woods 22.7.2005

Cave Hole — Desperado Cave

Desperado Cave

The three striking pillars of the massive Desperado Cave have long been responsible for scaring the hell out of the most seasoned of soloists, but hopefully up-to-date information and topos might provoke more regular interest.

Approach - Routes from *Desperado* to *Mike's Free Willy* are approached by dropping easily down to half-height ledges on the left edge of the cave. From here, a further down-climb gets you on your way. For *Lick of the Cat*, down-climb *Pirates'*. *Surface Tension* requires a short swim with a dry-bag. To gain the start of *Temporary Lifestyle*, walk to the massive crane, and down-climb the fixed rusty ladder to sea level.

Conditions and Tides - A mid-high tide covers your bases. You will ideally need a fresh breeze for best conditions.

1 Desperado 6b S0/1
18m. A lengthy, diagonal classic, taking on the 'beef' of the southern end of the cave. Start on the ledge system on the far left, and drop progressively down to traverse the white section of wall just above the barnacles (a decent high tide will threaten your boots here). Keep traversing towards a big flake system and head diagonally rightwards to gain the top jugs.
FSA. Mike Robertson 9.6.1995

2 Psychoman . . . . 6a+ S2
11m. There's a spiked boulder in the water underneath the top crux - take care and check the water depth carefully. Follow *Desperado* until its crux, and avoid this by blasting straight to the top. Exit past a huge stuck-on jug and a pocket.
FSA. Mike Robertson 10.6.1995

3 Mike's Free Willy 6c S1
12m. Better water than *Psychoman* but it has a similar feel of commitment about it. Follow *Desperado* through its low traverse crux, and climb out of the groove to arrive at a high roof. Take this boldly to exit.
FSA. Damian Cook 23.7.1995

4 Lick of the Cat . . . . 6b+ S2/3
12m. A seldom-repeated, classic scare. The holds are fairly generous, but the ground is steep and the water depth often worrying. With a big high tide it might prove difficult to keep your boots dry on the leftwards traverse to reach the starting point in the cave beyond the route. Blast up the left side of the superb hanging prow and swing right to arrive at big, questionable dinner plate holds. Sprint to the top.
FSA. Damian Cook 9.6.1995

Big Easy Face Cave Hole 85

5 Pirates of the Black Atlantic 6a S1
10m. A lesser route than its neighbours, often done (and originally climbed) as a down-climb to access *Lick of the Cat*. It takes the pillar in the centre of the cave, found just below the square stone set in the cliff top. Move rightwards to finish.
FSA. Damian Cook 9.6.1995

6 Surface Tension 6c+ S2
13m. Exhilarating. Slip your boots and chalk bag into a dry-bag, and swim across from the ancient ladder to gain a small ledge at the base of the massively steep prow. A series of vertical moves take you to the 45° upper section. Continue boldly on - using the many quaintly stuck-in 'dinner plates' - to the top.
FSA. Mike Robertson 4.8.1995

7 Temporary Lifestyle 4+ S0
13m. A fine introduction to the world of DWS. From the base of the old rusty ladder, climb the weakness to the left to gain the overhangs. Follow the generous holds across this steep band to emerge on the far side.
FSA. Mike Robertson 31.7.1994

Big Easy Face

8 The Big Easy 6a+ S0
18m. This nifty little mini-expedition is essential to gain access to all the Ixtlan face (around the arete to the right) but is terrific in its own right. The route ventures across the initial vertical face and abruptly changes angle for the slightly harder traverse across the leaning face on the flip side. Continue to a big sit-down shelf. Once there, either reverse it, reverse half-way and ascend *Big Easy Arete*, or continue on to ascend one of the other lines.
FSA. Mike Robertson 6.8.1994

9 Foxy Chicks 6a+ S0
6m. This little jug-romp starts from the middle of the ledge. Reach up for a huge side-pull (a big reach for shorties), cut loose, and continue up the face on big slots to the top.
FSA. Mike Robertson 6.8.1995

10 Reel 'Em In 6b+ S0
6m. Start just right of *Foxy Chicks*. Make a long move around the lower roof to gain a decent diagonal hold; share on this, and crank your way up the slotted face above. *Photo on page 6.*
FSA. Damian Cook 21.5.1995

11 Aquamarina 7a+ S1
7m. A crimpy little beast indeed. Good climbing on small holds. Start out on *The Big Easy* traverse, gain a big side-pull hold, and blast smoothly (yeah, right) to the top of the crag. One that stops plenty of strong folk!
FSA. Steve Taylor 11.8.1995

12 The Little Hard 6a+ S2
7m. The faint groove left of the arete offers some chirpy climbing. From the arete, swing left, tackling the wall above on small crimps and side-pulls.
FSA. Mike Robertson 15.5.1995

13 Big Easy Arete 5 S0/1
7m. A charming feature which is good as a route in its own right, or as an escape route/access down-climb to the *Ixtlan* region, especially when the swell is wetting the back of *The Big Easy* zawn. From the lower jugs, climb the arete, past a bit of a sloper move, to gain the top shelf.
FSA. unknown

Big Easy Face
The highly accessible Big Easy Face is a mini-gem, giving the DWS-merchant a great viewing gallery and offering routes in a relatively benign environment.
Approach - Climb easily down to sea level, where a traverse into the face becomes clear.
Conditions and Tides - A high one will do nicely; when the air space in the arch under the face is filled in, you have enough water. The face can sometimes be damp in the morning.

Big Easy Face

Cave Hole — Ixtlan Area

Ixtlan Area

The Ixtlan Area is just around from The Big Easy Face, although it is hard to view it from there. A walk along to the hanging descent rope at the Captain Haddock Area will give the best view.

Approach - This face is best accessed by climbing around from The Big Easy Face.

Conditions and Tides - A high tide will serve you best, ideally with a calm sea. The face gets sun all morning.

❶ Massive Amounts of Strength 7b S2
7m. An eliminate. From a ledge just to the right of *The Big Easy* arete, climb straight up and tackle the roof above directly.
FSA. Martin Crocker 2.10.1996

❷ Huge Reaches 7a+ S1
8m. The testing groove to the right of the roof. Stretch between small holds to finally get established in the upper groove. Don't forget to check the boulders below carefully.
FSA. Martin Crocker 2.10.1996

❸ Lunge or Plunge 7a+ S1
10m. A terrific challenge; the roof left of *Ixtlan*. From the incut bay left of *Ixtlan*, move leftwards and up to a roof, then pull up and right to gain the short hanging groove. Further feisty moves gain the upper wall, and success.
FSA. Martin Crocker 5.10.1996

❹ Ixtlan 6a S1
10m. A wonderfully classic flowstone route. It starts about 7m after the completion of the traverse of *The Big Easy*, where a flowstone feature shows the way to the top. Climb the feature, on amazing welded holds, until grasping the very top of the crag; fumble for a bit and then perform a character-building rock-over to finish it all off (or try the purist's mantel).
FSA. Damian Cook 23.4.1995

❺ Karma 6b S2
10m. To the right of *Ixtlan* is a vague triangular roof with a crack through it. Check the depth over the submerged boulder carefully on this one. Climb the vertical wall on good flat holds and then swing right to reach for a jug in the roof. Pull up and through this via a hard rock-over and continue up, trending left to the top jugs.
FSA. Mike Robertson 8.5.1995

❻ Mad About You 6b S1/2
10m. A groove provides the meat of this line. High in the grade. Climb up into the groove on small crimps; continue on more reasonably-sized edges to the top, moving left to finish.
FSA. Mike Robertson 15.5.1995

There have been some lines climbed between Mad About You and the next route, but they all rise above a shallow underwater shelf, so haven't been included here.

❼ Russian Roulette 6b+ S0/1
35m (total). A long and invigorating line, linking *The Big Easy* with the arete at the 'pirate rope' end of the face. Climb the entire length of the brilliantly-sustained face, on good edges all the way. When almost at the arete, climb straight up, where a handful of tricky moves up the flowstone crack finally allows you onto the finishing shelf.
FSA. Mike Robertson 11.6.1995. The name refers to the dilemma of the parents of the first ascensionist as they sat incarcerated in a Moscow jail accused of visa irregularities.

Now that looks fun! Amy Colson on the infamous Pirate Rope at Cave Hole, Portland. Photo: Mike Robertson.

Cave Hole — Captain Haddock Area

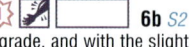

Captain Haddock Area

Walking south along the cliff top you will encounter a big, sunken hole in the ground. This is actually 'Cave Hole' itself - a huge blowhole, these days covered over with a people-friendly grid. A walk of a few metres to the cliff edge will get you to the Captain Haddock Area. This has a couple of good lines, and a quaint and exciting access arrangement - the thick, bolted-in knotted hemp rope was first planted here in 1995, and has seen a number of replacements since then.

Approach - Use the Pirate Rope! At its base, traverse right to reach the bulk of the routes.

Conditions and Tides - You will need a good tide here. This face can stay a little damp in the morning.

❶ Captain Haddock. 6b S2

10m. Surprisingly sustained for the grade, and with the slight jutting ledges below giving pause for thought. From the base of the rope, swing left and climb up to a steepening. Traverse back right to cross the rope and climb the face rightwards to the top.
FSA. Mike Robertson 19.5.1995

❷ Flipper Force 6c S0

9m. Traverse rightwards from the pirate rope, and do a hard move onto the wall above, just left of the stepped arete; a further technical move up and right enables you to reach the rather better top holds.
FSA. Damian Cook 19.5.1995. The third ascent was the scene of Joff Cook's hilarious cry of "take" as he plummeted towards the sea after pulling off a hold at the top (it would be a shame to leave that slice of history out!)

❸ Gourmet Shit Traverse. 6a S0

14m. The substance of this odd little outing is a clockwise traverse of the huge supporting pillar found down at sea level. En-route, climb through the rather enchanting 'window', and proceed back to your start point.
FSA. Mike Robertson and Mark Williams 26.8.1995

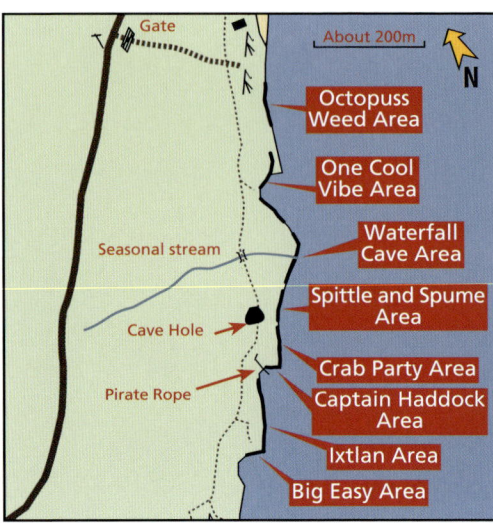

Crab Party Area **Cave Hole** 89

Crab Party Area

The Crab Party Area is found just north of the Pirate Rope, and offers a number of steep routes on great rock. The classic is the stunning *Crab Party*, which takes the huge roof flake on the right.

Approach - Down-climb the rope as for the approach to the Captain Haddock Area. At its base, traverse right to reach the first route on the arete.

Conditions and Tides - Take a decent one, and a calm sea if you can; the traverse over to *Crab Party* and *Andy Pandy* has been known to wet folk down, especially when there's a little bounce in the swell..! A dry breeze will make your visit more lucrative, especially with regard to *Crab Party*.

Up the Grotto (Mike Robertson, 19.5.95) originally climbed the inner recess of the big arete, but the demise of the huge roof flake has meant a deletion from the DWS register. The hard moves above the lower, jutting ledge are consider unjustified. But, of course, there's always something good to emerge from the ashes ... and we now have the excellent Water Wings.

❹ **Water Wings** . . . . . 7a+ *S0/1*
9m. Major 'slapsville' terrain with some terrific, somewhat baffling moves. From the ledges at the base of *Ooh Lovely!*, keep left to make hard moves to a horizontal rail. Get your ass right on the sharp, flying arete proper, and slap your way up the feature to the top. *See photos on page 27 and 71.*
FSA. Gavin Symonds 27.7.2001

❺ **Ooh Lovely!** . . . . . . 6b+ *S0/1*
9m. Good and sustained climbing, with every move a crimpy one. Climb up from the lower traverse ledge, heading slightly right, to gain a quick breather. Veer a little left to finish close to the arete (although a rightwards finish has been done at the same grade).
FSA. Mike Robertson 19.5.1995

❻ **Out of Yer Shell** . . . . . . 7a+ *S1*
9m. Climb up into the diagonal corner which leads to a roof. Use undercuts to reach over to poor holds. A couple more moves get you to an easier leftwards finish.
FSA. Martin Crocker 13.8.1998

❼ **Crab Party** 6c *S1/2*
20m (total). A mega-classic outing, tackling the alluring 7m roof flake. A tricky traverse approach and a committing position make this one of Cave Hole's finest adventures. You'll need reasonably flat water and a mid-tide for the low traverse around to the start of the route (or brave it at a big high tide with your shorts on your head for a steadier *S0/1* tick). Down-climb the pirate rope and traverse rightwards into the huge cave. Make a move up the back wall to gain a good resting ledge below the start of the roof flake-line. Off you go! *See photo on page 68.*
FSA. Mike Robertson 19.5.1995

❽ **Andy Pandy** . . . . . . 7b+ *S0*
25m. Fun. The cave traverse into the base of *Crab Party* has now been extended to gain the back ledges of the inner cave system. A low line, with the crux almost touching the sea. Pass the entry jugs to *Crab Party*, and continue on big holds, until drop-down moves gain a crozzly break-line. Keep on this to finally gain a big rest at the back of the cave. From here, either jump in or reverse the route.
FSA. Andy Long 13.8.2006

Cave Hole — Spittle and Spume Area

Spittle and Spume Area

A very popular venue, with a good spread of grades and packed with quality lines.

Approach - Find the single staple bolt near the edge of the crag: most folk use this for the down-climb, simply tying in a short rope and using it to hand-over-hand the 7m needed to get down to the sea level ledges. Once down, heading leftwards will take you along to *Intimate Dancing*; the remainder of the routes are to the right.

Conditions and Tides - A mid-high tide is perfect. Rough seas don't present too much of a problem here, but make sure you can use your tied-off rope to get out again, as the next option is the Pirate Rope, 20m away.

❶ Intimate Dancing . . . 6a S2/3
10m. The shapely, left-trending arete gives excellent but bold climbing, with barely sufficient water for an ascent (although a proper 2.3m spring tide actually does provide the necessary depth, giving an *S1/2*). Climb the arete diagonally leftwards, past a balancy, technical move, to find yourself on an easier top wall.
FSA. Mike Robertson 13.6.1993

❷ G-String 6b S3
8m. A bold eliminate up the slight prow left of *Robertson's Jar*.
FSA. Mike Robertson 22.7.2005

❸ Robertson's Jar 6a S1
8m. A short, direct route straight up the neat little groove. The top moves provide the entertainment, with the tiny, hard-to-find crimps giving the only solace.
FSA. Steve Taylor 13.6.1993

❹ Spittle and Spume 6a S0
12m. A nice 'entry-level' Cave Hole outing, offering excellent water and cool moves, and with the briny paying close attendance at all times. After swinging rightwards to the far wall, take a brief mid-route rest on flat holds, then trend slightly left and up to the top.
FSA. Mike Robertson 13.6.1993

❺ Bare Reputation 7a+ S0
16m. This brilliant and very sustained traverse is a guaranteed pump-out (so says all who sail in her). Start for *Spittle and Spume*, but continue traversing right (crux) to the protruding domed jug. From here, venture right and slightly downwards, to finally arrive at a line of good holds that lead you by the nose to the top shelf (there's also a slightly shorter but equally-hard-overall direct finish).
FSA. Mike Robertson 15.5.1995

❻ Under-Bare 7b S0
16m. An enchanting, largely footless route, found underneath *Bare Reputation*. The route traverses the continuous jug-rail, right on the lip of the cave. Start as for *Bare Reputation*. Climb the mother route to the last biggish hold (shared with *Spittle*), and drop down to the rail below. Follow this strenuously, with occasional possibilities for the feet, to finish as for *Bare Reputation*.
FSA. Dave Henderson 12.8.1998

❼ Under-Bare Extension
. . . . 7b+ S0
18m. *Under-Bare* has also received a thoroughly gratuitous extension, which pushes the grade to 'soft' 7b+. Just brilliant. Finish as for *Smile Please!*
FSA. Gavin Symonds 8.2005

❽ Smile Please! . . . . 6a+ S0
8m. A steady and pleasant little face climb above good water, finishing up a thin flake. Reach it either by a short abseil or a short '4' down-climb to the right.
FSA. Steve Taylor 7.97

❾ Hooked Like No Fish Before Me
. . . . 6b S0
14m. Great climbing. Access as for *Smile Please!*, then traverse the juggy break-line leftwards, to finish up a prominent flake.
FSA. Martin Crocker 5.10.1996

Waterfall Cave and One Cool Vibe Area — Cave Hole

Waterfall Cave
The shapely Waterfall Cave is a tough venue, but the routes here have seen plenty of traffic.
Approach - The cave is under the stream flowing below the walk-bridge, which empties itself through the roof of the cave during springtime. To see the cave's interior, walk just to the north and drop back down on good ledges.
Conditions and Tides - The *Swingin' Nineties* is almost a low-tide route. The ledge just to the south affects significantly the S grade of *King of the Swingers*.

❿ King of the Swingers   **7c** *S3*
16m. An absolute masterpiece and probably Cave Hole's most inspiring hard route. Take a huge tide along. Yard across the first half of the *Swingin' Nineties* and continue all the way along the horizontal break to gain a crazy leg-bar rest in a wide roof crack. From here, either follow a logical rising line of jugs up and right-wards (7b+), or keep to the bolt-line on the left (7c).
FSA. Andy Long (right finish), Gavin Symonds (left finish) - both 12.8.2006

⓫ Swingin' Nineties   **7b** *S0/1*
11m. A brilliant horizontal route giving a feisty thrash across a seemingly impossible roof. It has the most water of any route at Cave Hole. From a ledge / small viewing gallery close to the top of the cliff, swing down and left to gain the traverse break-line. Follow this until an undercut move gives way to a line of jugs heading towards the light.
FSA. Mike Robertson 12.8.1995

⓬ Law of the Jungle   **7b+** *S0/1*
9m. This less-climbed companion to *Swingin' Nineties* gives good climbing but features a 'proper hard crux'. Access the start by a simple down-climb just to the right (looking in). From sea level, climb up to the roof and cross it rightwards with difficulty, on sloping edges, to gain the top.
FSA. Dave Henderson 12.8.1998

One Cool Vibe Area

⓭ One Cool Vibe   **6c** *S3*
11m. The arete is something of an eliminate and requires deep water and a steady head. Some excellent moves; peruse them from the top shelf prior to your attempt.
FSA. Pete Oxley 11.5.1989

⓮ This is the Life   **6c** *S3*
12m. An excellent route, it is just a cryin' shame the water level isn't a little more generous. Take a 2.3m spring tide with you - nothing else will do. The strenuous rightwards traverse into the groove (brief rest here) leads on to a great finale on small holds.
FSA. Pete Oxley 11.5.1989

One Cool Vibe Area
The next two routes are found on a high, streaked arete just south of the Octopuss Weed cave. The rock is immaculate, but both require a big spring tide and they're not completely safe even with that.
Approach - Scramble down the fisherman's ledges to the south of the routes and find the traverse break which takes you rightwards onto the wall.
Conditions and Tides - There are no boulders on the flat shelf in the sea below the routes, but a fall will require a calculated 'armchair landing'.

Cave Hole — Octopuss Weed Area

Octopuss Weed Area

The next routes are in the Octopuss Weed Cave, one of Cave Hole's finest (and funniest) features. *Octopuss Weed* is one of the best traverses on the south coast.

Approach - Find the huge crane that sits above the cave, then down-climb the left edge (looking in) of it. This brings you to an accommodating ledge, from where it is possible to see what you're letting yourself in for.

Conditions and Tides - The water here is plentiful, so any mid-high tide will give you the confidence to go for it. Try to catch it with a dry easterly breeze, which should give optimum conditions.

❶ Octopuss Weed 6c S0
12m. Yep; satisfaction guaranteed or your money back! An exceptional little test-piece, and one of Damian's finest contributions. From the lower starting ledge, perform some funky gymnastics to gain and crawl onto the hanging 'shelf' feature (often referred to as the 'plank'). From its culmination, attack the hanging traverse line with gusto to finally pull onto the far wall of the cave. Note the two finishes available from here; the left one provides some solid, additional S0 entertainment.
See photo on page 19.
FSA. Damian Cook 8.5.1995

❷ Tentacle Master . . . 7a+ S0
10m. Beastly and baffling - sees very few on-sights. The line takes on the main challenge through the centre of the cave. After getting settled into the good holds on *Octopuss Weed*, climb up into the wickedly steep territory above (poor but essential side-pull) to finally gain easier ground above.
FSA. Joff Cook 27.7.1995

❸ Previous Top-Rope Problem . . . 6a+ S0
14m. A highly unlikely top-rope problem indeed - the humour might well remain an 'in' joke! This line spirals its way clockwise around the very lowest extremes of the cave, approaching as for *Octopuss Weed*. You'll need a calm sea and a low to mid tide.
FSA. Damian Cook 8.5.1995

❹ Killer Loop . . . . 6c+ S1
7m. Steep as! The back of the cave offers two weaknesses across its roof; this line ventures across the flake found on the left (looking in). Follow the roof/shelf crack (spotter advisable for the first few moves) until it finishes. A backwards span now takes you towards the plank.
FSA. Joff Cook 3.9.1995

❺ Skeleton Surfers . . . 6c+ S0
7m. Very similar to the last route, but safer, with good water all the way. Climb the opposing flake-crack until some tenacious undercutting moves gain the elusive plank.
FSA. Mike Robertson 3.9.1995

The Great Escape Wall

The wall immediately south of the Beeston routes is a decidedly complex DWS venue. This is down to a lack of a viewing gallery, no guaranteed dry ledges from which to start your chosen line, and routes which traverse, weave and cross all over the place. Add to this sub-surface boulders, tricky tide allowances, and bolted pitches more normally split with hanging stances... you get the picture! So, with a certain reluctance, fuelled partly by a continued lack of real interest in the wall since about 1996, I've decided to leave the crag out of this guide (the routes are listed in the Dorset Rockfax).

Beeston Cliff

❻ Krakatoa 4 S3
8m. Steady as you like, pulling on pretty sizeable conglomerate holds all the way. The one snag is the too-wide starting ledge - you'd need to clear that in the event of a fall.
FSA. Steve Taylor 3.4.1994

❼ Etna 3 S3
8m. More of the same - massive holds! The same lower ledge situation applies here.
FSA. Damian Cook 10.4.1994

Beeston Cliff Cave Hole

8 Popacatapetl 6a+ S2
8m. More flowstone, with the added problem of a slight shortfall of the stuff towards the top - you'll need to make one proper hard move to gain the finishing holds. The ledge is slightly narrower here, but watch out for it.
FSA. Mike Robertson 27.4.1994

9 Fifteen Minutes to Fame 6a S1
9m. Local lad bolted it (took him about quarter of an hour, would you believe…) then soloed it rather than bother to tie in - yep, they're all quite mad down there in Dorset. Good moves on great rock, and less cruxy than the previous route.
FSA. Steve Taylor 5.8.1994

10 Bay of Rainbows 6c+ S0/1
12m. Now we're right out there over the briny. A superb testpiece and one of the best DWS's of its grade on the island. Step off the right edge of the belay ledge and head diagonally rightwards, past a good but tough move, trending a little leftwards to reach the top.
FSA. Damian Cook 16.7.1994

11 Bay of Peegs 7a+ S0/1
12m. This excellent 'hard-un' starts from the small corner on *Belly Button Traverse* and forges its way directly up the face. The holds are small!
FSA. Joff Cook 8.2001

12 Cornflake Girl 6b+ S0/1
12m. Probably the most suitable continuation to *Belly Button Traverse*. Start from the far ledge system and wander up and left on various blobby holds. Slightly harder than it once was due to the loss of a flowstone jug.
FSA. Mike Robertson 3.6.1994

13 Bungle, Zippy and George 4+ S2/3
11m. For the last route on the face take steady, juggy conglomerate to the very top, then make the obligatory and tricky mantel to top out. Watch out for that starting ledge!
FSA. Mike Robertson 21.8.1994

Beeston Cliff
This charming little cliff offers some really excellent climbing, quite often on naturally glued-on, conglomerate holds. The rock is sound and the sea below is pretty deep; it's quite possible to jump off the top of this cliff at mid-tide, in fact. The easier routes on the left have the disadvantage of a jutting lower ledge, as does *Bungle*, over on the far side.
Approach - The easiest method is to make a short abseil from bolts on boulders on the top ledge. A downclimb is also quite common practice here.
Conditions and Tides - The crag is best enjoyed in the morning sun, as it can often get slightly damp here later in the day. Take a decent tide along; it will help!
Exit - It is not so easy to get yourself out of the water. It is recommended that a knotted rope is left in place right down to sea level, below the easier routes on the left. This will sort out all your exit difficulties.

14 Belly Button Traverse 6a+ S0
12m. A sweet introduction to the delights of Beeston, and one of the best solos in the area. It's a low-level traverse crossing the face to the far ledge, with the water always close to hand. Once relaxed, either continue up one of the previous two routes, or reverse back to your start point.
FSA. Mike Robertson 3.6.1994

Approach the next two routes by direct abseil from blocks.

15 Gyonyuru 6c S3
13m. A bold and daunting route, tackling the striking arete that forms the right edge of the square-cut sea cave. You'll need a very good spring tide to render it DWS ground, but there is just about sufficient water, maybe 2-3m at a good spring tide.
FSA. Damian Cook 8.1995

16 Gyttja 6c S3
13m. Another gripper, but again - a big spring tide will give confidence. Climb the right side of the prow to the right of *Gyonyuru*.
FSA. Martin Crocker 8.7.2000

Beautifully structured and colourful rock are trademarks of DWS'ing. Mark Glaister on an early morning crossing of *Rainbow Bridge* (7a+) - *page 102* - at Berry Head, Devon. Photo: Mike Robertson.

Devon

The Devonshire coast, made up of excellent, colourful and well-featured limestone, is one of the core areas of UK deep water soloing. There is a multitude of routes, plenty of good rock, and most of the routes weigh in at less than fifteen metres high. From the stunning traverses of *Rainbow Bridge* and *Magical Mystery Tour* to the looming pinnacles of Berry Head Quarry, from the alluring, sculpted archways of London Bridge to the isolated caves and zawns of Long Quarry Point - there is a great variety of colour, scenery, grade and of course, deep water. The normally sun-drenched Devon coast is ready-made for deep water soloing: solid rock, and soloing with an endless array of comfortable jugs and pockets. Devon's DWS history stretches back to the sixties, but has come into its own in the last decade or so, with many routes to go at across the grades.

Approach

Torbay is easily reached by car from the north via the M5 and then continuing on the A38 and the A380. Torquay has good rail and bus links which allow the crags to be reached using public transport. The closest airport is at Exeter which has cheap flights from many UK airports and European destinations.

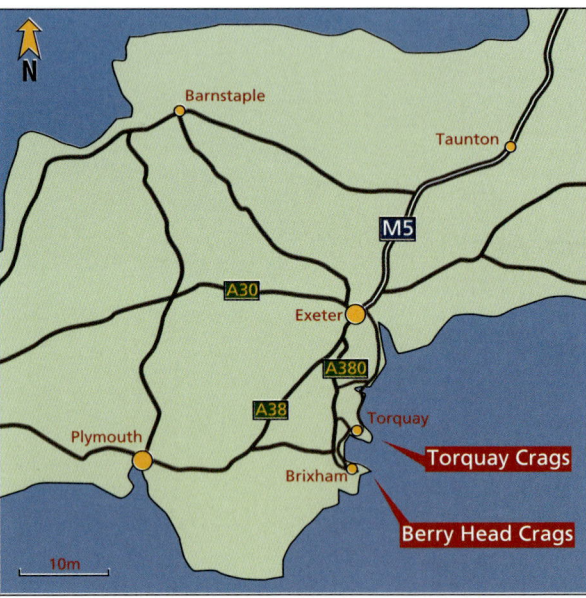

Conditions and Tides

Devon's tidal range is, on average, around three metres. The varied nature and height of Devon's routes and traverses means you can usually find plenty to have a go at, even during the lower neap tides. It's also worth noting that the longer traverse 'expeditions' are often better tackled at around mid-tide levels, when the available 'options' on the rock prove greater. The sea state is usually not a problem as most of the climbing is found in sheltered bays, but a strong easterly will usually increase the swell. Devon's rock varies from bone dry to minging damp - the best scenario is a drying breeze and a little sunshine, especially if contemplating routes in the caves and grottos.

Access

There is a restriction due to nesting birds at the Berry Head peninsula; see page 99 for full details of how this affects the deep water soloist. Bear in mind that a local bye-law still stands - meaning a £1000 fine is still in place for the offence of disturbing birds, which DOES include scrambling down into the Old Redoubt's Great Cave!
A brief mention should be made of the start/finish of the *Long Traverse* between Long Quarry Point and Anstey's Cove - the beach beneath Anstey's crags is officially closed, due to rockfall some years ago.

Elinor Currey stretching out on the pumpy *Aeronautics* (6c) - *page 105* - on the Pink Block area, one of the fine sections of crag rising above the stunning traverse of *Rainbow Bridge* at Berry Head, Devon. Photo: Mike Robertson

Berry Head

Welcome to Berry Head, Devon's deep water soloing Mecca, with its profusion of isolated grottos, incredible lines and pumpy traverses. The multi-coloured, jug-infested overhanging walls have long been a testing ground for deep water soloists, drawn to the headland's classic high quality traverses and numerous 'up' routes. The huge walls of the Old Redoubt Fort atop Berry Head date back to the times of the Napoleonic Wars, when Torbay was used for anchorage and served as a re-supply point for the British Channel Fleet. The headland was chosen to house a formidable battery of very large guns. You'll see the huge walls, built between 1795 and 1806, all around the headland, including the Berry Head Quarry area.

Approach

Berry Head is best approached from Brixham town or via the A3022 by-pass. Keep an eye out for the numerous brown signs (to Berry Head) posted on the main roads. From the traffic lights on the outskirts of Brixham, drive up the hill, taking a right turn. Pass a caravan park, with a small food store on the left. The narrow lane beyond the store takes you to the Berry Head car park (Pay and Display).

To reach the Great Cave - Walk out of the car park towards the sea, find the small gate in the fence (keep closed - there are goats inside this enclosure), and follow the winding path down and to the left and then back right (looking out). The gearing-up spot is here, by a cemented stake and a bird ban information sign. For access to the Great Cave, you'll need to drop down and right then down-climb a slabby ramp to the edge of the cave itself. For access to the Oz Wall, White Rhino sectors and the Quarry Pinnacles, see separate access notes.

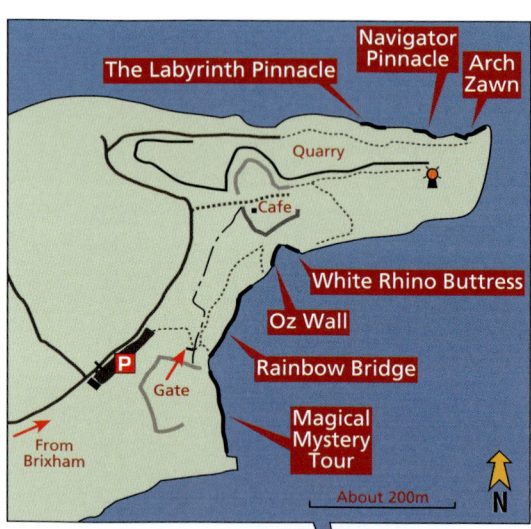

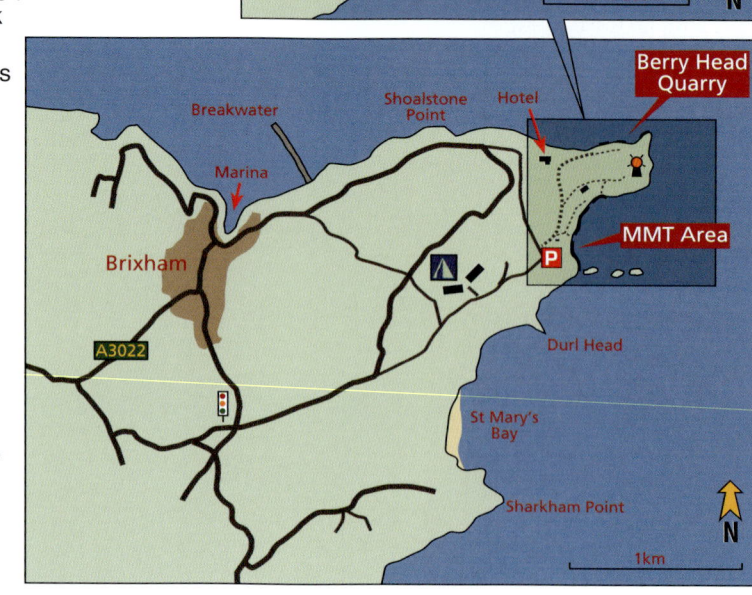

Berry Head

Conditions and Tides
Conditions are usually good in the summer. Expect morning sun on *Magical Mystery Tour* and *Rainbow Bridge*. Damp and humid conditions are worth avoiding, especially in the darker environs of the Great Cave and the Blue Grotto. Try to tackle *Magical Mystery Tour* around a mid-tide, and take a lightweight dry-bag if you expect to swim/part-swim the Green Grotto entrance. The routes along and above *Rainbow Bridge* are best tackled with a mid to high tide. For routes in the Oz Wall and White Rhino sectors, you'll find the sun stays around slightly longer. The routes on the White Rhino Buttress area are lower, and the tide state is less of an issue. For all routes, climb above calm seas whenever possible, and ALWAYS KNOW YOUR CLOSEST EXIT.

Seasonal Climbing Restriction
The cliffs of Berry Head's Old Redoubt are an important breeding site for a large guillemot colony, as well as supporting species such as kittiwakes, fulmars and shags. The section of coastline also forms part of a National Nature Reserve, and is designated as an Area of Special Protection under the Wildlife and Countryside Act (1981). Hence the seasonal climbing restriction, which operate between March 1st and July 31st inclusive. This restriction covers all routes in the *Magical Mystery Tour* and *Rainbow Bridge* area, as well as extending past the White Rhino Buttress and beyond. The routes in Berry Head Quarry are unaffected.

Variable Climbing Restriction
Torbay Coast and Countryside Trust and the BMC have now agreed that the climbing restriction on the central section of *Rainbow Bridge* will be lifted early if there are no nesting birds on the traverse. A red disk on a notice on the access path to the Great Cave will indicate whether the traverse is open or closed.
This arrangement is subject to the following conditions:
- The restriction applies to the section of *Rainbow Bridge* between the end of pitch 1 and the Terminal Zawn Ledge.
- No climbing in via pitch 1 of Rainbow Bridge and all routes in the Old Redoubt. This includes the scramble into the Great Cave, The Oz Wall and the White Rhino Buttress.
- Access to Rainbow Bridge is only by way of the marked access route, bringing the climber down to an in-situ thread at the start of pitch 2 (see Route 6 on page 104).
- Climbers must exit the route before the Terminal Zawn (for the last escape pitch, *Terminal Slab*, see page 108).
- In the event of a fall from the route, the Terminal Zawn ledges and the Great Cave are out of bounds. Either swim across to the Red Wall ledges at the far side of the bay, or regain the rock and climb out, most easily by climbing up the route *Eight Ball*.
- For any further queries, please call the local ranger on 01803 883262 / 882619

Accommodation and Food
The Berry Head and Brixham area has all the facilities to be expected in a seaside town; banks, post office, a collection of pubs and cafes, and the usual high street assortment of shops. The pedestrianised Brixham high street is home to the Lemon Tree Cafe, which offers a choice of breakfasts all day, and opens at 8am - a must for the tide-chaser! Also here, by the central Pay and Display car park, is the friendly Huckleberries Cafe. For an evening meal or beer, the Berry Head Hotel comes highly recommended, it has the best 'sunset patio' in the area, and does outside barbecues all summer, on every day the patio remains dry! For camping, the Century Touring Campsite is the best and most convenient, being within walking distance of all the Berry Head routes, as well as the Berry Head Hotel.

Berry Head The Old Redoubt

The Old Redoubt - Magical Mystery Tour
Berry Head's Old Redoubt crag is one of the UK's most impressive sea cliffs. The Great Cave is an awe-inspiring site, home to both the classic Hard Rock tick of *Moonraker* (HVS) and two Extreme Rock lines (*Dreadnought* E3, and *Caveman* E6). The severely overhanging nature of the crag is offset by the multitude of juggy rails that allow unbelievable positions to be had at 'reasonable' grades.

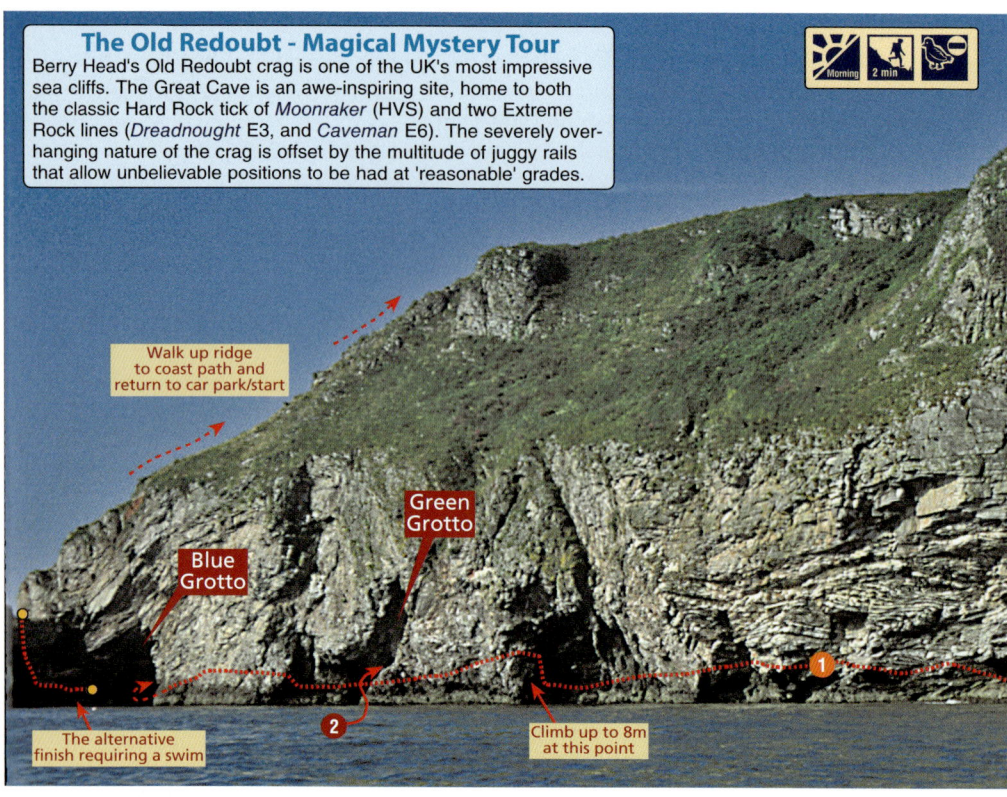

❶ Magical Mystery Tour .. 6a+ S1
(Part I, and Blue Grotto section of part II)
A titanic expedition, taking the intrepid soloist through moments of wetness, doubt, ecstasy and relief; this route could change your life! The route crosses the terrain from the Great Cave through to the slabs beyond the Blue Grotto - over 400m of huge jugs, gargantuan pockets and mighty dinner-plates.
Tides - The situation is rather complex and, instead of confusing things further with endless descriptions of variations and deviations, here is the simple choice:
a) It's slightly safer with more water, but often the climbing is a little harder, with less low variations possible;
b) Conversely, it's more intimidating with less water below, but often easier, with barnacles for feet often providing less beefy climbing;
c) At a big high tide, you won't get past the low jug rail leading out of the Great Cave;
d) At anything other than low-mid tide, you'll have to part or wholly swim to get past the Green Grotto.
420m. Start in the Great Cave. Climb across/around the easy reefs of the Great Cave, to regain the sunshine once more. Continue along a wall of endless jugs and dinner-plate holds, moving up and down a bit, to finally pass a hanging face, which is the crux (possible low barnacle variation, but still hard).

Continue along to the Green Grotto entrance, where you may well have to get damp, or briefly swim, to pass by (depending on the tide level). Follow the juggy wall all the way along to the bigger Blue Grotto entrance. Options here are a swim over to the ridge, or a higher traverse around a weakness, also gaining the big ridge. The normal method these days, however (providing the given length of 420m), simply continues on into the Blue Grotto, which is the perfect and quite delightful end to your adventure, featuring an amazing drop-across gully section on big pockets, as well as an exciting finale (care needed with lower tides). Finish by climbing up to the slabs just beyond the Blue Grotto.
FSA. unknown

❷ Green Grotto Traverse 6c S1
A courageous battle with the combined forces of gloom and steepness. A head-torch strongly recommended (6c+ without!). Victors will find themselves emerging, after some 40m or so, in the Blue Grotto, at the drop-over move on *Magical Mystery Tour*. Imaginative and gymnastic climbing throughout. Start where *Magical Mystery Tour* dives low; a speculative perusal of the Green Grotto cave entrance will leave plenty left to the imagination!
40m. Climb the relatively easy right wall, until you find yourself heading leftwards into a bay. A solid, 50° flake now soars away into the cave roof - get on board! Follow this up and then back down, where a crux move onto a protruding boss awaits you. More sustained, juggy climbing leads to a final bridging section, and out into the semi-light of *Magical Mystery Tour*.
FSA. Nick White 9.1991

The Old Redoubt Berry Head  101

❸ Caveman   7a+ *S3*

Caveman's first four pitches; wild, wild climbing across the hanging pink flakes, and above reasonable water all the way (expect a depth of around 3-3.5m at a decent high tide, but please check the depth over the solitary boulder). Pitch 4 is shared with *Lip Trip* and finishes some 20m above the sea on a big tide, whilst the hanging traverse sections of pitches 2 and 3 are around 15-17m. Use a BIG tide, and take your big guns!
40m. Climb across *Caveman's* easy lower traverse pitch to arrive at the hanging flakes. Follow these with commitment to a rest in the original belay niche, and flap across the rest of the pink traverse to gain a second 'almost' hands-off rest on the last protruding 'beak'. From here, climb up and left (probably the mental crux) to gain and finish on the stunning *Lip Trip* pitch. All recent solo ascensionists have reversed a short way down the trad route *Dreadnought* and jumped.
FSA. Dave Thomas 8.1989, using Terracotta *variation on pitch 4; original line soloed by Tim Emmett 8.2005.*

❹ Killa Gorilla  7b *S0*

9m. This diminutive but burly line is found below the first hard pitch of *Caveman*, fortunately it is very safe. Traverse through the Great Cave to the end of the slanting jug rail, and climb up and rightwards, to finally gain big holds. Finish by simply traversing left and easily back down to sea level.
FSA. Dave Henderson 8.2005

Magical Mystery Tour - THE RACE!

"The Race"! . . . Speed climbing on *Magical Mystery Tour*. Including a waist-deep paddle, with boots on, across the Green Grotto trench (shorts and chalk-bag on head).

Date: 16.8.05
Climber: Mikey Robertson
Time: 10.20am - 10.39am
Distance: 420m
Elapsed time: 19 minutes dead
Tide state: low to mid tide, rising
From: the gear-up ledge in Great Cave, climb the route along and through the Blue Grotto, finishing on the first grass on the slabs beyond the Blue Grotto
Slips: 4
Abrasions: 2
Falls: none
Verdict: Amazing! Anyone else want a go? This time could be beaten…

Berry Head   Rainbow Bridge

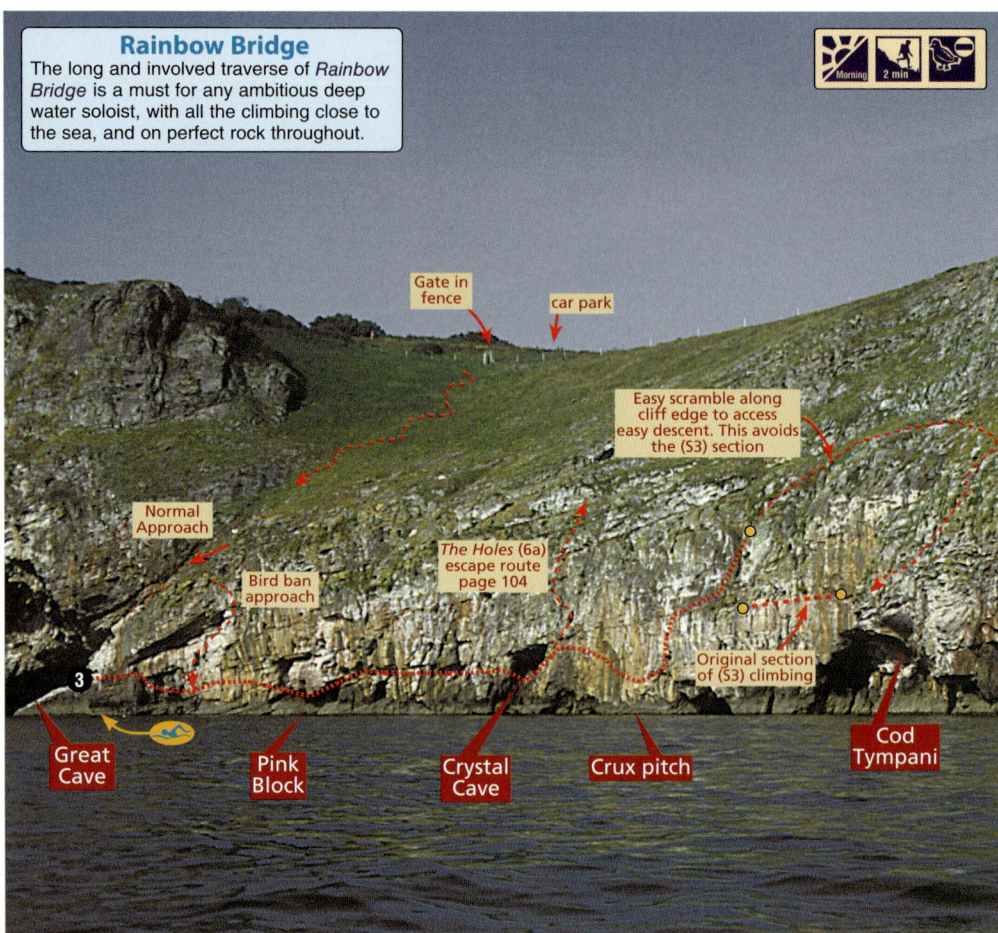

Rainbow Bridge
The long and involved traverse of *Rainbow Bridge* is a must for any ambitious deep water soloist, with all the climbing close to the sea, and on perfect rock throughout.

❸ **Rainbow Bridge** ...... 7a+ *S1*

280m. This route is an absolute MUST for any aspiring deep water soloist! It's very hard to describe the route blow-by-blow, as with *Magical Mystery Tour*. You would probably forget it all anyway, but here's some guidelines which should work with the photo to provide some illuminating information. I've taken the liberty of naming some of the obvious features - hopefully the terminology will stick. Rather than use the original pitches, which are very blurred whilst soloing (even to those who have done it dozens of times) I've set it into sections, using natural features. This should be better for the soloist, who's not going to be looking for any belay points. Although some of the features are only evident whilst on the route, the Cod Tympani Buttress is very obvious from the viewing ledges above the Crux Pitch.
In the Bird Ban season, please refer to the variable access agreement (page 99), which now kindly allows us to enjoy all *Rainbow Bridge* except the start and the Terminal Zawn finish.
See photo on cover, page 94 and page 109.

Great Cave - Pink Block
From the Great Cave, traverse steadily rightwards, to negotiate a tricky corner. Drop down, then gradually rise, to drop down again onto the stunning-streaky wall (still often referred to as pitch 2). Traverse this wall (6a+) on amazing pockets, then drop down and strenuously leave the wall for a low rest under the Pink Block.

Pink Block - Crystal Cave
From the Pink Block, continue along and a little up (sometimes pumpy, some tricky moves) to pass under a large white block. A further series of steady climbing gains the very deep Crystal Cave (you'll know when you're there!) and a large rest. From here you can contemplate the crux pitch (originally pitch 6) and retreat if necessary! Note: you can also choose this moment to escape upwards on *The Holes* (page 106).

Rainbow Bridge Berry Head

Crystal Cave - Crux Pitch
Swing out of the Crystal Cave and rightwards, to view the blank wall beyond. Climb across this, first up and then gradually heading downwards, and continue to a series of big slopers. Gain the last, horribly sloping one and stretch for a hidden finger-jug above, using this to gain the resting corner around to the right. Climb the technical groove up to the upper ledges.

Crux Pitch - Cod Tympani Buttress
Recommended is to escape from the cliff for this next section, then go back in down the line of *Eight Ball*. This will avoid the original (S3) traverse of pitch 7, which, although good, finishes over a jutting reef below the boulder-choke in the big corner. So … do as the locals usually do, and exit the crux pitch easily to the top, then walking along the hillside, gaining the top of *Eight Ball* (4+) - page 107. Down-climb this to reach sea level once more.

Cod Tympani Buttress - The Wave
Traverse easily, continuing under the roof of *Cod Tympani*, to reach the start of *The Wave* - a diagonal feature of textured strata, that soars diagonally rightwards. Either climb this (strenuous, at least 6b+), or stay low and take on the technical traverse (also about 6b+), staying very close to the sea.

The Wave - Terminal Zawn
Some steady traversing leads you by the nose to the Terminal Zawn. Traverse rightwards into the zawn (see Access notes on page 99 for the seasonal agreement) with a number of options to finally gain the hanging right/rear wall. The final moves to gain the big white finishing ledge are slightly unsafe; use discretion here, a short swim would not be too frowned upon!
FSA. Crispin Waddy 1989

Berry Head — Rainbow Bridge - Great Cave Descent Area

Great Cave Descent Area

The right-hand side of the Great Cave juts out over the sea and provides two impressive DWSs, whilst the initial section of the *Rainbow Bridge* wall provides a spread of lines, making it a good place to start exploring the vast potential on this crag.

Approach - The two highball lines are gained from the access scramble into the Great Cave; all other routes are reached by the traverse of *Rainbow Bridge*.

Conditions and Tides - Morning sun makes this a great place to hit early, but you'll need to be very early if the weather's hot, as it can get very sweaty. Any mid-tide or above will do for *Rainbow Bridge*; wait for a high one for the rest.

1 Hands Off Whizzy . . 6c S3
17m. This excellent and very airy DWS takes the left side of the high jutting prow. Traverse the break leftwards, to arrive in a very exposed position below a groove with a thread in it (this is on *Warspite in Brief*). Summon up some bottle, swing leftwards, and ascend slopers up the left side of the arete. Finish by moving right, then taking an easier descending line, to finally step back down to the start ramp.
FSA. Ken Palmer 1990's

2 Warspite in Brief . . 6b S3
15m. A wild trip and highly photogenic. Follow *Hands Off Whizzy* to its hanging jugs, and power straight up into the groove, past a thread, to gain a good rest. You may think about a jump - or use the down-climb, as with *Hands Off Whizzy*.
FSA. unknown

3 Drop Squad 5 S0
12m. A useful introduction to the crag. Climb the ramp, then swing up rightwards across to finish on good flat holds.
FSA. Martin Crocker 27.8.1998

4 The Gill 6b S0
12m. More meaty than *Drop Squad*. Climb into the horizontal niche below the big roof and use an undercut/side-pull under the roof to gain jugs on the lip. Swing out and find further holds (crux), before moving more easily to the top.
FSA. Mike Robertson 30.8.2005

5 Yokel Hero . . . . 6b+ S1/2
15m. Great rock and fine moves, with a spicy sequence or two thrown in for good measure. Keep an eye on the base ramp whilst moving through the easier mid-section; thereafter it is seemingly safe.
FSA. Ken Palmer 1996

6 Way Down 5 S1
15m. Most usually used as the down-climb during the bird restriction period.
FSA. unknown

7 Project 8a S1
15m. Crimpy moves, heading up the bacon-esque streaks.

8 White Meat . . . 7a S1
15m. Pumpy and hard with good, fingery climbing. Tackle the enticing crack/pocket feature to the left of *Rainbow Scoop*. The last move on the headwall is the crux.
FSA. Ken Palmer 1990's

9 Rainbow Scoop . . . 6c S0/1
11m. The pocketed scoop is brilliant, with impeccable rock, good moves and perfect water. Climb up into the right side of the over-hanging scoop via steep moves on good holds; continue slightly more easily, on well-formed buckets, to a sound exit.
FSA. unknown

Rainbow Bridge - Pink Block Area — Berry Head

Pink Block Area

Stunning rock and architecture are the backdrop for some great routes that only require a swift romp along from the floor of the Great Cave.

Approach - All routes here are best reached by way of the traverse of *Rainbow Bridge*. The exits from the top prove to be very straightforward but take care on the right-hand routes.

Conditions and Tides - Mid-high tide will do you nicely. Bright, breezy days are the best scenario on this wall.

⑩ High Tide Running 6b *S1*
12m. This route takes the steep brown pocketed wall a little left of *Pink Bus*. Climb off the pink block using a massive pocket, and trend gradually leftwards to finish.
FSA. Martin Crocker 27.8.1998

⑪ Pink Bus .... 6b+ *S1*
12m. This route finds its way up pockets and jugs in the upper wall above the big pink block. Start roughly in the centre on the big pocket/jug shared with *High Tide Running*. Trend up and rightwards (surprisingly sustained) to a good finish. Traverse leftwards onto easy terrain.
FSA. unknown

⑫ The Lost Locals ... 6b+ *S1*
13m. A superb piece of climbing! One of the most alluring lines on the wall. Climb up into the big niche on huge purple jugs, and bridge up the niche to its top. Move up and right to gain a big sloping jug rail, and continue up an obvious line of linked pockets. Continue direct on slightly crunchy rock (coral) to a tricky and direct finish.
FSA. Crispin Waddy 1992

⑬ Aeronautics 6c *S1*
12m. Exhilarating and sustained climbing up a slight groove-line, some 3m past the pink block. From undercuts between the two through-cave entrances, yard steeply up and right to massive holds. Finger jugs lead to a crack, where more strenuous moves lead to a massive bucket with a flower in it. Make one last move (rock-over, if you dare) to gain a solid, easy finish.
See photo on page 97.
FSA. Martin Crocker 27.8.1998

⑭ Show Goes On .... 6a+ *S1*
14m. The cracked groove 2m right of *Aeronautics*. Gain the rising ramp, and then the slim, right-facing groove above. Easier ground leads to the top.
FSA. Martin Crocker 27.8.1998

⑮ Inimitable Toenails 6b *S1*
14m. The black streak some 7m right of the pink block is unfortunately often a little wet. Climb the streak on pockets and jugs past a big hole, then trend right up the ramp. Either finish directly (with care) or traverse leftwards.
FSA. Martin Crocker 27.8.1998

⑯ Stripper Robertson 6b *S1*
14m. The cracked prow 3m right of the black streak. Climb up past two white ledges, and finish direct with care.
FSA. Martin Crocker 27.8.1998

⑰ Cyborg Crocker 6a *S1*
14m. The hanging groove right of *Stripper Robertson*. The groove leads to a steady upper wall. Take care with the rock.
FSA. Mike Robertson 30.8.2005

Berry Head — Rainbow Bridge - Crux Area

Crux Area

Home to the smooth, technical crux of *Rainbow Bridge* and a number of hard steep solos, including the excellent *Barrel Traverse*. For those exploratory folk, the big sea cave traverse has yet to be climbed.

Approach - The first routes here are gained by the *Rainbow Bridge* traverse. To reach *Look, Before You Leap* through to *Into the Fire*, you'll need to find a massive thread up in a goat's alcove on the cliff top for your abseil.

Conditions and Tides - Any mid-high tide will do for these routes; morning sun and crisp conditions will be your ticket to success.

❶ The Holes 6a S2
17m. This route is given a name here for the first time, as it is often used as an escape route. From the right arete of the Crystal Cave, swing out and up to a big in-situ thread and climb up and right to negotiate two large holes (crux). Continue up for a few metres, then traverse leftwards for about 5m, to gain a reasonable right-trending groove; follow this to the top, taking care with the rock.
FSA. unknown

❷ Barrel Traverse. 7c S0
15m. Hard, technical and ultra-blind; and yet to receive an on-sight, despite some very worthy attention. It's essentially a low-level continuation of the crux pitch of *Rainbow Bridge*, staying a few metres above the sea. From the rest in the base of the chimney after the crux moves on *Rainbow Bridge*, swing right at the same level and continue across the amazing hanging pillar on spaced pockets (and very few footholds!). The last desperate section leads up and right to marginally better holds. Climb strenuously up to join *Look, Before You Leap*.
FSA. Ken Palmer 1996

❸ Look, Before You Leap . 6b S0
11m. There's no low traverse to gain this line, access is by abseiling in from the huge thread in the goat's alcove, or by boat. Gain the HWM at the base of the route, in the big alcove. Climb up and left along the intimidating ramp/undercut feature, to finally sprint (past an in-situ thread) on good pockets, up to the traverse line. Finish more easily.
FSA. Nick White 9.1991

❹ Disco Inferno 7b S1
11m. A hard eliminate, battling with the pockets in the wall above the niche of *Look Before You Leap*. Access as for the last route; boat or abseil. Follow the mother route to the big hanging fang and use this to gain a short crack in the leaning upper wall. Continue up and left to finish as for the previous route.
FSA. Martin Crocker 12.9.1999

❺ Into the Fire 7b S1
11m. This powerful line is marked by a worn-out yellow thread some 4m above the sea. Abseil in as described above. Start in the sea level niche at the HWM. Climb up and left on small sharp holds (crux) to pass the knackered thread and gain better holds on the right in a wide crack (another thread). A few more big moves give you access to the higher break.
NYS

❻ Sea Cave Traverse .... ?
16m. As yet unclimbed, and as obvious as can be. This enticing possibility stays virtually at sea level, traversing the massive sea cave right of *Barrel Traverse*. May the force be with you.

Rainbow Bridge - Cod Tympani Area — Berry Head

⑦ Nor' Wind Blows.......... 5+ S0/1
9m. This vertical, steady face climb dives up the wall above *Eight Ball*, where the climbing allows for decent water below. Access by down-climbing *Eight Ball* to good ledges right of the chimney. Climb up the wall and pull on slots, moving gradually rightwards, to gain a short diagonal flake-crack. Use this to pull right to jugs, and move right to gain the right arete to finish.
FSA. Martin Crocker 12.9.1998

⑧ Eight Ball........... 4+ S0
11m. More often used as a down-climb to re-access *Rainbow Bridge* or reach *Cod Tympani*. Good climbing, and if you do find yourself 'off' the crux of *Rainbow Bridge*, you'll appreciate this steady exit. From the ledges to the right of the chockstone chimney, climb diagonally rightwards along a deep, comfortable crack to gain the nose of the prow; top out easily.
FSA. unknown

⑨ Cod Tympani ..... 7a+ S1
8m. This excellent and dynamic route breaches the big, brown roof that can be seen from as far away as the gear-up ledge. The feature is distinct and the rock is excellent throughout. Approach via *Eight Ball*. From the base of the down-climb, traverse *Rainbow Bridge* rightwards until below the big roof. Climb up to it and forge a path out and rightwards (pumpy) to finally gain big, flat jugs. Remember - it's not over until it's over!
See photo on page 3.
FSA. Ken Palmer 1994

Cod Tympani Area
The next section of cliff is on the other side of the boulder choke which forms the junction of the original 7th and 8th pitches. The boulder choke can be seen in the picture above, but not from the top of the cliff. What can easily be seen, however, is the big Cod Tympani Buttress - this is the large, brown jutting roof. *Cod Tympani* takes the right underside of the roof, whereas the very useful access/escape route *Eight Ball* follows the striking horizontal strata from the cliff-top to sea level. Also easily seen from the gearing-up ledges is *The Wave*, the white, rightwards curling feature just right of the Cod Tympani Buttress.

Approach - The line of *Eight Ball* (4+) is your way into these routes, and also the easiest way out, should you take a fall.

Conditions and Tides - Any mid-high tide will do fine; a crisp, sunny day will provide your best time to visit.

⑩ Variation / The Wave 6c S0
10m. This brilliant piece of climbing ascends the rising, pumpy jug rail, that can clearly be seen from the faraway gear-up point. Strenuous, and on great rock throughout; it is well worth seeking out. It takes the rising jug line above the lower, original traverse of Pitch 9. Start just right/north of the *Cod Tympani* roof. (If you want to climb the pitch as a route in its own right, use *Eight Ball* to access it.) Attack the traversing, rising jug rail with gusto, to end up at a standing rest on the far pillar. Continue by dropping down, to rejoin the lower traverse of *Rainbow Bridge*.
FSA. Dave Henderson 1997

Berry Head — Rainbow Bridge - Terminal Zawn Area

Terminal Zawn Area

The final section of *Rainbow Bridge* crosses the feature known as the Terminal Zawn (it's not really that bad!). The only way of taking a prior look at any of these routes in this zawn is from the finish of *Rainbow Bridge*; the big white ledge ('Terminal Zawn Ledge'). The first line is a useful way of escaping the zawn when the Bird Ban is on, and the rest are affected by this restriction, so should be avoided before August.

Approach - Routes from *Terminal Slab* to *Terminal Viscosity* are usually approached from the right/the finish of *Rainbow Bridge*, although they're also useful latched onto *Rainbow Bridge* when the bird bans are in force, giving a good choice of exits.

Conditions and Tides - Expect the zawn to offer some shelter; morning sun makes this area a great place to climb after breakfast (or before it...).

1 Terminal Slab . . . . 4+ S1/2

16m. This fairly steady 'out' pitch is an easy method of avoiding *Rainbow Bridges's* terminal zawn pitch, especially useful when the bird bans are in force - remember that £1000 fine! From the ledge, climb up easy ground, and climb the edge of the clean slab above.
FSA. unknown

2 Comeback Kid 6b S0/1

16m. A fun, safe 'snackette' which starts from the ledge at the south edge of the Terminal Zawn. Step off the right end of the long ledge and reach for a big undercut pocket. Move strenuously up to better holds, and continue up, stepping left to a short corner. Finish up the right edge of the slab on the left.
FSA. Martin Crocker 13.9.1998

3 Terminal Twelve . . . . 6b+ S1

16m. Excellent climbing to the right of the *Comeback Kid*. Climb the pockets up and rightwards until it's possible to swing back left to good ledges at about 12m. Finish more easily.
FSA. Ken Palmer 1991

4 Terminal Viscosity . . . . 6b+ S2

18m. This one's a bit of a highball, with a few weak holds above 12m, it does have good water, however. Start from the same ledge as the previous routes. Follow *Rainbow Bridge* for about 3m, then make hard moves up and right to get reach the rising flake-crack. Follow this to good jams, then, avoiding an obvious ledge out right, continue directly up on pockets to reach a protruding hold. Continue to the top, taking care with the rock.
FSA. Nick Hancock 1982

5 Gluteus Maximus 7a S0

20m. This line offers good and pumpy climbing. It is effectively a low-tide variation on the Terminal Zawn pitch, although most the climbing is very independent (and much harder). It can only be tackled at low tide, and can be climbed in either direction, although the first ascent was in reverse (of this description). From the ledge on the edge of the Terminal Zawn, follow the mother line until it's possible to drop strenuously down cracks to gain the edge of the barnacles. Continue climbing along the low grooves and roofs of the lower reaches, to gain the small, low inlet found in the corner of the Terminal Zawn. Continue traversing low down, to finally climb 'up' to the finishing white ledge.
FSA. Mike Robertson 1998

The Terminal Zawn Ledge is the big, white ledge seen from the gear-up ledges above *Rainbow Bridge*. This ledge gives access both to the finish (or reversal start) of *Rainbow Bridge*, and also provides the most common start to the Oz Wall Traverse, which should be high on any visitor's list. The traverse is mainly on vertical rock, as it weaves its way across to the White Rhino Buttress area.

Danie Rushmer on *Rainbow Bridge* (7a+) - *page 102*
Berry Head. Photo: Mike Robertson

Berry Head The Oz Wall

The Oz Wall

The Terminal Zawn Ledge gives access to the finish of *Rainbow Bridge*, and also provides the most common starting point for the *Oz Wall Traverse*.

Approach - To find the ledge, go through the gate in the fence line on the approach to the Great Cave and then head left along the cliff edge to a point about 20m before the corner of the Fort. Locate the top of a narrow and well-worn corner/ramp and descend this past a hammered-in metal spike and old wire handrail mid-way down. At the base of the ramp, descend the old quarried bowl to the Terminal Zawn Ledge.

Conditions and Tides - Any mid-tide or above will do for the *Oz Wall Traverse*; wait for a high one for *Lucid*. Morning sun makes this a great place for an early start.

❶ Oz Wall Traverse .. 6b+ *S0*
65m. A classic! From the Terminal Zawn Ledge, drop down and find your way across the lower section of the wall, all the way to a blank section just before the *Cavewoman* cave. Climb up and out rightwards to gain the top of the *Cavewoman* cave.
FSA. Nick Hancock 1985

❷ Lucid. .... 6b+ *S0*
8m. Start by traversing across the first 9m of *The Oz Wall traverse*. Gain the overhanging niche, then climb around a roof above on its left. Continue direct to the top.
FSA. Martin Crocker 13.9.1998

❸ The Groovy Gang 6c *S1*
10m. From the *Oz Wall Traverse*, gain the base of the steep whitish groove, and follow it strenuously to the top.
FSA. Martin Crocker 13.9.1998

❹ Cavewoman 6c *S0*
40m. From the rising finish of the *Oz Wall Traverse*, drop down the groove via some sandstone 'welded-on' jugs, and traverse powerfully rightwards for 9m into the inviting cave. After a sit-down chill, climb the amazingly clean, green-crystal chimney in the back. There's also an extended but inferior low-tide extension, tackling the crunchy barnacles on the opposite wall.
FSA. Ken Palmer 1992

White Rhino Buttress

❺ Barnacle Continuation Traverse
.... 6b *S0*
9m. A very steep traverse indeed! From the left edge (looking in) of the *White Rhino Tea* buttress, drop down on good holds to gain sea level. Swing right and attack the base of the grossly leaning buttress, to finally arrive on its far side. Either finish up the right groove of the buttress, or, more fun, climb on to gain the finish on the right wall, as for *Barnacle Traverse*.
FSA. Pete Biven and Frank Cannings 5.4.1968

❻ Edge of the Jungle 4 *S0*
5m. The very edge of the impressive prow gives an easy taster!
FSA. unknown

❼ Humanize .... 6a+ *S0*
7m. A bicep warm-up for the routes ahead. Follow *Barnacle Traverse Continuation* for 3m, then climb up the overhanging wall on massive plates, moving right as you go.
FSA. Martin Crocker 13.9.1998

White Rhino Buttress   Berry Head

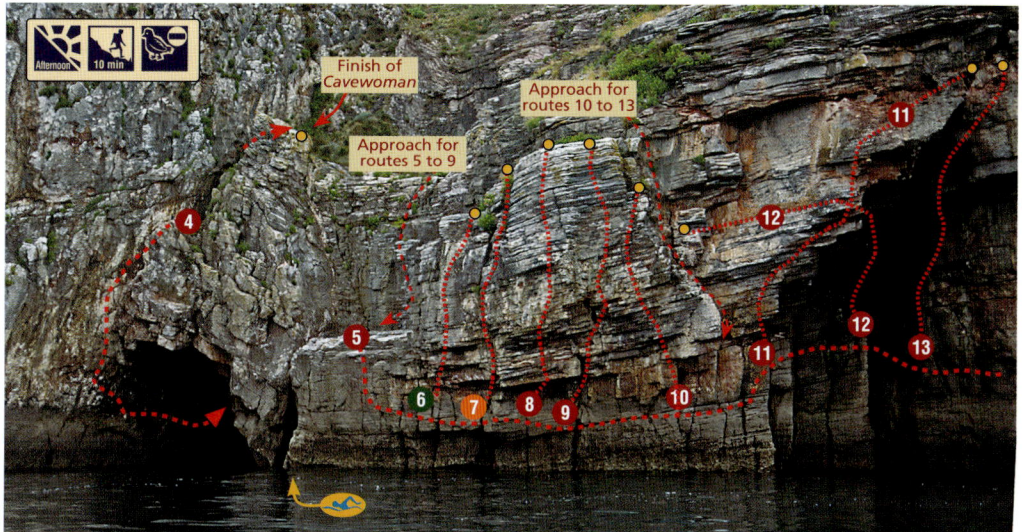

White Rhino Buttress

An excellent steep venue, with amenable low level routes that do not venture too far above the water.

Approach - From the cafe inside the Fort walls, walk towards the mast on the headland, then cut right and down to locate a park bench. From here, head down scree slightly leftwards to find the narrow fisherman's path through the thick bushes. Once down and out of this, swing back right to walk along to the top of the White Rhino Buttress.

Conditions and Tides - A mid-tide or above will offer enough water for any route here. Avoid greasy days, as those big dinner-plate holds might not feel so good!

⑧ Jose Sandeles .... 6c+ *S0*
9m. BIG holds, but ludicrously steep. Climb up the left side of the overhang, past a calcite-tufa feature, and continue with further difficulties to gain less steep rock.
FSA. Dave Henderson 4.9.1999

⑨ White Rhino Tea ... 7a *S0*
10m. This stunning route ventures up the leaning prow, which is easily seen from as far away as the Great Cave itself. Swing like a big monkey along *Barnacle Traverse Continuation*, until roughly beneath the centre of the prow. Yard up and slightly rightwards on dinner plate jugs; the crux is passing a hidden flowstone hold.
FSA. Dave Henderson 1.8.1998

⑩ Watting Yer Ouzel .. 6c+ *S0*
8m. Start from the right groove this time to save your arms. Climb leftwards on *Barnacle Traverse Continuation* to gain the right side of the *White Rhino Tea* prow. Continue directly up to reach the left edge of the access groove.
FSA. Dave Henderson 16.8.1999

⑪ Pink Roadster..... 7a *S0*
11m. Classic positions. Take the steep hanging arete, and follow it all the way to a massive jug below the final slab. Grasp the pink slopers on the very lip, and rock-over on these (crux) to go hands-off. Finish rightwards across the slab.
FSA. Mike Robertson 1.8.2005

⑫ Whoomze Got der Keys to me Beema
6c *S0*
8m. This line is essentially a hanging traverse accessed down the groove, as for *Watting Yer Ouzel*. Traverse rightwards into the tall cave, and clamber up to a jug rail. Follow this leftwards, around the overhanging arete. Finish in the easy groove.
FSA. Dave Henderson 4.9.1999

⑬ Hymenopteran Hippopotamus
6c+ *S0*
11m. From the base of *Whoomze*, traverse right and gain the vertical wall on the right. Climb this to the hanging 'V' feature in the roof then climb this out rightwards to the top.
FSA. Dave Pickford 2003

The final DWS interest here is found along some 90m to the east, where a big arete hangs above good water. Abseil in, or downclimb the easy corner immediately west of the feature.

⑭ Cod Direct .... 6b+ *S1*
14m. The arete is climbed by means of a boulder problem start, thereafter stick to the arete, on accommodating holds all the way. The original start came in from the left shelf, expect it to be 5 and S2/3.
FSA. Mike Robertson and Dave Henderson 14.8.2005

⑮ Barnacle Traverse 5 *S1*
90m. And last but not least, the original solo here; a low-tide barnacle-fest. Start by *Cod Direct*, and blast along leftwards for some 90m, to finally arrive at the shallow corner just to the right of *Hymenopteran Hippopotamus*; finish easily up that. Take a low-ish tide with you.
FSA. John Fowler and Fred Stebbings 9.9.1967

Berry Head

Berry Head Quarry - Arch Zawn

Berry Head Quarry

For those of familiar with the area, and who have ever wondered just what Berry Head Quarry really looks like, take a look at the picture above, snapped from a sea kayak a kilometre or so out in Torbay. The huge, shattered, quarried back wall gives some rather gripping trad climbing, but the sea level pinnacles are what attracts the deep water soloist to the venue. The rock here is wholly natural, solid, and offers some excellent climbs, with nothing at all above that magic height of 15m. There are four distinct pinnacles in the picture. On the left is the Arch Zawn area, second is the Navigator Pinnacle. The third is nondescript, with no routes, and the last is the Labyrinth Pinnacle.

Approach - From the car park, take the narrow tarmac road towards the cafe, then break out left to take the road down into the lower area of Berry Head Quarry.

Conditions and Tides - A mid-high tide scenario will be perfect. The headland is quite exposed, so be aware of the sea state.

❶ Wavewalker 7a S0/1
10m. The left-most line on the Gothic Face is approached via a low traverse in from the left, after an easy scramble down the left nose of the crag. Make hard moves to gain a collection of good slots (crux). Chill a little, then climb the cracked, slightly slanted feature above, moving slightly left to gain the arete above half-height. The route shares a few holds with the next route.
FSA. Martin Crocker 20.9.1998

The next three routes are best started either with a bench seat arrangement, or the more simple tape harness set-up. Rig the rope above the centre of the wall, off a Rock 10 placement/Hex, found in a slot a few metres below the summit edge. If using a seat, get someone to pull it up out of the way.

❷ Breathless 7a S1
14m. This brilliant line stays approximately on the mottled, scoopy features. Sustained and technical throughout, and on great rock. Approach with bench seat/tape harness rig. From the big pocket at the base of the wall, trend leftwards into the mottled scoops, and climb up to a natural brush with *Wavewalker*. Eschewing the easier finish to the left as for that route (about 6b+, and a worthwhile, easier option) step back right and climb direct past the final peg to a sustained finish on the upper wall.
FSA. Martin Crocker 19.9.1998

❸ Gothic . . . . 6c+ S1
14m. The same access as the above route. Superb climbing, giving quality, steep slab climbing up the black wall left of the corner; almost 3 stars. Catch it in the summer, when the sun raises its head well over the headland. From the same lower pocket as *Breathless*, move out right up a short diagonal break, and climb the balancy slab above, with some still-tough moves right at the top.
FSA. Martin Crocker 19.9.1998

❹ Man in Black . . 6b+ S1/2
13m. The big black corner is solid but somewhat intimidating. This line isn't likely to see much in the way of ascents, and has been graded for a possible clatter with the architecture on the way down! Make sure you tackle this when it is dry. One for corner enthusiasts only.
FSA. Martin Crocker 19.9.1998

Berry Head Quarry - Arch Zawn **Berry Head**

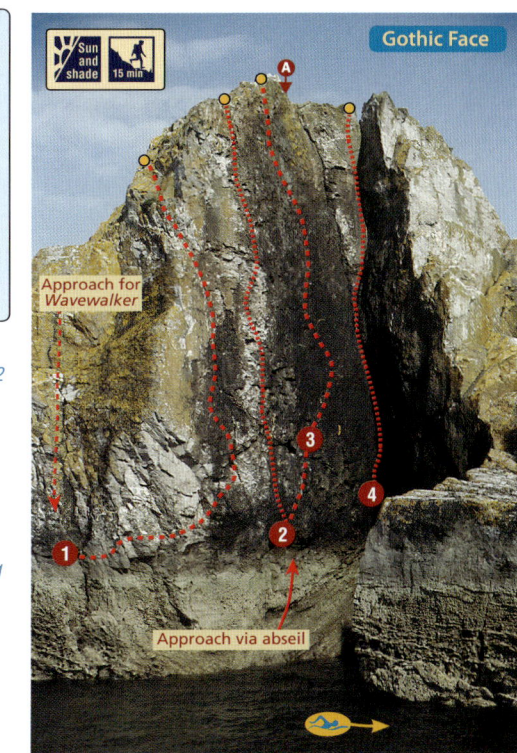

Arch Zawn

Arch Zawn harbours a fine collection of routes, with the airy *And All Because...* being the best highball in the quarry. The Gothic Face offers excellent, technical face climbing.
Approach - The approach to *And All Because...* is via the start of the *Arch Zawn Traverse*; to reach the Gothic Face, walk up the slope at the end of the quarry, turn left, and down-climb a short easy wall. A short rope (not in-situ) on a fisherman's spike will assist you.
Conditions and Tides - The sun hits the Gothic Face late in the day, and this is desirable, as the rock here can be greasy in the morning. Aim for high tide for all the routes here.

5 And All Because..   **6a+** *S1/2*
14m. The shapely arete offers amazing climbing throughout - you'll want a high tide on your side. The line is enticing, yet feels a little scary when you're up there (funny, that). Traverse in easily from the right to the arete, and follow it, on its right side, with judicious use of the crack. Escape the summit by carefully climbing across to the right and back down to the slope on that side.
FSA. unknown

6 The Arch Zawn Traverse   **6a+** *S0/1*
20m. A lovely dash of crab-wise activity covers the low ground from the start of *And All Because…* around to the ledge facing *Breathless*. The route (and the grade) is very tide-dependent, as the finish offers a multitude of possibilities through the various caves. A nice warm-up for the *Breathless* face!
FSA. unknown

Berry Head
Berry Head Quarry - The Navigator Pinnacle

❶ **Crunchie** 4 *S1*
9m. This small but good appetiser is found on the left side of the buttress. Traverse in from the fishermens' ledges, to gain the corner above. Climb it to the top.
FSA. Bruce Woodley 1983

❷ **Loftgroover** 5 *S0*
11m. A great piece of climbing; steady throughout. Probably the Quarry's best introduction to DWS. From the same access ledges as *Crunchie*, continue rightwards until on the edge of the sea cave. From here, climb the left side of the arete to the top.
FSA. Matthew Thompson 17.4.1997

❸ **Project** .... 7c+? *S0*
11m. The right side of the arete will be very hard.

❹ **Rhythm of the Night** 7a *S0*
13m. A dark undertaking, venturing up the slick black rock in the rear of the cave. Take a mid-tide, to retain some crucial footholds. Traverse left to a crack, and up to a flake hold. Continue up into the steep corner to finish.
FSA. Martin Crocker 3.10.1998

❺ **Deep House** .... 6a+ *S1*
12m. The back corner. From the small starting ledges, move leftwards to gain the corner, and bridge your way up to a roof. Take a deep breath and traverse rightwards beneath the roof, past one more hard move to get around the arete, then finish as for *Soul to Soul*.
FSA. Martin Crocker 3.10.98

❻ **Soul to Soul** 5 *S2/3*
12m. A slip from the hardest moves exiting the corner would have serious consequences on this one. The climbing, however, is damn good. Abseil to the small ledge at the base of the route. Climb up and rightwards on massive jugs, then follow the steep curling corner above to the top of the buttress.
FSA. Martin Crocker 20.9.1998

The Navigator Pinnacle
The Navigator Pinnacle, is the oddly-square, carved-out crag that is tricky to view. The superb lines of *Loftgroover* and *MC Navigator* are the most popular.
Approach - The abseil that services the central lines can be arranged with wires, set back from the top some way. Abseil in to small ledges just above the HWM. The outer lines are simple traverse-ins.
Conditions and Tides - High tide is recommended, although not crucial on all the routes, as the water is deep. A crisp, calm day will give the best friction, since the central section can be dank. The routes on the fringes of the crag will get morning sun.

❼ **Disco Babes from Outer Space** 7a+ *S1/2*
12m. A line that could really do with straightening, as it uses much of *Soul to Soul*, and finishes pretty much on *MC Navigator*. There is a boulder in the water that gives concern, and the route has yet to record an on-sight ascent. Climb up *Soul to Soul* to a flake at 4m or so, then break out towards a steepening. Surmount this using hard-to-find pockets, then move desperately rightwards to finish up the arete.
FSA. Martin Crocker 3.10.1998

❽ **M.C. Navigator** .... 7a+ *S0/1*
11m. The most popular hard route on the buttress. The line tackles the steep arete that forms the right edge of the sea cave. Access by a tricky 'crawl' across the lower break. Grapple upward for a good pocket, and then dive up the arete with verve, on pockets and side-pulls, to a move leftwards into an awkward rest. Pull steeply out of this to climb the final short scoop.
FSA. Martin Crocker 20.9.1998

The Labyrinth Pinnacle

❾ **Austin's Powers** ..... 6a+ *S0*
9m. Friendly and fun. Expect good water at pretty much any tide. From the descent steps, swing around the left arete with difficulty, and climb the right side of the arete above to a solid exit.
FSA. Dave Henderson 16.8.1998

Berry Head Quarry - The Labyrinth Pinnacle — Berry Head

🔟 Brown Paper — 6a+ S0
10m. The face right of *Austin's Powers* is an eliminate.
FSA. Dave Henderson 7.1999

🔟 Barefoot and the Hendersons — 4 S1
11m. The groove is pleasant, but unfortunately you'll need to do an English 5c move to gain the route. An alternative is to traverse in from the other end of the crag; this will keep the overall grade to about English 4c.
FSA. Phil Austin 16.8.1998

🔟 Labyrinth Pinnacle Traverse — 4+/6a+
40m. The traverse from the right, with a finish up *Barefoot and the Hendersons* gives the 4+ grade. The pure low traverse, usually undertaken from the left, will negotiate the hard move under *Austin's Powers*, thus giving a 6a+ start. *(S0/1)*
FSA. unknown

The following routes are almost always tackled by climbing in from the right side (looking in) of the pinnacle.

🔟 Pigeon Street — 6a+ S1/2
9m. From the steady approach traverse, climb up the streaked rock, past two holes, to finish slightly leftwards. Keep an eye on the reef below.
FSA. Dave Henderson 16.8.1998

The original route here, Labyrinth, dives into the crag and exits via the 'Squinting Rebirth Hole' and although providing some steady caving, is far from DWS territory!

🔟 Labyrinth Variation Start — 6b+ S0
5m. This enticing, low tide boulder problem is an alternative start to *Labyrinth*, entering the cave by way of a lower hole. The tide level will dictate the exact grade. Once in, you might take the easy (above your head) way back out.
FSA. Dave Henderson.8.1998

🔟 The Dulux Start — 6b+ S1
4m. This is an alternative start to *Shady Lane*.
FSA. Dave Henderson 9.7.1999

The Labyrinth Pinnacle
This upright feature offers some good climbing, although it's not in the league of the previous two venues, in terms of quality. It's also slightly spoilt by the lack of any viewing gallery, which tends to give your mates just as hard a time as you had.

Approach - The approach is logically from the left for the left-hand routes, and from the right for the routes at the opposite end of the crag.

Conditions and Tides - The morning sun pays a visit, so an early start is a great idea, although the rock should stay dry most of the day. Mid-high tide recommended.

🔟 Shady Lane — 6b+ S1
10m. Excellent climbing, getting involved with the leaning, open groove. A sequential start leads to a jug, from where the climbing gradually gets easier.
FSA. Dave Henderson 16.8.1998

🔟 T-Minus Ten — 6c+ S1
10m. The prominent arete gives a spicy pitch. Launch up onto the dark arete, and stretch for a hold above. Continue up and slightly rightwards to finish.
FSA. Martin Crocker 3.10.1998

The final route listed is a long traverse out of the quarry heading towards Brixham.

🔟 Hysoscella Sideways — 7a S1/2
You'll need a high tide to get the best out of this route, and it's slightly marred by a number of possible exit points. Rather than give you a blow-by-blow description, I'll leave you to work it out and have an adventure.
130m. Start from the big ledge found under the fisherman's parking area in the quarry, and make your way in the direction of the Berry Head hotel. After a good section through an overhung cove (some shallower water here), take on an excellent leaning wall, to gain a break at its culmination. Continue more easily along to the hotel.
FSA. Dave Henderson 18.7.1998

Torquay

The Torquay area is full of DWS surprises, all found on the eastern side of Torbay, the huge bay which is Devon's busiest tourist-trap. But this is the strange thing: despite the crowds that infest Torquay's beaches, the climbing areas covered here represent the absolute antithesis of this. Try a little soloing any summer day down at London Bridge or Long Quarry Point and you will probably have the place to yourself. The worst case 'rush hour' scenario is the odd fisherman scrambling through the bizarre architecture of the region's small inlets and zawns.

Approach

To reach the London Bridge area (including the *Five Star* and *Watchtower Traverses*) the free parking in Rock End Avenue is recommended, especially as it offers the chance to walk to Torquay harbour for food etc. To get down to the *Plimsoll Line Traverse* and the Aqua Marina Wall, the best parking is either in the Daddyhole Plain car park (currently free), or in free spaces along at the eastern end of Meadfoot Beach. To reach Anstey's Cove, with the Long Traverse and Long Quarry Point, you can do no better than stop at the DIY Centre car park, found in Babbacombe Road.

Conditions and Tides

The many crags detailed here have a variety of aspects so rock conditions vary considerably, but expect dry rock on warm sunny days. Allow some sun to arrive before your visit, and expect the conditions in the caves to be the trickiest to predict. It is true to say that Torquay has a degree of shelter from the real world, but it's a BIG bay, and the swell and sea state will always be variable. The most exposed venue here is Long Quarry Point. The tides have the usual Devon swings, and you'll need a tide timetable to get the best out of your visit. The traverses will need the most savvy with the tides, so don't expect to get it exactly right on your first visit!

Accommodation and Food

The Torquay area is not well-endowed with camping facilities, with most climbers tending to migrate over to the Brixham area at night. Expect a huge number of B&B's and hotels in Torbay - any search on the web will reveal these. Torquay itself has a massive selection of pubs, bars and chip shops, as well as a full selection of banks and suchlike. Try Ella's cafe, next to Torquay harbour, for breakfast. The quieter, 'suburban' Babbacombe offers a mini-Torquay, with banks, cafes, and pubs in good supply.

Johnny Woods on the excellent line of *Athiest* (6b+) - *page 121* - on the sea-arch of London Bridge, Torquay. Photo: Mike Robertson.

London Bridge Area

The superb and well-positioned London Bridge Area has an essential place in Devon deep water soloing. The striking, compact bridge itself is a geological delight - a hanging archway surrounded by water, and with grades running across the spectrum. Lovers of traverses need look no further than the region's three crab-esque offerings, including the striking and colourful *Watchtower Traverse*, whilst the wanderers amongst you might feel obliged to go and find the excellent Aqua Marina Wall.

Approach

South Devon car parks are legendary for their high prices; detailed in the map below are the free parking possibilities in Rock End Avenue and in the Daddyhole Plain car park, as well as the Pay and Display car park by the harbour.

From the Imperial Hotel, the twisting Rock End Walk footpath heads south-east, goes up a little, and then down through attractive trees and shrubs to reach Peaked Tor Cove (*Five Star Traverse II* starts here) and then Saddle Point (the Saddle Point outcrop is seen here down to the right, behind the trees). To reach London Bridge, continue on along Rock End Walk, turning left up steps between two bench seats, following the path until it drops back down steps. Turn right here down a wooded slope - the striking feature of London Bridge is apparent after 20m. For the outlying Aqua Marina Wall and the *Plimsoll Line Traverse*, see the separate access notes.

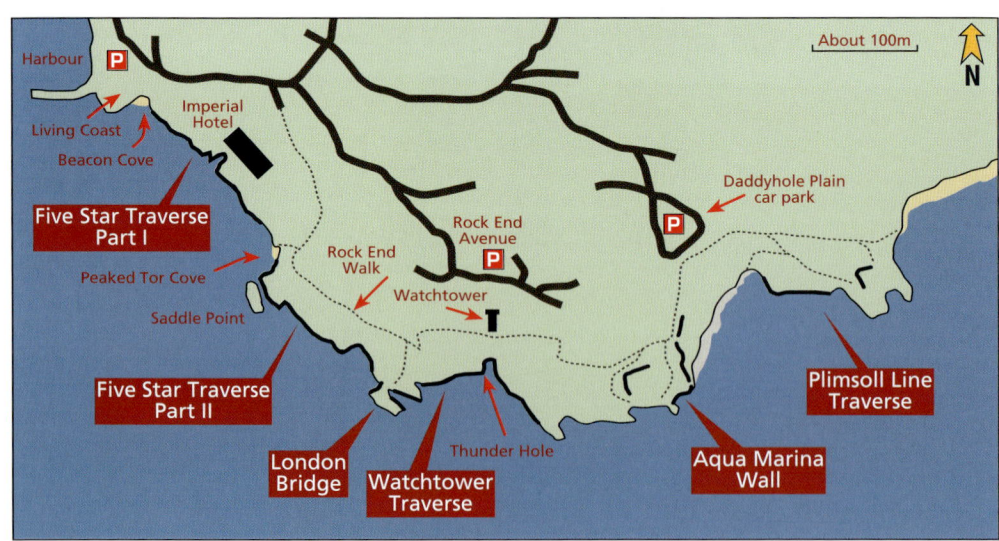

Conditions and Tides

You'll usually have plenty of routes in condition at anything between mid and high tide, with some of the traverses needing no more than mid-tide for an ascent. See individual route notes for your best timing. The rock is generally compact and the routes are fast-drying, although seepage does occur after prolonged rain. Most of the routes get sun by midday, although the sunshine aspects of London Bridge prove to be more complex.

Meilee Rafe tackling *Duck L'Orange* (3+) - *page 123* - on the Duck Face at the London Bridge Area, Torquay. Photo: Mike Robertson.

London Bridge Area — Five Star Traverse

Five Star Traverse
The first route covered here, the *Five Star Traverse*, was originally put up in the sixties in two sections, *Part I* and *Part II*. *Part I* presents a little more coasteering above shelves than is ideal, and should be undertaken with care. *Part II* is a much friendlier prospect, that generally offers fun climbing above good water, especially around a high neap tide or bigger.

❶ Five Star Traverse Part I 6a *S2*
200m. Start in Beacon Cove close to the harbour and work eastwards along easy slabs at first, before a couple of steep inlets must be negotiated. A little further is a square-cut zawn directly below the hotel. Once past this, the beach of Peaked Tor Cove is at hand. Has some sections of soloing above rock ledges.
FSA. Pat Littlejohn 1967

❷ Five Star Traverse Part II . . . . 5+ *S0/1*
200m. The recommended DWS of *Part II* begins at Peaked Tor Cove, and monkeys along to Dyers Quarry, with a further little bouncy extension to reach London Bridge if you like. Start at Peaked Tor Cove. Walk under the white wall of *Peaked Tor Cove Traverse* (or wade) then climb out of the Cove to pass Saddle Point. Continue on, with many excellent sections on steep slabs and walls, and keep down for a further low section to reach the middle of Dyer's Quarry. Climb out, and either walk to London Bridge on the hillside path (now obvious), or drop back in to negotiate the excellent, final bay.
FSA. Pete Biven, Mark Springett 1968

❸ Peaked Tor Cove Traverse . . . . 7a+ *S1*
15m. Good, hard face climbing; take a high tide, and please note - any knee-high paddling dramatically reduces the grade! Climb eastwards out of the Cove for 15m at a big high tide, on the beautiful white wall.
FSA. Nick White 1990

London Bridge
This unusual feature sits squat against Torbay's leafy coastline, with the big grassy connecting col giving the feature its 'bridge'. The whole thing is rather oddly formed and shaped; the overhead plan and the crag shots should reveal all its secrets easily enough!

❹ Project . . . . 7c? *S2*
12m. This horizontal possibility will require the guns (and the psyche). Start on the west side, and emerge on the east.

Atheist Wall London Bridge Area 121

❺ Luv-Groove-Dance-Party
7a+ *S0/1*

16m. A line requiring a little savvy. Good moves above excellent water. Traverse leftwards across the bottom of the groove of *Atheist*, and move up to reach a jug-line. The crux on layaways follows, delivering you to a finish up the groove formed by the bridge itself.
FSA. Martin Crocker 18.4.1997

❻ Atheist
6b+ *S2*

15m. Superb and pumpy climbing up the soaring groove. The difficulties begin down at the HWM and are beautifully unrelenting. A very logical rightwards move 2m below the top, stepping across to the finishing jugs of *Pumping'*, makes the final section more enjoyable. The original direct and unstable finish will feel closer to S3, with the reef closing in to your left/rear.
See photo on page 117.
FSA. unknown

❼ Pumping Dancefloor Energy
7a+ *S0*

12m. The fingery and very balancy arete to the right of *Atheist* offers wicked and well-positioned climbing. Traverse in from the right and attack the shapely arete direct.
FSA. Martin Crocker 13.8.1997

❽ Freddy the Frog Hits Torquay
6a+ *S0*

9m. The first line 'off' the traverse in, and a brilliant intro to the great game of DWS, with easy access, a mid-height crux and a solid top-out. Try to avoid a cheating sequence rightwards at two-thirds height; the top finishing groove is damn good!
FSA. Martin Crocker 31.3.1997

Atheist Wall

This fine and very compact face gives some of the best climbing hereabouts. *Atheist* needs some careful tide timing (but is well worth the effort) and the diminutive *Freddy the Frog...* is probably the best warm-up in the area.

Approach - Cross the bridge itself, then climb down and right (tricky) to reach sea level. Once here, the four routes are reached by way of a leftwards traverse. Please note that Route 4 on the topo is a project, and actually starts as for *Arch Temptress*, on the opposite side - see page 122..

Conditions and Tides - You'll ideally need a north-westerly breeze in here to crispen things up, as the wall only gets sunshine late on summer evenings. Wait for a good high tide for *Atheist*; a mid-high will be fine for the remainder.

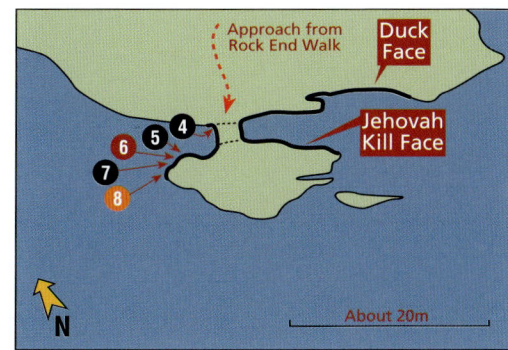

London Bridge Area — Jehovah Kill Face

Jehovah Kill Face

The Jehovah Kill Face is home to a selection of hard, fingery routes, the best of which might be the excellent traverse of *Long Dong Village*.

Approach - The routes are reached by crossing the bridge and heading leftwards over the stack, to gain sea level at the bottom/left (eastern) side of the face.

Conditions and Tides - A mid-high tide will give you all the water you need. Morning sun usually dries things out, but avoid damp conditions here - it's hard enough when it's dry!

❶ Long Dong Village **7b** *S0*
18m. The first line is the ubiquitous traverse, and it's a damn good 'un! Take a reasonable tide with that slight reef in mind, although the difficulties are always very low down. A pumpy line. Start as for *Jehovah Kill*. Climb that route to the rising section, and then continue to traverse the base of the crag, venturing up and down as necessary, to arrive at the far side.
FSA. Dave Henderson 8.2001

❷ Don't Fear the Reef . . . . **7a+** *S1/2*
11m. A hard, fingery line, that requires the cushion of a decent tide. Check the depth carefully. Start as for *Jehovah Kill*. Traverse as for that route, diving up early on to gain the slight rib and crack above. Move slightly left to finish with care.
FSA. Martin Crocker 3.10.1998

❸ Project . . . . **7b+?**
12m. The line to the right will go but it will be fingery and hard.

❹ Jehovah Kill **7b** *S1*
15m. This brilliant and persuasive line was once a sport route, though now it is firmly on the DWS agenda! Traverse rightwards on progressively smaller holds, and commit to a series of rising moves leading to a hollow flake at 8m. Finish by bridging up onto the bridge itself.
FSA. Martin Crocker 18.4.1997

❺ Project . . . . **7c+?**
12m. The left-hand finish to *Jehovah Kill*.

Duck Face

Arch Temptress and *French Kiss* are reached by scrambling easily down to sea level at the left end of the crag.

❻ Arch Temptress . . . . **6a+** *S1/2*
16m. A classic and fulfilling exercise; nowhere desperate, but it works your body all the way. Start on the big fin on the west side of the landward side of the arch. Undercut wildly rightwards, and battle your way across and up an almost endless series of welded flakes, emerging on the east side of the bridge. Have a big high tide for maximum security.
FSA. Martin Crocker 3.10.1998

❼ French Kiss **6c** *S1*
13m. A good recent addition, with some engrossing moves down low. Access as for *Arch Temptress*, but then drop down into the square niche, close to the sea. Make hard, 'au cheval' moves to get established on the lower face to the right, and climb small edges and side-pulls direct to the final undercuts on *Arch Temptress*. Finish as for that route.
FSA. Mike Robertson 8.8.2006

Duck Face — London Bridge Area

Duck Face

This south-facing steep slab offers some terrific climbing, with a good spread of grades. Take note of the varied angles of the routes on the face, and use your judgement carefully before trying your ascent.

Approach - Most of the routes are all gained by a walk down the grass, then by traversing the base of the face (right to left), starting from the end arete of *Duck L'Orange*.

Conditions and Tides - The face is usually dry and crisp, and the holds are almost always positive, even when they're tiny! Take a high tide with you for all the routes here.

❽ Chicken Head .. 7a+ S1/2

13m. A classic thrill, and very technical. From the base of *Dance on Dinkies*, do two moves and bridge left onto the face. Climb the line of perfect, tiny side-pulls all the way up to a chicken-head at 8m. Then either climb up and left, or left and up; either way, finish on the upper section of *Arch Temptress*.
FSA. Robbie Warke 1987, with hanging rope, FSA. Mike Robertson 8.8.2006

❾ Dance on Dinkies 6c+ S2

13m. The slim white groove is technical and bold. Enter the groove by some thin moves, and climb in the same fashion to a further desperate move at almost 10m, moving right to easier ground.
FSA. Robbie Warke 1987, with hanging rope; FSA. Martin Crocker 3.10.1998

❿ Duckless in Torbay .... 3+ S1/2

13m. The left-hand of the two grooves (the right-hand one NOT being a DWS) gives excellent climbing. Reach it via the traverse from the seaward ridge. Climb the straightforward groove direct, to a careful finish.
FSA. Mike Robertson 11.6.2005

⓫ Last Duck to Bombay 6a+ S1/2

9m. Fine, intricate climbing on small pockets and edges, up the wall just right of the square gully. Climb the wall, moving slightly right of the crack in the upper section, to finish on positive holds.
FSA. Martin Crocker 3.10.1998

⓬ Crispy Duck, No Noodles ... 4 S1

8m. The remainder of the wall is very steady indeed; this one's a good pocket romp! Traverse in from the seaward ridge and climb the wall on generous holds, past a steepening, to gain an easier finish. There are two variations in the mid-section.
FSA. Martin Crocker 3.10.1998

⓭ Something Ducky 4 S1

8m. Similar to the last route, tracing a line a little to the right. Climb up through a steeper bit to easier ground, finish direct.
FSA. Martin Crocker 3.10.1998

⓮ Duck L'Orange .... 3+ S1/2

8m. The right-hand edge of the Duck Face, on excellent rock. Climb up the steep slab to a crack, and continue to the top.
See photo on page 119.
FSA. Mike Robertson 11.6.2005

Torquay — The Watchtower Traverse

Photo labels: Watchtower on Rock End Walk; London Bridge Area; Thunder Hole

The Watchtower Traverse

The coastline immediately east of London Bridge is relatively low, and disappears off into a series of walls, bays and caves. The next route is found here, and heads in the direction of Telegraph Hole, the quarried bay along to the east.

① The Watchtower Traverse — 5 S1
(First third only, as far as Thunder Hole).
Even though the *Watchtower Traverse* in its entirety weighs in at 225m and 6c+, I've separated the post Thunder Hole half of the route. This is because Thunder Hole itself has one section that still uses a rope for aid (or protection) and the latter section of the route offers little in the way of good rock and nice positions, despite appearances. By contrast, the first section, across an almost endless tapestry of slanted diagonal cracks on a steep slab, gives some really superb climbing, burying the soloist within some really solid, colourful architecture. The final bonus; you'll rarely be further than 4m from the sea!
95m. Down-climb the slabs on the east side of London Bridge, and traverse all the way to the big cave feature of Thunder Hole, with good water all the way. There are sometimes a few moves on slabs that you'd probably need to 'push' away from, in the event of a slip. Be prepared for a swim back (dry-bag useful) - or doing the route twice, of course.
FSA. Pete Biven, Frank Cannings, Martin Springett 28.12.1968

② The Watchtower Traverse — 6c+ S1
(Thunder Hole to Telegraph Hole).
130m. But, for those who choose to seek the fuller experiences… the extension is added here for the full tick! It is a wee adventure, after all. At Thunder Hole, swim/dry-bag for some 10m or so, exiting onto a good ledge. Traverse all the way to the far quarried platform, at varying, confusing levels and with a certain element of vegetation. The final, sustained and technical wall gives the crux section, above deep water.
FSA. Pat Littlejohn 12.9.1991

The Aqua Marina Wall

③ Troy Tempest — 6c+ S0
12m. The wall on the left of the orange runnel features good hard climbing. Foot-traverse the lip of the shallow overhang rightwards, with a hard move back left for a jug. Climb up and rightwards on the left edge of the runnel on small holds, to gain the top ramp. Finish easily leftwards.
FSA. Nick White 1990

④ Barn Doors — 6c+ S0
12m. The traverse of the face is fun, and gives a method of reaching your start (albeit not an easy one). Start as for *Troy Tempest*, but continue along the breaks, finally dropping down and then back up to gain the big thread hold. Reverse the start of *Aqua Marina* to finish.
FSA. Mike Robertson 8.2006

Aqua Marina Wall — Torquay

Aqua Marina Wall

This nicely-situated wall, also known as the left end of the Daddyhole Main Cliff, is tucked well away and sees little attention, despite some great climbing. The classic of the crag is the brilliant *Aqua Marina*.

Approach - From Meadfoot Beach, walk in to Meadfoot Quarry, and drop down the wide groove formed by the blunt pinnacle to gain the excellent Plimsoll Line traverse (see next page). This takes you across to the boulder beach, from where you can hop along to the wall itself. Your alternative is to use the approach path down from Rock End Walk, which is tricky to find and not nearly as much fun. *Troy Tempest* and *Barn Doors* start from the base of the gully (easy descent, or abseil in) on the left side of the wall, with *Stingray* and *Aqua Marina* gained from the obvious reef on the right side of the wall.

Conditions and Tides - The water is so deep here, you may well fail to see the bottom, even at low tide. Morning sun generally keeps the rock fairly dry.

❺ Stingray **7a** *S0*
12m. This terrific eliminate line ventures up the beautiful orange runnel, gaining it from the right. Step off the lower reef and take the descending break until down low. From pockets, move up to gain a shallow overhang then use a big undercut to reach and follow good but hidden jugs up and left to a thin crack. Climb the orange runnel above to the top ramp.
FSA. Nick White 1990

❻ Aqua Marina . . . . . **6a+** *S1*
12m. Brilliant! The best route on the wall, and at a steady grade too. Step off the left-hand end of the lower reef, and follow the breaks to the right edge of the shallow overhang. Gain the big thread in the left edge of the groove above, and follow the groove on big holds up to the ramp of *Pinnacle Traverse*. Follow that feature diagonally leftwards (easy) to the saddle by the pinnacle.
FSA. Nick White 1990

The last two routes are found on the other side of the pinnacle, on a short steep wall above good water. After climbing Aqua Marina across to the top of the pinnacle, walk around the small bay to view these lines. Jam-Master is the crack/fin feature, and is reached by scrambling in to gain a ledge just above the sea.

❼ Jam-Master . . . . **6a+** *S1*
6m. Short and hard; take your jamming technique along. Climb the excellent fin-and-crack feature above the small ledge.
FSA. Martin Crocker 4.10.1998

❽ Devolution **6c** *S0*
6m. Hard and safe! From the same start, climb diagonally right up the bulging grey face.
FSA. Martin Crocker 4.10.1998

Torquay — The Plimsoll Line Traverse

The Plimsoll Line Traverse

The *Plimsoll Line Traverse* is essentially a sunlit and friendly steep slab, jutting from the sea between Meadfoot Beach and Daddyhole/Aqua Marina Wall. It is only 70m or so long, but offers good climbing, on superb rock, and in a pretty chilled setting. It's a pleasant but not gruelling example of Devon's traverses! That said, don't do it on a rough sea day.

Approach - The easiest option, especially for a shorter visit, is to use the Meadfoot Beach car park. Alternative (and free) parking can usually be found either in St. Mark's Road, above the main car park, or in the Daddyhole Plain car park, which can be reached by ascending the hill past the Imperial Hotel and following the signs for Daddyhole Plain. A further free parking area is found further along the beach road.

Conditions and Tides - Calm seas around a neap high tide recommended, as the low start moves would have to be tackled differently (higher, slightly harder) with bigger seas and bigger tides. In the event of a massive tide, just 'up' your line 2m or so! As with most of Devon's traverses, flexibility and a little ingenuity are the order of the day. Final note: the S grade depends on line taken, tide level and confidence, but there's plenty of water for most of the route.

1 Plimsoll Line Traverse. . 4 S1/2
70m. The picture above shows a blunt pinnacle rising from the platform just below Meadfoot Quarry, which itself is found a short walk from the beach's south-west end. Once by the blunt pinnacle, climb easily down to sea level (there are a number of grade 3 options), to gain the base of the cliff. Here a high neap tide and gentle water will allow the low start moves, which take crimps across a low, steep slab (feet on barnacle ledges). That dispensed with, climb across the big, engaging slab, at roughly the same level, to finally arrive on the boulder beach of Daddyhole. From here, either reverse the route, or head down to the Aqua Marina Wall for some further action. *Photo opposite.*
FSA. Pat Littlejohn 20.7.1967

Checking out the easy-going *Plimsoll Line* (4) - *opposite* - Torquay, Devon. Photo: Mark Glaister.

Babbacombe Area

The Babbacombe area of coastline comprises the beautiful Anstey's Cove, the endless jug rails of *The Long Traverse*, and the well-situated headland of Long Quarry Point. Better known worldwide for the discovery of some of the world's oldest human remains in Kent's Cavern in 1927, this stretch of coastline is perhaps more important in this guide for the diversity of its deep water soloing, ranging from the leisurely saunter of *The Long Traverse* (4+) through to the desperate, leaning test-piece of *Christine* (8a). The region is delightful, with many places to hide away from the ravages of Torbay's often overwhelming tourism, and the routes provide a perfect taster of Devon's outlying DWS treasures.

Approach

From Torbay, or from out of town, find your way to the lengthy Babbacombe Road, where you'll find parking in either the DIY centre (free), or in the Redgate Beach car park (Pay and Display). The DIY parking will provide your best base for the walk over to the Long Quarry Point path; use the Redgate Beach car park for an assault on *The Long Traverse* from its western end.

Tides and Conditions

Long Quarry Point is a headland, so note the sea state before you climb here. Crystal Zawn and Boulder Choke Zawn tend to be well sheltered from easterlies. Link your visit with a good mid-high tide, and you'll get plenty done; special care should be taken with Crystal Zawn, which does demand a well thought-out approach and a big tide.

Neil Gresham making the first ascent of the powerful *Once a Dogger* (7b+) - *page 130* - in Boulder Choke Zawn, Long Quarry Point, Torquay. Photo: Mike Robertson.

Babbacombe Area — The Long Traverse

The Long Traverse

The Long Traverse

The Long Traverse of Anstey's Cove is a gem indeed, linking the sprinkled craglets of Long Quarry Point with the easy-going tranquillity of Redgate Beach.

Approach - As for Long Quarry Point. An alternative is to approach by way of the sport climbing crag lower path, or Redgate Beach itself.

Conditions and Tides - Ideally, a high neap tide. A low tide will detract from the experience, as will a big high, which will give a desperate 7a+ roof in the mid section - although this is very obvious, should it happen to you!

❶ The Long Traverse . . . . 4+ S1
110m. This delightful excursion provides what Devon does best - cool traverse outings of the highest order. From Boulder Choke Zawn at Long Quarry Point, climb down the boulders to sea level, and traverse the various reefs, saddles and steep juggy breaks all the way to Redgate Beach. Or the other way, if you fancy, or even do it twice.
FSA. John Worsley 1962

Boulder Choke Zawn

This fine piece of rock rises brutally out of the sea on Long Quarry Point's south-facing side; it is home to one of the best solos in the area - *Arapiles, Oh Arapiles*. The rock is impeccable, and the water is almost always deep.

Approach - A simple walk gets you to the start of all three routes; the *Brutus Traverse* may well succumb to an assault from the left via a scramble into the zawn itself.

Conditions and Tides - The routes themselves are approx W/SW-facing, and get the sun from early afternoon onwards. There's rarely seepage, and any reasonable high tide will suffice.

Boulder Choke Zawn

❷ Brutus Traverse 7c? S0
12m. The low traverse of the crag will be nails. This hard possibility extends an old zig-zagging mixed-gear route known as *Et Tu Brutus*, giving it a finish on the start moves of *Arapiles*..... The rock is great, and it's super-safe.
NYS

❸ Once a Dogger . . . . 7b+ S1
10m. This superb and mega-steep test-piece starts as for *Arapiles*.... Take a big tide, as the sea level ramp behind you distracts just a little (the route has, however, been fallen from repeatedly, with no ensuing problems). From the moves onto the lichen-stained ramp, make hard moves diagonally left, to gain the peak of the grossly-leaning central prow. Two more moves gain the top. *See photo on page 129.*
FSA. Neil Gresham 20.8.2006

❹ Arapiles, Oh Arapiles 7a+ S0
9m. Just exquisite; a classy line indeed. This terrific line offers all those little niceties - an easy approach, a solid top-out, and nowhere too high. Low in the grade. From the iron-clad ledges on the right, traverse across leftwards to the slight ramp. From here, hard side-pull moves deliver you to an impasse on two small crimps - and a final, rather exciting dyno. You will be entirely forgiven for a sneaky peak down the line from the top, to check out your finishing hold!
FSA. Dave Henderson 14.8.1998

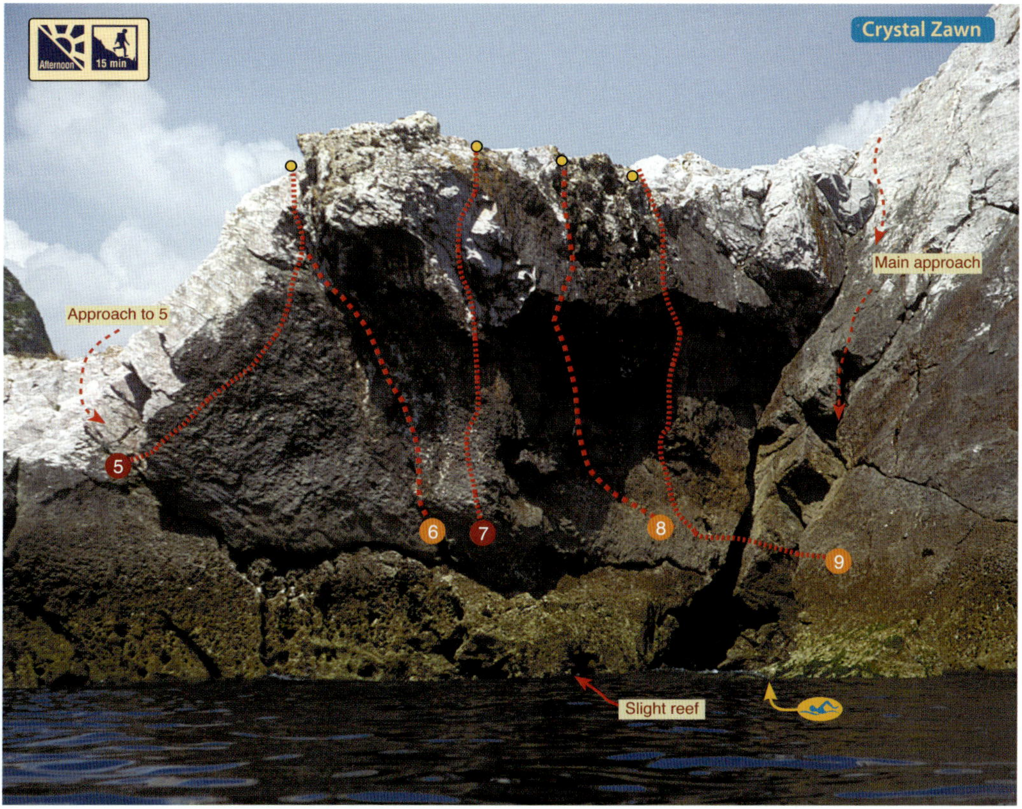

Crystal Zawn **Babbacombe Area**

Crystal Zawn

Crystal Zawn is neatly hidden from view. It's found over to the east of the more obvious Boulder Choke Zawn, and faces out to sea. The rock is terrific, and the routes are short but fun - your best introduction is *Crystal Pockets* (5+).

Approach - For *The Book of Laughter*, traverse in from the left. For all other routes on the wall, drop down the easy gully, and traverse in from the right - this approach is possible at high tide, which means you'll get the right water depth for your ascent.

Conditions and Tides - You'll need your tide timetable here, so please make sure you pick the best moment for your ascent, and check the depth if you're not sure. The wall gets plenty of sun, and is usually dry and in good condition.

⑤ The Book of Laughter .. 6c *S1*
7m. From the ledge, swing in and climb the sustained left edge of the buttress to a juggy finale shared with the next route.
FSA. Mike Robertson 20.8.2006

⑥ Honour Bright. . . . . 6a+ *S1*
7m. The curling corner offers some great moves. Traverse into the base of the steepening corner, and follow it all the way to the top, where a move right on big jugs gives an exciting finish.
FSA. Nick White 10.1989

⑦ Honour Bright Arete
. . . . 6c *S1*
7m. This excellent route is the hardest line on the face. Traverse into the base of the hanging arete, pull onto it with difficulty, and follow it strenuously to the top, where a final crux awaits.
FSA. Nick White 10.1989

⑧ Crystal Pockets. . . . . 5+ *S2*
7m. This line offers a great collection of jugs. Traverse in, keeping low, until you reach a big flake hold. Dive up the wall and through the roof on some truly massive buckets and pockets.
FSA. Nick White 6.1987

⑨ Midget Gem . . . . 6a+ *S2/3*
7m. Take care with this one - the gully below is as tight as a badger's bum, and it's not so deep! Swing into the face, and climb to the roof; stretch for a small pocket and step up for bigger holds.
FSA. Nick White 6.1987

Babbacombe Area — The Blowhole Pinnacle

Approach for Losing My Religion is through the blowhole opening at the back

The Blowhole Pinnacle
This wild cave is a must for any truly strong DWS'er. The compelling 8a line of *Christine*, with its straightforward access top and bottom and great water, must be one of the best hard solos in the county, with the brilliant *Losing My Religion* a close second, although this amazing 7b+ test-piece has lost some crucial holds (see below). The lines here are all identified by bolts.
Approach - *Blue Planet* and *Christine* are best gained by either a diagonal down-climb, or a short abseil from the top notch. To reach *Losing My Religion*, you'll need to delve into the cave through the blowhole opening (out of sight in the picture), and for *Waiting for Charlie*, you have to scramble easily down from the right.
Conditions and Tides - You will need optimum conditions for success here, so choose a crisp, dry day for your task. Take a high tide; all those upside-down antics on *Christine* will feel a little more amenable with the water closer to hand!

❶ Blue Planet . . . 7b+ S1/2
15m. Excellent climbing up the steep lower wall. Access is reasonable, with a down-climb across a ramp providing the way. From the start ledge, swing out across the lip of the cave on pockets and cracks, and continue rightwards up the steep wall, pressing on into a hanging groove. Climb up towards the crag's top notch, with easier moves to finish. *Photo opposite*.
FSA. Ken Palmer 2001

❷ Christine 8a S2
15m. What a gift! Mind-blowing positions and good water make this one of the most enticing routes of its grade to be found anywhere. Get a dry wind in the cave for your ascent. From the lower ramp just above the sea, climb up and right, and engage yourself in the hanging, grooved roof. Once through the roof itself, continue up the hanging face above to a junction with *Blue Planet*, and follow that line to the top notch.
FSA. Ken Palmer 7.2003

❸ Losing my Religion . 7c+? S3
15m. The original steep 7b+ monster here, and a brilliant pitch indeed. Unfortunately the route has lost a block, which provided much-needed undercuts where the line ventured out from the submerged boulder. This means that, as well as making the route considerably harder, it's not clear as to how safe it now is as a DWS. Go and find out. From a small ledge at the back of the cave (just above high tide) climb up, out and out again, finally reaching true daylight at the cave's lip by way of wild bridging and a '360' sequence. Finish much more easily.
FSA. Ken Palmer 2000

❹ Waiting for Charlie . 7c S1
15m. The shapely hanging prow on the right edge of the cave. The route tackles the very underside of the prow, and is a slight eliminate. Brilliant climbing throughout, with all the hard climbing dispensed with in the first half. From the base of the easy down-climb, sprint up the hanging diagonal prow, to gain the wall above. Finish more easily.
FSA. Dave Henderson 17.8.1998

Ken Palmer midway up *Blue Planet* (7b+) - *opposite* - on the Blowhole Pinnacle, Long Quarry Point, Devon. Photo: Mark Glaister.

Cornwall

Gavin Symonds tackling the sustained moves of *The Black Traverse* (6c+) - *page 144* - at Nare Head, Cornwall. Photo: Mike Robertson.

Cornwall

The isolated, sleepy county of Cornwall has always been renowned for its folklore, its alluring coastal towns, its ales and its big, atmospheric and traditional sea cliffs. For the deep water soloist there is surprisingly little to get excited about considering how much coastline there is, but the good news is the discovery of the DWS's of Nare Head, close to Truro, and the development of the friendly little crags of the Lizard peninsula. Although Cornwall may never be a major player in the great game of DWS, the region is highly recommended for a visit, especially if you combine it with some of the great trad sea-cliff routes.

Approach

Most folk approach using the combination of the M5, the A303 and the A30; all of these roads arrive at Exeter, where a spin along the A30, through Okehampton and Launceston, brings you down to Bodmin. After Bodmin, continue on the A30 and then turn south on the A3076, to reach Truro. This is the point where the directions for Nare Head start. For the crags of the Lizard, continue south-west and pick up the A394, which takes you to the town of Helston. This colourful town is on the doorstep of the Lizard peninsula, and a short drive down the A3083 will bring you to the approaches for both the Diamond Wall and Bass Point.

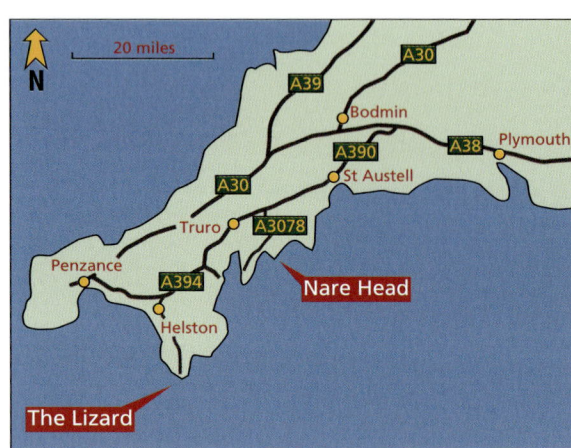

Accommodation and Food

Cornwall's south coast is well catered for, both with accommodation and camping possibilities. Expect a wealth of campsites in the immediate vicinity, with everything from appealing, rudimentary sites, right through to the ubiquitous, family-orientated caravan parks. The Cornwall Tourist Board can be reached on 01872 322900 and **www.cornwalltouristboard.co.uk**
At the Lizard, Henry's Campsite (01326 290596) comes recommended, with grassy terraces, a wickedly nice view and showers. Food-lovers need look no further than the charming Lizard village with its famous pasty shop, although a 15 minute drive to Helston will reveal further digs, plenty of chip shops, plus numerous cafes and supermarkets.
If you're visiting the more isolated Nare Head, you'll need to drive a little further for your requirements - look out for a number of accommodation and camping possibilities in the region of Tresillian and Tregony, with the large bustling town of Truro offering more in the way of sustained action.
For beaches within shooting distance of the crags, highly recommended is Kynance Cove - a spectacular series of west-facing beaches set amongst the Lizard's towering sea cliffs, and Carne Beach just west of Nare Head - the perfect chilling venue after a hard day at the crag!

Gavin Symonds on the deceptively difficult *Ong-Bak* (7b+), the hardest route in the area - *page 145* - on the Big Blue Face at Nare Head, Cornwall. Photo: Mike Robertson.

The Lizard

The Lizard, mainland Britain's most southerly point, is renowned for its warm weather, cream teas and the infamous Floral Dance, held in the main town of Helston. Also in Helston is the Blue Anchor pub; offered inside is one of the UK's finest

The dramatic coastline of the Lizard, Cornwall. Photo: Mike Robertson.

ales - 'Spingo', available in three strengths including a drop dead 7.6% variety!
The Lizard has always been a rarely visited outlying venue for trad climbers, despite the amazing diversity of quality rock on the peninsula - the best being the excellent Amphibolite, a high friction, often vertical rock, covered in good edges and split by many cracks. It's this rather sexy Amphibolite that provides us with the routes detailed below.

A massive sortie in 2006 (unsurprisingly, involving a sea kayak!) revealed two small venues on the Lizard Peninsula that proved ideal for DWS. With a number of routes at a very steady grade the south-west facing Diamond Wall, and the diminutive region of Bass Point, on the Lizard's southern tip are both worthwhile venues. It would be true to say that *A Girl's Best Friend* (4+), on the excellent Diamond Wall, is one of the best easy DWS's in the UK - this wonderful route features great climbing and perfect rock - all poised above a well-situated deep trench.

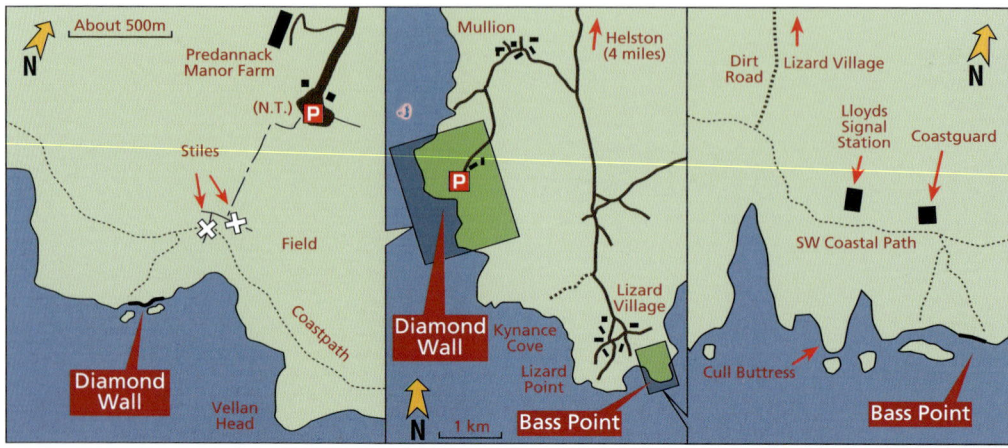

Just about as far south in the UK as you can go! Jason Porter on the delightful *Rangoon* (6a) - *page 141* - at Bass Point, the Lizard, Cornwall. Photo: Mike Robertson.

The Lizard — Diamond Wall

Diamond Wall

A fine buttress in an impressive location, with perfect rock and scenery. Although the number of climbs is limited, they are well worth seeking out.

Approach - From the A3083, make a turn and pass through the village of Mullion. Continue towards Mullion Cove until a left turn towards Predannack Head takes you down to the farm at Predannack Wollas. Park here at the National Trust car park, jump the stile, and walk down the hedged path through the fields towards the sea, to gain the main coastal path at a stile. Turn right and walk some 80m, then drop down and left to gain the top of the crag. Access is from the left or by abseil, and the 'swim-out' is just 5m.

Conditions and Tides - The south-facing rock here is usually dry and crisp. The sea state is always the main concern, of course - take a good look at this before committing to a climb. It's also worth noting that, to skip across the lower ledges on the left to gain the bottom of the face, you'll need a neap and not a big spring tide - those who prefer the maximum water will have to drop a rope down and get to the base in that fashion.

It is also worth noting that the horizontal break-line at about 13m (at a high neap tide) is essentially the limit of the hard climbing on the wall, with all cruxes situated below this (the cruxes of *Cut Diamond* and *A Girl's Best Friend* are dispatched within the first 8m, and the cruxes of *Koh-i-Nor* and *The Stone* are done and dusted before 13m). If you wish to avoid the higher, easier upper slab, leave a 'pull-out' rope in place - this will reduce all the S grades.

❶ **The Diamond Traverse** . . . . **6a+** *S2/3*
15m. The mid-height break on the wall is followed in from the left, and provides a ropeless entry to the crag in deep or heavy seas. The S2/3 is given for the first 3m which are steady and on solid rock, but over a lower shelf. The route would be most consistently finished via *The Stone*.
FSA. Mike Robertson 18.6.2006

❷ **Cut Diamond** **6b** *S1*
18m. The left arete gives excellent and very inescapable climbing with cool positions. From the holds at the bottom of the face, make strenuous moves up and left on side-pulls almost as far as the arete. Move up and then slightly right, to gain a flake system in light green rock and follow this to an easier finishing (4) groove in the upper slab.
FSA. Mike Robertson 18.6.2006

Bass Point — The Lizard

❸ Koh-i-Nor. — 6a+ *S1*
18m. A fine bit of climbing. From the starting holds, climb the face direct. Move slightly left to a fin in a pocket at half-height (a move right would head towards the 4+) and continue steeply up to the 13m break. Continue up the slab above at around 4.
FSA. Mike Robertson 18.6.2006

❹ A Girl's Best Friend. — 4+ *S1*
18m. A great line. For those breaking into DWS at the lower grades, there are so few available, so put this one on your list. From the start moves, either attack the crack from the high water mark directly (this is 5/5+), or weave in rightwards from the start of *Koh-i-Nor* (better and easier), to gain the crack. Follow the crack more steadily all the way to the upper slab, and continue to the top (the upper slab is about 3).
FSA. Mike Robertson 18.6.2006

❺ The Stone — 6b+ *S2*
18m. The right-most route is a slight eliminate, but has some excellent, well-positioned moves. The S grade is for the underwater shelf that sits out to your right/rear, although it would prove hard to reach that in a normal fall. From the first few moves of *A Girl's Best Friend*'s harder direct start, swing right across the spiky break to gain the thin and technical right-hand face. Climb this boldly on small edges to the 13m break, moving left to finish more easily.
FSA. Mike Robertson 18.6.2006

Bass Point
The Lizard's Bass Point is home to the charming *Amnesty* and *The Cull*, which cover some classic trad territory. The two solos detailed here are found a short distance from *The Cull*, down below the coastguard lookout. Both lines are a great introductions to DWS at the lower end of the scale, plus they enjoy plenty of water, and are on immaculate rock.
Approach - From parking in Lizard village, take the public footpath/wide track sign-posted for Bass Point. Walk down to the large white Lloyds signal station building, then briefly follow the coast path to the red painted wall beneath the coastguard lookout. Drop down the slopes, walking gradually leftwards, to find yourself at the top of the routes.
Conditions and Tides - As with the Diamond Wall, you won't want to be chasing the biggest tides; the sea you need is around a high neap - especially with *Rangoon*, which will prove quite inaccessible at a big high tide. Both routes are fast-drying and have no seepage concerns. There are various ways of gaining the base of the two lines here, most usually via the gullies. Look for the best method, or take a short rope and a few wires if you're unsure.

❻ Jessica Alba — 5+ *S0/1*
9m. The left-hand of the aretes is fun, solid and well-equipped with water. From the lower ledges on the left, climb out on the rising break to gain the prow, and follow it to the final (crux) move. There is a variation possible lower down, where climbing the line of holds below the rising break will give slightly harder climbing at about 6a.
FSA. Mike Robertson 12.5.2006

❼ Rangoon — 6a *S1*
13m. A cracker! An entry-level solo, with good water all the way. Given S1 for the top crux, which feels a little airy, so take a reasonable tide with you. From either the right or the left, traverse to the base of the odd-shaped prow, and climb it direct to the top, where a tricky mantel may make you squirm (just a little).
See photo on page 139.
FSA. Mike Robertson 12.5.2006

Nare Head

The deep water soloing of Cornwall's isolated Nare Head was discovered in July 2005, when the author spent nine days paddling a sea kayak from Sidmouth to Falmouth in search of fresh crags. Nare Head's climbing is actually found 1km east of Nare Head itself, and features mainly vertical walls offering technical climbing on small edges, mostly based around the aretes and walls of a sheltered, rectangular zawn. The zawn's entrance faces south-east, with the Black Tower getting light from dawn to mid-morning; the sun then swings around to bathe the Big Blue Face in sun from midday onwards.

Nare Head's rock is of volcanic origin, and, although similar in appearance to some of the Lizard's rock, is actually known as Greenstone.

The area is not yet fully developed (a small inflatable boat would facilitate a good crop of further prizes) and there are currently no bird nesting restrictions in place, although August 1st onwards is recommended for a visit, to avoid any unnecessary clashes with the bird population.

Approach

The OS map for Truro and Falmouth will help you with the convoluted drive in. On the A390, some 3 miles east of Truro, is the tiny village of Tresillian. Drive east out of the village, and follow the A390 for 2 miles, then take a right turn on the B3078, signposted to Tregony. Three miles gets you to Tregony village; continue on the B3078 southwards for a further two miles, and take the left turn just after the Esso garage, sign-posted to Veryan and Nare Hotel. Follow this small lane for just under a mile, then take a left turn signed to Trewartha. Follow the lane through Trewartha and go straight on at a cross-

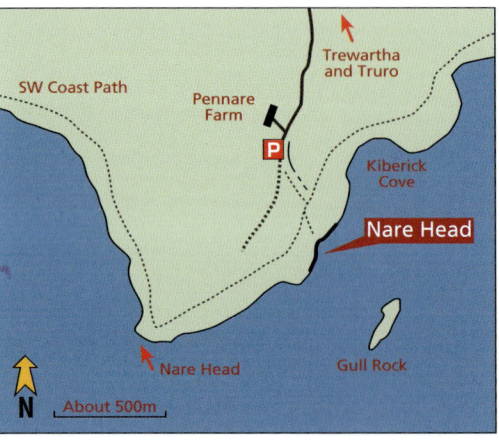

roads (marked Carne Beach 1.75 miles). Your last turning is a left, down a tiny, wing mirror-battering road signed for Nare Head. A further 0.75 mile gets you to the Nare Head and Kiberick Cove National Trust car park.

Walk out of the car park, heading west, on the well-travelled farm trail. After 100m, bear left, past a cattle trough, into the big, domed field. Follow the left/coastal fence until it dives left and runs out, and, after a further 80m, you'll see a vague, knobbly ridge appear on the left slope. After a further 40m, find the new 'path', down through ferns and gorse to head down the steep ridge, to a gearing-up spot just above where the crag disappears into the sea. The ridge below continues down to form Nare Head's Big Blue Face. The whole rough descent traces a line roughly towards the left (east) edge of Gull Rock - the big rocky island laying just off the coast here.

Conditions and Tides

As noted above, this venue is not actually on the headland, and you'll almost certainly enjoy a reasonable amount of shelter inside the main, rectangular zawn, especially from the prevailing westerlies. The tide swing averages around 3m or so, although the water here is very deep at most tides. Expect a little seepage early and late in the DWS season, particularly on the more shaded Black Tower.

Rosen Bay Nare Head

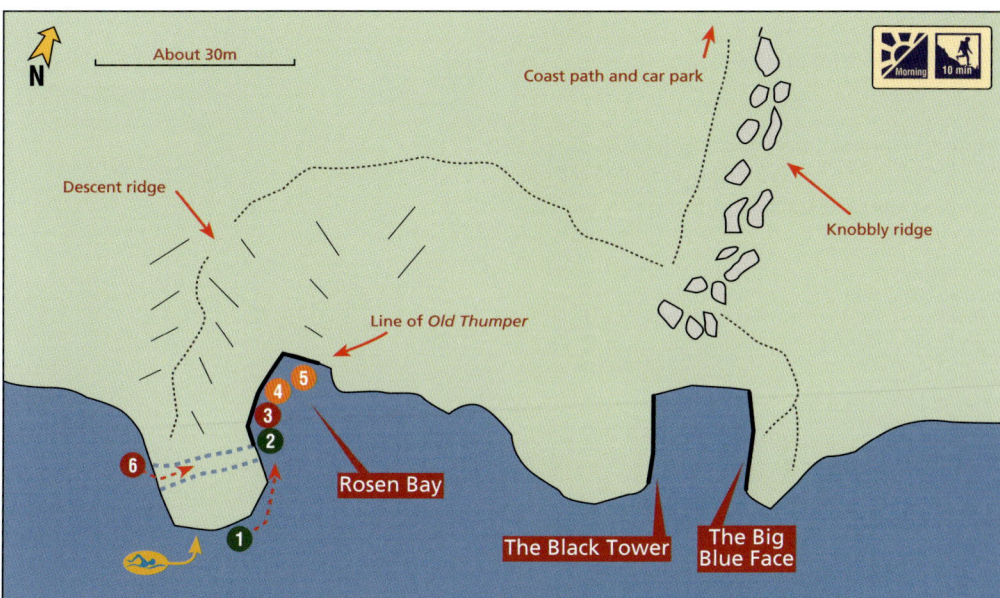

Rosen Bay

Rosen Bay is the big, curved bay found just west of the Black Tower. The climbs are on good rock.

Approach - The routes detailed below are all found by scrambling down the long ridge that forms the bay's western extremity. A few tricky moves (there's gear for an abseil, should you need it) will get you down to sea level, at a spacious promontory. The following routes (except *Old Jock's Tunnel*) are all gained by heading east, using the *Rosen Traverse*.

Tides and Conditions - The water depth is rarely a problem but a mid to high tide is ideal. *Old Jock's Tunnel* needs crisp conditions for success.

❶ Rosen Traverse 4 S1
17m. This fun little excursion takes you along the slab that bounds the west side of the bay. Follow the slab, keeping an eye on one or two sub-surface rocks, to reach good ledges at the far end.
FSA. Julian Lines, Mike Robertson 2.8.2005

The ledge system at the end of the traverse gives plenty of space to view the following routes. A little bit of planning is required to find the best way onto and off the routes.

❷ Old Peculiar........... 4+ S1
11m. From the ledge system at the end of the *Rosen Traverse*, head up and right on the hanging slab. This is followed to a good ledge at the top.
FSA. Mike Robertson 2.8.2005

❸ Brahma 6b S0
11m. This steep line is a harder way to gain the ledge at the top of *Old Peculiar*. Start as for that route, then swing rightwards to gain the overhung prow to the right, and follow it to the ledge.
FSA. Julian Lines 2.8.2005

❹ Bishop's Finger 5 S0
11m. The first ascent of this steep, juggy feature was a down-climb to link the finish of *Old Peculiar* with the start of *Old Thumper*.
FSA. Mike Robertson 2.8.2005

❺ Old Thumper 6a S1
14m. Brilliant moves; a hearty and out-there voyage up a very steep, juggy groove. From the base of *Bishop's Finger*, traverse rightwards to gain the base of the leaning groove and climb it all the way to the grass. Exit the long grassy slope with the utmost care.
FSA. Mike Robertson 2.8.2005

❻ Old Jock's Tunnel .. 6c+ S1
20m. This wicked route tackles the tunnel that dives all the way through the headland. Amazing climbing, and in a very unlikely place. You'll need good conditions to get involved. From the down-climb (as for all the routes above), simply swing northwards around the steep prow and take a look at the long tunnel in front of you. Climb into the tunnel on the right wall (crux) and continue on, mainly on the left wall, until further trickiness gets you back out into daylight.
FSA. Julian Lines 2.8.2005

Nare Head — The Black Tower

The Black Tower

The best routes at Nare Head are located on the Black Tower which gives excellent face climbing on good finger-holds.

Approach - The Black Tower's routes are reached by abseil from two points by the gear-up spot on the upper ridge. There are some good flakes and small outcrops to set up your rope from. For the first 2 routes, abseil down the southerly, open groove. For the remainder of the Black Tower's routes, set the rope down the tall corner found above the right side of the face - this will get you straight to the accommodating 'inset' ledge at the bottom right edge of the wall. This small ledge (2 people, 3 at a push!) is perfectly situated for access, sitting just above the high water mark and not jutting out into the line of fire.

Tides and Conditions - Very deep water. Mid tide or above is best.

❶ The Black Traverse   6c+ S0
12m. The brilliant and ultra-safe low traverse, starting from either side. If you start from the left, you'll have a route to do to escape, or simply reverse back! Technical, crimpy and sustained; finger-lickin' good.
See photo on page 134.
FSA. Mike Robertson and Julian Lines 2.8.2005

❷ Cafe Noir   6b+ S1
14m. The crux on this shapely little groove is actually getting across to it from the left, which is also the hardest single move on *The Black Traverse*. The lower groove itself is *S0*. Beyond its end, you'll probably need to add an S grade or so for a left-hand exit, or give your fingers a further workout if you continue higher/rightwards above water.
FSA. Julian Lines 2.8.2005

❸ Night Shift   6b+ S1
14m. Superb and sustained climbing up the left-most diagonal twin flake-line. It's not as hard as the next route, keeping below and parallel to that line all the way. The hardest moves may well be on *The Black Traverse*. From the abseil ledge, climb up into the flake-line and follow it all the way to the left edge of the face. Move up and left with care to reach the big ledge above. It can also be started from the left.
FSA. Julian Lines 2.8.2005

❹ Lemoria   6b S1
14m. A classic, striking flake-line; possibly the best route at Nare Head. Sustained throughout. You'll find the name on some of the area maps - it seems this outcrop really does have a local name. Leave the incut ledge, and climb diagonally leftwards - gradually easing - to finally finish on the left edge of the face, just by a bright green plant (in the right season!).
FSA. Mike Robertson 2.8.2005

❺ Dolphins Always Make Me Cry   6b+ S1/2
16m. This excellent line traces a path, parallel to and to the right of *Lemoria*, finishing on the clean-cut square ledge just left of the narrow top face. Climb up the very edge/arete of the lower right recess (technical) to gain the face proper. Continue up the ever-more-obvious flake feature, paralleling the previous route, to finish some three metres higher than that line, by rocking onto the handy, big flat ledge.
FSA. Mike Robertson 2.8.2005

❻ Su Doku   6c S2
19m. This intimidating line ventures into (and out of) the baffling narrow recess behind the start ledge. From that ledge, climb rightwards 'around' the cave recess, then bridge across onto the right wall of the chimney. Continue into the narrowing, then traverse leftwards to finish on *Dolphins'*.
FSA. Julian Lines 2.8.2005

The Big Blue Face Nare Head 145

❼ Project .... 🔖 ☐ **7a+?** *S3*
25m. The jutting face/corner set high up and left of *Jean Reno* looks amazing - and utterly gripping. Expect around 7a+, with a crux at over 20m.

❽ Jean Reno .... 🔖🧗🪝 ☐ **7a** *S0*
15m. A very hard start gives way to some great moves up the low, hanging prow. Abseil down to start in the black open groove, some 6m left of *The Big Blue*. Traverse leftwards, past a desperate sloper move, to gain the prow. Climb this with gradually easing difficulty, to the easy upper slab.
FSA. Julian Lines 2.8.2005

❾ Luc Besson .... 🧗 ☐ **6a+** *S0*
13m. The start is shared with the next route and the route eases considerably after a tricky start. Locate the small, slanting groove just above the sea (just above a small, sloped 'boss' at the waterline). Abseil in with a tape harness. Move up and left (crux) to gain the small prow just right of the slim, black groove. Climb more easily to the top slab.
FSA. Mike Robertson 30.8.2005. Named after the director of the classic film The Big Blue.

❿ Ong-Bak .... 🔖🪝🧗 ☐ **7b+** *S1*
13m. Nare Head's hardest route is also one of the best. A classic crank, based around the overlaps in the centre of the west face; powerful climbing on undercuts, with poor footholds. Start at the base of the face as for the last route (sling harness). Climb up and right to gain the undercut territory, and continue in the same theme to an easing of difficulty at 7m or so. Climb the easier slab to the top. *See photo on page 137.*
FSA. Gavin Symonds 30.8.2005

The Big Blue Face
The Big Blue Face is easy to identify, being much lighter in colour and more ochre-stained than its opposite neighbour.
Approach - To reach the routes, walk down the ridge and set up a 16m abseil from a big, prominent flake set in the top of the ridge. This will get you down to all routes from *Jean Reno* along to *Ong-Bak*.
Tides and Conditions - Mid-tide and above; take a big tide for *Carlo Varini*.

⓫ Link-up: Ong-Bak - Big Blue . . . ☐ **7a?** *S0*
13m. This excellent link-up is, as yet, unrealised. Follow the initial holds of *Ong-Bak* rightwards, until it's possible to arrive at *The Big Blue* arete; follow this to the top.

A tweak of the abseil rope will drop it into the orange, south-facing groove. Abseil down to a good ledge at its base.

⓬ The Big Blue ..... 🔖🧗🪝 ☐ **6b+** *S0*
13m. The arete in the centre of the east face is striking, and the climbing tricky and technical. After your abseil down the orange corner (the corner itself is not a DWS), swing left and tackle the tricky arete direct and remember, it's not over until it's over.
FSA. Mike Robertson 2.8.2005

The last route on the Big Blue Face can be easily reached by a scramble traverse in from the right.

⓭ Carlo Varini ... 🔖🧗🧗🪝 ☐ **6c** *S2*
12m. The seaward arete is named after the genius of The Big Blue's camera maestro. Take a high tide for the traverse in; climb the sustained arete direct to the top.
FSA. Mike Robertson 2.8.2005

Pembroke

Meilee Rafe approaching the crack of *True Blue* (4+) - *page 153* - at the amazing Barrel Zawn, North Pembroke. Photo: Mike Robertson.

Pembroke

The vast, magnificent area of Pembrokeshire needs no introduction for sea cliff lovers - it's been at the very top of the UK sea cliff hit-list for decades. This stunning strip of Welsh coastline is littered with limestone and sandstone cliffs of all shapes and sizes, many of which are hanging right out there over the sea.

Our journey starts with the recently developed Barrel Zawn, a perfectly-formed, small sandstone zawn, and just two miles out of St David's, in North Pembroke. Next we jump south to Bosherston, and to the pumpy, eventful Breakfast Zawn, with a further stroll east giving us the eclectic venue of Stennis Ford, with its compact, tilted walls providing all manner of high jinks. Just around the corner comes the well laid-out Newton Head, a festival venue with more viewing galleries than you can shake a fish at ... whilst over at the beautiful Broadhaven Beach we find the atmospheric and challenging Broadhaven Cove.

A short drive east takes us to the diverse Lydstep area - a mighty collection of solos, and in a region so quiet you could hear a chalk bag plop! Take a look here at the Skomar Arch routes, the Cavern Promontory routes, and the incredible Alien Cave. Last but not least we venture even closer to Tenby, where the Penally region provides a sprawl of inlets, caves and zawns, including the marvellous Kato Zawn.

That sums up Pembrokeshire: you'll need to master the art of reading tide timetables, and you'll need your wits about you in some of those crazy blowholes, but it'll all be so worth it. See you at the Olde Worlde Cafe in Bosherston!

Access

The army still hold much of Pembrokeshire in a death grip, so you'll need to plan around them to some degree. The Range East region is usually shut weekdays, but is generally open weekends and bank holidays. You can usually get in during the evening after 5pm, but Thursdays are often shut for night firing. Call the range booking office on 01646 662287 for up-to-date firing times. The Penally region is sometimes shut for localised firing - see page 182 for more details.

Conditions and Tides

Pembroke's tide swings are problematical and their vagaries are often enough to confound an unplanned solo visit. Briefly, the difference in water level between a Pembroke low tide and a Pembroke high tide can be as much as 8m. This is known as an 8m 'swing'. That said, an average swing, somewhere between a spring and a neap tide, would offer a swing of around 5m or so. This lower figure is still much higher than Devon and Dorset's average swings, which are about 3m and 1.5m respectively. The above situation means that a steady, deep S1, say *Restraint of Beasts* (6b+) at Lydstep, might have no water at all on a low spring tide - I've walked across the sand under the route more than once.

What all this means is not that Pembroke is unsuitable for DWS - it's more that you'll need to get a handle on what the tides mean for each area, and get wised-up on how to time your visit. The usual natural laws apply to Pembroke: THE BIGGEST HIGH TIDES OCCUR EARLY AND LATE, ALWAYS! So go to the less water-dependent venues on more regular tides (Barrel Zawn, for example, better suits neap, midday tides) and visit the more serious venues (Stennis Ford is an example) on the weight of the big morning and evening spring tides. GET A TIDE TIMETABLE, AND PLAN!

Conditions vary from crag to crag in Pembroke. Expect the sunlit, vertical faces generally to be in better nick, and visit the caves and overhung areas when humidity is low or when there's a good dry southerly breeze.

Ruth Taylor on the crinkly groove of *Flashing Eyebrows* (6a) - *page 161* - in Stennis Ford, Pembroke. Photo: Mike Robertson.

Pembroke

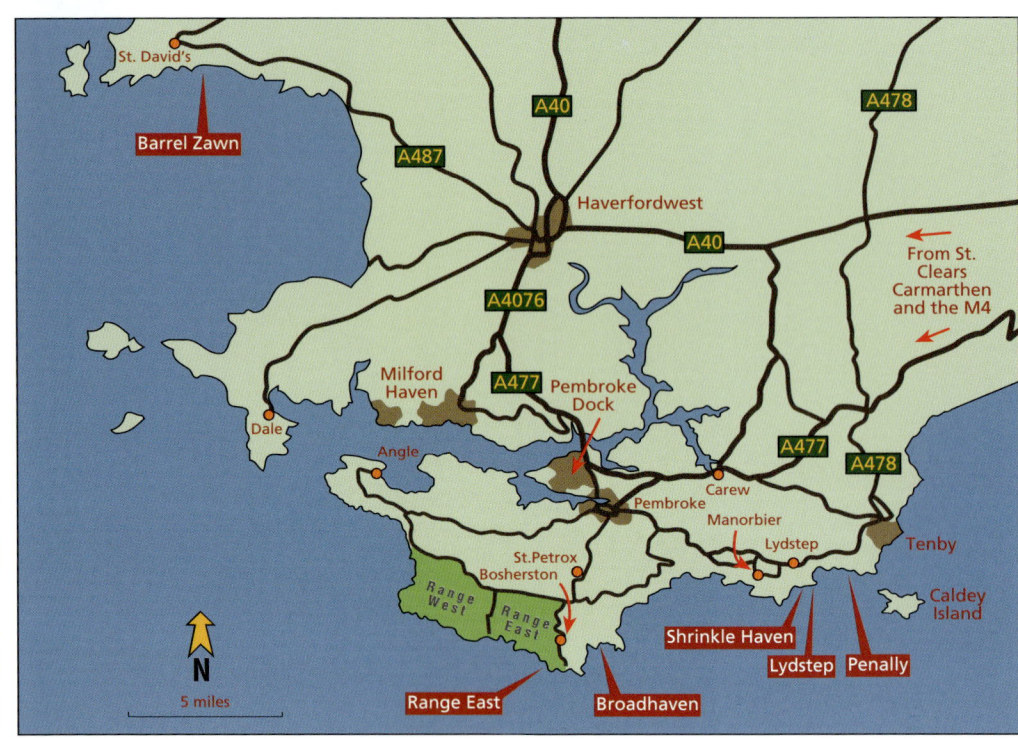

Approach
From the western end of the M4, continue west on the A48, to Carmarthen. Join the A40 and continue to St. Clears. From here, North Pembroke and Barrel Zawn are reached by staying on the A40 to Haverford West, where the A487 is picked up. For all the South Pembroke crags, get on the A477 at St. Clears, and keep on this to its junction with the A478 to Tenby. Turn left to Tenby here for the approach to Shrinkle Haven, the Lydstep area, and Penally Training Camp. For all the other crags, you'll need to get to Bosherston village. So keep on the A477 all the way to Pembroke town, and pick up the B4319, following it south until a left turning for Bosherston.

Accommodation
There are a wealth of hotels and B&B's in the area - any web research will readily conjure up these. For the average deep water soloist, of more importance is a decent campsite. If you're staying in the Bosherston area, a good bet is the Glebe Farm campsite, with friendly owners and plenty of space; whilst a few miles up the road at St Petrox is the Old Rectory campsite, which is more expensive but better-equipped. If you're heading over towards Tenby, you'll find stacks of camp-sites along the A478 north of Tenby. If you're up at St David's, you need look no further than the two huge campsites on the Caerfai Bay road, although these sites are pricy. There are a number of terrific unofficial dosses in Pembrokeshire - use your loaf and seek some local knowledge.

Food and Booze
In Bosherston, you'll almost certainly migrate towards The Olde Worlde Cafe, which is still Pembroke's most popular meeting place, with firing times and suchlike posted outside. Next door is the St Govan's Inn, which is a handy evening meeting spot. There are all manner of take-aways, restaurants and pubs in Pembroke and Tenby. Up at St David's, the Jones' Cafe is a great spot to meet, with the Farmers Arms pub providing an evening spot with outdoor terrace.

Julian Lines on the stupendous *The One-Eyed Man* (7a) - *page 178* - at Blind Bay, Pembroke. Photo: Mike Robertson.

Pembroke — Barrel Zawn

Barrel Zawn

Barrel Zawn's sunny walls, perfect viewing gallery and solid, straightforward exits make this a must-visit venue. The icing on the cake is that the climbing that seldom exceeds nine metres and is on bullet-hard sandstone that has amazing friction.

Approach - The turning for the crag is just west of St. David's on the A487 but it is unsigned and difficult to spot. Usually you will overshoot it and have to continue to St. Davids (for a cup of tea!). From St. David's, drive south, past a Texaco petrol station and a 12% gradient sign. Go down the hill and, when driving up the next hill, take the next, small unmarked road on the right. Drive for 200m to a big grassy car park on the right (the same parking that is used for Carreg-y-Barcud). Walk down the road for a further 300m, and right turn on to a 4wd track on the bend. Follow the track for 500m, and take the left fork uphill. This is the coast path. Follow the path past a green house and continue to an isolated fence above a deep zawn. Walk down the grassy ridge to the viewing spot. To access the crag, walk back along the coast path from the fence for 75m, where a slight path can be found dropping down the overgrown hill to reach a gearing up area. The crag is just down and to the left (looking out) to sea.

Conditions and Tides - There are no seepage problems apart from a single wet streak that crosses the *Barrel Traverse Extension* at its right-hand end. Climbing is possible at most tide states. The zawn is usually sheltered.

1 Barrel Traverse 6c S0
30m. The crag's best line; it's absolutely stunning. The 30m traverse of the continuous, gently rising break-line is well-positioned, pumpy and completely safe throughout. From the easy way down (or *Private Dancer*), follow the break to the far end of the grassy break above, using a short diagonal crack to get stood on the grassy break to the left. Walk easily off leftwards.
FSA. Mike Robertson 19.7.2006

2 Private Dancer 5 S0
7m. The slim, leftwards corner is a must. It's also the best start for the *Barrel Traverse*.
FSA. Mike Robertson 19.7.2006

3 Owen Meany .... 6b+ S0
6m. The wall is taken on small edges and slopers.
FSA. Mike Robertson 19.7.2006

4 Student Grant 5 S0
6m. The wall just right leads into a white corner.
FSA Grant Wright 20.7.2006

5 Hippy .... 4+ S0
7m. The left-hand of the two cracks is good. After the tricky traverse in, make use of a brilliant 'hip' rest in the wide slot at the base.
FSA. Mike Robertson 19.7.2006

Barrel Zawn Pembroke 153

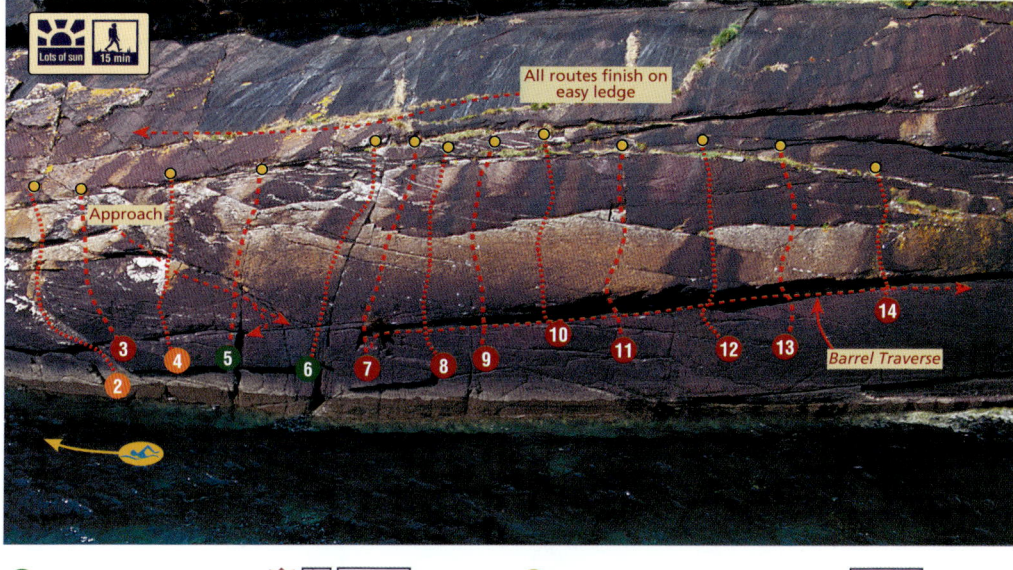

6 True Blue .... 4+ S0
7m. The right-hand crack is the best easy route here. Great climbing! *See photo on page 146.*
FSA. Mike Robertson 19.7.2006

7 Mouse Claws 6b S0
6m. The seams just right of the crack provide some sustained entertainment.
FSA. Mike Robertson 19.7.2006

8 Welcome to Jamrock 6b+ S0
6m. The crimpy wall right again, with some wicked moves.
FSA. Dave Pickford 20.7.2006

9 Giant Farts 7a S0
6m. First of the desperates. From the shallow vertical slot, get crimping.
FSA. Tim Emmett 20.7.2006

10 Snake Pass .... 6b+ S0
6m. A good hold on the headwall… that turns into your foothold. Just stand up.
FSA. Tim Emmett 20.7.2006

11 Voyage of the Parrot Fish
.... 6c+ S0
6m. The swirling seam needs a concerted effort.
FSA. Dave Pickford 20.7.2006

12 Drake's Drum 7a S0
6m. The black streak. A hard rock-over/press move provides the goods.
FSA. Dave Pickford 20.7.2006

13 Wreck of the Zephyr ...... 6c+ S0
6m. Another curling seam. Hint: get a crafty heel-hook.
FSA. Dave Pickford 20.7.2006

14 The Eternal Golden Braid 6c S0
5m. Get into (and out of) the curved, lichen-stained headwall seam.
FSA. Dave Pickford 20.7.2006

15 Terrapigeon ... 7a+ S2
8m. The blank-looking upper right wall of the crag is taken by way of a leftwards-rising line. An excellent and daring proposition, and Barrel Zawn's only bold route.
FSA. Dave Pickford 20.7.2006

16 Project 7b S0
8m. The enticing diagonal line, crossing an oft-wet streak. Brilliant climbing, leaving the lower groove and heading up and left. It's nailed two protagonists so far. Briefly known as *Muppet Splash*.

17 Barrel Traverse Extension
.... 6c S0/1
40m total. The 10m continuation of the *Barrel Traverse* is worthwhile, both as an addition, and to reach the starting groove of *Muppet Splash*. It's the longest line on the crag; down-climbing *Private Dancer* and taking on the whole crag, finishing in the lower section of the end groove, will give at least 40m of climbing! Either try *Route 16* or reverse out.
FSA. Mike Robertson 19.7.2006

One further, small buttress exists here. Dubbed the Boater's Buttress (see picture opposite), it's reached by a dry-bag swim or by boat, as there's no path available to reach it.

18 Curly Mick 6a S1
9m. The upper, diagonal crack-line is a delight.
FSA. Mike Robertson 19.7.2006

19 Mad Mei .... 5+ S0
9m. The lower of the two breaks; move up and left over the bulge to finish.
FSA. Larry the Limpet 1900

Range East

The cliffs immediately west of the main Bosherston car park have been popular with trad climbers for decades, with the many zawns, caves and headlands providing probably more entertainment than most folk can squeeze into a lifetime.

For the deep water soloer, the lesser-known Hollow Caves Bay houses Breakfast Zawn, tucked into the Bay's western boundary - a relative newcomer which is now firmly seated in the DWS hall of fame. Further east, the fabled giant slash of Stennis Ford has two well-featured, opposing faces and an impressive spread of routes with a few still in the planning stage! Next up is Newton Head, which is now familiar to anyone who attended the DWS festival in the summer of 2004. The crags here are variable in height, the rock is solid, and mostly have super-clean finishes with the final advantage that the crag is the nearest crag to the Bosherston car park. Not that I'm implying deep water soloists are lazy.

Access

The area is part of the army range and suffers from certain restrictions. Refer to the main Pembroke introduction for full details.

Approach

For Newton Head, head south-west across the grass from the Bosherston car park, to arrive at a series of higher tiers. All the faces here can be accessed easily, although you'll need to walk up via the high ground to get around to the Big Hair Wall.

For Stennis Ford, walk past the army flag and sentry box, and follow the tarmac road west-

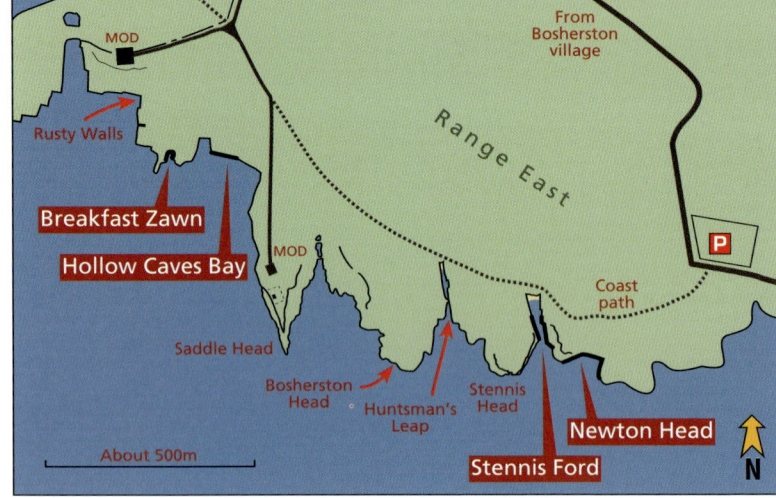

wards. Stennis Ford is the first very large slot in the ground on the left, after some 200m. To continue along to Hollow Caves Bay and Breakfast Zawn, pass Stennis Ford and carry on down the tarmac road. After a further 500m or so, you'll see a concrete building over to the left, at the top of the cliff; this is the top of Saddle Head, and the Hollow Caves Bay crag picture was taken from here. To reach Hollow Caves Bay and Breakfast Zawn, walk a little further, skirting the top terraces to find the top of the San Simeon Face. A further 150m walk, skirting Box Zawn, provides an entrance to Breakfast Zawn.

Conditions and Tides

The region is very tide-dependent, as is the whole of Pembroke. Always seek calm seas, and get well-acquainted with your tide timetable - you'll need it! With good planning, you'll have plenty of routes to climb. Remember the golden rule: all huge spring tides occur early and late!

The maestro at work! Crispin Waddy on the excellent corner climb *Hash Brown* (6c) - *page 157* - in Breakfast Zawn, Pembroke. Photo: Mike Robertson.

Swanage
Lulworth
Portland
Devon
Cornwall
Pembroke
Scotland
Rest of UK
Portugal
Costa Blanca
Mallorca
Rest of Europe
Australia
Rest of World

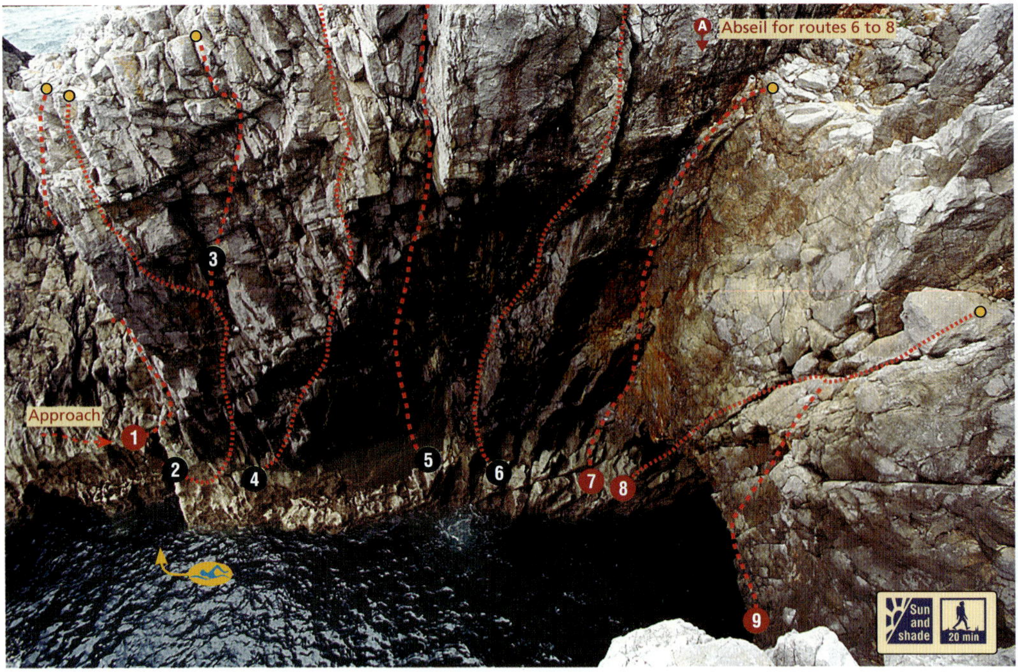

Breakfast Zawn

Breakfast Zawn is a delightful and shapely zawn, found tucked away in the headland at the western edge of Hollow Caves Bay. The sun catches the *Instant Black* face in the morning, with the classic *Traverse Tea* getting sunshine at around midday. The rock is terrific, and climbing excellent, but a word of warning - the *Instant Black* face is a lot steeper than the picture suggests!

Approach (See map on page 154) - From Saddle Head, continue west along the coast path. Walk across the top of Hollow Caves Bay, then drop down a series of terraces to reach the top of Breakfast Zawn, marked with a small sandpit. This is your gearing-up spot.

Conditions and Tides - The trickiest thing about Breakfast Zawn is finding it in good condition, so time your visit for a crisp, southerly wind. The sun comes and goes quite quickly, due to the surrounding architecture, so expect to climb in the shade more often than not. Expect a degree of shelter in the zawn.

The routes on the left end of the face are accessed by easily downclimbing the ridge towards the sea, and swinging down to sea level by the left arete of the Instant Black face.

1 The Pepper Man 1 6b S1

15m. The left arete of the face is an eliminate, offering some great positions. Climb across the lower face to a big jug-line about two meters above the barnacles. Climb the steep left edge of the arete, moving progressively rightwards to the very top.
FSA. Mike Robertson 27.8.2005

2 Project . . . . 7b+? S1

15m. The left-hand finish to *Instant Black* will be superb.

3 Instant Black 3 7b S1

15m. A classic DWS pump-out, and on immaculate rock. An easy approach via the ridge and a swing down to sea level gains the start holds. Climb the sustained groove to a poor side-pull rest, and continue (the crux is on an array of unhelpful slopers) to gain better holds. Continue rightwards to finish on the ridge.
FSA. Mike Robertson 7.2003

4 Project . . . . 8a? S1

15m. This line, starting as for *Instant Black* and rising slowly rightwards, may well be a hard classic in the making, but can suffer a little from seepage. Aim for a dry spell and morning sun.
NYS.

5 Project . . . . 8a+? S1

15m. A hard, direct line up the wall to the left of *Cereal Killer* - desperate moves may well lead to the hanging, jagged crack. Catch it dry for your attempt.
NYS.

The next three routes are best reached by abseiling down the corner of Hash Brown, with a little swing at the base to gain the juggy cave entrance.

6 Cereal Killer 3 7b S1

15m. From the cave, climb left across the base and then up the slim corner, to finally gain the steep hanging crack in the upper headwall. Get stuck in!
FSA. Steve McClure 28.8.2005

Hollow Caves Bay - San Simeon Face Range East

⑦ Hash Brown 6c S0/1
12m. A technical corner, with all the hardest climbing finishing at about 7m. Rock-over into the base of the corner, and tackle a further hard sequence to gain easier ground. *See photo on page 155*.
FSA. Crispin Waddy 7.2003

⑧ Coffee Anan 6b+ S0
12m. This line starts from the base of *Hash Brown*. Pull up and steeply out, to a junction with *Traverse Tea*. Follow *Traverse Tea* more easily to the top.
FSA. Adam Wainwright 7.2003

⑨ Traverse Tea 6b+ S0/1
13m. The original solo here, and a perfect introduction to the zawn. Abseil down the corner/gully to the right (east), to access the start. Climb across the lower face, on terrific rock (crux), to finally reach easier ground in the obvious crack feature on the back wall. Climb more easily to the top. Superb!
FSA. Ben Bransby 2001

San Simeon Face

⑩ Great Dane / Ringolino 6b+ S2/3
19m. A combination of these routes, using the best water, might give a terrific highball. Spring tide only; check depth carefully.
NYS

⑪ Super Galactic Hammy 6a+ S2/3
19m. A good line up the left side of the San Simeon Face. Check depth carefully.
NYS

Hollow Caves Bay - San Simeon Face
The San Simeon face of Hollow Caves Bay offers the deep water soloist a mix of bold and hard. The rock is generally good, and the routes are usually on sustained, overhanging territory. It's a serious venue, and would demand an abseil inspection from almost every visitor.
Approach - The picture above was taken with a long lens from a vantage point close to Saddle Head, so a look from that angle will provide a useful introduction to the crag's geography. A walk around the top of the Bay will enable you to reach the routes. You'll need to arrange any required abseils by following your nose.
Conditions and Tides - You'll almost certainly want the biggest spring tide you can muster for the occasion. Take a calm sea, and make sure you're absolutely sure about your swim-out points; these are very limited - you might need your ab rope and jumars.

⑫ The Fine Art of Surfacing 7b+ S2
18m. A great prize; tall, but above good water. Pick your tide carefully! From the tiny ledges at the base of the face, climb the slim groove, thereafter trending gradually leftwards to an easier top section.
FSA. Neil Gresham 7.2003

⑬ San Simeon 8a S3
21m. An absolute stunner. This wickedly good steep face route stays hard all the way to the top, so you'll need to do some proper groundwork to consider this one. Get a ridiculously large tide, while you're at it. If soloed, it'll be the biggest DWS tick in Pembrokeshire.
NYS

Range East — Stennis Ford - West Face

Stennis Ford - West Face

The tilted walls of Stennis Ford's West Face are better known for trad routes such as *Mysteries* (E3) and *Ghost Train* (E7). Yet down at the seaward end of the Ford, the walls decrease noticeably in height (and the water gets a lot deeper) giving a number of excellent deep water solos, with the classic tick here probably being the superb *Overexposed* (6c). Expect stiff S grades. Any pre-route inspection can be easily carried out from the other side of the Ford - such convenience!

Approach - You'll need to abseil in from good blocks to gain a ledge for the routes from *Skelis* through to *Bingo*'. All the other routes need either a tape harness or a bench seat arrangement.

Conditions and Tides - Condensation in the Ford is common, so time your ascent to coincide with a good dry southerly breeze and take a BIG tide with you.

Exit - Scope your swim-out in advance - your best exit will prove to be either on the beach at the landward end (fixed rope ideal for the scramble out), or a swim towards Newton Head, if the sea conditions are calm.

❶ Skelis 6b *S1*
16m. From the left end of the ledge, climb leftwards and up, to gain a slim groove. Follow this to the depression, and scramble out with care. A pre-placed rope would be forgiven for the upper section.
FSA. Crispin Waddy 1999

❷ Goblets 5 *S1/2*
16m. The big groove. From the left end of the ledge, climb up the deep groove above, to finish in a depression. Scramble out with care up a pre-placed rope if necessary.
FSA. Crispin Waddy 1999

❸ Bingo Master's Breakout
.... 7a *S2*
21m. Excellent, and with a very low crux. Start on the accommodating ledge. Traverse rightwards and down slightly, crux, to gain the face on the right. Climb this to the wide top crack and follow this to the top.
FSA. Crispin Waddy 1999

❹ Living on Air .... 7b+ *S3*
21m. This excellent existing route still awaits a solo. From a bench seat belay close to the HWM, climb the lower face, trending slightly leftwards to a big flake rest (about 7a+ to this point). Attack the thin headwall above with verve and confidence, to finally reach good holds just below the grassy top.
NYS

❺ Overexposed 6c *S2*
21m. A real beauty. The holds just get bigger the higher you climb - very convenient! Tackle the curling line (low crux) and traverse into the soaring flake-line. Follow this, with an almost supernatural easing of difficulty, all the way to the top.
FSA. Mike Robertson 8.2001

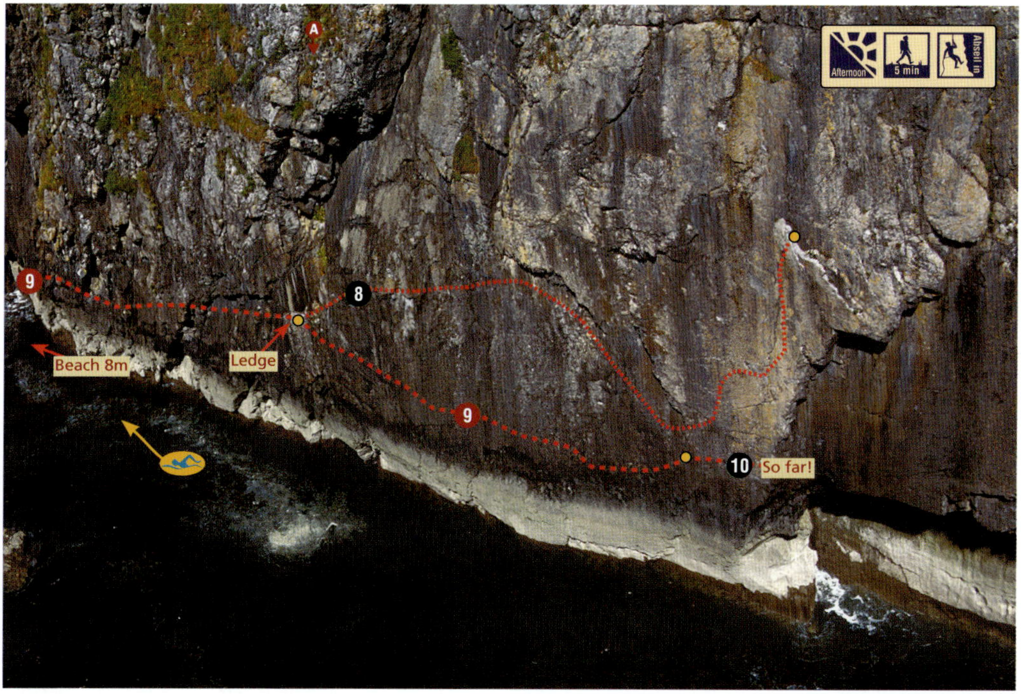

❻ Feersum Endjin 2 7b S3
23m. A spicy offering. From small ledges above the HWM, head off up a leftward-leading flake. Harder climbing awaits above, taking the steep headwall direct.
NYS

❼ Excession . . . . 1 7a+ S3
22m. This striking line starts from a belay quite a way above the HWM, so is a little more convenient to get going on. From the ramp, climb to the crack and follow it to the top, with the crux moves found slightly right of the crack's upper 'narrowing'.
NYS

Stennis Ford - The Shield

❽ The Shield . . . . 3 7b+ S2
22m. This magnificent line takes the immaculate grey pillar of rock jutting from the Ford's East Face. A lengthy rightwards traverse leads to a climactic crux finish - the moves are baffling, thin and technical. From the marked ledge on the topo, climb the traverse across to a rest beneath the left edge of the big grey shield. Climb onto the shield and cross it, finally gaining the crack above; an extended crux sequence leads you to the finish ledge. A jump from the 17m high finishing ledge should form an integral part of the route - the alternative is to jumar out on a pre-placed rope.
FSA. Julian Lines, Mike Robertson 30.5.2005

Stennis Ford - The Shield

The landward end of Stennis Ford's East Face is home to the technical complexities of that big grey shield of rock, which now provides us with *The Shield* (7b+). It also gives us *The Stennis Traverse*, which one day might link with the seaward section.

Approach - *The Stennis Traverse* starts from the beach, gained by a short abseil from the wall at the landward end of the Ford. Recommended for *The Shield* is an abseil in, which enables you to use a bigger tide, as the beach start is almost impossible at high tide.

Conditions and Tides - The Ford is almost always calm, so most important are crisp conditions - a southerly breeze will assist you here.

❾ The Stennis Traverse . . . . 1 6c+ S0
25m. The lower traverse on this face, starting from the beach, is a fine route in its own right, although it's a little sharp in places. To finish the job, either reverse it, jump in, or see below!
FSA. Mike Robertson, Julian Lines 30.5.2005

❿ The Stennis Traverse Extension 7c? S0
85m (total). The currently unclimbed, lengthy extension of the above traverse seeks to conquer the first crux around the right arete of the shield, and ought to then carry on down the east face to the very end. It has been previously climbed by Crispin Waddy from the seaward end and there is only about 6m of rock left unclimbed in the centre section.
NYS

Swanage Lulworth Portland Devon Cornwall Pembroke Scotland Rest of UK Portugal Costa Blanca Mallorca Rest of Europe Australia Rest of World

Range East — Stennis Ford - East Face

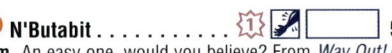

Stennis Ford - East Face

The seaward end of the East Face gives a great collection of routes, across the grades. The classics are *Exultation* (6b+) and the slightly easier *Godliness* (6a).

Approach - The juggy *Way Out!* (3+) is your best bet, and gets you fired up for all the Ford has to offer. You might consider an abseil into the big bowl itself, especially for familiarisation, and maybe even to reach that project!

Conditions and Tides - Take a decent high tide along. Calm seas are usual in here; a perky southerly breeze would pay dividends.

Exit - Decide on your exit before climbing - either swim into the landward end; swim to Newton Head end; climb up *Way Out!*

❶ Project .... 7b? S2
19m. The first line is a project. You'll need a dry spell to be in the running, as it suffers a drainage streak low down. The crux is found in the first half of the route.

❷ Exultation .... 6b+ S2
18m. A really classy DWS face climb; a must-do. Swing around the base of the *Godliness* 'bowl', to find yourself under a bulging wall. Take a breath and take on those small edges to gain bigger holds above. Continue, with constant interest, all the way past an in-situ thread to the top.
FSA. Mike Robertson 1999

❸ Gateaux Thief.. 7b S2/3
18m. Good, hard, and yet to be repeated. Tucked in between the 'bowl' cave and *Exultation* is this daring proposition up the very left edge of the cave.
FSA. Tim Emmett Aug 2001

❹ The Heckler ... 6c+ S2
16m. A precarious and demanding line. Climb *Godliness* past its crux (exiting the bowl), then traverse into the wide upper scoop on the left. Technical moves lead horizontally left to the arete; continue more easily past the break to the top.
FSA. Crispin Waddy late 90's

❺ Godliness 6a S1/2
16m. A well-positioned feature. Nip up the upper right wall of the bowl-shaped cave to a horizontal break, and keep on venturing up and right to gain bigger holds. Just brilliant.
FSA. Crispin Waddy 1990's

❻ Clean Ass .... 6b+ S1
17m. The left groove variation of *Cleanliness* is a little harder than the mother route (see below). Expect a low and obvious crux; steady ground above.
FSA. Jonathan Woods 7.2004

❼ Cleanliness .... 6a+ S1
17m. Another good helping. Drop down out of the *Godliness* cave and traverse right for a few metres, then make hard moves up and into the right-hand of the two grooves above. Continue straight up more easily, to finally join *Godliness* for the easy top section.
FSA. Crispin Waddy 1990's

❽ N'Butabit.......... 5 S1
17m. An easy one, would you believe? From *Way Out!* climb up the groove, swing boldly onto the left face, and move on up the buttress to progressively easier ground.
FSA. Unknown

Stennis Ford - East Face Range East

9 Way Out! .... 3+ S1

16m. Just insane! Massive holds throughout, ascending an almost pillar-like feature that can be observed from the other side of the Ford. So do it historically and downwards … or even upwards; as you please.
FSA. unknown

10 Flashing Eyebrows . 6a S1

17m. This crinkly line ascends the attractive, slim orange groove to the right of the last route. Named after a Bristolian with entirely out-of-control features. *See photo on page 149*.
FSA. Mike Robertson 8.2001

Range East   Newton Head - Splashdown Buttress

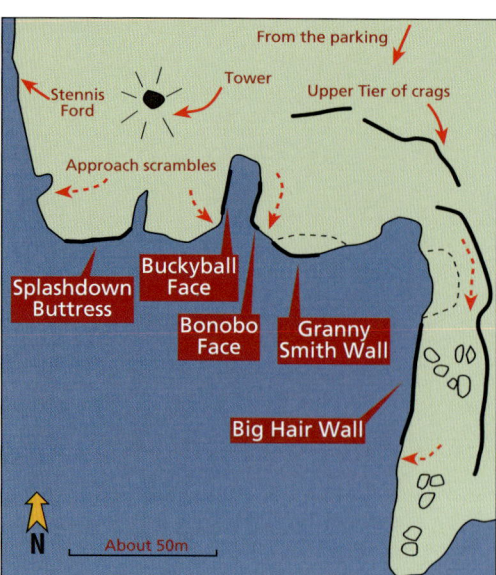

Splashdown Buttress

This face is high, and spice is guaranteed.
Approach - Descend the wide gully on the west side of the buttress and a traverse in.
Conditions and Tides - Newton Head's rock is almost always dry and crisp, and there is very little in the way of seepage. For the Splashdown Buttress, a big high tide is mandatory!

❶ Double Dragon **4** *S2*
18m. Great climbing, good rock, but a little high. A good intro to the slightly highball DWS. From a position just left of centre (looking in), climb the buttress by way of a long groove system. The top 5m is about 3, and very solid indeed.
FSA. unknown This received 30+ ascents during the 2004 DWS Festival.

❷ The Ceaseless Tide . **6b+** *S2*
18m. A little harder than it looks. From the base ledges, traverse rightwards until under the centre of the buttress. Climb quickly past a low crux, and continue up the buttress to the top.
FSA. Ruth Taylor 8.2003

❸ Splashdown . . . **6b+** *S3*
20m. Beautiful moves on perfect rock, and with a gripping finale! The zawn below is almost too narrow. From the base of the centre of the buttress, traverse right and upwards (crux) to reach a juggy rail below a small corner. Climb up this to gain a flat ledge, and press on up the stunning top arete with commitment (a leftwards shuffle into *The Ceaseless Tide* reduces the grade).
FSA. Mike Robertson 8.2003

Buckyball Face

This deep little inlet is full of water and good rock. The cruxes are low down on the harder routes.
Approach - An abseil is required, with a tape harness arrangement the best method of entry.
Conditions and Tides - Plenty of water, so any reasonable high tide will do. A calm sea is useful for *Buckyball*.

Splashdown

❹ Buckyball **7b** *S0*
12m. The west face of the zawn; it's the enticing crack-line easily viewed from the other side. From the barnacle line, seize the hold in the very base of the crack, and climb up and through the overhangs above; finish more easily.
FSA. Adam Wainwright 8.2003

❺ 9 ½ Weeks . . . . . . **7b+** *S0*
11m. Very steep. From a start on a spike-sling above the barnacles, climb up the face and pass the overhangs en-route to an easier finish.
FSA. Neil Gresham 10.7.2004

❻ Candy Trail . . . . **6a+** *S1*
8m. This line starts high in the gully. First climbed the day of the DWS Fest 2004. Swing out across the breaks and make a couple of powerful moves to gain easier ground.
FSA. Neil Gresham 10.7.2004

Buckyball

Tim Emmett on *World of Bonobos* (6c+) - *page 164* - on the Bonobo Face, Pembroke. Photo: Mike Robertson.

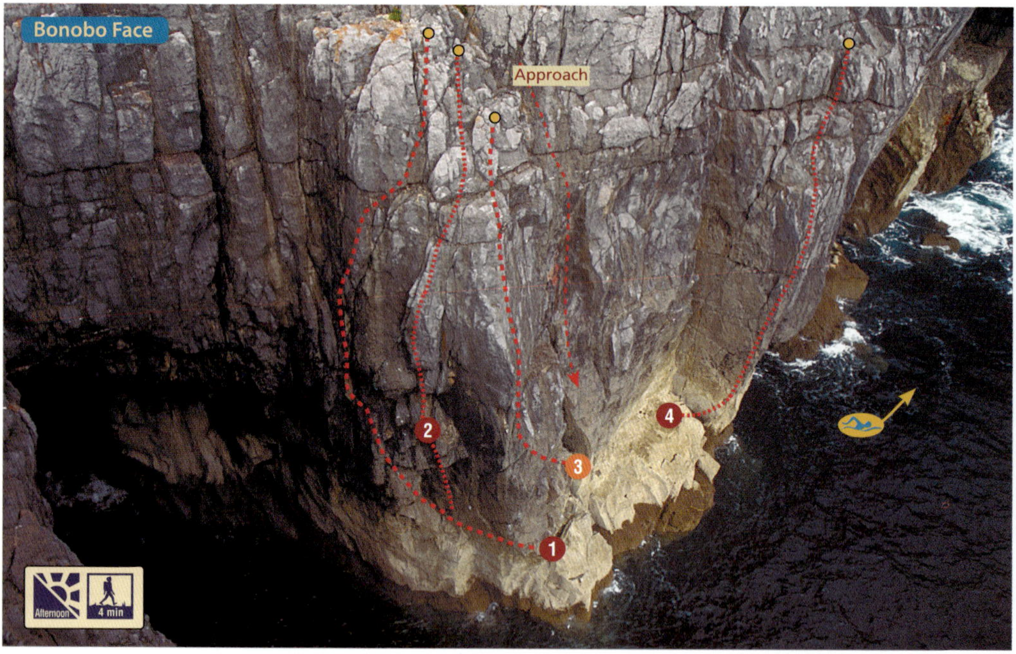

Range East Newton Head - Bonobo Face and Granny Smith Wall

Bonobo Face

The Bonobo Face gives good, technical climbing on side-pulls and small holds.

Approach - A 4+ down-climb will access the lines, or a short abseil, if you please.

Conditions and Tides - A huge tide makes it hard to get across underneath *World of Bonobos*, so select a mid-high tide. Climb later in the day, when the face is likely to be drier.

❶ Heimlich Manoeuvre 6c S1
13m. The line just right of the vague corner in the back/east side of the zawn. Start as for *World of Bonobos*, but continue the traverse leftwards to gain the line.
FSA. Crispin Waddy 2001

❷ World of Bonobos . .  6c+ S1
12m. The shapely prow on the east side of the zawn is a gem. Swing out of a slight corner at the base of the face, and ascend the prominent flakes and side-pulls direct. *See photo on page 163.*
FSA. Mike Robertson 8.2002. This featured as the DWS Fest 'speed route' in 2004.

Granny Smith Wall
This wall is instantly recognisable as the steepest wall in the area! The rock is somewhat crinkly in nature.

Approach - Reach these lines by traversing in from the left.

Conditions and Tides - Take any high tide that will accommodate your traverse into the base - too much water will wet your shoes!

Newton Head - Big Hair Wall — Range East

③ Bonobo Arete 5 *S0/1*
10m. This prominent feature proved popular at the 2004 Festival. Escapable, easy to access at all tides. From the lower ledge, climb the well-positioned arete to an easier finish.
FSA. unknown

④ The Surrealist . 6c *S2/3*
12m. The crinkly, well-positioned left arete; bold and digitally complicated. From the lower ramp, climb the arete past a tricky move right. Easier ground above.
FSA. Mike Robertson 8.2002

Granny Smith Wall

⑤ Southern Rain . . . . 6b+ *S1*
12m. Traverse the bottom of the steep stuff with difficulty, and ascend a cracked, crinkly groove.
FSA. Mike Robertson 8.2002

⑥ Galileo's Balls . . . . 6b+ *S1*
12m. Same approach; traverse on a little further to gain the long groove, and follow it to the very top. Crinkle world at its best!
NYS

Big Hair Wall

⑦ Big Hair. . . . . . 7a+ *S1*
11m. A quick roped dangle to the prominent flake ledge gets you in place. Move out rightwards across an obvious thin break, and climb the wall above direct, to an easing finish.
FSA. Mike Robertson 8.2002

⑧ Underwater Love . . 6c+ *S0/1*
11m. Start as for last route, but forge out right to avoid *Big Hair's* complexities, climbing to a steady finish. Good stuff.
FSA. Tim Emmett 7.7.2003

Big Hair Wall
This vertical, west-facing wall offers good, technical climbing on very small holds.
Approach - An abseil in to a spiky ledge gets you to *Big Hair* and *Underwater Love*; the remainder are all reached by way of an easy scramble on the right.
Conditions and Tides - A mid-high will be perfect, but take a low tide for the traverse. A calm sea is advisable.

⑨ Thoughtcrime. . 7a *S0/1*
16m. This one features a l-o-n-g traverse in and up, there's no sprinting this one. Low-mid tide required. Traverse leftwards, keeping low and using some barnacles, then keep heading diagonally up and left, on an endless series of sloping holds.
FSA. Mike Robertson 8.2002

⑩ Uncovered Rock . . . 6b+ *S2*
12m. The shorter, higher traverse in. Don't slip onto the slab when entering the groove. Style (not) across the upper break and make tricky moves to get into the groove. From there, head up and right to a 'flyin' finish.
FSA. Mike Robertson 8.2002

⑪ The Newton Traverse!
. . . . 7a *S1*
40m. The traverse of the eastern wedge of Newton Head, starting in the far groove, as for *Thoughtcrime*, and finishing up *Bonobo Arete*. You'll need a low-ish tide and a calm sea.
The crux on the sustained first wall is shared with *Thoughtcrime*. You might also find a few bold moves above boulders below the Granny Smith Wall, depending on the state of the tide.
FSA. Mike Robertson, Steve Findlay, Jude Spancken and Matt "Ug" and others during the 2004 Festival - 10.7.2004

Broadhaven Beach

This region has two main points of interest. The first and smallest is the bizarre tubed Confucius Hole, which is found 'inside' the edge of the headland to the south-east of the beach. This cave is home to the superb, weaving *Confucius*.

The second is the big, open, curved face of Broadhaven Cove. This crag has reasonable access to the bottom, and a useful jutting, viewing promontory at its eastern edge. What is doesn't have is solid rock in its upper reaches, so you'll need to know the cleaned exits before you embark on one of the central routes. That said, the hard routes are terrific, especially the steep arete of *Jaws*.

Approach - From the Broadhaven Beach car park, go down the steps and walk across the beach to the far side. A possible brief paddle of the small inlet (depending on your timing and the height of the tide) leads to the big headland on the far side. Walk along to the tip of the headland to find Confucius Hole. For Broadhaven Cove, continue east until you see a jutting promontory below. This forms the east edge of the crag, and serves as your viewing gallery.

Conditions and Tides - Confucius Hole requires dry conditions and a reasonably flat sea, as the entrance can get feisty in rough seas. Broadhaven Cove is less particular. A high tide is definitely recommended here, along with gentle enough water to swim out to the promontory after your fall from *Jaws* (there have been plenty!).

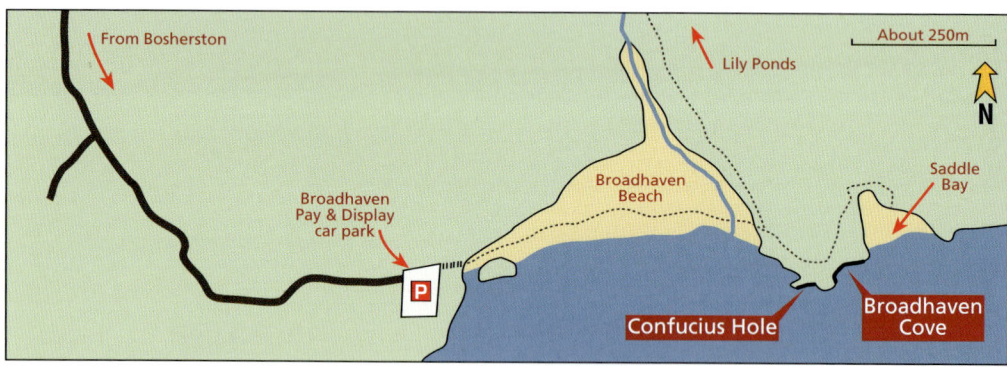

Confucius Hole

Confucius Hole is a small cave, or, more correctly, a open 'tube', or barrel. The original line of *Confucius* traverses in, with the other two routes offering further climbing within the hole itself. Find your way easily down to the beach side of the hole's entrance.

❶ Confucius .... 6b+ *S0*

10m. Brilliant, and very unusual. From the outside, traverse rightwards into the hole along a break. Once into the cave, spiral gradually up and leftwards, to gain the arch above.
FSA. Crispin Waddy 1990's

❷ Hole in One .... 6b+ *S0*

18m. Once into the hole, traverse the whole interior in a clockwise direction.
FSA. Crispin Waddy 1990's

❸ The Classical .. 6b+ *S2*

15m. The inner arete is tricky and not without interest; take a good tide and a flat sea. Start as for *Confucius*, and continue to the arete. Climb it to the top, keeping an eye on the lower wall to your right, and then trend left to finish.
FSA. Crispin Waddy 1990's

Broadhaven Cove **Broadhaven Beach** 167

Easy but fractured slab

Broadhaven Cove
An exciting and atmospheric venue, with a good collection of steep, mid-to-hard routes.
Approach - The central lines of the Cove are best tackled from the left side of the crag, via the Broadhaven Cove Traverse. This approach offers the most straightforward climbing.
Conditions and Tides - A big tide proves useful, as does a calm sea.

❹ Broadhaven Cove Traverse 7a S0
40m. This terrific crab-wise route offers a lot of good and well-positioned climbing. It's usually started from the left side, as you'd approach the routes. Continue all the way to the far side, where a pumpy section finally gets you to the viewing ledges.
FSA. Trevor Massiah 2003

❺ The Shotgun ... 6b+ S2
17m. This route heads up to the two prominent holes in the hanging prow on the left side of the bay. Climb to the holes, then trend leftwards to an exit which might give cause for concern.
FSA. Ian Parnell 2003

The next three routes give solid climbing, but a less-than-perfect upper section. They all share a cleaned white slab finish, at least as far as the real climbing goes. A hanging rope to assist your finish would be forgiven.

❻ Wet T-Shirt Contest .... 7a+ S1
14m. Great positions. From the traverse, climb up into the groove right of *The Shotgun* to a good rest. Then sprint out across the hanging arete to gain the upper white slab.
FSA. Neil Gresham 7.2004

❼ Jaws 8a S1
14m. The Cove's central hanging arete is a true classic, and offers exceptional, very steep climbing. Low in the grade. From the traverse, tackle the shapely hanging arete direct to the white upper slab.
See photo on page 170.
FSA. Tim Emmett 10.7.2004

❽ Renaissance 7c S1
14m. The grooved right side of the *Jaws* arete; steep and enticing. Climb the groove to the right of *Jaws*, trending leftwards to finish on the same upper slab.
FSA. Neil Gresham 7.2004

Shrinkle Haven

Shrinkle Haven is the delightful area found to the south of the village of Manorbier, near the popular Mother Carey's Kitchen. The area is essentially a western extension of the Lydstep area, but as the crags are right next to the Shrinkle Haven car park, I've grouped them together here. Forbidden Head constitutes the headland just south of the car park and has a number of lines, including some very steep projects. Bridge Buttress is its more benign neighbour, with a good handful of routes, including some great crack climbing. You'll need a 40m rope to do any of the Shrinkle Haven routes; they all need an abseil to access them.

Approach

From Pembroke, take the A4139 towards Tenby. Turn off the A4139 at the (second, eastern-most) sign for Manorbier, which includes a sign for Shrinkle Haven. Follow the road for about 1km, and turn left at another sign for Shrinkle Haven. Follow the road down through the de-restricted signs, and around a sharp left bend by the Royal Artillery Range gate. Continue to a 'group' of car parks, and park at the last one, at the top of a short flight of steps. Forbidden Head is found on the headland south of the car park, and Bridge Buttress is found on the other side of the massive Frontier Zawn, which is below and immediately east of the car park.

Forbidden Head - From the car park, drop down the steps and turn right along the cliff path. After about 80m, drop down the headland on a vague path, then trending to the right, past a big wire cage. Follow your nose downhill to the crag.

Bridge Buttress - From the car park, drop down the steps and turn left. Follow the path around the big bay and take a smaller path to the right, towards an old concrete shelter. From here, drop down sloping grass ledges to the crag. You'll find enough gear (thread, block) to abseil into a good 'yellow' ledge on the bottom of the arete. In the event of a fall, you will need to scramble up the ledge system (take care) on the right of the buttress. The first line is shown on the topo. The feature you're looking for is the hanging groove found below/in the arete, on the last south-facing bit of rock here.

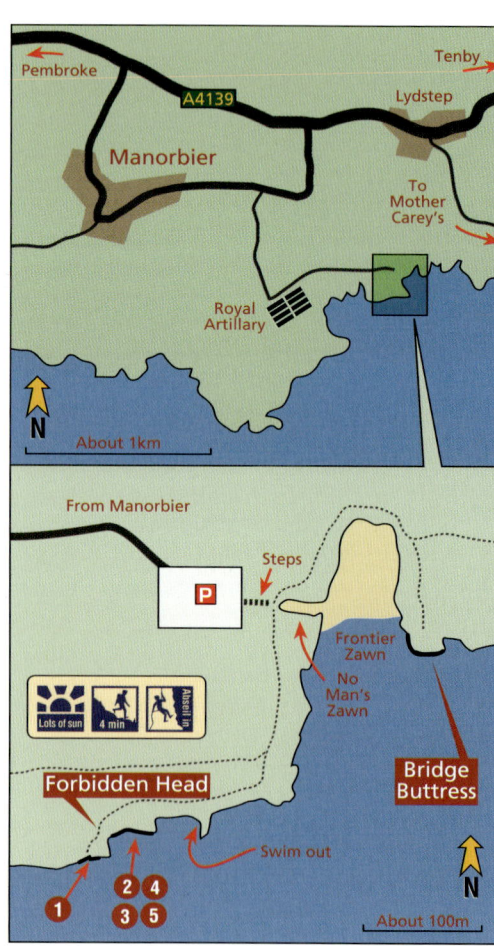

Conditions and Tides

Forbidden Head will need some proper large tides, so expect to climb early or late. A calm sea is advisable, as it's a 50m swim to regain the rock on easy get-out terrain. Bridge Buttress also needs a decent tide. The rock of both venues dries quickly after rain; expect crisp rock and positive holds throughout.

Forbidden Head and Bridge Buttress — Shrinkle Haven

Forbidden Head

The first line is shown on the map. The feature you're looking for is the hanging groove found below/in the arete, on the last south-facing bit of rock here.

1 Iron Pirate .... 6c+ S2
15m. The hanging groove in the very steep arete of the south face is brilliant. Abseil down a steep slab to gain a ledge. Swing right into the hidden, hanging groove, then climb it until it disappears. Make hard moves onto the hanging arete and finish up the arete in a great position, and with a solid exit.
FSA. Julian Lines 7.9.2006

The next routes start from a corner. You'll need to check your depth and arrange a rope to get you down to sea level; tape harness advised. The grades of *Love Action* and *Strange Love* will be affected (made easier) if you don't start from the left corner. A calm sea will make the lower traverse much easier with the footwork! The impressive steep leaning wall just left of *Fooled by a Smile* is unclimbed at the present time.

2 Fooled by a Smile.. 7a S3
15m. A brilliant corner climb, but a spring tide-only route. From the corner ledge, traverse right and climb the cream streak direct to the corner. Continue up the corner all the way to the top.
FSA. Julian Lines 7.9.2006

3 Blue Mood 6c S2
15m. A crimpy start finally gains the blind layback flake in the upper section. Follow this to a tough move and a left exit.
FSA. Julian Lines 8.9.2006

4 Love Action ... 7a? S1
15m. All the hard moves are low down. From the start corner on the left, follow a bewildering series of crimps across the wall, and move up to gain the base of the big slot in the layback flake above. The remainder of the route should prove to be easier.
NYS

5 Strange Love .. 7a S1
16m. This excellent line nibbles across the crimpy lower face, before taking the beautiful hanging arete above. The climbing eases towards the top.
FSA. Julian Lines 7.9.2006

Bridge Buttress

6 Kelpie Poodle........ 6a S2
16m. The hanging, cracked prow is good value. There's a direct and a right-hand finish available; take care with the rock at the top. Approach as for *Bridie Girl*.
FSA. Julian Lines 6.9.2006

7 Bridie Girl .... 5+ S2
16m. The corner. From the start ledge, traverse left for about 4m (crux), and head up into the big corner above. Top out rightwards, taking care with the rock.
FSA. Julian Lines 6.9.2006

8 Angry Child 6a S1
15m. The left arete of the face is delightful. From the start ledge, climb the arete, starting on the right. The delicate upper arete is taken mostly on the left.
FSA. Mike Robertson 6.9.2006

9 The Cutting Edge .. 6a+ S1
15m. The leftmost crack in the face. Superb, sustained climbing. From the yellow ledge, swing right and climb the crack all the way to the top; finish on the left.
FSA. Mike Robertson 6.9.2006

10 Musketeer .... 6b+ S1
15m. The terrific and poky crack in the centre of the face. Traverse out and climb the crack, past a hard move at half-height. Move leftwards to finish.
FSA. Julian Lines 6.9.2006

Bridge Buttress

Tim Emmett high on the classic arete of *Jaws* (8a) - *page 167* - at Broadhaven Cove, Pembroke. Photo: Mike Robertson.

Lydstep Area

This complex area is remarkable for its plethora of walls, caves and buttresses, many of which give excellent and relatively safe solos, with very few routes venturing higher than fourteen metres. It has the added attraction that almost all the approaches are by way of easy down-climbs or scrambles, so you can leave your ropes in the car. Unlike many of the other areas in Pembroke, the Lystep area is not affected by seasonal bird bans or the movements of the army - now you just have the tides to worry about!

Approach
From the A4139 Pembroke to Tenby road, drive into Lydstep village and find the Lydstep Tavern pub. 50m west of the pub is a small road heading south/downhill; take this and follow it (rough in places) all the way down to a sudden left bend. Turn right on this bend (blue sign: 'headland') and drive up over a cattle grid into the car park. All the Lydstep Cavern crags are described from the Mother Carey's Kitchen car park.

Conditions and Tides
The six crags described here all need the usual Pembroke savvy with tides, and mostly need a reasonable high tide, although the level is not always critical. The routes can usually be easily accessed with no ropes or harnesses, and they all have a viewing gallery of some description. Expect coarse, high-friction rock with little seepage, but bear in mind humid or damp conditions can exist, especially for the early morning visitor. There are no particular sea problem here - but take a calm one if you can.

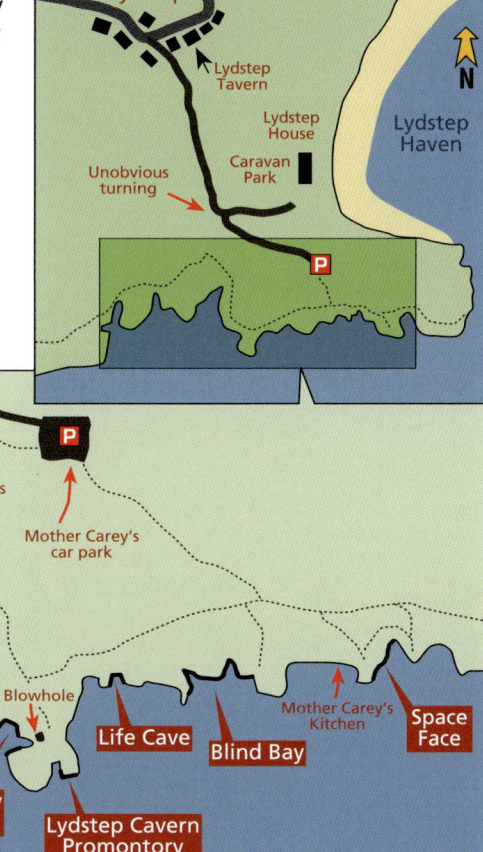

Lydstep Skomar Arch West

Skomar Arch West

This west-facing wall is found directly below the access ridge. It's steep, and generally has very sustained climbing.

Approach - *Dynamite* to *Scotch on the Rocks* are easily reached via a scramble down from the left, and routes from *Captain Caveman* through to *The Medic* are reached by walking down the ridge and scrambling in from the right.

Conditions and Tides - Climb here on a big tide if you can; a low spring tide visit will give a sunbathing beach instead! Of note is the reef found below *Vamos* and its neighbours - check the depth carefully, and swim it if necessary.

❶ **Dynamite** 6b S1
16m. Terrific and steep climbing. From the lower slabs, forge out rightwards to gain a steep wall, then trend back towards the prow on the left. Follow this and take on a hard sequence to finally finish rightwards.
FSA. Mike Robertson 7.2002

❷ **Project** . . . . 7a+? S1
16m. From the lower section of *Dynamite*, continue directly up to pass the roof on its right.

❸ **Scotch on the Rocks** . . . 7a S1
16m. A somewhat frustrating crux! From the same start as Route 2, climb the hanging prow, then make a couple of baffling moves to get established in the bottomless groove. Easier climbing gains the ridge.
FSA. Julian Lines 8.2006

The remaining six routes on this face are accessed from an easy way down on the right. Please note the submerged reef below; take a good high or a spring tide, and check the depth!

❹ **Captain Caveman** . . . . . 6c+ S1
11m. This wicked bat-style route ventures into the upside-down-ness of the arch itself, and in an amazing position. From the jug-rail, climb strenuously leftwards into the edge of the cave, and proceed up to a welcome double knee-bar rest. Follow the inner archway right across to the far (north) end. Phew!
FSA. Andy Cave 2003

❺ **Isostacy** 7b S2
16m. Out there. Climb *Captain Caveman* in from the jug-rail to gain the knee-bar rest. Pull through the roof above using crozzles, to gain the face above.
FSA. Julian Lines 16.6.2006

❻ **Vamos** 6a S2
14m. Start from the big jug-rail; take a fairly direct line up the face to the top. Check the depth on the reef very carefully.
FSA. Julian Lines 6.2006

❼ **Sea Leg** . . . . 6a+ S1/2
14m. From the big jug-rail, make hard moves directly up, and continue on to reach the crack/groove feature above. Follow this to the top. Check reef depth.
FSA. Julian Lines 6.2006

❽ **Nobody's Hero** . . . . 6a+ S1
13m. From the left end of the slim ledge, climb the groove above, then trend rightwards into a series of good flakes. Continue to the top.
FSA. Julian Lines 6.2006

❾ **The Medic** . . . . 5+ S1
12m. The easiest of a gradually-easing bunch. From the slim ledge, climb the appealing flake-line all the way to the top.
FSA. unknown

Skomar Arch East **Lydstep**  173

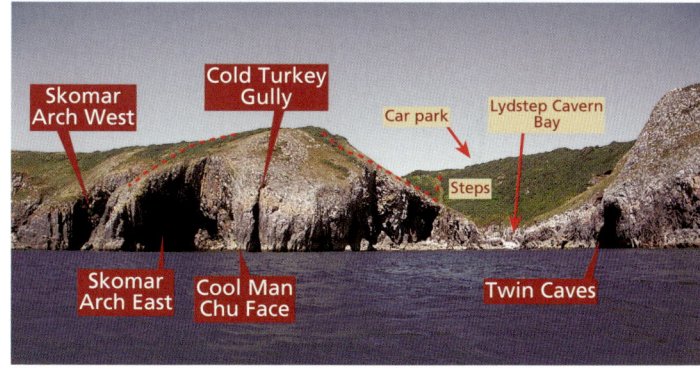

Skomar Arch East

This east-facing wall has an annoying reef positioned along its seaward end, but still manages to squeeze some good routes into the region of the arch.

Approach - *Reef Walker* and *Patch's Shorts* are found by walking along the reef, and *Restraint of Beasts* is reached by traversing in from underneath *Dynamite*.

Conditions and Tides - Take a big-ish tide along. A calm sea will give a lot more flexibility with your approach.

⑩ Reef Walker 　　　　　　　　　 **7a** *S3*
14m. The oft-eyed hanging arete has now been fondled for the first time. An S3 start; sprint for the upper section! From the start reef, make a precarious move to gain a hand jam; stretch right to the jug on the arete. Continue up the arete, veering rightwards above the apex of the arch. You'll gain more confidence with height (a rare experience).
FSA. Julian Lines 22.9.2006

⑪ Patch's Shorts . . . . 　　　 **4/6** *S?*
16m. Very hard to grade; the top blowhole is definitely size-ist! Steady climbing up inside the arch leads to a top blowhole - simply squeeze through it!
FSA. Patch Hammond (one point of aid) 7.2002. The 'point of aid' was three burly guys dragging the first (and only?) ascensionist through the blowhole, whereupon his shorts got dragged down to his ankles. One of Lystep's funniest moments.

The next two routes are reached by way of the traverse under Dynamite, continuing around to gain the east side of the arch.

⑫ Project . . . . 　　 **7c?** *S0*
14m. A tempting proposition and as safe as houses. A diagonal traverse leads to some burly roof action and an easier upper wall.

⑬ Restraint of Beasts . 　　　　　 **6b+** *S1*
14m. A fine route and safe all the way. From the lower arch, traverse rightwards and climb the pillar above, gradually trending leftwards up the vague groove system, all the way to the ridge.
FSA. Crispin Waddy 2000

Lydstep Cool Man Chu Wall

Cool Man Chu Wall

This wall forms the eastern edge of the main cave, and is recognised by the triangular reef lying below its left edge. The established routes all avoid this, and the S grades are as cosy as can be.

Approach - The routes are all accessed by way of the easy *Way Down* (3). This vertical down-climb is best (and most easily) tackled by climbing down the left arete of the easy groove, as you'll then be fully over the drink. A short abseil is easy to set up if preferred.

Conditions and Tides - Expect afternoon sun and plenty of dry crisp rock. Any mid to high tide will give plenty of water.

❶ Project .... 7a+? *S2*
13m. This one should be a corker; powerful and sustained.

❷ Cool Man Chu. .... 6a+ *S0*
12m. From the base of the way down, traverse leftwards to gain a line of undercuts; when they peter out, climb the wall above on bigger holds. Finish more easily.
FSA. Julian Lines 6.2006

❸ Planktonitis .... 5+ *S0*
11m. Traverse left to reach the left end of a cream streak, and climb it into a vague groove; join *Big Screen* for the top face.
FSA. Julian Lines 6.2006

❹ Big Screen. .... 4+ *S0*
11m. Delightful! We need more solos like this. From the base of the *Way Down*, look for a diagonal line of holds up and left. Get your hands on these and follow 'em all the way to the top.
FSA. Mike Robertson 7.2006

❺ Way Down 3 *S0*
10m. The left arete of the groove is excellent and solid.
FSA. unknown

❻ Reso's Nose. 5 *S2*
10m. The right arete of the face is dandy, but check the depth carefully. From the way down, traverse right until below the arete. Climb the arete on its left side, all the way to the top.
FSA. Mike Robertson 7.2006

Cold Turkey Gully Lydstep 175

7 Cocko — 5 S0
10m. The left arete of the gully is climbed to a solid exit.
FSA. Mike Robertson 7.2006

8 Crill Wars — 4+/6a+
9m. This split-grade route finds itself negotiating the left wall of the gully, and the difficulty depends on your height - high is 4+ and S2 (rock on the other side beckons), and low is 6a+ and S1. Once at the back of the gully, simply reverse out.
FSA. Mike Robertson 7.2006

Extras and Cold Turkey are accessed by down-climbing easy ground to arrive at a groove at sea level on the east edge of the gully. Remember that a fall from either of these routes will NOT require a 'push-out'! The gully here is just wide enough for a straight drop only.

9 Extras — 6a+ S1/2
10m. The face left of the arete. From the first moves up the arete, swing leftwards to gain jugs, and climb direct on good holds to the top.
FSA. Mike Robertson 7.2006

10 Cold Turkey — 6a+ S1
10m. The arete is a solid and engaging proposition. Climb the sustained arete on its left side all the way.
FSA. Mike Robertson 7.2006

There's a further route on its own, go and give it some company.

11 Sex-pack on the Beach — 5+ S0
16m. A fine traverse, finishing up a wide corner; good value. From the cliff top, drop down an easy slab, and swing rightwards across a steep wall on good holds. Finish up the corner.
FSA. Julian Lines 7.2006

Cold Turkey Gully
This gully can be seen in the overview photo below - it is the slice of shadow on the very eastern edge of the cavern. The S grades are slightly higher than it's neighbour, partly because the gully is a little too narrow for flying folk and partly because the gully culminates in a blowhole, but that caving stuff is a little beyond the jurisdiction of the S grade!
Approach - *Cocko* and *Crill Wars* are accessed from the route *Way Down*.
Conditions and Tides - A mid to high tide is desirable.

Lydstep The Twin Caves

The Twin Caves

The final bit of cave-style action at Lystep Cavern Bay is this rather attractive cave set-up, found immediately east of the boulder beach of the bay itself. It's all packaged quite nicely with good access and a rather fetching viewing gallery.

Approach - The path that follows the contour of the hill up from the bay will get you to the top of the wall; access the routes easily from here.

Conditions and Tides - A calm sea and some afternoon sun should see you on your way. You'll need a dry day and a breeze to discover the innermost secrets of *Calm* and *Charm*.

❶ Offshore Drift . . . . 6a+ *S0*
14m. This exciting route takes you along the higher traverse line, and is a gem. From the entry ledges at just above half-height, forge across the perfect upper break. Exciting moves slightly down lead to a bridge across the final groove of the arch; step left and finish up the groove. The route can be done in either direction.
FSA. Julian Lines 7.2006

❷ Cellar Deck . . . . 6a+ *S0*
18m. A grand outing; the lower traverse. From the easy ground on the far right end of the crag, drop down and traverse on good holds into the recess. From here, move up and left, to join *Offshore Drift* in reverse for a flying finish.
FSA. Julian Lines 7.2006

❸ Wreck of the Hesperus . 6c *S0/1*
8m. Another good 'un! Follow *Cellar Deck* until all routes meet at the prow, then climb directly through the overhang above, past two plants located in (thankfully) big holds.
FSA. Julian Lines 7.2006

❹ Flotsam . . . . 6b+ *S0/1*
7m. Another steep finish awaits on this one. From *Cellar Deck*, break out and up a weakness, cross the upper traverse and take the roof on for a finale.
FSA. Julian Lines 7.2006

❺ Jetsam 6a *S0/1*
6m. A little chap for a warm-up. From *Offshore Drift*, swing up into the V-feature, and pull over to finish.
FSA. Julian Lines 7.2006

❻ Aperitif 6a *S1*
5m. Short and sweet. From the higher traverse, break out and up to the right edge of the roof system. Negotiate the roof above with a pull right followed by a pull left.
FSA. Julian Lines 7.2006

The final two routes at the Twin Caves are, not surprisingly, found in the second cave, just a few metres to the north. The west wall of the cave is solid and rough - almost grit-like - and provides two atmospheric crack climbs. Go in there when the conditions are good. A ropeless approach is to climb down the seaward edge of the central arch and then traverse the inner west wall (this will be a little harder than the routes themselves) along into the second cave.

❼ Calm . . . . 5+ *S2*
12m. The left-hand crack is a crack. Teeter up a ramp to gain the vertical crack; finish the route slightly rightwards. Check depth over the boulder carefully.
FSA. Julian Lines 7.2006

❽ Charm 5 *S1*
12m. The right-hand of the two cracks is terrific. The start is the crux.
FSA. Crispin Waddy 2000

Cavern Promontory Lydstep 177

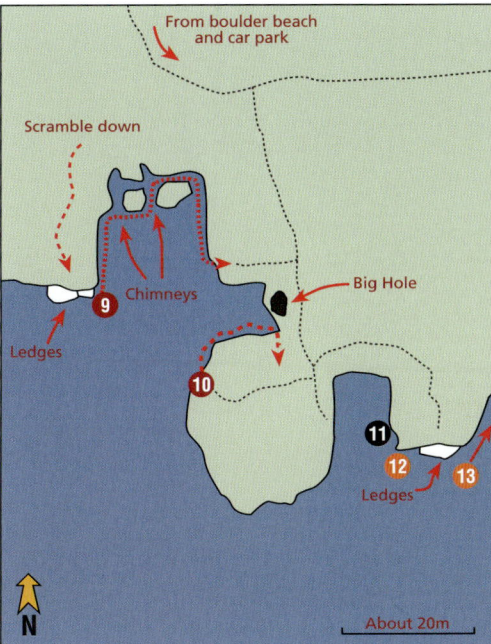

Lydstep Cavern Promontory
This rather bizarre bit of geography is found just to the south-east of the main bay, and gives some extraordinary little adventures.

Approach - From the steps, follow the contour of the hill around, to pass a large hole in the ground (this is the infamous cavern itself). A walkabout from here will familarise you with both the *Topology* zawn and the *Perfect Pitch* zawn. To gain the start of *Topology*, you'll need to retrace your steps and drop down slabs about 25m west of the zawn, to gain ledges. The alternative, especially at high tide, is a short abseil.

Conditions and Tides - A calm sea would be ideal. Take a decent tide along.

⑨ Topology 7a *S1*
20m. Absolutely brilliant. The route traverses all three sides of the north zawn, and gets harder all the way. Traverse easily across the east-facing slab, and continue past a chimney in the south-facing wall, to gain a second chimney. Down-climb the left arete of the chimney, and drop into it; continue past a hole and get established on the wide ledge in the steep west-facing wall. From the ledge's right end, swing down and then up into a short groove; finish up rightwards with difficulty.
FSA. Crispin Waddy 1990's

⑩ Strangeness 6c *S0*
9m. This ace little crank tackles the north-facing wall of the east zawn. Down-climb the wall (easy) just south of the arete to the HWM. Traverse leftwards to the arete, and swing under it into a strange slot-cave feature. Follow this leftwards until it ends, and undercut through an overlap to gain pockets. Step left and finish direct on juggy conglomerate.
FSA. Crispin Waddy 1990's

A walk out onto the east side of the promontory will give you a good view of *Perfect Pitch*, and found immediately to its left, in the shadowed, very steep groove, is *Fancy Claps*.

⑪ Fancy Claps ..... 7a+ *S1*
12m. The steep hanging groove just left of the face is spicy indeed. Good dry conditions required. From the base of the face, swing around the arete and make hard moves into the base of the groove. Continue up the groove to the top.
FSA. Tom Briggs 2003

⑫ Perfect Pitch ..... 6a+ *S1*
12m. The route up the left edge of the face is fantastic. Excellent rock, amazing positions and perfect climbing make this one of Pembroke's best deep water solos. Take a good high tide. From the access ledges on the right side of the face, traverse left and climb the face on its left side all the way to a solid finish.
FSA. Crispin Waddy 2000

The last route in the vicinity is a dashing little cave roof, found in a cave about half-way along towards Blind Bay, some 45m from the Promontory. The cave is, in effect, an isolated, inner 'pool'.

⑬ Life .... 6a+ *S1/2*
11m. Ace, and mad territory for the grade; a good find. Step right into deep cracks, which lead to a ledge. Continue up across the cave roof on massive threads, finally swinging down to jugs. Step right and down-climb the easier groove with care, ending up close to your start point.
FSA. Crispin Waddy, Dan Donovan 8.2006

Lydstep Blind Bay

Routes from White Fang to The Abyss are started from the big corner ledge, often referred to as the 'Beat Ledge', named after the E5 trad route up the corner, Beat Surrender.

❶ White Fang .... 6b+ *S1*
20m. From the Beat Ledge, traverse left to the arete recess, and climb the arete on its right side past a white flake to a ledge. Jump from here; the *S2* corner above is unnerving.
FSA. Julian Lines 31.8.2005

❷ El Lobo .... 6b+ *S2*
20m. From the Beat Ledge, move left to gain a wide crack, and climb this to a wild move leftwards to join *White Fang*.
FSA. Julian Lines 31.8.2005

❸ Project .... 7c? *S2*
20m. The continuation seam above *El Lobo*.

Aristocrat and Toffee Nose can be tackled at S3, but are described here with their S1 format using the reversal of Snobs to avoid the upper wall.

❹ Aristocrat 7a *S1*
12m/25m. Traverse out rightwards from the Beat Ledge to pockets, and climb the thin wall above (crux) to the half-height ledge. Reverse down *Snobs*, or take the superb crack-line above to the very top (*S3*).
FSA. Julian Lines 1.9.2005

❺ Toffee Nose ... 7a *S1*
12m/25m. Traverse rightwards to the sharp arete, and climb it precariously on its left side (crux) to gain the half-height ledge. Reverse down *Snobs*, or take on the scary upper arete (*S3*).
FSA. Julian Lines 1.9.2005

❻ Snobs 6a *S0/1*
12m. A fine route in its own right and a great way to get off the last two routes. Traverse right around the arete, crux, into the corner; continue up this for 6m, then take a rising line of jugs leftwards to the arete, and the half-height ledge. The grade is given for the first half; the high continuation is 6a+ and *S3*.
FSA. Julian Lines 30.8.2005

❼ The One-Eyed Man
.... 7a *S2/3*
35m (total). This line is one of the best-positioned DWS's in the UK - it's just stupendous. Brilliant and sustained climbing throughout. Abseil to the square ledge at the base of *Beat Surrender*, and traverse just above the high tide crinkles, as for *Snobs*, to arrive at the base of a corner. Thereafter heading rightwards and gradually upwards, to trace a crazy, intimidating line up the left side of the arete. Swing right around the arete to gain a big rest and the easier, fossil-like chimney. This finishing corner is around 5+. *See photo on page 151.*
FSA. Crispin Waddy 1991

❽ The Blind Man's Traverse
.... 7a *S0*
25m (total). A pumpy and stylish method of gaining the inner cave. Traverse all the way from the Beat ledge, to arrive at the very edge of the main cave. Traverse the technical wall on perfect rock, to gain a resting ledge at the start of *The Abyss*. An accommodating and not-too-high tide will allow you to continue to finally gain the Alien ledge.
FSA. Adam Wainwright 2003

Blind Bay Lydstep

Blind Bay

Blind Bay consists of the vertical walls around the Beat Ledge feature, and the deep, intimidating Alien Cave, found over to its right. The routes on the left side of the bay are quite a proposition, but the routes found within the Alien Cave itself are something else. This architecturally-stunning cave is one of the absolute bastions of S3 climbing in the UK.

Approach - To reach the Beat Ledge, drop down the slope from the cliff top, and set up an abseil rope, use this to access the ledge. For the Alien Cave, drop down a small winding path to gain the right edge of the cave. A further downclimb (4+) gains good ledges at sea level.

Conditions and Tides - The water here is very deep, and the higher routes described are best undertaken at a good spring tide, where careful timing will reduce the S grade to a more manageable level. The Alien Cave can be greasy at times, a southerly breeze brings the best conditions. The bay is fairly sheltered.

❾ The Abyss 7b S2/3
50m (total). An astounding voyage into the roofs above; one of Julian Lines' very finest contributions to the genre. From the Beat Ledge, climb all the way across to the *Blind Man's Traverse*; use this to enter the cave, to gain the slab rest. Move up and rightwards into the hanging 45° off-width and follow this, then swing left to reach a hanging 'tunnel' for a well-earned rest. Drop out of the tunnel and move left on undercuts to gain a huge thread at the lip of the cave. The easier, upper corner awaits.
FSA. Julian Lines 11.9.2005

The rest of the routes in this cave all start from the approach ledges, on the right side of the cave. The access traverses in and out of the cave are well-positioned and on perfect rock.

❿ The Anti Matterhorn 7b S3
35m. A mammoth outing. The committing crux is at around 15m at a good spring tide. From the lower traverse in, climb the groove to a short face, then climb outwards and then back left, to gain a shake-out under the biggest roof. From here, drop down and bridge onto the horn, and get established on it using a distant undercut. Follow a line of undercuts to gain the corner above; finish up this more easily.
FSA. Julian Lines 9.9.2006

⓫ Abduction 7a S2/3
35m. Another crazy piece of climbing, threading its way through the cave. Traverse into the back of the cave, move left onto the wall, then traverse left into a groove. Move out and leftwards to cross a pillar feature, then take the groove up and leftwards. Swing blindly up and rightwards into space (crux) to eventually arrive at a rest in the upper cave niche (*S1/2* so far). Climb directly outwards along the downward-pointing roof, to reach a huge thread on the lip (a possible double leg-bar no-hands rest), then pull round the exposed lip on good but hidden holds. From here, a step right into a groove takes you to a finish up the easy wide crack-line.
FSA. Julian Lines 3.9.2005

⓬ Deep Water Alien .. 6c S1/2
40m. This escapade is slightly more amenable, with a possible early rightwards exit at hand. Traverse the wall into a cave, bridge left and down across the chimney, then move left round the arete; then either make a hard low traverse across the wall (not possible at spring tides) or a slightly higher and marginally easier traverse to gain the *Alien* ledge. Move up and right on shelving holds to the roof, then take the traverse line diagonally rightwards, to gain the very edge of the cave. Escape can be made out right here, at *S1*. For the higher and rather more gripping finish, step left and get established on the awkward seat, then pull up through the roof on big holds and traverse left across the lip into the deep finishing corner of *One-Eyed Man*.
FSA. Julian Lines 1.9.2005

⓭ Boomerang 6b S1
18m. After the lower traverse into the cave, take on the hanging traverse line in the roof above, which takes you all the way back to the start ledge.
FSA. Crispin Waddy 1990's

Lydstep Space Face

Space Face

This venue will usually leave the most hardened deep water soloist reeling in his or her rock shoes. Mother Carey's famous and grossly leaning Space Face houses *Hyperspace* and *Just Klingon*, to name just two of the classics here, but the face is over 30m of overhanging rock so what can it possibly offer the deep water soloer? Below is enough information to get involved with this face WITHOUT the high top-out! You won't ever have to climb over 20m at a big spring tide - how does that sound? For an added bonus the collection of routes at the right end of the crag, in the *Tiger Tiger* cave, all have low cruxes.

Approach - One approach is to abseil down the main seaward face of the tall buttress left of the Space Face (known as Brazen Buttress) and traverse in (the height of this traverse varies according to the tide level). Alternatively, a boat/dry-bag approach can be made to gain the dry-bag ledge. This watery approach will be better at big spring tides, as the traverse in from Brazen Buttress is desperate when fully waterlogged! This ledge can also be reached by abseil using the fixed threads to pull yourself in.

Conditions and Tides - A BIG spring tide is essential for all the biggies; a lesser tide will be okay for the routes on the far right. Take a calm sea, and scope the swim-out, which gains the fisherman's ledges over to the right.

Finishes - For the *S2* finish at the level of *Hyperspace's* second belay, abseil in, using the threads on *Just Klingon* to pre-place your bench seat. Or finish the routes by reversing *Hyperspace* to below its first belay, followed by a jump at the level of your choice.

For the higher, *S3* finish above the shattered pocket on *Hyperspace*, pre-place a hanging knotted rope, or (ideally) a bench seat with harness and jumars. This should be about 2m above the pocket to give the full grade.

❶ **X Factor.........** 7a+ *S1*
15m. A new addition. Move leftwards around a bulge (crux) and up to a rest under the roof. Pull through the roof on hidden finger jugs, just left of the wide slot.
FSA. Julian Lines 25.9.2006

❷ **Hyperspace.......** 6c+ *S1/3*
15m / 32m. The first pitch is a spring tide *S1* and is a stunning, classic solo in its own right, with the last hard bit at around 13m (the first pitch goes at 6c+). Jump or down-climb/jump. The whole route is *S3* and 6c+, to a pre-placed bench seat set just above the shattered pocket.
FSA. (all 3 pitches) by Julian Lines and Mike Robertson 7.2006

❸ **Fireball XL5...** 7a *S2*
17m. First half only gives this grade. Truly brilliant climbing. Would be an incredible full-height solo; watch this space.
FSA. Julian Lines 26.9.2006

Space Face **Lydstep** 181

Julian Lines taking on the crux of *Tiger Tiger* (7b)
- *below* - on the severely overhanging Space Face,
Pembroke. Photo: Mike Robertson.

4 Just Klingon... 6c *S2*
17m. First half only. Takes the stunning, steep grey face all the way to the traverse line.
FSA. Tim Emmett 2005.

5 Mother Night.. 6c *S2*
17m. First half only of this magic route gives this grade. Pumpy, technical and totally classy.
FSA. Julian Lines 9.9.2006

6 Zoony....... 7a+ *S3*
18m / 23m. This meaty line features both hard moves and lots of technical bits. It joins *Hyperspace's* third pitch; top-end *S2* if you turn left at that point, turning right to continue past the shattered pocket gives *S3*.
NYS

7 Unconscious .. 7c *S3*
23m. An absolute beast; you won't be queueing! This crazy-steep line blasts up the steep overlapping slabs to reach *Hyperspace's* shattered pocket direct.
NYS

8 Tiger Tiger....... 7b *S1*
13m. This also joins *Hyperspace* at its third pitch, but it is cool to tick the grade by jumping off at the jugs at the end of the hard bit. Using this method the crux is at 8m or so - and let go at the jugs at about 12m. That's *S1* in anyone's book! *Photo above*.
FSA. Julian Lines 6.2006

9 Bagpuss ..... 6c+ *S1*
12m. Break away from *Tiger Tiger* below its crux, and traverse across the severely overhanging wall. Gain the grossly steep flake-crack, climb it to a grey boss foothold, and jump off.
FSA. Julian Lines 11.9.2005

10 The Laughing Hygena
.... 7c+ *S1*
12m. Don't be put off by the grade, you strong folk. All the hard moves are as low as can be. Exit early, as above. It will need dry conditions, ideally a neap high tide and a calm sea.
NYS

Penally

The Penally Training Camp region is a remarkable and diverse collection of caves, zawns, walls and blowholes, all found close to the Lydstep to Tenby road. It offers a number of high-quality traverses, leaning walls and tunnel escapades. The brilliant Kato Zawn heads the line-up with its impressive spread of grades, but also worth seeking out is the hilarious Scoop Wall.

Access

There are some special considerations when entering the Penally region. Scoop Wall and Concrete Wall are open all the time, but all crags from Marble Zawn through to Kato Zawn and Dawn Bay are in an army training area, and when the red flags are flying (visible from the road, if you're passing through) you can't get in. So dial 01834 845950, and get the following month's closures - this number is usually an ansaphone message with the dates, and goes to the Penally guardroom. A quick visit here (just 200m from the parking) is quite acceptable - indeed, the guardroom staff have recently suggested that climbers let them know their plans.

Approach

From Tenby, drive west down the A4139 coast road for 2.5 miles. Park on the grassy verge just before the Penally Training camp entrance, and walk left/south on the footpath. This takes you under the railway line. Then swing right and follow the path past the sentry box, to finally arrive at the second sentry box, on the cliff edge. All the individual crags detailed below will be approached from this second sentry box.

Conditions and Tides

A southerly breeze and a little sunshine would be just the ticket for a visit. A calm sea and a high-ish tide are ideal, but remember venues like Kato Zawn can be climbed on neap tides, (ie. the smaller midday high tides) this proves a lot more convenient!

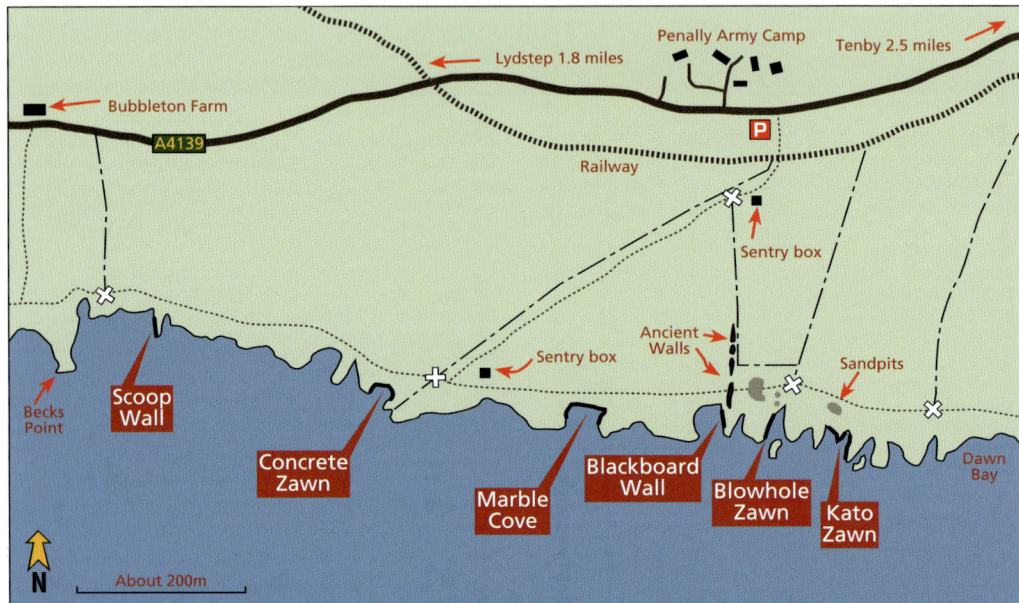

Scoop Wall and Concrete Zawn — Penally

Scoop Wall
This fine crag has just three lines, but they're absolutely brilliant. The rock is scoopy, as the name suggests, but also full of enormous holes. Access is easy.
Approach - From the coast path (second) sentry box, walk west for 500m to a fence. Jump the stile and swing left past a blowhole feature, to then view Scoop Wall back behind you. Once recce'd, go back over the stile and walk for 50m to reach the crag. Drop down the slopes; the grade 3 access down-climb is just right (looking out) of a prominent white block on the cliff edge and please note that the leftwards traverse all the way to the base of *Magic Flute* is about 6a+.
Conditions and Tides - Expect plenty of afternoon sun and dry rock but avoid those damp days. A mid-to-high tide will give you a great time on this excellent little wall.
Exit - If you take a fall, the swim-out here is long, about 40m - see above for exit point.

Concrete Zawn
The Zawn appears to be made up of concreted blocks that for the most part is entirely solid. It is really more of a cove than a zawn. There are lots of up routes that are not described but pride of place must go to *Nice but Dim*, the long traverse of the entire zawn.
Approach - Walk along about 60m from the coast path sentry box, to drop down slopes to the crag top (see map opposite). An easy down-climb gains the start of *Nice but Dim*.
Conditions and Tides - Any high tide will give enough water depth. The zawn is tucked in and gives some shelter. It also gets plenty of sun.

❹ Nice but Dim ..... 6b+ *S1*
45m. The traverse of the whole zawn is long, and quite an expedition. From the west side of Concrete Zawn, find your way down to sea level and traverse east/rightwards all the way across the massive zawn, on some of the oddest rock at Pembroke. When at the impasse, make wild moves to hang a big slopy jug, and perform a mid-air 'twist' to land on the small ledge on the other side (crux). Continue traversing the east wall until a easy way out becomes clear.
FSA. Tim Emmett and Crispin Waddy (varying leads) 2001

❶ Magic Flute ......  6a+ *S1*
16m. The line of the massive holes; brilliant. This route will get you laughing, guaranteed! From the lower, left end of the traverse in, climb up to and into the first tube/hole feature. Once you've hung gaily out of the first window, climb up to the second one, and repeat the experience. Joking aside, climb the final wall on deep slots to a solid exit.
FSA. Julian Lines 5.9.2006

❷ The Scoop ....  6b+ *S1*
15m. Another gem; wicked, powerful moves all the way. From the traverse, make hard moves to gain the deep, diagonal groove. Follow it all the way to the top.
FSA. Julian Lines 5.9.2006

There's one other line here, just to the east of Nice but Dim. It's clearly visible from the top of Concrete Zawn, taking the diagonal parallel cracks soaring left through the south-west facing wall:

❺ This Nation's Saving Grace
.... 6c *S2/3*
22m. A great line. Gain the base of the wall by abseil. Traverse in from the right to gain the double fault-lines, and follow these strenuously leftwards. When they end, climb the wall above to gain a left-trending ramp with difficulty. Move up and left to an easier finish.
FSA. Crispin Waddy 2000

❸ The Piano ....    6c *S1*
11m. Shorter, but with more excellent moves (every move on this crag is ace). From the earlier section of the traverse in, slap your way up the big, hanging prow to the top.
FSA. Mike Robertson 5.9.2006

Penally — Marble Cove and Blowhole Zawn

Marble Cove

This feature is a big, broad cove, which has a marble texture to it. The main event is the lower traverse, *Giraffes*. The best viewing point is from the eastern edge of the crag, which is also where *Giraffes* starts.
Approach - From the coast path sentry box, walk east for about 200m, then drop down the slopes to the crag.
Conditions and Tides - A good high tide is necessary. It is worth avoiding hot and humid weather, as the friction on offer isn't a patch on its close neighbours.

❶ Giraffes 6c S1
40m. The traverse across the cove is a fantastic expedition if you catch it in the right conditions. Expect one move which seems to offer a reach problem for anyone less than about 5'9" (1.75m). The route is usually climbed right to left.
FSA. Crispin Waddy 2001

❷ The Audi . . . . 6c+ S0
9m. Gain this line from the left. The steep wall left of the *Down and Out* tunnel gives some good moves. Climb the edge of the scoop to the upper slab.
FSA. Tim Emmett 2001

Found at the top of the crag is a small access blowhole. Dropping down this (pleasant, with no nasty squeezes) gets you down to the rather wacky tunnel in the lower left side of the cove. You're now in place for the next route.

❸ Down and Out . . . . 6b+ S0
12m. This crazy and most excellent line features bottomless body bridging along an incredible conglomerate tunnel. From the bottom of the blowhole, make your way out towards the light, mostly by way of the west wall, and full-on body bridging moves. Finish is for *Giraffes*.
FSA. Crispin Waddy, Mike Robertson 2001

❹ Mad Angus . . . . 7a+ S0
9m. The very steep wall right of *Down and Out* gives some steep and poky moves. Approach from the right, via *Giraffes*. From the pillar resting ledge on the right side of the *Down and Out* tunnel, climb steeply up to climb the bulge above direct.
FSA. Mike Robertson 2001

Blackboard Wall

This square bay just west of the lone broken wall has a single route up its east face. **Approach - See map on page 182.**

❺ Blackboard Wall 6a S2
17m. The black wall on the east side of the bay offers this atmospheric but slightly scary line. From the south-east tip of the bay, traverse easily leftwards to gain the base of the wall. Traverse across the base, and then climb it to the top, via an upper set of pillars.
FSA. Mike Robertson, Elinor Currey 2001

Blowhole Zawn

This well-hidden feature is found right below the fence - in fact, the fence runs right down into it. There are two routes in there, and you'll need an abseil rope for one of them.
Approach - See map on page 182.

❻ Matt Black . . . . 6b+ S0
11m. Brilliant. Traverse into the narrow zawn from the west, and climb the faint groove up the steep wall above.
FSA. Lancashire Matt 2001

The second route in the zawn can be viewed from the base of the clean blow-hole. But you'll need an abseil to get to it. Abseil from the left (west) side of the block at the top of the zawn, down a slab, and to a spike a little above sea level.

❼ Damocles 6c S1
11m. The inner west wall of the narrow zawn. From the spike, climb up steeply past a series of large hanging fangs; a final steep pull gains the much easier finish, on the upper slab.
FSA. Crispin Waddy 2000

Jason Porter enjoying perfect conditions on *Love* (6a) - *page 187* - Kato Zawn, Pembroke. Photo: Mike Robertson.

Penally Kato Zawn

Kato Zawn

Now here's a venue that offers a little of everything. Kato Zawn, the crag that most soloists have failed to find on at least one occasion. The zawn offers climbing up to 13m high and the rock is as good as it gets. The absolute classic here is *The Wizard*, which goes into the history books as the first ground-up 8a new DWS route in the UK. For normal humans, the right / east side of the zawn gives some surprising grades, with *Way Down* and *Hate* providing the perfect introductory 5 circuit.

Approach - From the coast-path sentry box on the cliff edge, turn left / east and follow the coast path eastwards for about 400m to a fence and an old, short broken wall. Cross this fence by way of the gate and walk a further 80m. Kato Zawn will now be down on your right. You'll need a 20m rope and a few wires and cams to set up an abseil for Kato's harder routes, on the south-facing *Wizard* face.

Conditions and Tides - The easier, west-facing wall is just about always dry and sunny. The *Wizard* face, although south-facing, is so steep that it fails to get a direct hit from the summer sun. This means that condensation is sometimes a problem on the hardest routes. Take a dry southerly breeze with you if you can. The sea state is not usually an issue here, but obviously a calm sea is best. The deep water below doesn't need too much in the way of tide research - any mid-high tide will be fine.

The first six routes all start from small ledges underneath Waterland and Rusty Dog, where it is possible to move around and lose your harness without too much of a problem. Abseil from cams and wires down a line just right (looking in) of Rusty Dog.

❶ The Wizard  **8a** *S1*
12m. This is just classic sustained territory. It takes the monumentally-steep groove on the left side of the overhanging face. From the abseil landing spot, traverse easily left and make some hard moves to gain the groove. Follow it all the way to the top.
Photo on page 28.
FSA. Neil Gresham 7.2004. A slice of history in the making - the route constitutes the UK's first ground-up 8a DWS new route, after some nine splashdowns.

Kato Zawn **Penally** 187

❺ Not Now, Kato! 6b *S1*
12m. The cracked groove 3m right of *Rusty Dog* offers some really excellent and sustained climbing. From the first section of *The Stairs*, keep climbing direct up the crack/groove feature, all the way to the top.
FSA. Crispin Waddy 1999

❻ The Stairs 6b *S2/3*
13m. The route features some rather unusual DWS territory; it's steep overall, but... is something of a staircase. Climb the stairs to a final resting place, finishing off by way of the short, steep upper wall - perky territory for a moment or two.
FSA. Mike Robertson 2003

The next batch of solos, on the east wall, are all easily accessed by the Way Down - a terrific and very handy 4+ break-line. This gets you down to a small start ledge just above the sea.

❼ Love 6a *S1/2*
12m. A really nice route, although slightly scary on the few moves above the narrow trench. From the very base of the wall, climb up and left to step into the vague corner feature. Absorbing moves lead you up; swing off right at the horizontal break to a safe finish. *See photo on page 185.*
FSA. Crispin Waddy 1999

❽ A Thin Line 7a *S0*
11m. Steep and fun with one very hard sequence. From the small ledge, climb up to the overlap on the arete above. Make a very hard move to gain better holds, and gain the horizontal break to finish rightwards.
FSA. Crispin Waddy 1999

❾ Project .... 7c+? *S0*
10m. The tempting, v-e-r-y thin headwall move has seen off a few protagonists. One 'very' hard move.
NYS.

❿ Mad World .... 7a+ *S0*
8m. Great moves. A thin headwall crack can be seen from the other side of the zawn; the route takes this on. Down-climb *Hate* until at jugs just down and right of the thin crack. Make hard moves up leftwards into the crack, and continue on crimps to finally gain the upper break.
FSA. Mike Robertson 7.2004

⓫ Hate 5 *S0*
9m. A perfect intro to DWS! From *Way Down*, climb up to gain the diagonal fault; follow it rightwards all the way to an easy and solid exit.
FSA. Crispin Waddy 1999

⓬ Way Down .... 4+ *S0*
9m. Why don't all DWS crags have an access route as well placed as this? If only... Find the diagonal fault from the top, and climb it all the way across to the base of the wall. There's just one tricky move, and it's right at the bottom.
FSA. unknown

The Stairs

❷ Project .... 7c+? *S1*
12m. The left-hand finish to *Waterland* will be tough terrain.

❸ Waterland .... 7b+ *S1*
12m. Steep, sustained, and excellent. From the lower ledges, fire up on jugs and side-pulls to a crux on the even steeper upper section.
FSA. Neil Gresham 7.2004

❹ Rusty Dog 7b *S1/2*
12m. Another marvellous and pumpy route. Climb the right side of the base pedestal (take care, here), and gain the ramps above. Tip toe onto the second one, and sprint up the upper sloping jugs (crux) as fast as you can.
FSA. Mike Robertson 7.2004

Perfect granite: Julian Lines on the superb *Please Rub Salt into my Wounds* (6b+) - *page 201* - Paradise Wall, Isle of Erraid, Scotland. Photo: Mike Robertson.

Scotland

by Julian Lines and Mike Robertson

Scotland

Welcome to Scotland, this guide's most northerly venue. It wasn't an immediate choice for inclusion, but the crags in the far north of the UK are beautiful, tranquil and seductively remote, and offer an isolated experience far removed from the flesh pots of Torbay and Pembroke! There has been much pioneering around the Scottish coastline and islands over the years, but the most usable venues have been described here to give a taster of what the far north has to offer.

The diversity of Scottish DWS rock is startling, both in colour and in texture, with the golden granite of Erraid's Paradise Wall and Aberdeen's Red Tower vying with the bronzed, curling sandstone bulges of the more recently developed Baby Taipan Wall. Surprisingly, in amongst all this variation you won't find any limestone.

So now we've established that Scotland's cliffs are not all huge, tottering adventures, undertaken only with a rope and twenty hours of graft. I'll grant you the sea temperature might not be as comfortable as it is further south, but a late season visit will still give enough degrees to make your trip worthwhile. As for that ambience - I can only say that camping on Erraid for a few days, complete with utter isolation (save for the odd yacht or two), a campsite to die for, and scampering minks for company... need I say more? And not a big hairy kilted man in sight.

So here's the information you'll need. Explore, enjoy, and go and try a few of those enticing projects.

Approach

Scotland's crags are a fair distance apart! If you're driving up from the south and heading for the east coast, your journey to the Aberdeen area is likely to bring you up past Edinburgh and on to Dundee, where the A90 takes you up to Stonehaven (Craig Stirling) and on to Peterhead (Red Tower). For the west coast, you'll need to get to Fort William for the road down to Oban, the ferry to Craignure on Mull and the isle of Erraid. For the Baby Taipan Wall, you'll be heading up the A835 from Inverness towards Ullapool, continuing to Reiff for the final leg.

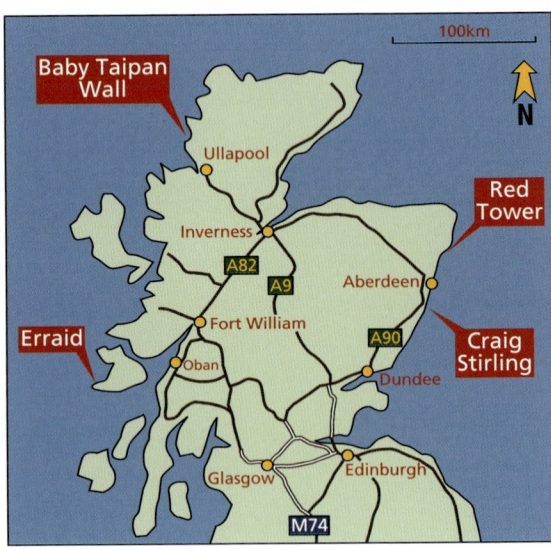

Inverness and its airport is central to all the crags covered here, and it's possible to get reasonably-priced flights to this airport - the web will turn up details on these but a hire car will also be needed.

Conditions and Tides

Be prepared for a 2-3m swing in the tides, although the spring tide variations can nearly reach 5m. It's usually best to choose a high tide, ideally to fit in with a little sunshine. Since most of the venues face northwards to some degree, this generally favours morning climbing. Remember that sea temperatures are at their warmest in September - although splashdowns have occurred in May!

Mike Robertson enjoying sea-washed granite at its best on *Tarka* (6c) - *page 201* - Erraid, West Coast of Scotland. Photo: Julian Lines.

Craig Stirling

In 2006 this crag became the venue for Scotland's first ever deep-water soloing festival. The cliff is split into two buttresses, the water is deep, and the crag reaches eighteen metres in height; thankfully the cruxes of all routes are below 13m - perfect for soloing. The rock is a contorted and banded schist, with amazing texture.

Approach
The crag is 10km south of Aberdeen, between the villages of Portlethen and Newtonhill. Driving south from Aberdeen on the A90, pass the Portlethen turn-off, and then take the road marked East Cammachmore. Follow the single lane road to a Y-fork after 800m. Take the left turning, passing a large house and continue along the track to find parking space by a barn or a little further. Looking out to sea from here, there are two little peaklets - this is the top of the crag. To reach the crag, follow the fence through the field directly down to the coast (5 mins). Alternatively, drive into Newtonhill, park above the harbour and follow the coast path north (10 - 15 mins) to the crag. There are two buttresses split by a bay containing a fallen block, generally known as Fallen Block Bay. The East Buttress is approached by way of either a short down-climb on the left, or an abseil down the central corner. The West Buttress is gained either by an abseil down to one of two ledges, or a 6a+ traverse in (shallow water) from the Fallen Block Bay. Note that the descent down to the Fallen Block is an easy scramble, but take care in damp conditions.

Conditions and Tides
Try to choose a day when there is a gentle northerly breeze, as the rock, especially lower down, can suffer from dampness. A high tide and a calm sea is desirable for all that Craig Stirling has to offer.

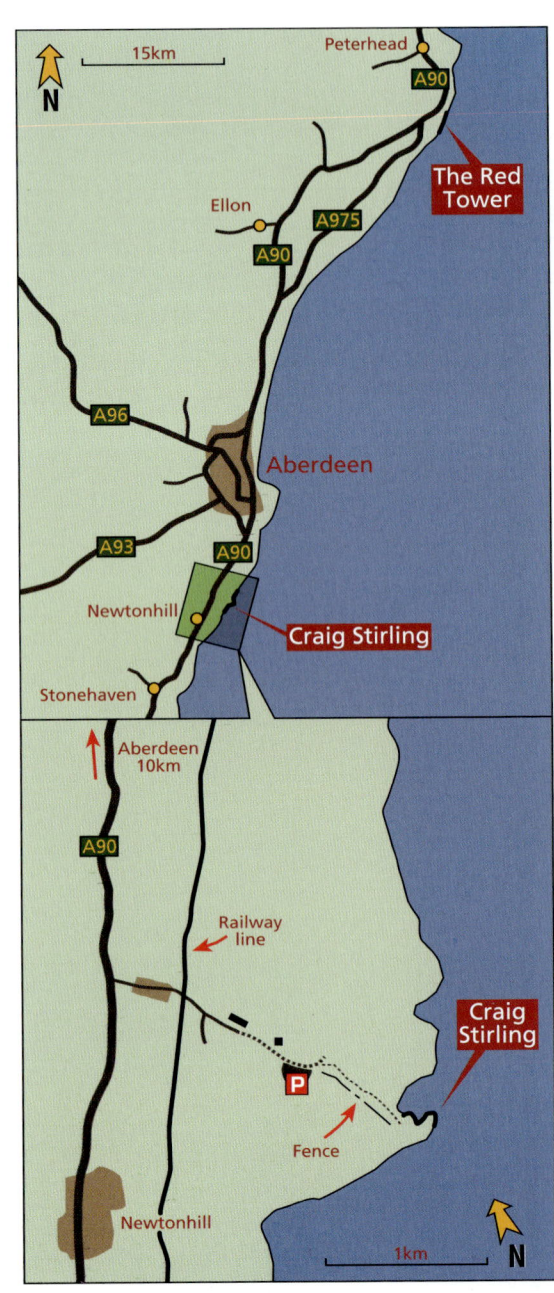

Wilson Moir on the space-walking *Depth Charge* (6b+) - *page 194* - East Buttress, Craig Stirling, Scotland. Photo: Julian Lines.

Craig Stirling — East Buttress

East Buttress

A well-textured schist crag, offering some excellent climbing in a lovely setting.

Approach - An easy traverse in from the left will get you in place; your alternative is to use the *Eastern Girdle*, to traverse in from the right.

Conditions and Tides - Use a big high tide if possible. The crag catches a little morning sun; time your visit to catch it if you can.

① Wet Pussy 6c *S3*
18m. Climb the enticing square cut arete through the overlap, before contemplating the easier upper wall. Take a good look at the sea/ledge beforehand … jump out if it all goes awry.
FSA. Julian Lines 6.2003

② Depth Charge 6a *S3*
20m. A stunning line across the impending wall to gain the hanging arete, first sniffed out, amazingly, by a young Pat Littlejohn. A remarkably popular solo, considering the first section is above a ledge. After gaining the flat ledge on the arete - the 'diving board', the final corner is only grade 4.
FSA. Pat Littlejohn 1978

③ Sea Cat Direct Project .... ? *S3*
18m. The right edge of the fantastic wavy wall surely deserves some attention for those with the confidence. A blind, fingery start gets the juices flowing.

④ Depth Charge Direct 6b+ *S1*
18m. Absolutely classic deep water soloing territory. Jump onto the flying arete to join the parent route. Easier when it's chalked, or harder when it isn't! *See photo on page 193.*
FSA. Wilson Moir 1993

⑤ War Without Tears . 7b *S1*
20m. This fun but burly offering leaves *Jeux Sans Frontieres*, and improvises along the lip of the roof to gain the huge jug out in space. From the jug, power upwards, utilising the arete … alarming!
FSA. Julian Lines 26.8.2006

⑥ Jeux Sans Frontieres ... 6b+ *S1*
20m. Takes on the twin converging cracks in the overhang, and then the easier crack in the wall above. Good fun at a high tide, and it catches the late afternoon sun.
FSA. Wilson Moir 1994

⑦ Upper East Girdle 5 *S1*
25m. A good find, with some exposed climbing at an amenable standard. Traverse in from the Fallen Block Bay, taking the corner initially - before swinging leftwards around a rib to gain a jug rail. Continue to the arete and further exposure.
FSA. Julian Lines 7.2006

⑧ Eastern Girdle 4 *S1*
15m. Pleasant climbing. Heading west-to-east gives a good entry to *Depth Charge* and the rest.
FSA. unknown

West Buttress — Craig Stirling

West Buttress
A great piece of rock, with tasty routes of all grades.
Approach - Abseil from a large block to one of two ledges. Note: there is often a herring gull nest on the Upper Ledge. An alternative approach is to use the last section of *Western Girdle* to traverse in from Fallen Block Bay, at 6a+; take care with this approach, as not all of it is above the sea.
Conditions and Tides
Take a northerly breeze with you if you can, as this dries out the lower sections of the crag. A good high tide is desirable. The wall only gets sun in the very early morning.

9 Stirling Bomber 6b *S0*
6m. A dinky little arete, starting from the lower ledge. It couldn't be any safer... go on, take the challenge! From the upper ledge either traverse left and out or try another route.
FSA. Wilson Moir 8.2002

10 Lean Meat . . . . 6b+ *S1*
20m. The mind-numbing overhanging flake is THE classic tick here, another Scottish plum picked by Pat Littlejohn. Step on, don't look down and sprint for the monster jug on the arete. The upper arete is easy (4) but scary; alternatively reverse *Jack Sprat* to the starting point.
FSA. Dougie Dinwoodie around 1985

11 Raw Meat 6c *S2*
20m. Half-way across *Lean Meat*, take a deep breath and forge up the wall, to a wobbly rock-over onto the yellow slab, finish up the upper arete of *Lean Meat*.
FSA. Julian Lines 15.5.2003

12 Red Meat 7a *S1*
10m. Pull on as for *Lean Meat*, crimp rightwards into a scoop before snapping for the hold on the arete, and continue up the arete.
FSA. Julian Lines 15.5.2003

13 Jack Sprat 6b *S1*
20m. A short, safe and thoroughly absorbing finger-tweaking traverse, which needs a drying breeze. Can be reversed (*S0*), or, veer out from the groove onto the arete.
FSA. Dougie Dinwoodie 1980's

14 Roaring Forties . . . 7a+ *S0*
10m. Leave the *Jack Sprat* traverse and step up a gear to pull swiftly through the overlap, sidle rightwards under the monster roof.
FSA. Julian Lines 15.5.2003

15 Sushi 7c *S1*
15m. Crikey, this isn't the route you came to do…is it? The monster roof above the *Roaring Forties* is outrageous. One measly pocket leads the way to further inverted difficulties to get established in the scoop. The first ascent finished up *Raw Meat*.
FSA. Julian Lines 3.6.2003

16 Project . . . . 7? *S0*
10m. A barnacle grovel is required, before attacking the roof. A low-ish tide and a northerly breeze would be very helpful.

17 Hell and High Water 7a *S2*
30m. Apt - wait for high water, I'm not so sure about hell! Make a diagonal traverse away from *Jack Sprat* to gain a perch; the left end of the slender overlap succumbs to a cheeky left hand layaway. The remainder is easier; scramble out to finish.
FSA. Julian Lines 2.6.2003

18 Between the Devil and the Deep Blue Sea
. . . . 6c *S2/3*
30m. Classic boldness; sorts the men out from the boys. Take the rising traverse out from *Jack Sprat*, and, at the cul de sac, look down very carefully at the submerged boulder below… Commit to the overlap; the exposed wall above isn't as difficult as it looks. Scramble out to finish.
FSA. Julian Lines 6.2001

19 Western Girdle . . . . . . 6b+ *S3*
30m. Added here for completeness; it provides good climbing but is not entirely above water at the start and finish. Abseil onto the mid-tide, tidal ledges at the west end of the crag. Climb the black roofed corner, and exit left to join *Jack Sprat*, reverse *Jack Sprat* (crux - safe) to the higher ledge. Climb down the crack (4) to the lower ledge, before traversing into fallen block bay.
FSA. Wilson Moir 1993

The Red Tower

The beautiful east-facing wall of vertical granite is truly amazing, and the routes are some of the best in north-east Scotland; the classics include *Hole in the Wall* and *Shere Khan*. The wall is ready-made for soloing; around 16m high, and with most of the cruxes just above mid-height - but remember to push out a little if you fall. Sadly there aren't any lower grade routes here.

Approach

Travel north from Aberdeen for 30km (22 miles) on the A90 towards Peterhead. 6km (4 miles) south of Peterhead is a small hamlet called Longhaven, there is a shop and phone box on the left, a useful stop for provisions. Continue for 300m, to a wide quarry entrance on the right, turn down this and follow the track to a ruin/car park by the second right-angled bend. Look in a north-east direction and you will see a solitary derelict wall on the cliff top; the crag is below this wall. Take the twisting coastal path to the wall, and then descend steep grass in a south-west direction to walk over a natural rock arch to access the cliff's flat top (15 mins). To access the routes, either descend easily south and traverse in, or abseil straight down the wall to ledges.

Conditions and Tides

The place is usually sheltered and calm. Take a decent tide, and avoid hot sun for the harder routes, as the rock can feel a little sweaty.

Julian Lines on the classic *Shere Khan* (7c+) - *opposite* - The Red Tower, Scotland.
Photo: Dave Cuthbertson.

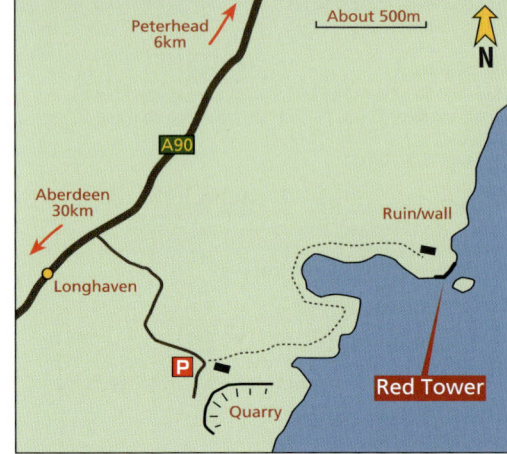

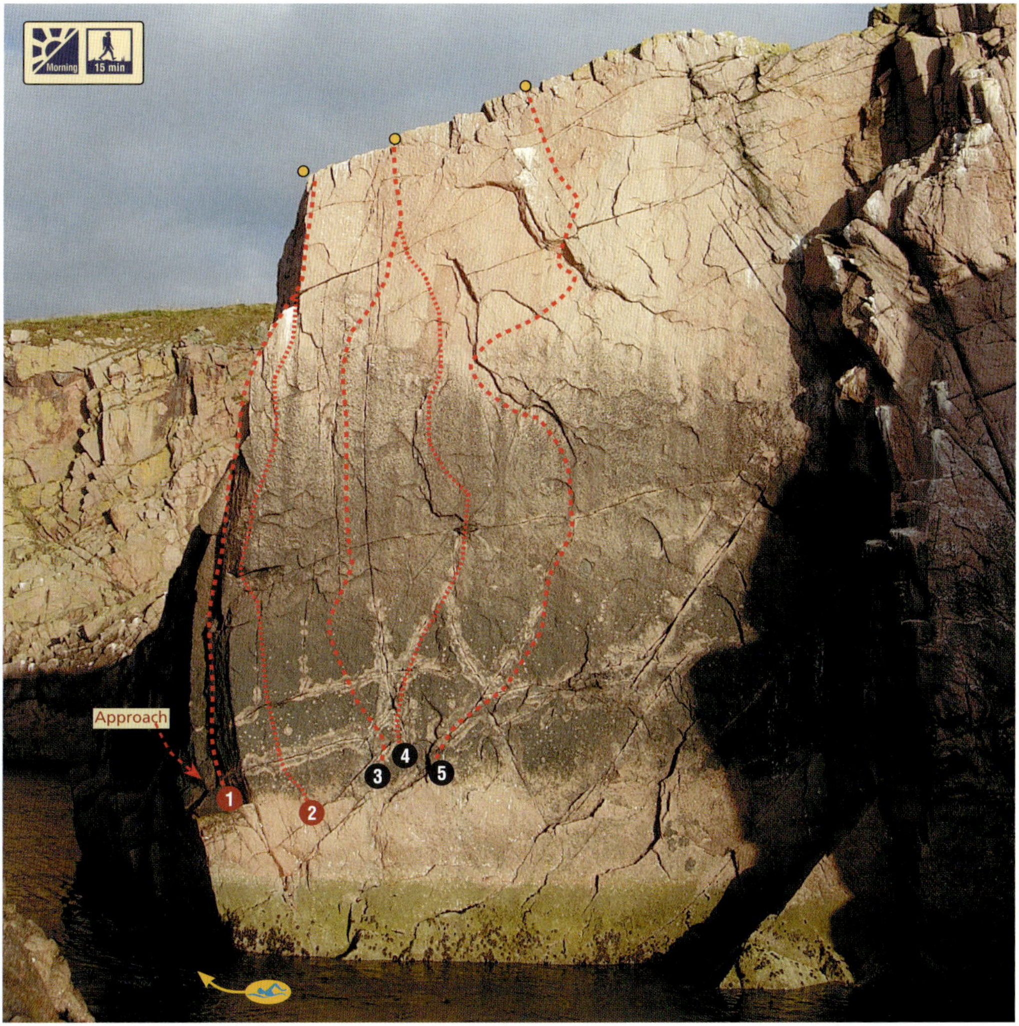

Swanage
Lulworth
Portland
Devon
Cornwall
Pembroke
Scotland
Rest of UK
Portugal
Costa Blanca
Mallorca
Rest of Europe
Australia
Rest of World

1 Mowgli . . . . 2 **6c+** S2
15m. The deceptive, slim tapering groove above a tiny ledge, which gradually eases. Jump backwards if the technicalities defeat you!
FSA. Julian Lines 6.2001

2 Baloo 1 **7a** S1
15m. A great, striking line, but a little contrived. Take the thin crack and then adhere to the arete as best you can.
FSA. Julian Lines 8.1998

3 Shere Khan . . . . 3 **7c+** S1
15m. Stunning. The most coveted deep water solo in Scotland to date. If you've got what it takes, gain the twin parallel cracks and power up them via a sequence of sustained fingertip slapping. *Photo opposite.*
FSA. Julian Lines 21.6.2001

4 Hole in the Wall . . . . 3 **7a+** S1
15m. Inspiring; this is an absolute must. Gain the hole and take a deep breath, then step up and span left before summoning up all your strength to snatch for the elusive jug. The remainder is much easier.
FSA. Wilson Moir 9.1998

5 Bagheera . . . . 3 **7b+** S2
18m. The black purring cat is probably the best and most dangerous route here, giving technically exquisite and absorbing climbing. Sustained moves up the lower wall gain the flake, a blind span is required to negotiate the crux, after which keep a close eye on the water … high tide only.
FSA. Julian Lines 13.6.2001

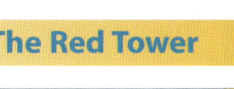

Baby Taipan Wall

The Baby Taipan Wall (GR 996171 on O/S map 15) is located on the Rubha Coigeach peninsula, just to the north of the village of Reiff. This superb wall of 20° overhanging sandstone is a cross between Taipan Wall and Mallorca's Diablo! Although it has been known about for some time, it was only developed as a DWS venue in 2006. The cliff is fifteen to eighteen metres high, with the meat of the routes generally found in the lower portion. Being south-east facing, the crag catches all the morning sun and the outlook to the peaks of Suilven, Cul Mor, Stac Pollaidh are priceless. The drawback is …err… the approach!

Approach

Take the A835 north out of Ullapool for about 15km and turn left onto the single-track road, signposted to Achiltibuie. Continue along here for about 20km, absorbing the stunning scenery all the while, until you reach a T-junction. Turn right and continue into a small hamlet. Turn right again and go past the campsite, to park at the end of the road, close to Achnahaird beach.

Now for the downside; the walk-in takes about an hour. You'll need to head in a north-westerly direction, and it's best to keep to the high ground. Additionally, there is no path and the ground can be boggy. So amble along the vague ridge, passing some cottages, before reaching a high point. From here, follow the shoulder in a north-north-west direction to gain the crag. Alternatively, kayak in from the beach - there is a camping spot on a rocky dais, just above the high tide zone. At the north (right) end of the crag is a large boulder above a black corner. A straightforward abseil down the corner at the right side of the crag is the best way to gain the lower traverse of *Milk and Honey*. This traverse will enable you to reach all the other routes here.

Conditions and Tides

Sheltered, and almost always calm, but don't visit when easterly winds are blowing. Time your visit for late summer, to get the best conditions and avoid the wet streaks of early season. The crag gets the morning sun. Take a reasonably high tide.

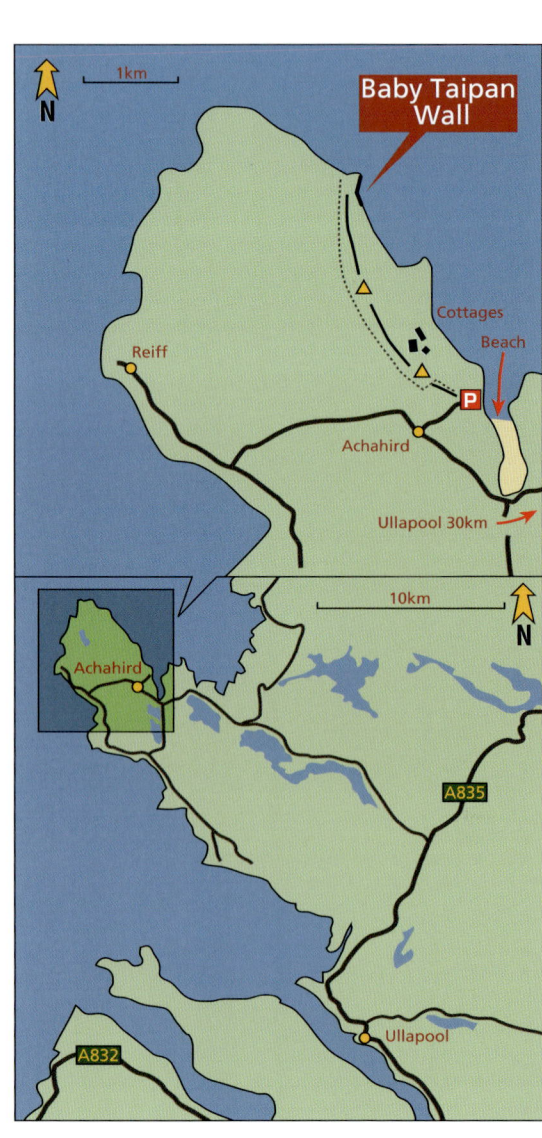

Baby Taipan Wall   199

❶ Land of Milk and Honey. 6b S0
30m. The excellent and pumpy break-line gives access to the other routes here. Great climbing along the perfect traverse, tackled with a sequence of jams and stamina. Can also be reversed.
FSA. Julian Lines 23.07.2006

❷ Project .... 7? S2
20m. A deceptive scoop will be one day reached via crimpy overlaps … deserves attention, good luck!

❸ Project .... 7? S1
30m. The upper traverse will be an energetic affair.

The next three routes take on the central section of the face. You may consider jumping off at the upper break feature. Dry, serious types should finish up the upper section of Acacia.

❹ Semi-skimmed 6c S1
20m. The left-most line of holds on the central face. Expect slopers, layaways and dinner plates. A pleasurable grapple.
FSA. Julian Lines 24.07.2006

❺ Manuka .... 6b+ S1
10m. A most enjoyable climb taking the left hand crack-line, just keep on pulling.
FSA. Julian Lines 14.10.2006

❻ Cyber Pimp ... 6c S1
15m. The fine crack-line runs out at a shield; forge past this with vigour to a rest under the roof.
FSA. Julian Lines 14.10.2006

❼ Project .... 7? S2
15m. A desperate line that cleaves the headwall … only talented and brave hearts need apply for this one.

❽ Acacia .... 6b+ S1
15m. The stunning flake-line cleaving the face. Muscular moves lead to a decent rest, and delicate shuffling out rightwards through the overlapping slabs completes your journey.
FSA. Julian Lines 23.07.2006

❾ Project .... 7? S1
15m. Tiny holds and breaks lead leftwards to a right-facing flake.

❿ The Ganges .... 6b+ S1
15m. A superb and varied route, tackling the black overhanging flake feature; the finish is wonderfully delicate. Can suffer from a little seepage, but it doesn't affect the climbing.
FSA. Julian Lines 13.10.2006

⓫ Project .... 7b? S1
15m. The overhanging face left of the arete has one strangely appealing, powerful move to gain the break; either continue via an odd scoop, or move out right to the arete.

⓬ Project .... 8? S1
15m. The awesome lower arete will succumb … maybe!

⓭ Project .... 7? S1
15m. The black overlap on the north-facing wall. Vicious crimping. Finish up the upper arete.

Erraid

Erraid is stunning, providing a landscape of absolute serenity, golden granite and crystal-clear water. The island's southern bay houses the deep water solos, and goes by the name of David Balfour's Bay, after the character in Robert Louis Stevenson's novel 'Kidnapped', in which David Balfour finds himself shipwrecked on the isle.

The routes are found on the north-east-facing side of the bay, and attract sunshine until about 9.30 am in the summer. The stunning Paradise Wall provides the main action, with the Otter Wall offering a few stylish extras.

Approach

From Fionnphort on the Isle of Mull, drive south to reach the tiny hamlet of Knockvalagan. Park at the farm (free), and walk west, to reach the tidal beach separating Erraid from Mull. Cross this (only presents a problem at whopping spring tides) and walk west across the bogs for about 30 minutes or so, to finally drop down into David Balfour's Bay itself. There's amazing wild camping here, and the crag can be seen from your tent!

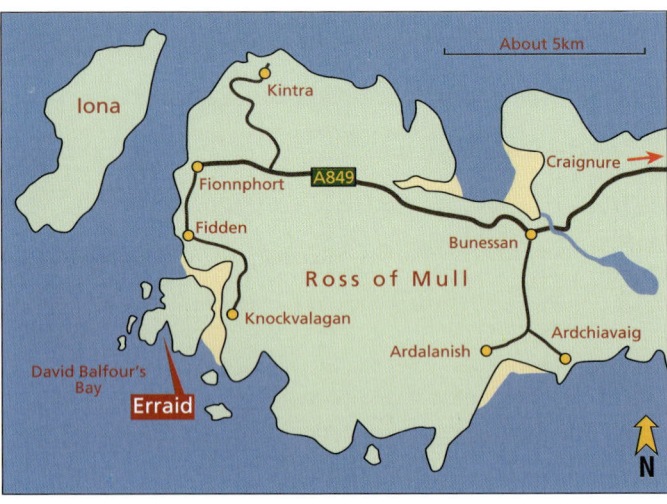

To reach the crag, follow the vague path around the beach/bay and follow your nose, until you reach a deep gully (this forms the inner/right edge of the Paradise Wall) with a makeshift plank across it. The routes on the Otter Walls and the Paradise Wall are reached by crossing the plank and continuing through ferns, to gain the top of the Otter Walls. *Drowning in Adrenaline* and *Monkey Business* are reached by dropping down the ridge facing the Paradise Wall, which also serves as your viewing gallery. The mega-classic *Brine Shrine* and the rest of the routes are reached by walking around and either abseiling in from blocks or down-climbing a groove some 9m left of the *Project Route 3*.

Conditions and Tides

The bay is well-sheltered, so generally expect calm seas. The rock is usually dry; good weather in late season should provide the goods. An early start finds the sun on this wall, select a decent high tide for any climbing here.

Erraid

Paradise Wall

Otter Wall

1 Ring of Bright Water ... 6a+ *S1*
35m. The traverse of the well-featured Otter Wall. From the seaward end, traverse all the way in to gain the edge of the box inlet. Reverse out for the given grade, or alternatively, continue on, possibly using boulders for the feet, to gain the corner beyond. Finish up the right arete of the corner (grade for the extension tide-dependent; between 6c+ and 7b).
FSA. Julian Lines 21.8.2002

2 Tarka ... 6c *S0*
11m. The bulging nose in the wall provides the spice. From the left, traverse in, moving up to gain the prominent chockstone. A pull up and right gains a flared flake-crack, sprint up this to easier ground. *See photo on page 191.*
FSA. Julian Lines 21.8.2002

Paradise Wall

The following routes all start by either a short abseil or a steady down-climb, in a groove located some 9m left of the Project.

3 Project ... 7c+? *S0*
8m. The desperate seam splitting the left edge of the wall will respond to the right person. Can't win 'em all ...

4 Brine Shrine ... 6b *S0*
10m. Total class; one of Scotland's finest. The burly off-width crack is less off-width than you'd think! From a 'lie-down' rest at the base of the route, tackle the crack directly and with vigour; from a sneaky hands-off rest at just above half-height, continue up to a pumpy leftwards finish. There is also a right-hand finish at a slightly harder 6b+.
FSA. Julian Lines 16.7.2001

5 Please Rub Salt into my Wounds
... 6b+ *S0/1*
11m. Brilliant; another forearm-pumping little number. Throw yourself at the central crack, and continue, with sustained interest, to exit via a deep groove at the top. *See photo on page 188.*
FSA. Andy Spink 1996

6 Dreamline ... 7a *S1*
12m. The right-hand of the three cracks is another absolute gem. The tide level does affect foothold choice - and the easiest sequence will give shallower water than really desired. From the traverse in, make hard moves to gain the crack, and follow it all the way to a solid exit.
FSA. Gary Latter 17.7.2001

7 Drowning in Adrenaline
... 7a *S1/2*
15m. The absolute business; a pumpy rising traverse of the highest order. You'll need a less-than high tide to get started, as, much as above, the tide level does affect foothold choice - and also the S grade and the overall grade. From the lower gully perform a huge bridging move to gain the base of the wall, and aim yourself confidently towards the finish of *Brine Shrine*.
FSA. Julian Lines 18.7.2001

8 Monkey Business ... 6a to 6c *S0/1*
28m. The traverse of the right-most section of the crag is long and fun. Expect the grade to vary according to the tide.
FSA. Mike Robertson, Julian Lines 6.2005

Rest of the UK

Further promises: the intrepid Julian Lines on fresh rock near Rhue, Ullapool, north-west Scotland. Photo: Cubby Images.

Rest of the UK

Neil Gresham on the classic *Bathtime* (7a) - *page 209* - Bathtime Wall, Vivian Quarry, North Wales. Photo: Jerry Moffatt

The UK section of this guide was by far the hardest to catalogue, photograph and document, despite it all sitting right here on our doorstep. There's a good reason for this - here in the UK, we have an incredible amount of rock above the sea, and so much of it fits within the parameters of what is considered generally acceptable for DWS. Of course it wasn't possible to accurately document the lot, and many surprises undoubtedly remain - this section is to remind you of your obligation to go out and find some more!

So here are a few pointers as to what's still out there in the UK. It includes detailed information for the Vivian Slate Quarry - this guide's only UK fresh water venue. The other areas are given brief coverage only; nothing solid, and no grades, just some ideas. Go and play!

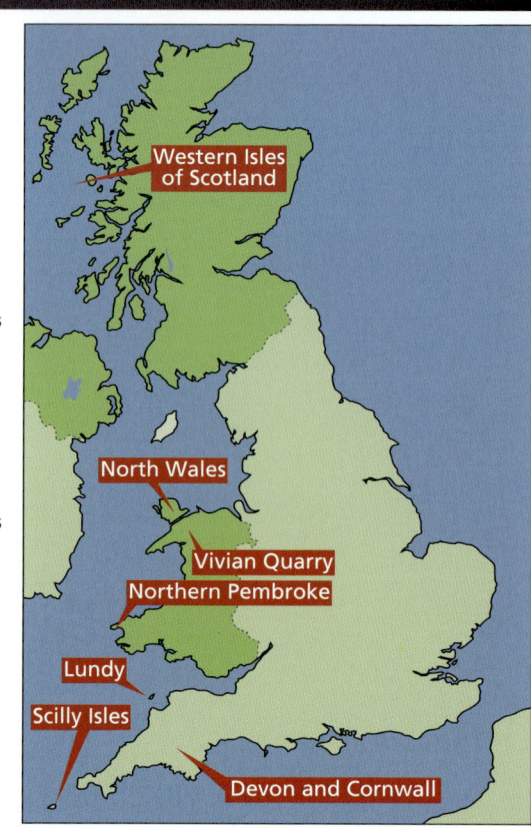

Granite perfection: Neil Gresham on the first solo ascent of *The Flying Dutchman* (7b+) Lundy, Devon. Photo: Simon Cardy.

Devon and Cornwall's South Coast

The south coast of Devon and Cornwall probably still harbour some little gems, although it does seem likely that any big, accessible areas have already been found. Boat owners might need to pay a visit to the bays found to the south of Kingswear, where a kayak foray by myself turned up some rather stunning rock, located in a bay that looked like it belonged in Thailand. There may well also be snippets in the regions of Chapel Point and Dodman Point (both found close to Mevagissey).

Scilly Isles

The low-slung, orange-granite islands found some 40km off Land's End have long been known for their tranquillity, their crystal clear seas, and their two-hundred or so islands. Most of these are not what you'd call high (or large) but information indicates the possibility of deep water solos on at least two of the larger islands. You can take a ferry to the isles from Penzance, or fly from Land's End. It is recommended that you take an ocean kayak. There is camping next to the accessible tidal beach on the island of St Agnes.
Find general info at **www.islesofscilly-travel.co.uk**.
Also recommended is nipping off down there on a settled high pressure forecast, and avoiding the bird season, when most of the smaller islands are banned from visitors. Your best bet is a visit at the end of August or early September.

Dave Pickford on the highly entertaining *Gawain's Arete* (6a) Tintagel, Atlantic Coast, Cornwall. Photo: Mike Robertson.

Atlantic Coast
The wild and atmospheric Atlantic Coast, comprising of Devon and Cornwall's upper, west-facing coastlines, has long been regarded as the bastion of big trad adventures, but there are DWS possibilities remaining. In the region of Tintagel, a huge block dubbed 'Merlin's Thumb' gave a small number of solos, including the very photogenic *Gawain's Arete* (6a) - *see photo left*.

Lundy
Granite often suffers from one considerable drawback for deep water soloists: the general slabbiness of the rock. It goes without saying that the *Devil's Slide* is not going to be on your DWS list! But there is steep granite on the isle: how about Starship Zawn, where a summer 2006 trip saw the seamed, technical face of *The Flying Dutchman* (*see photo on page 205*) finally go down, and at a grade of about 7b+. The route was described by the first solo ascensionist as being truly outstanding.

North Pembroke
2006 saw the development of the amazing new venue of Barrel Zawn - discovered in August by some bloke in a kayak - lucky bugger! But this kayak exploring idea really does work. So why not plan a trip from Milford Haven, heading all the way around the beautiful St. Bride's bay, past St. David's, to finish around in Fishguard Bay? This would give three or four days of sheer pleasure, and you'll almost certainly grab some brand new solos.

North Wales
There's a wealth of DWS gems in North Wales that are unsung and usually known only by the local contingent. In the vicinity of Lower Pen Trywn and Pigeon's Cave, the 160m traverse *The Water Margin* (5) might prove to be a good DWS, but only if you abseil in to find the appropriate tide level (fairly high). Just around the corner, a look at Dutchman's Zawn, TMS Zawn and Gateau Zawn will reveal some excellent possibilities, including the three-star 7b *Truly, Madly, Steeply*, and the tasty *Riders in the Chariot* (about 6c). Take the North Wales Rockfax and check these out, but bear in mind that, in addition to making up the S grades as you go along, extended wet weather does sometimes render these north-facing venues damp. On the Little Orme, there's certain to be many routes lying in wait for the dedicated, whilst over in Gogarth there's all sorts of potential, with some of it already realised. *Electric Blue* (6b+) has proved to be an absolutely classic DWS, with dozens of solo ascents to date. See also the Vivian Quarry section on page 208.

Scotland
Scotland is just massive, and with a lengthy and diverse coastline to match. In addition to the major venues described already in the guide, there have been bits of DWS development all over the east coast, which is more sheltered from the Atlantic, but maybe the future main event has to be the monumentally wild west coast. Who out there can claim to have really explored islands such as the architecturally amazing Staffa (home of the amazing Fingal's Cave), set just a little north of Erraid (see page 200). And to the south-east of Erraid, you'll find the big and beautiful island of Jura (60 miles west of Glasgow), where there are definite murmurings of solo-style adventures to be had. But possibly the most potential I can highlight here must go to the breathtaking chain known as the Western Isles. This stunning spread of islands will give views seen nowhere else in the natural world, and its southerly chain of Mingulay, Pabbay and Barra hold more unexplored secrets than can be imagined.

Vivian Quarry

The beautifully positioned Bathtime Wall in Vivian Quarry has long been the scene of DWS shenanigans. Indeed, tales tell of intrepid soloists breaking contact with its rock way back in the lycra-clad eighties! The protruding lump of slate itself is known as the Vivian Prow, with the south-east face known as the Bathtime Wall. It's all nicely suspended above water, the rock is generally pretty good, and the sun hangs around about until early afternoon.

The water itself is at least 20m deep, so don't even consider the possibility of hitting the bottom (rumours abound of a Volkswagon Beetle residing on the very distant bottom; scuba divers only need apply). The drawback is the slightly lofty height of the wall, hence the perky S grades and the even spread of heart 'flutter' symbols. You'd better add to this the unnerving 'flatness' of the water's surface - the Llanberis tombstoners have long been known for their rock-hurling practices prior to the jump off the highest point, known as 'Nicky's Leap' (the rock breaks the surface tension, thus easing your entry.)

The height itself, with the routes touching around 16-19m on the finishing holds, means the venue is only going to be of interest to dedicated soloists, but please note that many of the cruxes are not higher than about 14m above the drink, and the finishes, once given a quick clean, especially around the heather cornices, should be a bit of a formality. Use an exit rope if unsure, and also bear in mind that the grades of the routes are yet to be set in stone - this is due to lack of traffic, so please leave a little in reserve!

Access
The Bathtime wall is currently shut to climbing during the opening hours of the Vivian Diving Centre, although this exclusion might be stretched to 'active' hours, as diving often gets underway as late as 1pm. Call in at the centre for further info, or call them on 01286 870889.

Approach
From the east edge of Llanberis town, on the main through road (the A4086), take the road signed to the Welsh Slate Museum and Padarn Country Park. Follow the road northwards for a kilometre or so, taking a left, and continue past the museum to arrive at the huge Padarn Park car park. From the 'Llanberis Lake Railway' building, walk past the Vivian Diving Centre and through the adjacent arch into Vivian Quarry. A look to the left will give you a perfect view of the Bathtime Wall. For access to the top of the Bathtime wall, locate the upper tarmac link path, which will take you to a short path that leads to the Vivian Prow itself.

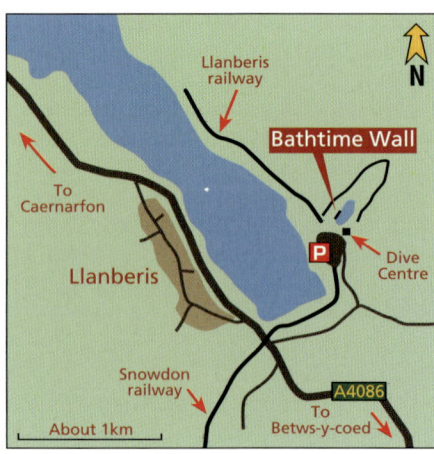

Where to Stay
There are lots of options locally, ranging from plentiful camping to huts and B&Bs.

Conditions
The wall is sheltered and fairly fast-drying, and conditions in the summer season will usually present no problems. Avoid climbing after heavy rain, when the finishes might prove troublesome.

Bathtime Wall Vivian Quarry

The first two routes both start from ground level. Access is via the base path, along the left edge of the pool. There's a slight ramp under the water here - watch out for this, and also observe the old railway track protruding slightly at the water's edge.

❶ The Order of the Bath
7b S3
24m. A high, rising traverse of the Bathtime Wall - an intimidating outing. Climb the stepped feature (easy; not DWS), and continue on, now above water, to cross the next four routes. Finish as for *Soap on a Rope*.
NYS

❷ The Wishing Well
7b S2/3
18m. A slanted seam marks the path of this excellent and sustained line. From the small tree, make hard moves up into the seam, and follow it all the way to the top.
FSA 'almost' Simon Bull 1980's

The next two routes both start from an ancient (but very substantial) bolted-in bracket, a couple of metres above the drink. Abseil from the top trees to the bracket; the 'tape-harness' arrangement might prove useful at the base, although not essential.

❸ Sucked Away with the Scum
7c S2/3
18m. A very powerful and sustained bit of climbing. The crux is high, and there's a very slight chance of touching the bracket in the event of a low fall - be aware of this. From the bracket, step left, and climb the white-streaked wall, past three bolt runners, to finish at the gnarly tree.
NYS?

❹ I Ran the Bath
7b S2/3
18m. Brilliant. From the bolted bracket, climb up and right, to cross a shield feature. Climb the centre of the wall, into a slight groove, and make hard moves to gain a massive jug rail. Continue more easily, to two possible exits (left to the small gnarly tree is recommended).
FSA. Trevor Hodgson 1987

The final three routes all rise from the spacious, vegetated ledge on the right/lower edge of the wall - an easy place for a couple of DWS loons to chill and jettison a harness.

❺ Bathtime
7a S3
19m. Enticing ground. From the ledge, traverse down and left for some 5m towards the ancient protruding bracket, then climb the wall above to gain a flake-system. Either finish directly past a pink-ish scar (cleaning recommended), or finish back right on *Soap'* at around 6c+. *See photo on page 204.*
PFSA Neil Gresham 1980's

❻ Dope on a Rope
6c S2/3
21m. This route is good, but is basically a link between *Bathtime* and *Soap on a Rope*. From below the base of the flake-system on *Bathtime*, move up and right to join *Soap on a Rope*. Finish as for that route.
FSA. By various Llanberis slateheads, 1980's

❼ Soap on a Rope
6c S2/3
19m. The best route on the face, with excellent climbing all the way; an absolute classic. From the start ledge, climb up the right arete of the face, using good side-pulls to get onto the face proper. Move up past the bolt (blue tat), and continue up the very arete of the Bathtime Wall to good jugs about three metres below the top. Top-out more easily. Superb!
FSA. By various Llanberis slateheads, 1980's

Portugal

DWS perfection. Julian Lines on *Anthony Hopkins* (6b+) - *page 230* - the Garcia Wall at Ponta Garcia, Portugal. Photo: Mike Robertson

Portugal

Welcome to Sagres, Portugal's gateway to all the rugged Atlantic coast has to offer. The town of Sagres is found on Portugal's south-west tip, and provides the deep water soloist with Ingrina and Ponta Garcia - two magnificent and well-catalogued limestone venues, which have seen all their development packed into the last few years. Couple their accessibility with warm, late season seas, and you have what amounts to a DWS paradise. You wouldn't expect the Atlantic Ocean at Sagres to offer only a 0.8m tidal variation, much like the Mediterranean, but that is what Portugal's south coast provides. More essential than tide watching is grabbing the days when the surf is down, however with both crags enjoying some form of shelter from the Westerlies, this can be easier than you'd think.

Getting There

The town of Sagres is found on the far west end of Portugal's famous Algarve coastline, and is about an 80-minute drive from Faro international airport. Flights to Faro are plentiful and usually very good value. Try the usual low-cost airline websites.
From Faro airport, follow the blue signs to the A22 motorway. Get on the westbound carriageway, signposted to Portimao and Lisbon. Head west and stay on the A22, eventually picking up signs for 'Vila do Bispo' and Sagres. The route takes you around the western edge of Lagos, on the N125. Carry on to Vila do Bispo, and take the signs south to Sagres. The route is a little over 100km.

Getting Around

With two crags now on the agenda, it's not likely you'll manage easily without a hire car, as Ingrina Beach is a 17km drive from Sagres. The usual cheaper pre-booked deals on small hatchbacks are available, and Sept/Oct prices tend to be more sensible. What is sure is that you won't spend much on petrol! Sagres is fantastically chilled, and the town will probably provide you with everything you'll need.

When to go

At the end of the summer is ideal - this gives slightly cooler climbing weather, cheaper flights, and warmer water! (The sea is somewhere between 20°C and 24°C at the beginning of September depending on the summer they've just had.) Early-September to mid-October is probably the optimum time to pay a visit.

Gavin Symonds going for it on the crux of *Super Bock* (7c) - *page 219* - in the Main Cave at Ingrina. Photo: Mike Robertson.

Conditions and Tides

As you'd expect, any area which offers surfing on the menu must sometimes be rough! That said, you'd be surprised by the number of relatively calm days here, and also by the amount of shelter the crags get, especially the east-facing bay that houses Ponta Garcia. So take a good team, scope your swim-outs well, and have a rest day when the sea gets choppy. The tides on Portugal's south coast are surprisingly benign too; this is the mighty Atlantic Ocean but the tidal movement is always less than 1m.

Accommodation

Cheap accommodation is quite easy to find, with a massive number of cheap-ish guest houses and apartments in town - brush up on your Portugese and try to do a deal. The Ingrina campsite and the Orbitur campsite near Garcia both offer shower facilities, so if your only concern is personal hygiene, consider the problem solved.

There's also a wealth of beautiful cliff-top bivis in the area. The sandy area just on the town side of Garcia is great, and for somewhere nicely close to the water, try the low cliff-top at Martinhal, just the other side of the harbour - it's wonderful (beach dossers/lovers will adore Martinhal's lovely beach for the same reason).

Food and Beer

There's plenty of choice in Sagres for sustenance. 'Pastelaria Marreiros' in the town square is perfect for breakfast/coffee, and cheap - try the 'Sandes Mista' (delicious cheese and ham sarnies, available hot). The 'Dromedario Bistro' is a fine venue for that evening meal and drink, and also houses a 'new routes' info file. The climbing Bar/Cafe of choice is the 'Bubble Lounge', just off the square. The AliSuper supermarkets offer just about everything in the way of food and beverages. As for the rest of town, there's a market, a pharmacy, a shop that sells face masks, rubber shoes and kiddy boats, a total of three internet outlets, a very quiet police station, and a Tourist Info that sells Algarve maps.

What to Take

A few pairs of boots, and a large collection of chalk bags. A 15-litre dry-bag is the next most useful bit of kit; this facilitates access to some of the most bizarre cave 'starts' known to man. It's also worth buying a cheap inflatable boat in town (two shops sell these in Sagres), because this will give you some additional viewing scenarios and a social scene to die for.

Pure 'SO' pleasure. Elinor Currey enjoying perfect rock on *The Smile* (6a+) - *page 220* - Ingrina, Portugal. Photo: Mike Robertson.

Ingrina

Ingrina is an amazing place. With a massive batch of S0's, a crag that rarely touches 12m, and angles that are often a little more 'steady' than the canted, gutsy angles of Ponta Garcia, the venue's position in the DWS history books is fully guaranteed. Add to this easy access almost everywhere, brilliant gear-up ledges and excellent viewing and beta points, and you have a world-class arrangement. The main Ingrina beach is simply beautiful, with a palm-tree surrounded bar and good parking. The walk-in to the crag from the cliff-top car park is no more than 5 minutes. The camp site is a pretty chilled-out example, with its own bar and restaurant, and some colourful clientele.
I can't sing the crag's praises highly enough.

Approach

From the Fortaleza roundabout in Sagres, drive out of town, past Vila do Bispo, to the first set of traffic lights (about 11km). Turn right, and take the first tarmac right turn, marked 'Ingrina Beach'. Drive this road for about 6km, passing the turn signed 'Camping Ingrina' on the right, to arrive at the beach, where a right turn finds the small car park on the western edge of the beach. Look for the dirt track up the hill to the right, and follow it up to the rise. If you have low clearance on your car, park in the first car parking area - if clearance is no problem, continue to the second. From the red-soiled, second car park space, walk along the main trail heading south-west, skirting a valley to the left, and heading for the high point of the promontory ahead. Once beyond the high point of the headland, you'll find some very big holes in the ground, and you'll also have your first view of Ingrina's Main Cave, seen down and to the right. Walk down the series of easy rocky shelves to reach an excellent gearing-up spot. This spot is actually between the Main Cave and the Smiley Face. Get amongst it!

Conditions and Tides

Ingrina's tides are tiny, so focus instead on the sea state, which is infinitely variable. Visit on warm, crisp days, when the main cave will be in best condition.

Main Cave - Left Ingrina

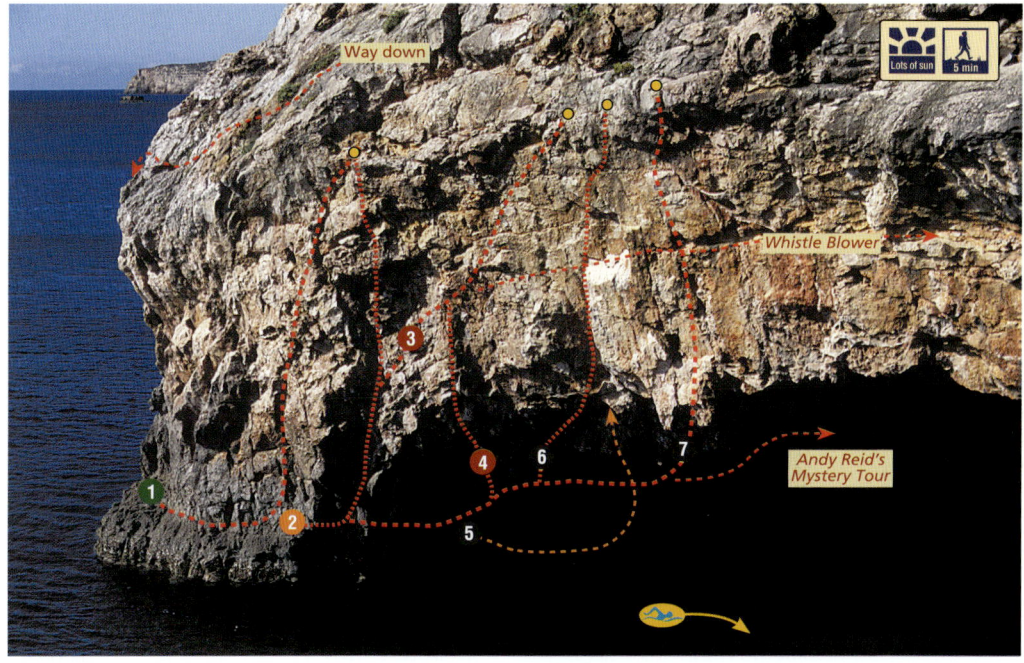

① In the Flesh . . . . 4+ *SO*
11m. From the lower traverse, take the easy jug, passing just right of a jutting, tall block. Finish up the big flake/groove feature.
FSA. Julian Lines 23.9.2005

② The Stripper . . . . 6a *SO*
12m. Some burly moves at the bottom give the crux. From the traverse, continue steeply under the last route, to climb up to a rest at half-height. From here, climb leftwards, to finish easily as for the previous route. Don't forget your shorts.
FSA. Mike Robertson 23.9.2005

③ Dromedario . . . . . . 6b *SO*
13m. A pumpy little classic! Brilliant, sustained climbing all the way, with no real rests. The holds, however, are all BIG. Traverse in as for *The Stripper*, and attack the rising line of jugs to the right, crossing the top of a steep corner on your way to a final rock-over onto a small, arched slab.
FSA. Mike Robertson 23.9.2005

④ Comedy of Errors . . 6c+ *SO*
14m. A dynamic crux should see a few flyers! The low face under *Dromedario* is very steep and sustained. From the low traverse of *The Stripper*, keep low, past a glued-in white fang hold, to gain a comfortable 'wedged-shoulders' rest. Dive up and left (crux), to finally join *Dromedario*.
FSA. Mike Robertson 23.9.2005

⑤ Project . . . . 7c+? *SO*
18m. A very powerful line, taking the grossly steep face below *White Dove's* twin slab feature. From the white fang described in *Comedy of Errors*, attack the roof above to emerge onto the twin slabs; finish up *White Dove*.

Main Cave - Left
The left side of Ingrina's Main Cave is packed with quality routes and great rock, and with a useful spread of grades.

Approach - All routes are approached from the left, by way of the end face. Either climb down the face on good rock and good holds at around 3/3+ (NOT DWS), or put a short abseil rope in (wires/slings) to abseil to good sea level ledges.

Conditions and Tides - Expect plenty of sunshine on the upper section of the cave, and try to get crisp conditions for venturing down into the shadows. The tides will prove irrelevant; a calm sea is more important.

⑥ Project . . . . 7b+? *SO*
15m. This amazing line has yet to be climbed. Follow *White Dove* to the second rest, swing left and up to the perfect corner and take this to the top. Will one day be a classic.

⑦ White Dove . . . . . . 7a+ *SO*
16m. An absolutely stunning line, taking on all the features of the cave's left flank. From the 'shoulders rest' on *Comedy of Errors*, press on across the two hanging slabs to the right. A hard-to-find rest above the second slab leads to a jug romp around the roof above. Continue up the steep wall above, until it's possible to move right, into a final flake-line.
FSA. Julian Lines 23.9.2005

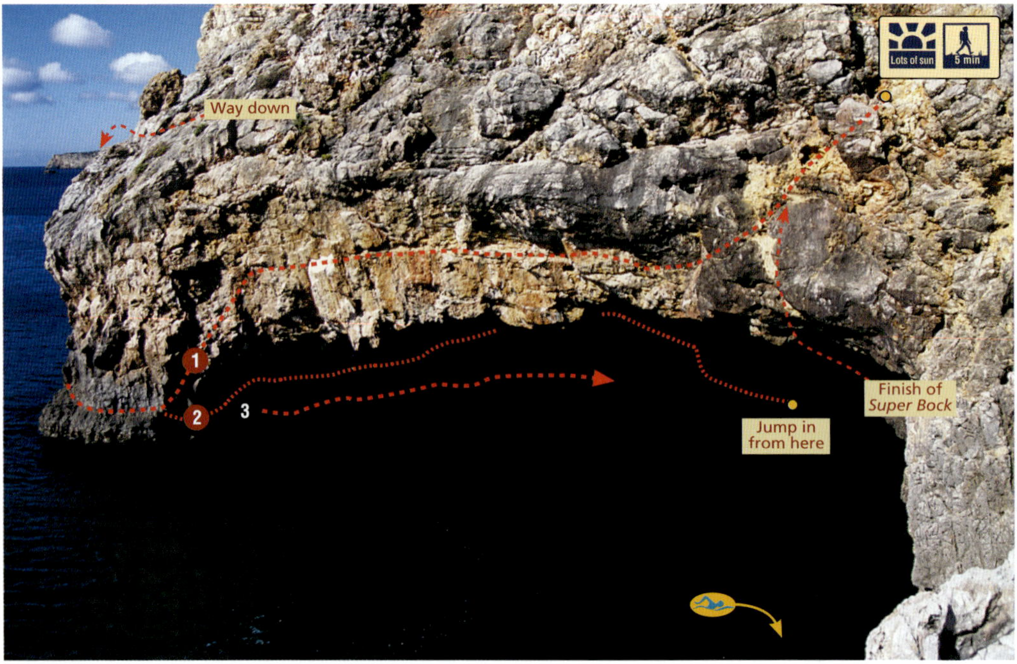

Ingrina Main Cave - Centre

Main Cave - Centre

These lines take on the beefiness of the whole cave, and are essentially traverses. They are long and involved, and require a little savvy to find the correct line on, especially the gloriously wandering *Andy Reid's Mystery Tour*.

Approach - The routes are all reached from the Main Cave - Left as detailed on the previous page.

Conditions and Tides - You'll only need a sunny, dry day and a calm sea for your chosen outing.

❶ The Whistle Blower. 6c+ S1
22m. The upper traverse of the cave. The line is fairly obvious, taking the sunlit area in the upper section, starting from the left side. The drawback is one or two wobbly holds - not the usual state of affairs at this crag! The final 6m will feel quite unnerving. Start by down-climbing the last 3m of *In the Flesh*. Cross all the left routes to gain the top of the short corner, and keep on traversing right at about the same level. Finish on *Super Bock's* slab.
FSA. Julian Lines 27.9.2005

❷ Andy Reid's Mystery Tour
.... 6c+ S0
25m. A weaving and absorbing line, dallying with the spectral light of the atmospheric inner cave. Start as for *White Dove*, gaining that route's rest on the second slab. From there, continue rightwards, following your nose, at about the same level. You'll eventually find, after a wacky series of ups and downs, rests and ripping body moves, a way back down to sea level, where a couple of green scars are found just above the water-line. Jump in and swim out.
FSA. Julian Lines 23.9.2005

❸ Project .... 7b+? S0
22m. The engaging sea level traverse, starting as for *Comedy of Errors*. Stay low on the barnacle line to gain the lower, inner cave. Very steep and pumpy.

❹ Stab in the Dark ... 7a S0
11m. A riveting and energetic voyage, up the dark side of the preposterously steep, hanging prow. Start beneath the prow on a ledge just above the sea. Climb the inner side of the prow, with a series of massive locks, to eventually gain an inviting through-cave and a rest. Slip in here for a nice lie down, and then drop out, traversing down a ramp to finish up the final moves of *Queen of Cool*. Ace!
FSA. Mike Robertson 23.9.2005

Finding Ingrina
Mike and Ju arrive at Sagres, after their epic 1000km drive all the way from the Spanish Costa Blanca. They pop in for a beer at Dromedario Bar where they carefully line their stomachs with Super Bock, the local brew. They pull the 'new route book' down from the shelf, and find a small sketch from Andy Reid, veteran of countless trad new routing trips to the Sagres area. "Here you go, lads" begin the words next to the tiny penciled map. "Some DWS possibilities for you". The Reid-map shows the location of Ingrina Beach and the caves, and the next day the two DWS addicts climb a total of 24 new lines.

Main Cave - Right Ingrina   219

❺ Super Bock 7c *S0*
11m. What a beast; this undertaking will confound all but the very strong. Start at the base of the blowhole. Climb the first few moves of *Queen of Cool*, nip up its ramp to gain the through cave rest shared with *Stab in the Dark*, and then climb out, heading out and out. Desperate moves get you to the outer/sunny edge of the cave and then climb up a tiny slabby groove. *See photo on page 213*.
FSA. Gavin Symonds 30.9.2005. Named after the local brew.

❻ Queen of Cool .... 6c+ *S1*
10m. Steep, steep. A terrific route! The start moves do, however, have a distracting ledge; a spotter here will provide a little security. From the base of the blowhole, climb up and out on powerful locks, to gain the ramp-line (a deviation to rest in the hole on the left gives a 6c variation). Head up and right, to a final hard sequence, gaining the slight cut-out at the very top.
FSA Mike Robertson 23.9.2005

❼ Cerveza, Por Favor . 6b *S1*
9m. This excellent, slightly less wilting line is found ascending some big scoops high up, just right (looking in) of the access blowhole. Access is recommended from the right (see above), as the start moves will feel safer from that side. Climb the steep wall up to the scoop features, and finish directly above.
FSA. Julian Lines 23.9.2005

Main Cave - Right
More top fun to be had here, mainly in the form of very steep stuff, although the right-hand routes are a little more amenable.
Approach - To get down to sea level, simply scramble down the accommodating blowhole feature - it takes you straight there! The quicker alternative for the right-most routes is to traverse in easily from the right.
Conditions and Tides - A calm sea will help when negotiating the lower ledges, and crisp conditions will help when climbing on the routes in the shadows. The tide level is unimportant.

❽ Ilvico 6a *S0*
9m. Steady at last! This safe line climbs the prominent crack. From the slab on the right, traverse left across the lower reef/ramp and enter the left-trending crack. Follow it all the way to the top.
FSA. Julian Lines 23.9.2005

❾ Clear Cut 6a *S1*
8m. Another amenable little number; fun, and very photogenic. From the right-hand access slab, swing left onto the reef and climb the arete, staying slightly on its left for the best water.
FSA. Elinor Currey 25.9.2005

Ingrina Smiley Face

Smiley Face

The well-formed face below the gearing-up ledge is home to some fine routes, consisting of mostly steep climbing. The highest point of the wall is 12m high, the water below it is mostly excellent, and the rock of impeccable quality.

Approach - The routes are easily accessed from the left gully (looking in), with the exception of *White Teeth*, which is reached comfortably from the gully on the other end. Both approaches are about grade 3.

Conditions and Tides - Plenty of water and plenty of sun; the wall is usually in good condition.

❶ The Prow 7a S0
6m. The first route found after the descent is a tight line, taking the left prow of the crag very direct. Swing around from the descent, grasp some small holds, and blast up the prow to arrive at the finishing shelf of *The Smile*.
FSA. Julian Walker 25.9.2005

❷ The Smile 6a+ S1
9m. A solid, steady intro to the delights of DWS! From the down-climb, traverse right-wards to a steep, juggy groove. Yard up this, and follow the shelf around to the left, to a easy finish. *See photo on page 215*.
FSA. Mike Robertson 23.9.2005

❸ Smiley's People 6b S0/1
12m. The delightful collection of jugs in the steep, upper groove is 'lotsa' fun! Start up *The Smile*, then ignore the easy left finish to head off steeply into the hanging, right-trending upper groove.
FSA. Mike Robertson 23.9.2005

❹ Hot Lips 6c S0
14m. Brilliant; very pumpy indeed! A bit like *Octopuss-weed* at Cave Hole (see page 92). Traverse the lower section of the crag (some 3m or so above the sea) to arrive at jugs located close to the right arete of the cliff. Contemplate the 'hanging' line of jugs to your left, and get on with it! Finish on *The Smile*.
FSA. Mike Robertson 23.9.2005

❺ Brown Sugar 7a S0/1
13m. You'll have to pull on a few small holds on this one. Perform the left to right traverse as for *Hot Lips* to the jugs, then climb straight up, on small edges, to finally gain a decent horizontal break-line. Further tricky moves, up and left into a groove, lead to an easier finish.
FSA. Mike Robertson 23.9.2005

❻ White Teeth 7a S0
14m. The right to left, low traverse is hard, safe and enjoyable. Perfect for those strong, nervous types! From the right-hand gully, take on the crimps at the top of the low, leaning headwall, to arrive at jugs on the arete. Traverse the whole crag back to the left gully. The entire route is well above the barnacle line.
FSA. Mike Robertson 23.9.2005

White-Lips-People Link-up, 7a
This lengthy 3-route amalgam starts as for *White Teeth*, but takes *Hot Lips* up and over to the far side, before finishing up *Smiley's People*.

Also worth mentioning here is the right-hand line on the wall which has been eschewed due to the jutting reef found below. So don't go there!

❼ Fashion Victims 6b S2
12m. The odd-shaped, stepped-out arete in the gully, roughly central between the Smiley Face and Nude Boy Wall, has been climbed. Challenging for the grade, and slightly unnerving. Access by down-climbing the crack feature to the right, at about 4. Traverse across the barnacle line and climb the oddly-featured arete direct, with a crux at two-thirds height.
FSA. Mike Robertson 23.9.2005

Nude Boy Wall — Ingrina

Nude Boy Wall
The Nude Boy Wall consists of a wall that starts within sight of the gearing-up ledge, but disappears off in the direction of the Romeo & Juliet Face. The routes on the west-facing bit are usually technical and around vertical, with the south-facing section offering some steeper, more cruxy challenges.

Approach - From the top ledge system, drop down the easy grooved arete to gain the base of the wall.

Conditions and Tides - Plenty of water and plenty of sun; the wall is usually in good condition.

⑧ 'Ladies Only' Tunnel .... ⬜ 7? *S0*
14m. The tunnel looks amazing. Open to female new-routers ONLY (see Bristol Biters Cave - page 223).
NYS

⑨ Bolshy Bridesmaid . 🔲 ⬜ 5+ *S1*
10m. The rising traverse above the cut-out, low cave is steady ground, and a good intro. From the easy way down, climb leftwards, and follow the general weakness across the left face, to finish just above a smooth grey feature.
FSA. Julian Lines 23.9.2005

⑩ Scarlett Tiger ..... 🔲 ⬜ 6b *S0/1*
9m. Another fun trip. Follow the last route until beneath a tiny groove feature. A hard move up through this leads to a crimpy, vertical wall; climb this to the top.
FSA. Julian Walker 29.9.2005

⑪ Down for an Hour .. 🔲 ⬜ 6c *S0*
8m. After all the feistiness of the 6c's in the main cave, this one will stretch some different muscles. From the easy way down, climb across to the left face, and pull out of the shallow cave on small pockets. Continue direct to the top.
FSA. Julian Lines 23.9.2005

⑫ White Pocket Arete . 🔲 ⬜ 6a+ *S0/1*
8m. The very compact wall here is characterised by the 'aero rock' of the next route, and the more blank-looking rock of the last route. This line climbs the edge of the blank stuff. From the easy way down, swing left across the base and climb a tricky section (hidden pocket), to emerge on the left edge of the rounded arete. Stay true to the arete, moving slightly right at the top.
FSA. Julian Walker 29.9.2005

⑬ Gone in Twenty Seconds 🔲 ⬜ 4+ *S0*
8m. The low arete is climbed by way of its left face. The rock is curiously pocketed, a little like an aero bar. Down-climb the easy access groove and swing left under the low prow, climbing direct to the top. The prow has been climbed direct, but the main line here is as described.
FSA. Julian Lines 23.9.2005

There are three more routes on the Nude Boy Wall which are described on the next page.

Ingrina Romeo & Juliet Face

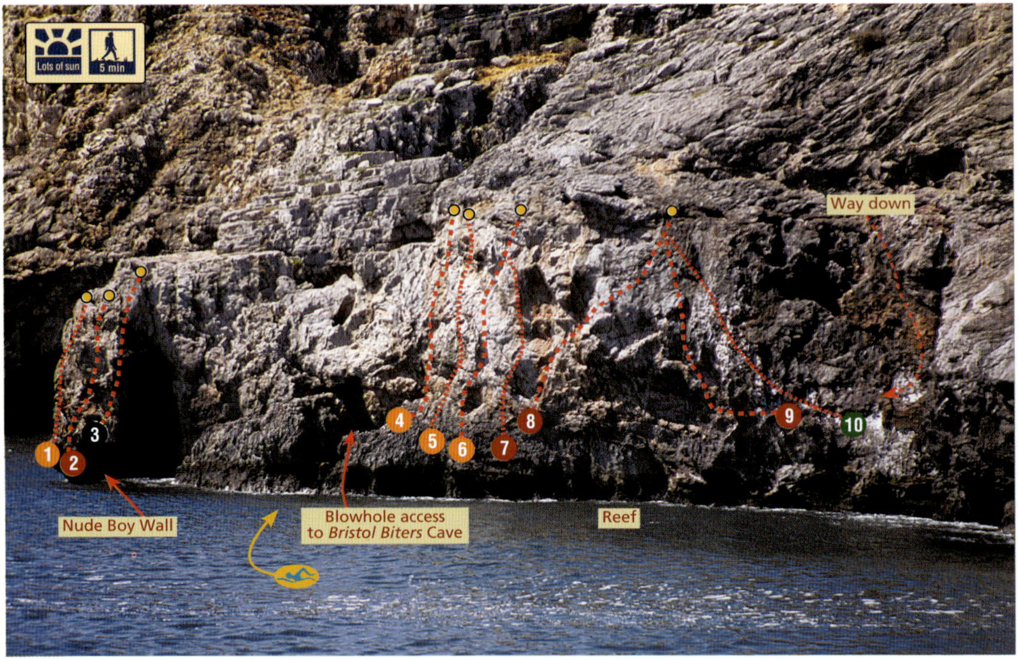

The first three routes are just around the arete from the Nude Boy Wall and are harder to recce in advance. They're a little shorter, with plenty of water below. They are easily reached by down-climbing the arete as described on the previous page.

❶ Rock Lobster 6a *S0*
7m. The right edge of the scoop offers good climbing. From the easy way down, swing across and tackle the scoop's edge with a flourish.
FSA. Julian Lines 23.9.2005

❷ Tulula 6c *S0*
8m. A great bit of climbing. Traverse across the face from the easy way down, and climb up to the hanging fang. Pass this and continue to the top.
FSA. Julian Lines 23.9.2005

❸ Nude Boy Slim 7b *S0*
8m. A gripping little boulder problem, and the scene of Ingrina's first splashdown! Climb across to the bulging arete, get beneath it, and reach for a pocket in its left side. A few slaps up the right side should (might) get you to easier terrain, and the top.
FSA. Julian Lines 23.9.2005

Romeo & Juliet Face

❹ Hazelnut Surprise 6a *S1/2*
11m. A line venturing up the steep slab on the compact right-hand wall of the low access cave. It is most easily described by its proximity to the next one - climb the steep, compact slab 2m left of *Romeo & Juliet*, moving right to join it in the upper section.
FSA. Julian Walker 27.9.2005

Romeo & Juliet Face
The Romeo & Juliet Face, split from the adjoining Nude Boy Wall by a big blowhole, is characterised by mostly vertical climbing. Expect to find a combination of face climbing and steep slab moves, often on small, rounded bumps and layaways. The slight shallower reefs might give cause for concern, so don't expect the total safety of the other sectors at Ingrina.
Approach - From the top ledges, drop down the easy ramp, passing the big blowhole en-route. This brings you down to the jug rail at the start of *Hazelnut Surprise*.
Conditions and Tides - Don't climb here in the hot sun - the rounded holds will make life awfully tough for the grade! The tides will not make much difference, but take a high tide if you can.

❺ Romeo & Juliet . . . 6a *S1*
11m. Traverse out of the low cave along the jug-rail. Where this rail ends in a big jug, rock up on the jug and climb the wall/steep slab direct, passing the left end of a long 'hazelnut cluster' feature en-route.
FSA. Mike Robertson 23.9.2005

❻ You and Me, Babe . 6a+ *S1*
11m. Climb the technical wall right of the last route, passing the right end of that same 'cluster'. Thereafter bear right, to climb gradually rightwards, on steeper ground, to the top.
FSA. Mike Robertson 23.9.2005

Bristol Biters Cave — Ingrina

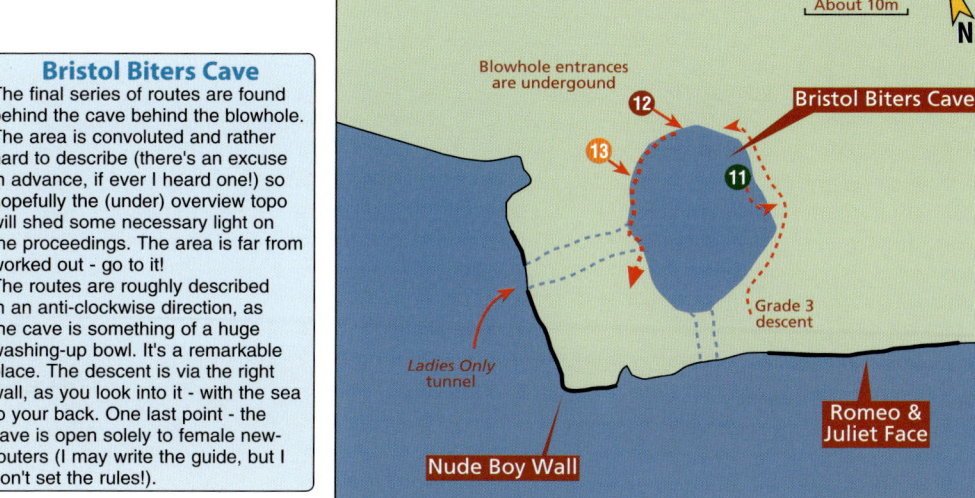

Bristol Biters Cave

The final series of routes are found behind the cave behind the blowhole. The area is convoluted and rather hard to describe (there's an excuse in advance, if ever I heard one!) so hopefully the (under) overview topo will shed some necessary light on the proceedings. The area is far from worked out - go to it!

The routes are roughly described in an anti-clockwise direction, as the cave is something of a huge washing-up bowl. It's a remarkable place. The descent is via the right wall, as you look into it - with the sea to your back. One last point - the cave is open solely to female new-routers (I may write the guide, but I don't set the rules!).

7 How About It? 6b S1/2
11m. From the lower traverse jug line continue further right, dropping down to another line of jugs. From here, climb up a technical wall/scoop (past another, lower 'cluster') until it's possible to move left into the last route for the finish.
FSA. Mike Robertson 27.9.2005

8 Farewell Jim .. 6b+ S2
12m. This one's a diagonal, hanging groove. Technical and somewhat scary. Start/access as for *How About It?*, but break immediately right, to gain a golden scoop feature up and right. Make further, tricky moves up and rightwards to gain easier ground, and a scoop (*Street Serenade* also finishes in this scoop).
FSA. Julian Lines 27.9.2005

9 Laying Everybody Low .. 6c S1
12m. From the easy slab down-climb, swing down and left to sea level, where a hanging arete forms the right edge of a low (not-DWS) scoop. Climb the arete direct, exiting right, and finish up on *Street Serenade*.
FSA. Gavin Symonds 27.9.2005

10 Street Serenade ... 4 S0/1
14m. Now here's a rarity! An easy route, and without any catches. The line takes the diagonal, right-to-left, white-patched interface between the top slab on the right side of the wall, and the overhanging scooped area beneath (the climbing is right on the edge of things). Great stuff! Down-climb the easy slab as for the last route, and climb the very edge of the slab leftwards. Keep left towards the top, finishing in the easy scoop feature.
FSA. Mike Robertson 27.9.2005

Bristol Biters Cave

11 Pink Flamingos .... 4+ S0/1
6m. The back bowl feature has a juggy wall set in it, and it's short and sweet. Access by down-climbing the 3 wall at the very back. Climb out of the east side of the bowl to an easy exit.
FSA. Amy Colson 29.9.2005

12 Mad Dogs and Englishwomen 6c S0
6m. A couple of sharp tugs are required on this one. From the base of the same easy down-climb, traverse leftwards (looking in), to arrive at a technical sequence, to climb diagonally leftwards to the top inner shelf.
FSA. Elinor Currey 29.9.2005

13 Bristol Biters ..... 6a+ S1
10m. Ouch! They do. Ladies' teams only need apply, of course. From the finish of *Mad Dogs*, climb leftwards (spotter required for first move), with feet on the base of the three huge, hanging fangs, to circumnavigate the main cave bowl. Finish the journey, after a bridging session, back up on the sea-side of the cave, on a white-ish finishing ledge.
FSA. Elinor Currey, Ruth Taylor, Amy Colson 29.9.2005

Ponta Garcia

The atmospheric venue of Ponta Garcia, just a few kilometres outside Sagres, was Portugal's first DWS discovery, with routes established between 2001 and 2006. Garcia offers two distinct features: the wacky Fossil Cave, with tufa jugs and steepness guaranteed; and the three-piece Garcia Wall, with more jug-fests on superb rock. It's a great venue, with the approaches to the routes using either a traverse in, or a dry-bag swim-in - although I hear the local shops are now doing a roaring trade in kiddy play boats! Add to this plenty of unrealised projects, the Beliche Beach (some 300m distant) and a clutch of local cafes and restaurants, and you have a DWS spot that will stand the test of time. Although it might never rival the more recently developed Ingrina for steady grades and ease of access, Garcia is now firmly on the more advanced deep water soloists away-list.

Approach
From the roundabout at the Fortaleza, follow signs for 'Beliche Praia' (Ponta Garcia's very excellent local beach), heading west out of town. Drive out of Sagres for about 3km, pass a small, beige building on the left, and park on the start of a 'twin track' dirt road on the left.

Walk along the rocky, wide road southwards for 150m until it closes down, then hang a right down a narrower continuation. After 150m of that section (ignoring 2 small leftwards tracks) the path takes you gradually leftwards, to the head of a distinct valley.

Follow a smaller trail down the centre of the valley, dropping down to a carved-out niche after 150m or so. This is the main gearing-up ledge, and from here you can easily see the Garcia Walls (the Fossil Cave is out of sight, around to the right).

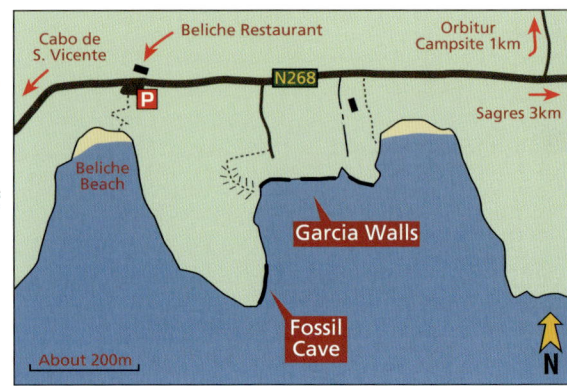

Conditions and Tides
Expect the tide movements here to be less than a metre. Your main concern is the ocean movements; avoid climbing on rough days, and be aware of currents. The rock is generally dry, but allow for a little dampness when deep in the Fossil Cave.

Neil Gresham above the blue-green Atlantic on *Portuge'E'zergood* (6c) - *page 230* - on the Garcia Wall, Ponta Garcia, Portugal. Photo: Mike Robertson.

Ponta Garcia — Fossil Cave

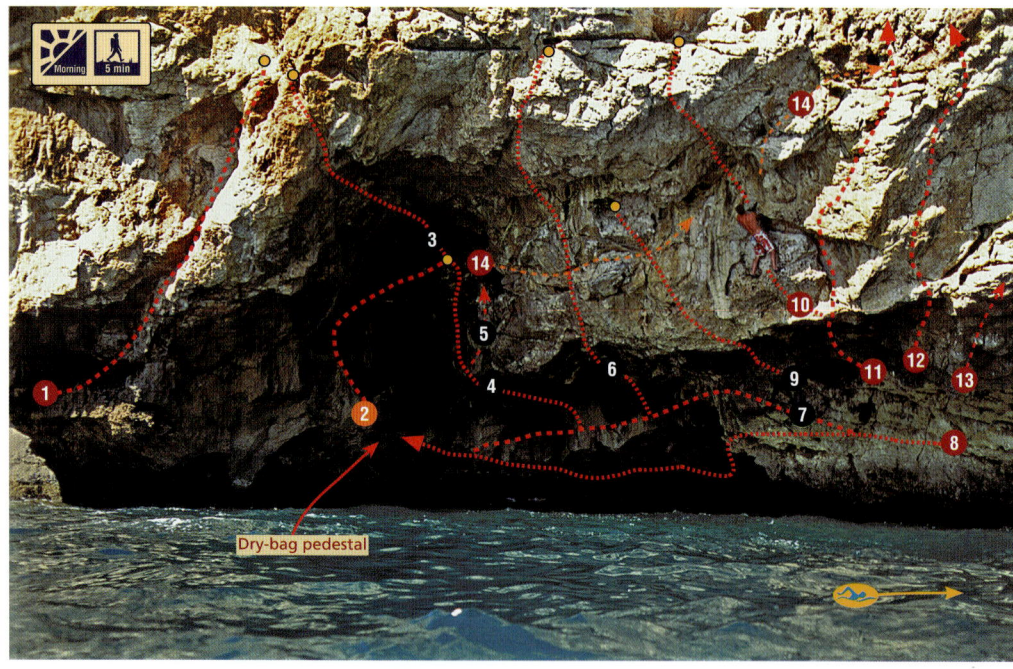

Dry-bag pedestal

Fossil Cave

This amazing cave is littered with buckets, pockets, prows, grooves and roofs. It's simply stunning, and gives any reasonably strong climber the chance to do countless moves in almost complete safety. It's the closest thing you'll ever find to a steep bouldering wall above a swimming pool! The highballs are also stunning, but give that extra sense of commitment, with three lines topping out at 20m, although on perfect rock. The best viewing platform is the very well-positioned boulder/viewing island lying off the left side - it just couldn't be in a better place, and it's big enough for a small picnic.

Approach - The viewing island is reached by dry-bag, kiddy boat or swim. To reach the routes, use a combination of the traverse in from the gearing-up ledge and the dry-bag approach arrangement (or kiddy boat). The finishes of the routes are a combination of jump-ins, top-outs, and traverse-off scenarios. Use your ingenuity here.

Conditions and Tides - The water depth here is around 8m, so you can forget all about hitting the bottom!

❶ Amphibian **6c** *S0*
12m. This cracking line tackles the diagonal groove-line on the far left of the cave, just inside the viewing boulder; gain it with an abseil and a brief scramble. Climb the curling groove, past a precarious crux at 7m, to reach the big ledge system. There's also a higher, unclimbed finish.
FSA. Julian Lines 10.2004

The next two routes start from the dry-bag pedestal in the centre of the cave's lower back wall.

❷ Coprolite . . . . **5+** *S0*
9m. The back wall of the cave offers this truly remarkable route, and at an outrageous grade for the territory. It's simply littered with buckets. Start from the back pedestal and climb up and left, and out, and up, and right, and out. The finish ledge is shared with *Cabelo Loco*. Jump in to finish.
FSA. Julian Lines 10.2004

❸ Magnum **7b** *S0*
12m. Stupendous. One of the best solos in Portugal. Takes the hanging traverse out of the cave, with a wicked finale on the leaning prow at the left edge of the cave. Climb *Coprolite* to the upper ledge system, and traverse leftwards across the very brink of nowhere, to gain a final poor rest. Move left, then dyno wildly rightwards to grasp a good pocket. One more sequence gains the big ledge. Jump off to complete the experience!
FSA. Mike Robertson 29.9.2005

❹ Cabelo Loco **7b** *S0*
7m. The first of the truly steep routes in the Fossil Cave, this one plunges out from the low-level traverse to take on a roof equipped with numerous, massive threads and pockets. The finish provides the crux, although the line is hard all the way.
FSA. Julian Lines 10.2004

❺ Cabelo Locko **7b** *S0*
7m. There is also a same-grade right-hand variation finish to the route, employing a dyno to the same finishing ledge.
FSA. Neil Gresham 10.2004

Fossil Cave Ponta Garcia

6 Project .... 8a?
12m. This one's been fallen off plenty. Very steep!
Photo page 228.

7 Trench Warfare. 7b S0
13m. The burly low-level traverse is usually climbed right to left, and involves an amazing collection of body bridges, funky rests and outright weirdness, all undertaken on pipes, threads and fat slopers! Start from the ledge system that runs in from the gear-up point.
FSA. Julian Lines 10.2004

8 The Speleologist. 6b S0
15m. The ultra-low traverse can be used to gain the dry-bag pedestal, but only when the sea is calm and the tide low.
FSA. Julian Walker 9.2005

9 Bill Piscod .... 7b+ S0
8m. This superb line is truly, truly steep, but stops low, giving a very powerful and gymnastic test-piece, and all in complete safety. An 8m 7b+ above 8m of water? It doesn't get much better than that. Jump off to finish.
FSA. Charlie Woodburn 10.2004

10 Faro Fawcett Finish. 7a S0
12m. Excellent. This leftwards line provides *Best Seller* with an *S0* finish. From the mother route, climb diagonally leftwards, and up through the roof stack to the ledge/break.
FSA. Charlie Woodburn 10.2004

The next three routes are incredible; the Fossil Cave really is one of the best DWS caves on the planet. They're all highball and all utterly memorable.

11 Best Seller. 7a S2/3
20m. One of the coolest routes in town. Takes the steepness on, and combines it with a stunning and much easier wide groove system in the top wall, with buckets where you need them most!
FSA. Charlie Woodburn 10.2004

12 Cult Classic ... 7a S3
20m. Intimidating but superb, taking you to the very top. The lower roof leads you to the well-formed prow; climb this, trending gradually left, to an airy and exhilarating finale.
FSA. Charlie Woodburn 10.2004

13 True Grit ..... 6c+ S3
20m. This brilliant high-riser takes the big, steep arete on the right side of the cave. It offers generous pockets and jugs all the way to the top - but it's a pumpy beast. Start on the left entry shelf. Climb quickly up to a small cave and a rest; continue to the second hole, another possible rest. Strike out up the twin grooves above, keeping to the right one; big pockets lead you up to and through the final roof, to a clean exit.
FSA. Mike Robertson 10.2004

14 Pick n' Mix. 7a S0
50m. A long and pumpy link-up. Solves the problem of exploring the cave without swimming! Climb *The Speleologist* to the dry-bag pedestal. From here, climb *Coprolite* to the upper ledge system, at the finish of *Cabelo Loco*. From here, traverse rightwards, out and up, crossing *Cult Classic*, to finally enter and down-climb (crux) the steep lower section of *True Grit*.
FSA. Julian Walker 26.9.2005, Crispin Waddy 2001 (the higher section only)

Ponta Garcia — Garcia Wall

Charlie Woodburn attempting the project (Route 6) - *page 227* - in the Fossil Cave, Ponta Garcia. Photo: Mike Robertson.

Garcia Wall

The splendid Garcia Wall is home to a great bunch of classics, including the brilliant traverse of *Fishing Line*, the long escapade of *Anthony Hopkins*, and the ultra-steep *Match of the Day*. The wall here has been spilt into three parts, which the topography somewhat dictates - the crag is split roughly into three by the two largest caves.

Approach - You'll need to get down the approach Grade 3 down-climb, to arrive at sea level. From here, see the separate approach notes, including the dry-bag swim-ins, which are an essential part of a visit! If you intend to finish a route at a ledge or a low terrace (*Anthony Hopkins* is a good example of this) then take a lightweight dry-bag, clipped to your chalk bag cord/elastic. Once the climbing's finished, you can load your bag and boots into the drybag and jump off with it - why get all that gear wet when you don't have to?!

Conditions and Tides - Conditions on the Garcia Wall are generally good, but avoid rough sea days or hot days - this will make your quest either wetter or stickier! The entire area of the wall is suspended above a perfect bed of sand, with barely a boulder in sight (the only boulder IS 'The Submerged Man'). This beautifully flat ocean floor is rather handy, as the water level averages about 3m or so - if this depth sounds barely adequate, please bear in mind it's been fallen off and jumped off on plenty of occasions.

❶ Falling into Fish . . . 6c *S3*
20m. This one's a bit of a highball, taking on the big, steep buttress direct. Look out for a cunning rest with your head in a hole. Climb across the lower section, and take on the buttress direct, with steep moves pretty much all the way. Finish on fairly solid rock at the very top of the buttress.
FSA. Mike Robertson 10.2004

❷ Brown Nose 6c *S2*
20m. This line takes the wild steepness just to the right of the previous route, thereafter finishing more easily rightwards. Climb the prow feature right of *Falling into Fish*; trend right to finish up the *Portugeezers* easier groove system.
FSA. Crispin Waddy 2001

❸ Portugeezers . . . . 6a+ *S0*
9m / 20m. This route is most often used as an entry route to somewhere else; the extended version is high but steady *S2* territory, and the shorter version gets you over to the start of the higher lines to the right. From the easy gully, climb down and right (looking in) keeping close to sea-level. Traverse right across a big groove, and up onto the big, bulging roof. The less-often climbed top section forges up the groove above.
FSA. Crispin Waddy 2001

❹ Portugalz 7a *S0*
9m. The first of the true steepness here. This line climbs the very edge of the low bulging roof, approached from the left.
FSA. Neil Gresham 10.2004

Garcia Wall - Left   Ponta Garcia

Garcia Wall - Left

There's some great routes at this end, with both highball and lower options available. Take your guns for those ultra-low roof routes!

Approach - Garcia Wall's left section is easily accessed by dropping down the Grade 3 approach down-climb. From the ledges just above sea level, you'll be able to tackle *Falling into Fish* and *Brown Nose*, and for the rest of the routes, you'll need to climb the first half of *Portugeezers*. To reach the start of routes 4 to 7, you'll have to traverse the lower back wall - there are good holds along that section of rock.

Conditions and Tides - Plenty of sun, so expect good conditions most of the time; a calm sea will keep the lower routes a little drier. Select a high tide for the highest lines.

5 The Linesman .... 7a+ S0
9m. A fine route; steep as you like - almost downhill, really! The route breaches the roof right from the back of the lower wall. Very steep territory indeed, but with every hold a good pocket or bucket. Yum yum!
FSA. Neil Gresham 10.2004

6 Let's Give It 7c S0
9m. ..... as opposed to merely having it, or taking it. A brilliant and powerful test-piece, firing across a roof of huge jugs and pockets (except that single two-finger pocket, of course).
FSA. Neil Gresham 10.2004

7 Project .... ?
9m. Very hard.

8 Faroway Finish 6b S1
10m. A good finish above the ledge of *Portugeezers* - probably the most logical finish out and up to the terraces. The route takes you off the right end of the bulging roof, through the steepness below a big orange scoop. Finish by traversing left back to the gear-up point.
FSA. Neil Gresham 10.2004

9 Project .... ?
10m. Another desperate piece of steepness. You'll have to make up your mind as to how you get started on this project - either from the left, or from below.

10 Cruel Sea .... 6b+ S1
10m. The weakness through the roof about 3m to the right of *Faroway Finish* offers a similar outlook. Climb up to a prominent, purple-ish jug, and pull through the roof to a rock-over onto the upper slab, and easier ground.
FSA. Julian Lines 28.9.2005

11 Fishing Line .... 6b+ S0
16m. A madcap traverse of ever-increasing steepness - crazy! Has proved very popular since its inception, partly because it's lengthy but very safe - all the tricky stuff is within 9m of the sea - and partly because of its accessibility. Traverse along the bulging roof, and set off across the steep terrain to the right, taking the lowest line. The final hard bit is getting across and up into the slanted groove. Either keep left to the groove, or swing right here to finish over on the slabby recess.
FSA. Crispin Waddy 2001

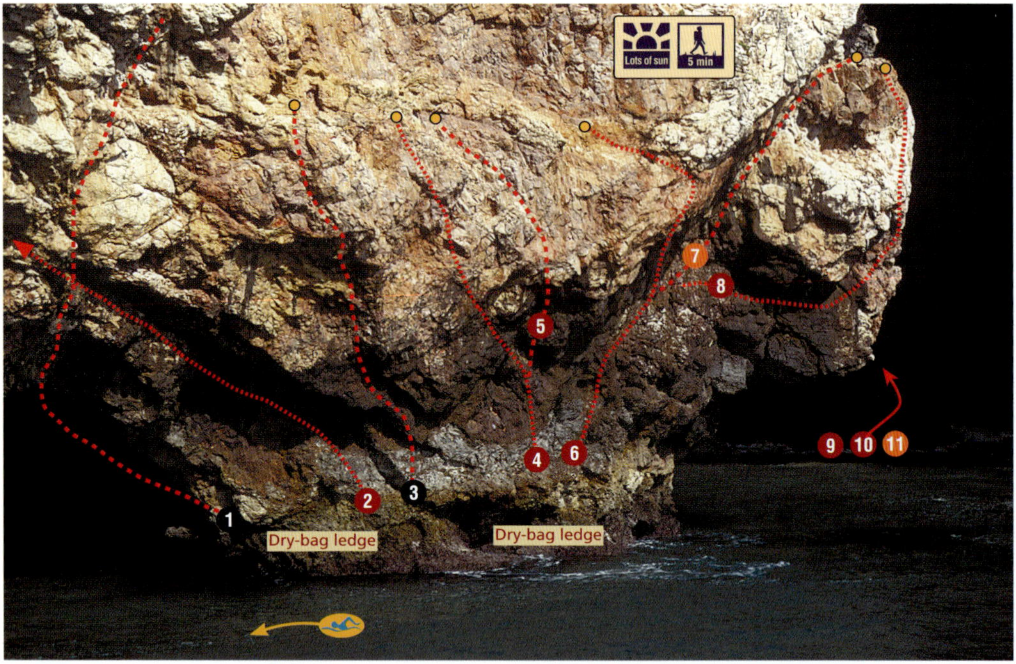

Ponta Garcia Garcia Wall - Centre

❶ Lotta .... 7a+ S0
11m. A powerful and superb line, starting in an exquisite sea cave low down. The monkey-man antics in the cave lead to pumpy climbing on good holds. Climb out of the right side of the cave's apex, and climb diagonally rightwards, into very steep terrain indeed, finally finishing on good ledges, from where the terraces can be easily reached.
FSA. Julian Lines 10.2004

❷ First Blood 6c S0
14m. A brilliant and almost endless diagonal jug-fest. From the dry-bag ledges, jump on board the rising right-to-left break-line - it's steep! Continue until it's possible to squeeze into a slim groove; a few more moves gain the terraces.
FSA. Julian Lines 10.2004

❸ Project .... 7b+?
11m. This looks most excellent.

❹ Dave's Restaurant..... 6c S0
11m. A fine, sustained eliminate, staying on ground just to the left of the next route, on small pockets and edges. Climb straight up the wall to join *Sea of Holes* for its leftwards traverse to the terraces.
FSA. Neil Gresham 10.2004

❺ Sea of Holes 6c S0
11m. A voyage of discovery, on massive holds. Take your biceps for all those funky undercut moves. The route is a fast series of big locks. From that same scoop, climb up the big hole features above your head, finally heading left to easier ground.
FSA. Mike Robertson 10.2004

Garcia Wall - Centre
Garcia's central section offers brilliant and steep climbing on good holds.
Approach - The two dry-bag ledges provide the start for the routes, and are about a 40m swim from the main gearing-up area.
Conditions and Tides - A calm sea is desirable for the dry-bag approach, as waves around your ankles will prove to be a distraction when you're getting dressed. Any tide will suffice.

❻ Portuge'E'zergood.. 6c S0
11m. A hanging arete, and great positions. Start as for *Heaven Scent*, but gradually trend leftwards, to find yourself on the steep hanging arete. A couple of pull-downs gives you easier ground.
See photo on page 225.
FSA. Neil Gresham 10.2004

❼ Heaven Scent..... 6a+ S0/1
13m. A delightful line, with just one burly undercut move. Swing right and climb the lower, grey wall, climbing up into the wide groove. Follow this to finally arrive on the jutting ledge high on the right. Either jump off, or, if you prefer to stay dry, make one 5+ move up and left, to gain the terraces.
FSA. Mike Robertson 10.2004

❽ Anthony Hopkins... 6b+ S0
14m. Ought to win an Oscar, this one. Marvellous, sustained climbing, and on great holds all the way. Follow *Heaven Scent* until the way is clear to traverse right, under the hanging roof. Climb directly up the far wall, to finish leftwards to the same final ledge as *Heaven Scent*. *See photo on page 210.*
FSA. Mike Robertson 10.2004

Garcia Wall - Right   Ponta Garcia   231

9 Liverpool Lady 7a *S0*
13m. A shapely and very steep hanging groove, with a well-positioned pocket hanging in the left-hand side, just where you need it most. It's a dry-bag start from the ledges in the left side of the cave, traversing leftwards out to the route. Grapple your way up the ridiculously steep groove, say a silent prayer for that well-placed pocket, and continue up until it's possible to head left towards the finish ledges, shared with the previous two routes.
FSA. Julian Lines 10.2004

10 The Dogfather 6c *S0*
13m. Found in the groove to the right of the last route. Very steep indeed, but on huge jugs and undercuts. Climb the very leaning, bucket-infested groove/wall to the right of *Liverpool Lady*, finally traversing across to join that route for the ledges. Finish leftwards, onto the spacious ledge system.
FSA. Mike Robertson 10.2004

11 Anchana .... 6a+ *S0*
15m. A bucket-fest; expect the full pump all over again! From the low, inner reef inside the cave, climb up on large holds and then leftwards across the overhanging inside wall of the cave, to gain a flake-line. Continue leftwards, to join *The Dogfather* and finish to the same ledge.
FSA. Julian Lines 9.2006

Garcia Wall - Right

12 Project .... 8c?
18m. Just not the done thing, to apply stars to an unrealised route, but just this once... the utterly stunning hanging arete is world-class.

Garcia Wall - Right
More of those big holds on this end of the wall.
Approach - One dry-bag ledge serves these routes, and it's approximately a 60m swim over.
Conditions and Tides - A calm sea is useful for these routes. Any tide is sufficient for the climbing.

13 Match of the Day .. 7a+ *S1*
14m. A mega-classic. The holds are sizeable, but finding them proves problematical. Start beneath the centre of the grossly steep central face, and follow it directly up (out?) on a host of hidden jugs, to gain a crazy sit-down rest in a big niche. From here, head leftwards around a hanging flake system, to swing back rightwards to finish to a small slab.
FSA. Neil Gresham 10.2004

14 The Submerged Man 6c+ *S0/1*
23m. A veritable juggling match of pockets and jugs, with a final wilting rock-over onto the top slab. Start in the dry-bag recess. Climb up and right, with various deviations, to arrive at an odd rest in a high cave/hole feature, just before the final crux move. Swing right and grab that exciting rock-over, to gain a long, technical traverse rightwards - follow this all the way to the far prow. Excellent! Either jump, or scramble easily up to the top of the cliff.
FSA. Mike Robertson 10.2004

15 Marine Life 7a *S0*
23m. Wicked. Climb up until the appealing rightwards traverse line is reached. The rest is an out-there line of holds in the most outrageous positions! Follow the line of jugs all the way across the crag (at a level of around 7m), until you reach the final prow; pull up this to join *The Submerged Man*.
FSA. Julian Lines 10.2004

Costa Blanca

The bizarre, hidden caves of Spain's Costa Blanca. Julian Lines on the first ascent of *Shaft of Light* (7a) - *page 243* - Secret Lagoon, Cala del Moraig. Photo: Mike Robertson.

Costa Blanca

The Spanish mainland, and the Costa Blanca in particular, is better known for its sport climbing and big mountain routes, with Mallorca being the prime destination for deep water soloists. 2005 changed all that and we now have Cala del Moraig and the Moraira region, which is now one of Europe's best hotspots for the deep water soloist.

Cala del Moraig is the real plum: short leaning walls, atmospheric cave routes and long traverses make up this fresh new area, with good access and a friendly climate. Whilst a little further south can be found the colourful, vertical walls of Moraira East Bay, and the promising yet undeveloped jewel of the Moraira Caves. Whatever the future for deep water soloing in Europe, it's fair to say that this region of the Costa Blanca is set to endure.

When to go

As with other European DWS destinations, it's probably best to time your trip for the end of the summer, when the water's warm, the tourists thin out a bit, and the prices are lower for most things, including your accommodation.

Flights

Any search for flights should include both Alicante and Valencia's airports, as the Moraira region falls between the two. Expect some good deals to these airports, especially out of season from September onwards.

Accommodation

There's all sorts of deals available on apartments, which seems to be the preferred choice for most small groups on a visit to Costa Blanca. Check the Rockfax web site for a whole series of possibilities - www.rockfax.com . As far as camping is concerned, you'll usually have to make it up as you go along; the Spanish are less inclined towards this and although there are campsites along the coast, they usually have a short summer season.

The Orange House

www.theorangehouse.net

Your base camp on the Costa Blanca

The Orange House courses
- Introduction to Rock
- Trad Climbing and/or Multi-pitch
- Improvers/Coaching Holidays
- Advanced Rope Work
- Women Only Weeks

Course Venues
The Orange House run courses in the Costa Blanca*, the Costa Daurada, Croatia and the UK.

*Accommodation is included in the price for Costa Blanca courses.

The Orange House Accommodation
We offer all levels of accommodation from camping or the bunkhouse to en-suite rooms, for individuals or large groups. All visitors can make full use of the facilities; TV lounge, 2 kitchens, bar and pool...

Costa Blanca
One of the best climbing destinations in the world for sport and trad climbing. Sea cliffs, immaculate inland crags and multi-pitch routes for the full alpine experience.

Contact
sam@theorangehouse.net
rich@theorangehouse.net
Main booking line
0034 965 878 251
Sam mobile 0034 686 044 003
Rich mobile 0034 619 807 515
UK mobile 07919 467049
Ptda de la Foya 31, Finestrat, 03509 Alicante

Steve McClure on Tortuga Island, 7c
Pirates of the Caribbean sector

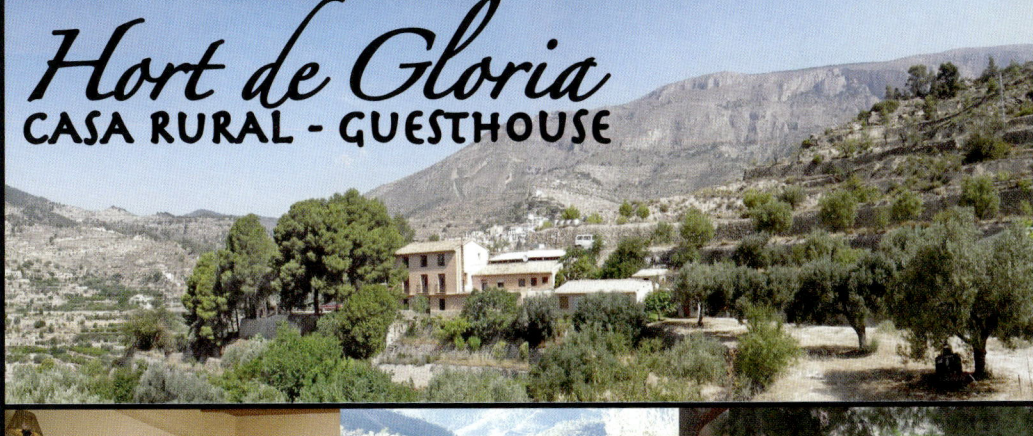

Hort de Gloria
CASA RURAL - GUESTHOUSE

info@aqua-ventura.com - www.aqua-ventura.com - 5 min from Sella crags
Tel. +34 680 206 221 / +34 96 587 9000 - Hort de Gloria - Sella - Alicante - Spain

Moraira

This hidden bay on the quiet side of the Moraira headland is well worth a visit; it offers some fine soloing, in a very quiet setting. It's a square-cut bay, found sheltering on the north-west side of Punta Moraira (Moraira Point). The solos are all less than 12m high, on good, mostly vertical rock, and with good water throughout.

Approach

From the centre of Moraira, follow the signs to 'Platja del Portet'. It's a beach area just short of the huge Moraira headland, with a cafe stretching along the promenade next to the beach. From here, drive up the steep road, heading north - its purple signposts point to the 'Cap d'Or'. Turn right at the first junction, and left at the second. Follow the road up to the right; continue steeply left, and park at the dead end, underneath an orange-pink house (with concrete dogs on pillars). On foot: follow the wooden sign 'Torre Vigia Cap d'Or 800m' and at the small col, swing left over the rise, and head downhill (following the green and white painted bands marking the path), and on past some colourful, orange-streaked walls on the left. Continue skirting the hillside, following the same 'bands', to drop down below a large cave (bolts evident, although currently banned), and then go right/down at a fork in the path. Follow the path roughly east, and drop down once again, this time to a vegetated headland, where an eastward 'look' down into a bay reveals Moraira East Bay. Take a trail down into the bay.

Sam Mayfield on the first ascent of *Lady's Ladder* (4+) - *page 247* - Cave of Pets, Cala Moraig. Photo: Mike Robertson.

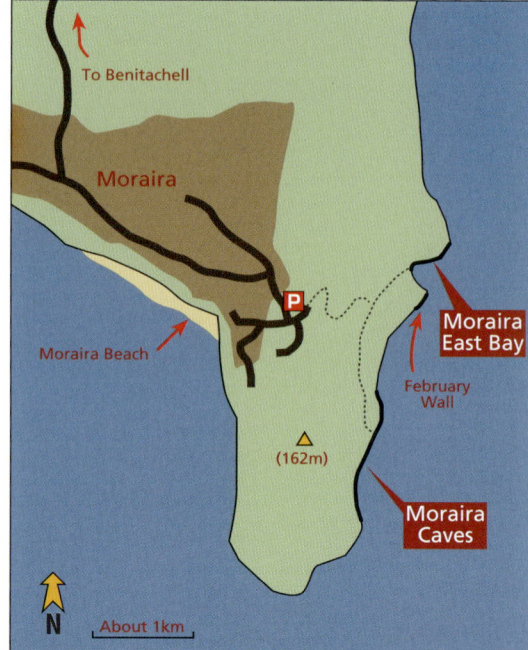

Conditions and Tides

The routes in the bay do get a fair amount of shelter, but the usual rules apply; avoid rough seas. The rock gets a full hit of afternoon and evening sun, and, being vertical, doesn't attract the dampness sometimes found in the caves of Cala del Moraig. There are no real tidal variations to speak of.

Perfect rock at Moraira East Bay. Ruth Taylor on the second ascent of *The Hipster* (6c) - *page 239* -. Photo: Mike Robertson

Swanage
Lulworth
Portland
Devon
Cornwall
Pembroke
Scotland
Rest of UK
Portugal
Costa Blanca
Mallorca
Rest of Europe
Australia
Rest of World

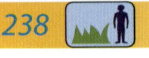

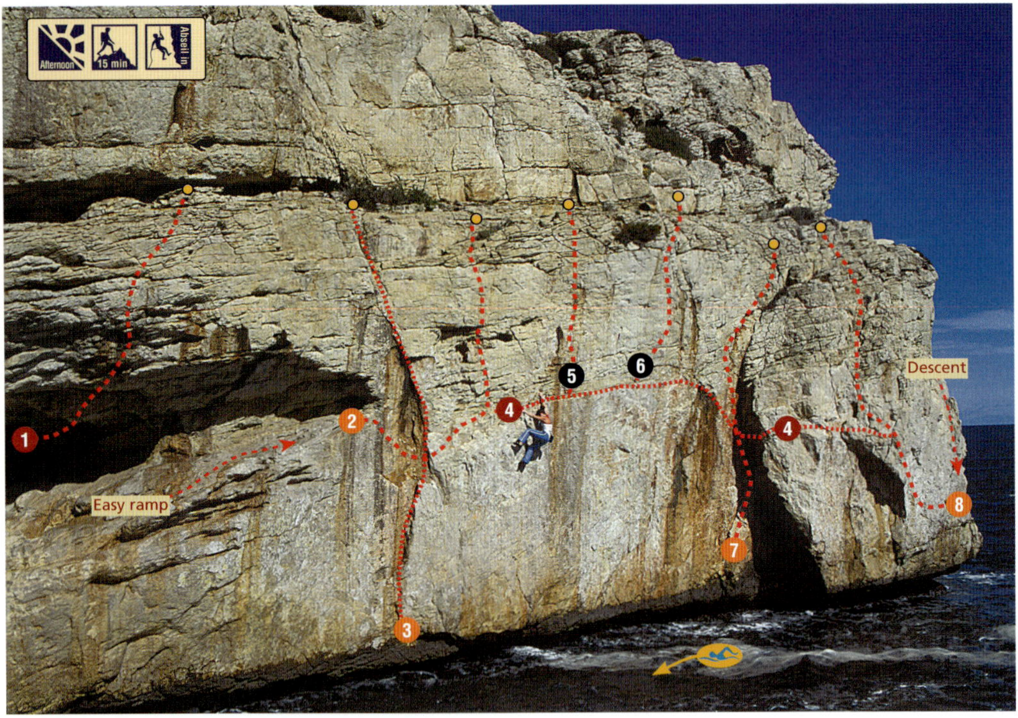

East Bay

The East Bay is located on the quiet side of the Moraira headland and offers some fine soloing, in a peaceful setting. The solos are all less than 12m high, on good, mostly vertical rock, and mostly above good water.
Approach - From the path down into the bay, a walk slightly rightwards onto a broken promontory gives a great view of the wall (the crag shot above was taken from here). All routes on the wall are reached either via a simple walk into the long niche, a tape harness abseil, or straight out of the water! *Rags to Riches* is reached by way of a scramble, and an easy down-climb.
Conditions and Tides - Expect any sunny day to provide dry rock and good conditions, but avoid hot sun. The tides are not really very important here; the water appears to be deep everywhere.

1 The Art of Reinvention .... 2 ☐ **6b+** *S2*
7m. The roof stack above the traverse in offers excellent, pumpy climbing, but you'll need a spotter for the first few moves. Once out there, you'll have good water below. Climb the roof stack on good flat holds, continuing gradually rightwards, to a solid top-out.
FSA. Mike Robertson 2.2005

2 Rich Tea Biscuits .... 2 ☐ **6a+** *S0*
9m. The upper face to the right of the long recess section succumbs to a few tricky moves. Good climbing and excellent rock throughout. Traverse out of the recess ramp and take the jugs above to a final hard bit.
FSA. Rich Mayfield Spring 2001

3 Striking it Rich .... 2 ☐ **6a+** *S0*
12m. The long groove is terrific, although tricky to start. Climb the curving groove all the way to the top.
FSA. Zoe Tate, Chris Thornton, Rich Mayfield, Chris Thornton, Adam Hocking and James McHaffie Spring 2001. The huge first ascent team swam over together and did it wet!

4 Little Mac Traverse . 2 ☐ **6c+** *S0*
18m. The traverse of the crag at mid-height is a fun outing. The mid-section proves pumpy, with no rests and poor footholds - then locate the elusive pocket hold to gain the groove.
FSA. Steve McClure 2.2005

5 The Silent Man .... 1 ☐ **7b** *S0*
8m. Hard moves up a vague side-pull rib.
FSA. James McHaffie Spring 2001

6 Project .... ☐ **7?**
9m. Desperate face moves.

East Bay and Caves Moraira

Path from Moraira Town

Descent

February Wall - 80m

Small slabby wall, with some good climbing at around 6a.

7 That's Rich .... 6a+ *S1*
11m. Start this one either from the water or by way of a tape-harness arrangement. Climb the wide groove direct, finishing more easily on the right.
FSA. Chris Thornton, Zoe Tate and team, Spring 2001

8 Rags to Riches .... 6a+ *SO*
12m. Down-climb an easy groove to the right, and traverse leftwards. Hard moves past the right edge of a slanting rib gets you to easier ground.
FSA. Chris Thornton, Zoe Tate Spring 2001

9 The Bunkhouse .... 6b+ *SO*
12m. From the easy groove down-climb, traverse rightwards and move into the big groove. Hard moves get you to an easier finish.
FSA. unknown

10 The Hipster .... 6c *SO*
8m. The end face is approached via a down-climb from the right. Once on the lower face, climb up to the top continuation face, and climb it direct via a hard move. *See photo on page 237.*
FSA. Steve McClure, Ruth Taylor 2.2005

11 The Hipster Extension - Project. 7? *SO*
14m. This possibility gives a harder and longer start.

February Wall
There are a number of little bits and pieces to be found around the corner to the north, although nothing electric. Moving the other way (to the south), there's a couple of items - where a well-placed block offers two lines. One of them is a very amenable wall, and there is a project just next to it. The grades are somewhat disparate!

12 February Wall .... 5+ *SO*
8m. Big holds and steady ground. Approach the front face of the block from the left (looking in). The wall is played out on good holds, to a good solid exit.
FSA. Mike Robertson 2.2005

13 Project .... 8b? *SO*
8m. The hard, very leaning 8m prow just to the right ideally needs both flat water and a low tide to get in to the base. It's very safe indeed, and the climbing looks superb.
NYS

Moraira Caves
A boat ride southwards towards the main Moraira headland is a total eye-opener. If you aren't wow-ing at great length, you ain't a true deep water soloist! The caves here offer up some truly amazing lines, many of them obvious three-star propositions, with the order of the day being lines of great purity and character - hanging pocket lines, flake-lines, corners and cracks. Most of the routes seem to be a maximum height of 15 to 20m, and the top-outs all look to be solid. This area will one day host at least 40 routes, from 6a+ to 8b+. Some of the routes will prove to be accessible with an abseil; take a boat to reach the remainder.

Approach - The caves are best approached from a wandering fisherman's track - you'll need to follow your nose a little, as the trail is not well-used. From the main track over to Moraira East Bay, break out right towards a big, prominent upper cliff, skirting the base of this to arrive on ledges above the caves.

Conditions and Tides - Expect conditions to vary considerably in the caves themselves, with the more vertical buttresses offering more sun. The water seems to be deep everywhere, but choose a calm sea day, as this spot is about as atmospheric as it gets!

Cala del Moraig

Julian Lines on the boulders of Firestarter Bay, Cala Moraig. Photo: Mike Robertson.

Cala del Moraig, developed totally from scratch in 2005, is a real DWS plum; an enchanting region of caves, crags, tunnels and leaning walls. It also harbours the hidden feature of the bizarre Secret Lagoon. You shouldn't find it too difficult to negotiate yourself around the place, with all routes within a 1km stretch of fairly quiet coastline. It even has a bar, a toilet and a nudist beach (in summer). The highest crag in the area is about 12m high - a textbook ideal height, with many of the region's S grades reflecting this.

Cala del Moraig is set around the central beach, with the coastline here providing you with something like a south-east aspect, although the crags themselves offer a variety of aspects, including late afternoon sun. To the south-west of the car park you'll find the Jellystone Buttress, the Bruce Lee Buttress, the Secret Lagoon and the Firestarter Traverse, and to the north-east you'll discover the excellent Cave of Pets, the Spring Tide wall and the Hidden Beach area.

Cala del Moraig

Approach

Cala del Moraig is a straightforward 25 minute drive from the A7. From junction 63, follow the Teulada signs, picking up the N332 / CV740. Drive into Teulada, and at the far edge of town, take a left at a roundabout, following the CV740 / Benitachell signs.

Some 9km from Junction 63 brings you to the village of Benitachell; look for a brown 'Cala del Moraig' sign. Keep straight on, then turn right at the lights. Keep following signs for Cumbre del Sol (green) and Cala del Moraig (brown).

Take the road up the hill for 2km or so, which then drops down into the residential development of Cumbre del Sol. Pass through this and continue downhill for about 4km, to finally arrive at the beach of Cala del Moraig. The journey from the A7 to the beach car park is about 16km. Some maps, including the useful Michelin Costa Blanca map, have Cala del Moraig marked as 'Cala de los Tiestos'.

Conditions and Tides

Cala del Moraig's limestone is usually dry, but the cave areas do sometimes suffer from a little moisture, and that effect will be heightened by a big swell. The tides are fairly incidental here, unless you want to try your hand at developing the Spring Tide Wall. Yep, it's the Mediterranean - but the sea can still be choppy and unpleasant - so please avoid the rough sea days and go sport climbing instead. Expect warm seas in late summer.

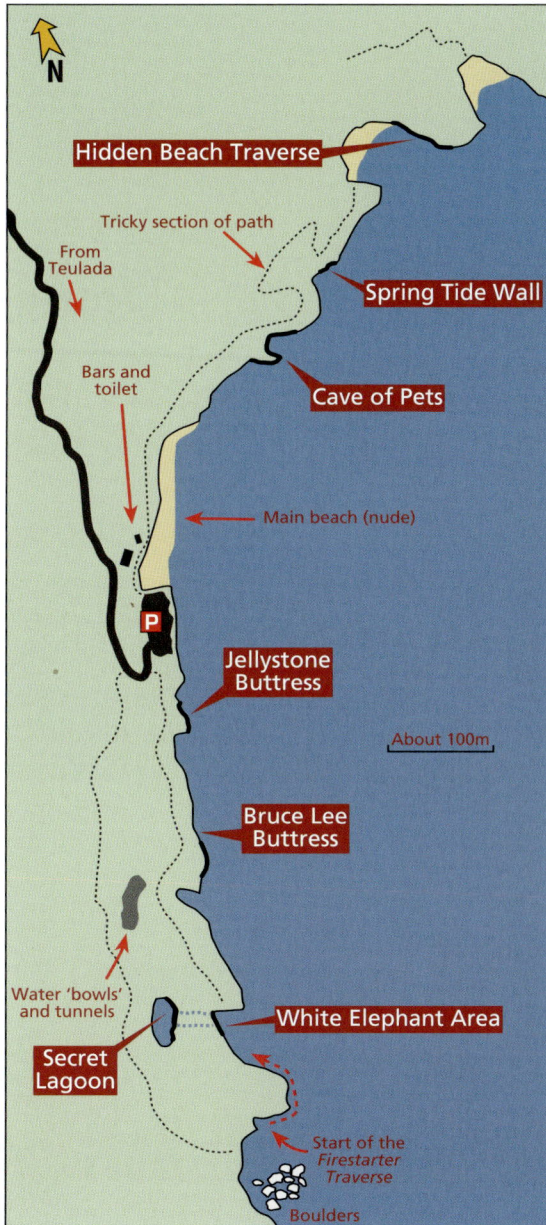

Special Consideration

ALWAYS SCOPE OUT YOUR EXIT IN ADVANCE. This is especially important at Cala del Moraig, as the concrete fisherman's ledges are surprisingly hard to get back onto from below. Use a short exit rope if in doubt, especially on the Bruce Lee Buttress; without a hanging rope set here, the swim-out is a long one - all the way round the headland and back to the car park.

Cala del Moraig — Firestarter Area

Firestarter Area

There's some nice bouldering to be found over in the Firestarter Bay, with big boulders set in the sea giving some excellent little climbs. But the main event here is the 350m traverse, starting from the beach and heading north-east. It's a blast, with many rests, great positions, and good water throughout.

Approach - The bay can easily be found, by walking up the road to the first bend, and taking the footpath past the Secret Lagoon.

Conditions and Tides - Calm seas and any tide will give great conditions for this escapade. Expect plenty of sun until into the afternoon.

❶ **Firestarter Traverse**........ 6b *S0*
350m. A great expedition. From the boulder beach at the base of the gully, climb the face out of the bay and on. Essentially, the route takes you through a series of bays, past the White Elephant Area, continuing on to pass a number of cleverly-built fishermen's concrete ledges. The natural finish is at the ladder to the right of the Bruce Lee Buttress, and the grade will depend on your exact line as you pass through the White Elephant Sector.
FSA. Julian Lines, Mike Robertson (swinging leads) 9.2005

White Elephant Area

The low cave entrance that leads though to the Secret Lagoon is roofed by an assortment of concreted-in wooden cross-poles; the *Firestarter Traverse* passes here. The very steep leaning wall to the left of the poles contains two routes.

Approach - The approach to this area is tricky to describe, as there are a number of options, some of them exposed scrambles on fishermen's wires. But highly recommended is the sea level traverse in from the Bruce Lee Buttress.

Conditions and Tides - Any tide will do fine since there is plenty of water everywhere! Avoid hot sun on the rounded rock you'll find here.

❷ **White Rino**.......... 6b *S0*
11m. That's not mispelt; it's a Dutch nickname. The left side of the leaning buttress is good, pumpy and rounded. Avoid easier ground in the left groove.
FSA. Marijne Lekkerkerker 9.2005

❸ **White Elephant**.... 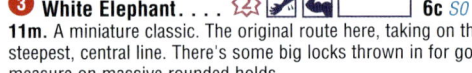 6c *S0*
11m. A miniature classic. The original route here, taking on the steepest, central line. There's some big locks thrown in for good measure on massive rounded holds.
FSA. Mike Robertson 9.2005

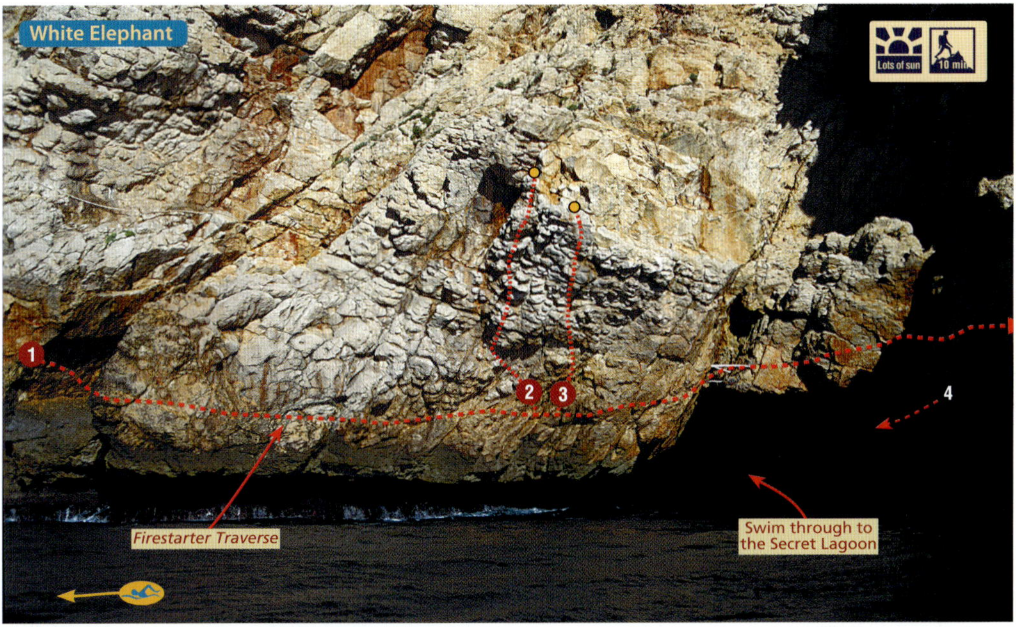

White Elephant Area and the Secret Lagoon — Cala del Moraig

White Elephant

Firestarter Traverse

Swim through to the Secret Lagoon

Secret Lagoon

A crazy place. In September 2005, the lagoon was 'discovered' by way of the swim through the cave and back out through a rear 'window'. If the fellows in question had simply walked the tourist trail, however - it's not so secret after all! The Secret Lagoon is marked by a stunning, towering smooth wall, which is taken by *Shaft of Light* to a cave at 16m; *Oasis in Flames* flanks the wall's left edge. Everything remaining is either very hard or very high. The cave system and lagoon are simply amazing to be inside, and just cry out for a mask and snorkel - so don't leave home without them.

Approach - From the tourist trail, scramble down on the right side of this remarkable feature, where a short down-climb (take care) gets you to sea-level boulders. A better alternative is to simply swim in through the tunnel from the wooden poles of the White Elephant Area - it's quite incredible.

Conditions and Tides - Calm sea is needed for the swim-in approach. Tides are unimportant here. Try to catch *Shaft of Light* as the sun splashes it, sometime around mid-afternoon in September. It's worth the wait!

❹ Project .... ☐ 7c? *S0*
18m. The traverse into the right side of the cave and back out underneath the central feature (finishing on the wooden poles) is awaiting completion. All the moves are right above the sea, and it's already seen plenty of splashdowns!

❺ Oasis in Flames ...... ☐ 6a+ *S1*
13m. This exploratory route takes the left edge of the towering smooth wall, thereafter scuttling left into the far left cave. It's a straightforward dry-bag approach to gain the sea level cave recess; start from there.
FSA. Julian Lines 9.2005

❻ Shaft of Light .... ③ ☐ 7a *S1*
16m. A cool, quality find indeed, although with some obvious logistical problems! You'll need a hanging bench seat for the start, suspended from some medium/large wires, all easy to place from the water. Get equipped on the bench seat, and follow the line of pockets and side-pulls up the wall (crux) to gain a rest in a niche at 9m. Continue up and slightly right to get into a cave and a finish in a slot. From here (16m up), jump off.
See photos on page 18 and 232.
FSA. Julian Lines 9.2005

❼ Secret Lagoon Traverse ...... ☐ 9a?
20m. This outrageous girdle of the smooth, leaning face should go, and might one day be one of the best hard solos in the world.
NYS

Cala del Moraig — Bruce Lee Buttress

Bruce Lee Buttress

This is the buttress found above the last stretch of the *Firestarter Traverse*. It is named after the watery exploits of a certain Lee Meadows, and also dedicated to a guy called Bruce Lee, who would have probably flashed the whole lot just using his abs. The routes are steep and powerful for their length, but are correspondingly all S0!

Approach - *Enter the Dragon* from the left; for the remaining lines, it seems more logical to approach from the right.

Conditions and Tides - Expect plenty of sun and dry rock as a rule. Tides are unimportant here.

Exit - The most important point here is that the swim-out is lengthy - 40m at least. So take a rope along and attach it to the ladder if you are unsure how to get past that lower hard bit.

1 Enter the Dragon .... 6a+ *S0*
13m. This terrific route takes you through a pair of holes - starting at the old ladder to the south of the route, the line can be easily seen. Traverse rightwards to gain the first hole, and climb through the second hole, direct to the top.
FSA. Julian Lines 9.2005

2 Fisheries of Fury .. 6c *S0*
12m. This one's a little more burly; probably the hardest on the wall. Come in from the right, and attack the wall via some powerful locks on slopers, to gain easier ground.
FSA. Rich Mayfield 9.2005

3 The Big Boss 6c *S0*
11m. Brucie was! Climb the left side of the scoop, using some sloping crimps. Continue to the top.
FSA. Julian Lines 9.2005

4 Bruce Lee .... 6a+ *S0*
10m. The last route is slightly less burly. Climb the right side of the recess, using a couple of big slopers, to an easier finish.
FSA. Mike Robertson 9.2005

Jellystone Buttress

5 Wilma 6a *S1*
12m. The face's left arete is exciting; stay right on it for best water. From the traverse, climb the arete direct to the top, finishing slightly on its left.
FSA. Rich Mayfield 9.2005

6 Dino 5 *S1*
12m. The cracked groove has a couple of wobbly, jammed jugs, but is otherwise fun. Climb the groove directly, with a little care, to a solid finish.
FSA. Rich Mayfield 9.2005

Jellystone Buttress **Cala del Moraig**

Jellystone Buttress

The Jellystone Buttress is a fine little section of crag, within easy reach of the car park. It is a maximum height of 12m, and has good water throughout. The only reason there are any S1's is that the face is a fraction slabby, and there's a rattly hold or two.

Approach - Routes 5 to 9 are accessed from the useful ladder found just to the left of the crag - the very height of accessibility!

Conditions and Tides - The most important consideration here is a calm sea, as waves tend to blast into the cave, creating merry hell.

⑦ Clockwork Orange . . . . 6b+ *S0*
12m. A gem! Solid rock and great positions. From the lower traverse, climb up to the steep, upper headwall, and climb it past a pint-glass handle thread, and on to an exciting, solid finish.
FSA. Rich Mayfield 9.2005

⑧ Twisting by the Pool . . . 5 *S1*
13m. This one's seen plenty of traffic. From the traverse, climb diagonally rightwards, finding yourself on that big flake. Taking care with the rock, finish direct up a twin crack to a good finish.
FSA. Rich Mayfield 9.2005

⑨ Poet's Eye 6b *S0*
14m. The tucked-away groove is steep and committing, although safe throughout. Climb the lower face rightwards, staying low, passing a hole (or passing through it!) to swing into the base of a very steep corner. Climb the corner/groove, swing left onto the arete, and yard on up spaced holds to the top.
FSA. Mike Robertson 9.2005

The final routes here are accessed by way of an easy, slabby wall, which is discernable by the presence of concreted footsteps and a few old metal spikes. Either abseil in, or climb down to the platform, where you'll find:

⑩ Jellystone . . . . 5+ *S2*
13m. Great positions on this one. Keep an eye on the sub-surface reef. From the fisherman's ledge, climb up and leftwards to gain a break-line; follow this leftwards (crux) to gain a rest on the upper wall. Continue up the less steep wall direct to the top, on an array of good side-pulls. *See photo on page 251.*
FSA. Rich Mayfield 9.2005

⑪ Old Dog, New Tricks . . . . . . 3+ *S2*
7m. The open groove is approach by a traverse from the lowest ledge and followed on good holds.
FSA. Chris Craggs 3.2007

⑫ Farewell Mrs L . . . . 4+ *S0*
7m. The arete can be seen from the beach - it's short and safe, and a good intro to the area. From the fisherman's concreted ledge, traverse rightwards to get under the arete. After a pull into a slight groove, climb the arete direct to easier ground.
FSA. Julian Lines 9.2005

⑬ Woof Woof Splash 4 *S2*
7m. The rounded chimney groove on the right is reached by a low traverse past the arete of *Farewell Mrs L*. Exit left at its top to rejoin the descent route.
FSA. Chris Craggs 3.2007

Cala del Moraig — Cave of Pets

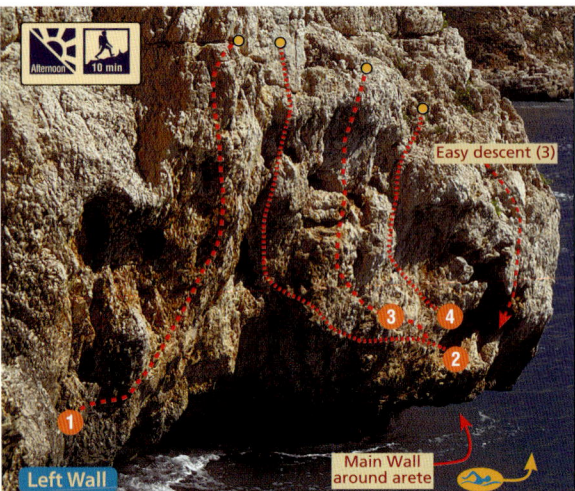

Left Wall
Main Wall around arete
Easy descent (3)

Cave of Pets
The first area encountered to the north-east of the beach is the shapely and very enticing Cave of Pets. The cave is a delight, with good water and a relaxed feel to it. The viewing is great, the access usually easy to arrange, and there's even a central access blowhole! The final treat is the excellent running-jump from the top platform.

Approach - The left side of the cave can be seen from the car park, and the cave can be reached in less than ten minutes. Cross the nudist beach (eyes down), scramble up to the higher ledge (in-situ, large fishermen's rope), and walk easily along to the cave itself. The blowhole provides access for the central routes in the cave; the remainder can be traversed into from the wings. Recommended is a short exit rope here, as it can sometimes prove tricky to get back out of the water.

Conditions and Tides - Take a calm sea, especially for the right-hand section, which features a low traverse. The tides are fairly unimportant.

Left Wall

1 Brutus Stanton . . . . **6a+** *S1/2*
11m. Good climbing, though the tidal shelf down to your left distracts greatly! Swing in from the left, and climb the steep left-hand prow direct.
FSA. Mike Robertson 9.2005

For the remainder of the routes on the face, simply down-climb easily into the small rounded depression on the right.

2 Trouser Snake **6a** *SO/1*
10m. The best outing on the wall. From the recess, traverse leftwards, dropping down when things get tricky. Gain the base of the steep groove, and follow it on good holds to the top.
FSA. Mike Robertson 9.2005

3 Sleek Pussy . . . . **5+** *SO*
8m. Start as for the above route, but continue leftwards, thereafter finishing up the steep, juggy wall.
FSA Mike Robertson 9.2005

4 Blackie Collins . . . . **5** *SO*
6m. Climb leftwards to gain good pockets; another tricky sequence should get you directly to the finishing holds.
FSA. Mike Robertson 9.2005

Main Cave

5 The Velcro Twins . . . . . **6b** *SO*
14m. The traverse of the main cave's left wall is excellent. From the blowhole feature in the centre of the cave, drop down onto the left wall and traverse steeply leftwards on big holds, to a rest just before the left arete. Reach blindly for a good hold in a crack, and swing onto the arete to finish.
FSA. Mike Robertson 9.2005

6 The Holes . . . . **6b** *SO*
10m. A proper little gem. From *The Velcro Twins*' traverse, climb up the series of holes in the left wall, to a leftwards exit with a final sting.
FSA. Julian Lines 9.2005

7 Project . . . . **7c+?** *SO*
11m. The line to the right of the holes may one day succumb. It has been fallen off plenty of times.

8 Sapphire . . . . **7b** *SO*
12m. A tough cookie. From the blowhole, climb across onto the right face, reach for a slot (check its location from the water first) and pull desperately up the wall above, wriggling your body into a slight rest in the cave's apex. A final sequence rightwards gains the top.
FSA. Julian Lines 9.2005

9 Project . . . . **7b+?** *SO*
11m. The shapely prow that starts low and down to the right of *Sapphire* will prove slappy and hard!

The following routes (with the exception of Lady's Ladder) often utilise the slim purple shelf at the base of the routes, depending on the tide level. This means that their starts are marginally unsafe, although it hasn't proved a problem so far - especially as the crux moves are always found much higher up, and out over good water. So don't be precious about your boots - or use a buddy! (See Circus Dog for a possible tip).

10 The Funhouse . . . . . **6c+** *S1*
11m. From the slim, lower purple shelf (wet boots yet?!) climb carefully up the groove to a rest at 3m. Move up and left on small side-pulls (possible kneebar) and continue on crimps to the top.
FSA. Mike Robertson 9.2005

11 Circus Dog **6b** *SO/1*
11m. Another line which just might use a wet boot or two! A terrific line, and probably the cave's best. Climb up from the lower shelf (ask Silvia Fitzpatrick about her naked 'hired help' who assisted in keeping her boots dry) and tackle the very overhanging prow, on (almost) always great holds. *See photo on page 23.*
FSA. Julian Lines 9.2005

Cave of Pets and Spring Tide Wall — Cala del Moraig 247

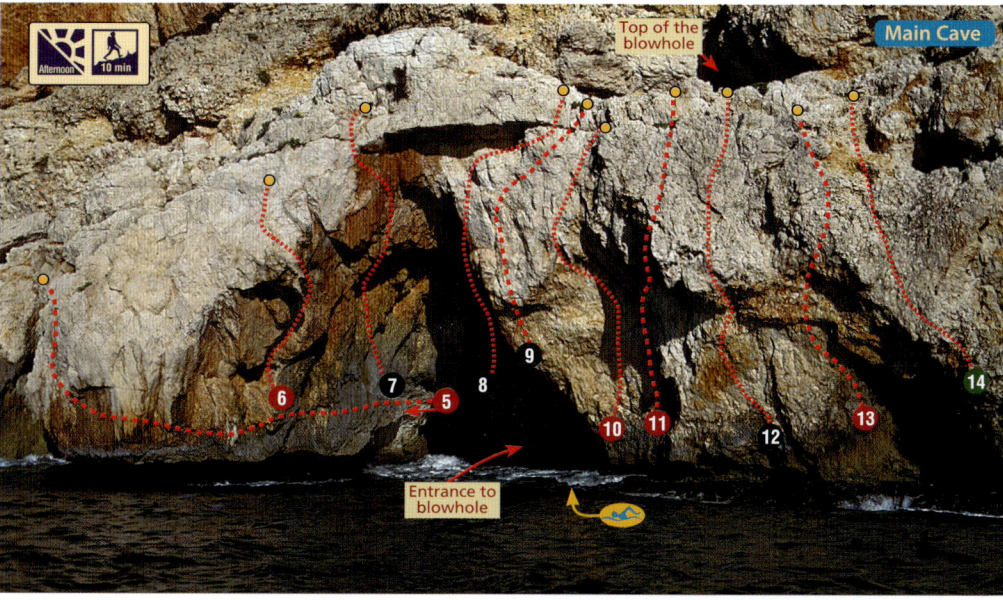

12 Project .... 7a+? *S2*
11m. This one's been fallen off once or twice, but watch out for that lower purple shelf. From the orange patch, battle it out on crimps for the top.

13 Fear of Flying 7a *S2*
10m. Another feisty one. Traverse in from the right, making a tricky (and unsafe) move into a groove. Move up and slightly left, and throw yourself dynamically at the prow up to your right. The slappy, upper crux moves appear to be safe.
FSA. Mike Robertson 9.2005

14 Lady's Ladder .... 4+ *S0/1*
10m. At last an easy one! A terrific little number. Use the leftwards traverse to arrive at the low hard stuff. Bypass this by performing a leftwards rising traverse to gain the top shelf.
See photo on page 236.
FSA. Sam Mayfield 9.2005

15 Millie 6a *S0*
8m. This micro-traverse is best tackled by finding the next shelf around rightwards (north-east) of the main cave. Traverse back towards the cave, keeping low, to pass a technical last move.
FSA. Sam Mayfield 9.2005

Spring Tide Wall

16 Project .... 7b? *S1/2*
7m. The ultra-low traverse, from left to right, has the hallmarks of a gem in the making!

17 Project .... 7c+? *S2/3*
7m. The excellent, full-height line will need the best tide possible.
NYS

Spring Tide Wall
The next feature here is the small but alluring Spring Tide Wall. There are no completed routes at present. Take a full moon with you. The rock features small pockets and edges, and it's VERY steep.
Approach - Follow the easy path along the cliff from the Cave of Pets, until faced with a tricky bit of path; the wall will now be right in front of you.
Conditions and Tides - Use any positive tidal variation you can get your hands on! The Best of British!

Cala del Moraig — Hidden Beach

Hidden Beach

The final feature here is the Hidden Beach. The beach in question is not the one seen when looking north from the car park - rather, it's located one 'bay' closer to the car park than that one. The main event here is the world-class *Hidden Beach Traverse*, which is one of the best traverses in this guide, and easily a match for anything Devon has to offer. You can scope the line from the approach path.

Approach - Take the wandering path past the 'tricky section', and continue along to the Hidden Beach itself. A short down-climb drops you to the shingle; walk the beach to the start.

Conditions and Tides - you'll need dry rock for this route, so tackle it when things are dry and crisp. The tides are not really an issue.

❶ Hidden Beach Traverse 7a+ *S0*
50m. An amazing voyage. The climbing is sustained, powerful, and absolutely brilliant. Climb up into the starting cave, situated right above the edge of the shingle (it's easy to wade in, with towel and rock shoes on your head). Get your boots on, swing out of the cave, and traverse at that same level, to reach a hard move passing a hanging boss (massive jug awaiting). Continue on until a diagonal flake-crack is reached. Climb up this for 2m and continue traversing, to gain the top entrance of an amazing through-cave/tunnel. Drop down the tunnel for a well-earned rest, and then fall out of the bottom of the tunnel, swing through the low cave to a bridge rest, then attack the hanging terrain to the right, via a very hard move to gain a finger jug. The remaining 17m is about 6a+, with brilliant, steady climbing at the same level, on big holds. Finish on the arete; you can either swim out or walk around the top path.
FSA. Mike Robertson, Julian Lines (alt leads), Silvia Fitzpatrick, 9.2005

❷ Three-legged Tufa 6b+ *S1*
11m. A right little dash. The line pulls out of the main traverse's start cave, thereafter venturing up the very steep prow above.
FSA. Julian Lines 9.2005

❸ Project 6c+? *S0*
10m. The shapely prow found right in front of the traverse's through-tunnel is steep, and looks fun. Pull out over the roof, just above the sea. A dry-bag approach might be the easiest way to get on board.
NYS

Isla del Descobridor

This amazing, sausage-shaped island is set just a few metres off the coast, about 4km west of the massive headland feature of Cap de la Nau. The island crag is accessed by way of another nudist beach, by the name of Playa de Ambolo. The beach in question is found by dropping down off the Cap road. Boaters, simply get paddling - the beach is your base and the Evening Light Wall is only 30m from the mainland. For dry-bag explorers of the Evening Light Wall, just boulder-hop the pebbly beach south-westwards until the end of the island closes in, then swim the 30m to get there. The island is about 400m long with all sunny aspects covered. The areas described here are approximately divided into the individual crags' sunshine times. One day a fully-boated and equipped crew might hit the isle and do the lot, but in the meantime, here's a taster. All routes established so far have been jumped from, almost always from good finishing ledges or small caves. Nothing highball has been established, and all routes so far have been around S0/1.

Morning Light Wall
The long, north-east face opposite the beach. Mostly slabby, but the obvious steep section in the middle has seen some quality action. There's more to go here, including a wild, hard traverse.

❶ Disco Labrador . . . . 6a+ *S1*
15m. The steep prow in the centre of the wall is taken to a niche; finish direct over a hanging roof and up to a cave, where a jump is the order of the day.
FSA. Mike Robertson 15.9.2005

❷ Jazz . . . . 6a+ *S1*
15m. This one starts further right, and takes a leftwards-trending groove, to finish up on the same steep prow, with the same cave finish as *Disco Labrador*.
FSA. Julian Lines 15.9.2005

Lunchtime Light Wall
The east-facing tip of the isle is festooned with grooves and cracks. Access is tough, though. For the well-equipped, there's a lot of very fine rock. The main drawback is getting out of the water and onto the rock - the starts are hard! Maybe a solid boat with a gangplank arrangement?

Afternoon Light Wall
There's some excellent potential on the long south-west face, some of which has been realised. The obvious, low V-cave in the face has been breached, and various face and arete climbs have been done. The larger cave further to the left is beautiful, with the amazing, hanging highball arete yet to be bagged! Here the routes are described from right to left - as you'd find them if you're paddling clockwise round the island.

❸ Amos . . . . 6c+ *S0*
15m. The brilliant V-cave, climbed direct from the back wall. The best completed route on the isle to date. Keep to the right wall once involved, then swing across to the left wall after the apex; continue leftwards up to a ledge system at 11m. An excellent, lengthy left start has been tried out of the water.
FSA. Julian Lines 15.9.2005

❹ Boat People 6c *S0*
14m. The crinkly orange groove, trending gradually rightwards to an arete. Technical and fingery climbing, with the crux at 10m. Finish on a good ledge.
FSA. Mike Robertson 15.9.2005

❺ Disco Traverse . . . . 6a+ *S0*
80m. The lower face here has been traversed for some distance. Mostly technical, always safe.
FSA. Mike Robertson 15.9.2005

The massive cave leers at you now; very appealing, in a highball sort of way. It's been fully scrutinised! The left edge of the cave is formed by a shorter arete, beneath a towering groove.

❻ Disco Arete . . . 6b+ *S0*
16m. Tackle the striking arete by traversing rightwards onto it at 5m, then continue up it; finish when you've got the hands-off bridge in the groove at about 14m.
FSA. Mike Robertson 15.9.2005

Evening Light Wall
This west/north-west facing area, as already stated, is very close to the mainland. The obvious lines have yet to be climbed (excuses: end of day; only day; lots of hard swimming; not enough food; not enough water). So go pay a visit; and if you get some lines bagged send me details!

Cala Ximo

The micro-crag at Cala Ximo is diminutive, but fun! The cliff itself consists of the steep cut-out in the right side of the bay, opposite the headland parking area. There's enough madcap soloing to occupy a few hours, especially if you have your work cut out with mid 6's (the four routes give a spread from 6b to 6c). The lines are steep, and always out above water. One word of warning: there are some spiky sea anemones present in the water here, so take care when wading about!

Approach - From the northern end of Benidorm's huge, 3km beach, get on 'Avda del Mediterraneo', or the parallel road of 'Avda de Madrid'. At the very northern edge of town, at the end of Avda del Mediterraneo (note Centauro hire car office, and an odd green 'island' in the centre of the road), take the road of 'C/. Berlin' up the hill (past the black Triangle Pub). Take a right turn at a T-junction into a road called 'Sierra Dorada'. This road winds around a great deal; follow it, looking for a sign on the right, giving a turn for 'Castell del Mar'. Take this right turning, following the road through various hairpins, to arrive at a prominent, concrete-walled headland. This headland is above Cala Ximo, and it provides the parking. A short walk around the bay will get you easily to the small cliff, found at the far side.

Conditions and Tides - The crag gets plenty of morning sun. If the weather's too hot, you'll find it a little easier to climb here in the afternoon, when things cool down a bit. This especially applies to the traverse of *Sticky Vicky*, which is affected by a dust layer at times. Take a high tide for this crag, as the water here is not super-deep.

❶ Sticky Vicky 6c *S0/1*
10m. The traverse is spicy, and more so with the unusual amount of dust usually found on the main rail. Do it in the shade and in either direction.
FSA. Rich Mayfield and Ewan Lyon 7.2005

❷ Miss Layton . . . . 6b+ *S0/1*
7m. The left-most and hardest of the 'up' routes. Smaller pockets - same angle! Climb direct to the top; the crux is low down.
FSA. Ewan Lyon 7.2005

❸ Dog's Bollocks 6b *S0/1*
7m. The middle line is just right of centre. Good pockets and locks provide the fault-line; as with its neighbours, continue steeply to the top.
FSA. Rich Mayfield 7.2005

❹ Benidorm Bender 6b *S0/1*
7m. As steep as. From the lower shelf, climb on massive pockets to gain the fault-line rail. Continue to the top.
FSA. Ewan Lyon 7.2005

Riding the wild surf: Rich Mayfield on the first ascent of *Jellystone* (5+) - *page 245* - Jellystone Buttress, Cala del Moraig. Photo: Mike Robertson.

Mallorca

by Mike Robertson and Daimon Beail

Mike Weeks aiming for the tufas on *The Might of the Stalactite* (7a) - *page 273* - Cala Barques, Mallorca. Photo: Mike Robertson.

Mallorca

The emergence of Mallorca onto the DWS scene in 2001 set the tongues wagging, and with good reason. The island, better known as a tourist venue and a top sport climbing destination, had always been known for its near-perfect limestone, but the island's low-slung, south-east coastline had been slow to show its true potential.

In summer 2001, local climber Miquel Riera invited a team of DWS hitmen to an almost-forgotten crag he "hopes is worth the visit". Five carloads of deep water soloists turn up, inspired by a single picture of Miquel soloing a 7a at Diablo in the late 80's. The rest, as they say, is history. Today, after the attention of soloists from the UK, Austria, France, U.S. and Australia, the island is certainly the most cosmopolitan destination in this guidebook.

Getting There

Flights to Palma, Mallorca's capital, can be found on the internet, with better deals for out-of-season folk like us.

Getting Around

A hire care is pretty essential. Your best bet is to search the internet for a deal, although simply turning up is rarely a problem, especially out of season. Bear in mind that if your flight lands you in the middle of the night, your car hire company might charge you for a call-out, which could be expensive.

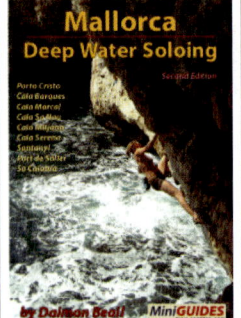

Mallorca DWS MiniGuide

Such is the pace of development on Mallorca that Daimon Beail is producing a second edition of his PDF MiniGuide. This also covers all the main areas in this book. Most of these venues are along the south east coast with some more remote locations on the wilder north coast. The flexibility of the MiniGuide system means that we will be able to keep this PDF download up-to-date as new areas are developed which, on an island with as wonderful a coastline as Mallorca, seems to be absolutely certain.

More information
www.rockfax.com and **www.dwsworld.com**

Lauren Matthews getting her share of a *Slice of Heaven* (5) - *page 266* - on Cova del Diablo, Mallorca. Photo: Mike Robertson.

Conditions and Tides

Mallorca's tides are not an issue with the deep water soloist. The tidal variation, or 'swing', is usually around 0.4m, so that's a concern to cross off your list! More important, as with all crags in this guide, is the state of the sea. So climb with your mates, use a rope when needed for exits and safety, and retire to the cafe when the sea gets angry.

Mallorca's crags are prone to mid-summer condensation. This has thwarted many a summer visit, and is due to a combination of high temperatures and crags that are often too steep to attract the overhead summer sun. So recommended is a visit in the autumn, when the temperatures drop, the rock is cooler, and the conditions are almost always superior. And let's not forget that a September trip is likely to give a sea temperature of around 26°C.

Daimon Beail 'off' the classic line of *Strangers in Paradise* (7b+) - *page 275* - Cala de Barques, Mallorca. Photo: Andrew Chapman.

Accommodation and Food

Cheap accommodation can be tricky to find. There are stacks of hotels in the gungy pits of west Palma, but if you want to stay nearer the climbing in Porto Cristo, you either have to discreetly camp, or indulge yourself in one of the local hotels, which can be a little pricy. The best way to enjoy a trip, however, takes a little organising - search the internet for a villa, and fill it with people! This will be affordable and highly sociable.

Recommended for general eating and drinking is Porto Cristo, which is a lively town and harbour, found just around the corner from the mighty Diablo. The town has banks, kiddy boat shops (highly important), and lots of supermarkets and cafes. It's a delightful town, with none of the ugliness of suburban Palma. The best place to meet in the morning is the excellent S'assecados Cafe in the town square; the Flamingo Bar, found above the north end of the superb beach in the harbour, is a great place to eat and drink, with a good chance to 'move' all the tables together! The best bakery in town (essential stuff, this) is just up the hill from the local Tourist Info Office.

SERAC OUTDOOR SPORTS

- GUIDED ROCK WEEKS
- PRIVATE GUIDED CLIMBING
- GUIDED WALKING HOLIDAYS
- FULLY INCLUSIVE PRICES

See website for full details
WWW.SERACOUTDOORSPORTS.CO.UK
Tel: +44(0)191 5194495
Mobile +44 (0)7930 180 828

Walker on the Caval
Bernat Ridge
Photos: Chris Craggs

Rock Climbing on Mallorca

Foracorda Climbing Shop
www.foracorda.com

CRAZY FOR CLIMBING
MALLORCA

foracorda

Miquel Marquès.20
.07005.Palma.
Mallorca.
.Baleares.España.
Tel.Fax.+34 971 463004
foracorda@foracorda.com

Cova del Diablo

Mallorca's Cova del Diablo is a masterpiece of architecture, an eye-catching monument to what is conceivable in the fantastical world of DWS. It would be fair to say it's almost certainly the best-formed slice of DWS rock yet found on the planet: a huge, streaked amphitheatre of pocketed limestone, poised above a deep sea of green. It's quite breathtaking, especially on first acquaintance.

Of course nothing's that perfect and Diablo has its fair share of snags, just like any crag. It's a little too high and the exits can be tricky, especially when the sea is rough. The routes themselves offer a profusion of pockets and buckets, the angle generally dictates the grade, as the holds are almost always huge! It's worth mentioning that the cove itself, and especially the harder, steeper routes, are prone to considerable condensation in the summer months, so recommended is a later visit, around September-October, when the sun is lower. Also of note is the fact that almost all of the routes here have a crux at less than two-thirds height.

Approach

Most folk approach Porto Cristo from the Mallorcan capital of Palma, which brings you along the C-715 to Manacor. From here, take the PM-402 eastwards to Porto Cristo. The town of Porto Cristo is easy to find by following the signs, but slightly trickier is the baffling one-way system between town and the crag. So follow your nose to the eastern edge of town, where parking below a set of large villas gets you to a curve in the road very close to the cliff. A small path through the shrubbery brings you to the very top of the crag, where you will be soundly forgiven for whooping and shouting for a few minutes or so.

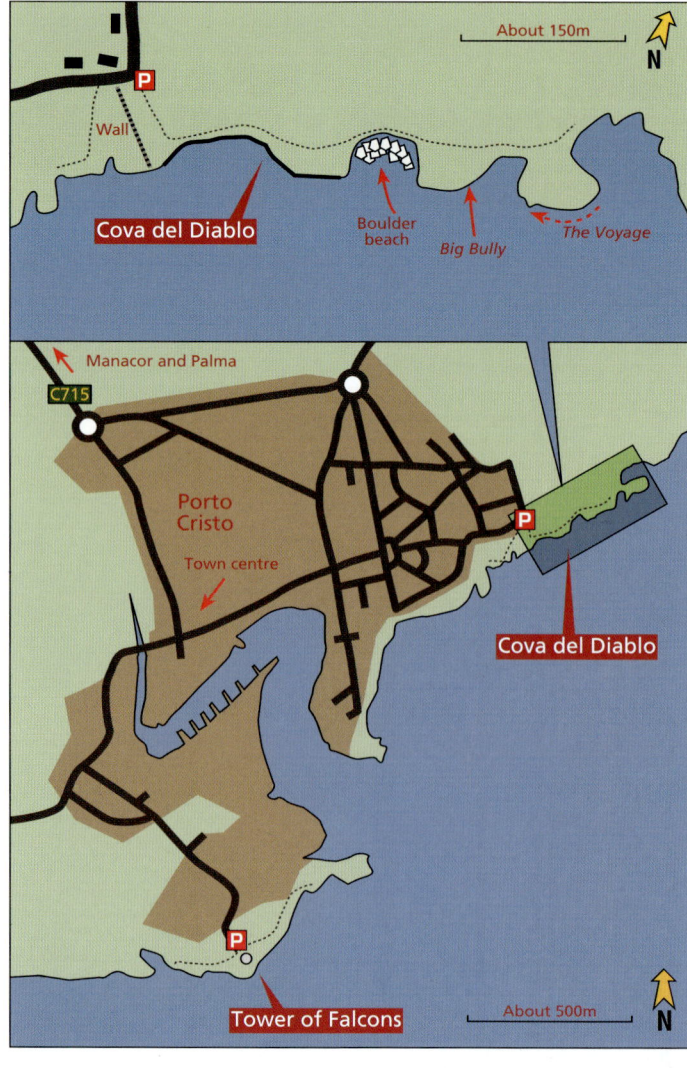

Local DWS legend Miquel Riera on the brilliant *In the Night, Every Cat is Black* (8a) - *page 264* - Cova del Diablo, Mallorca. Photo: David Torres.

Cova del Diablo

Conditions and Tides

Don't expect any tidal problems at Diablo, as the tidal variation on the island ia usually less than half a metre. Of more concern is the sea state, so observe the exit notes carefully before you proceed. As a general rule, leave it well alone if things are rough, and, if in any doubt, arrange a rope down to the sea with an inflatable wotsit on it - anything from a kiddy boat to a big ring. This contingency plan will prove a godsend if things get rough whilst you're down there.

Swim-outs

There have been problems with the exit from the water at Diablo, when the sea is a little rough. The boulder beach exit along to the north-east (at the right end of the *White Noise Traverse*, looking in) is the easiest exit from the water, but can sometimes become a no-go area in rough or choppy seas. So any effort to make your exit from the water easier, at the base of the easy way down, are of paramount importance. If the sea is less than smooth, take a rope and some wires/slings, and set it up - and knot up the hanging end where it reaches the sea. The preferred position for your knotted exit rope is marked on the photo-topo on page 265, right under the easy way down; the 'free' exit, ie. 'leaving' the sea without rope

Neil Gresham on *Ejector Seat* (7c) - *page 264* - Cova del Diablo, Mallorca. Photo: Mike Robertson.

assistance, feels like 6b/6b+, and is very testing with tired, wet hands. An alternative exit (although not enabling you to reach the top of the crag) is the threaded low cave, found just under *The Lobster*, where a short rope can be left in place.

This Diablo exit difficulty has become an significant safety issue and the life of a very experienced DWS'er was lost - please don't let this happen to you.

Mike Robertson on the steepness of *Afroman* (7b+) - *page 265* - Cova del Diablo, Mallorca. Photo: Neil Gresham.

Cova del Diablo Surfing Bird Area

Surfing Bird Area

This left (west) end of the crag provides a good selection of grades, and the finish of the girdle of *Superwoman*. The rock here offers an incredible number of huge pockets and buckets.

Approach - *The Italian Job* and *Swing Both Ways* are tackled either by a long traverse in from the circular basin found to the south, or by abseiling in from threads to gain the base of the wall. *Surfing Bird* requires an abseil into its niche start, with *Blue Tuna* and *Let's Have It* best approached by dry-bag or boat. To reach the start of *Iguanodon*, traverse leftwards along *Superwoman*, dropping down into the lower cave to gain the route's start (about 6a). The upper wall routes *Microdot*, *Sunshine* and *Shadow* (above *Iguanodon*) are most easily reached via a short abseil.
Routes from *Hip Hop* through to *In the Night...* are best approached either via *Superwoman* (from the right) or by an abseil, alighting down at the base of *The Lobster*. You'll need to swing in a bit, and clip a thread with a 'biner on the way down (Tip: abseil in on a double rope, clip one in on the way down, and attach your harness to the loose half - then get your partner to haul both ropes out of the way). The remainder of the routes are reached via the easy way down, on the right side of the amphitheatre.

Conditions and Tides - Wait for a calm sea. The small tide swing will not affect anything except perhaps the start of *Let's Have It*. Avoid climbing here when the rock is damp, as it often is in the summer when the sun is high.

Exits - Read the details on page 260 for your best exits from the water here.

❶ **The Italian Job** 6b *S1*
16m. Grossly bulging territory for the grade; how big can handholds get? Climb the wall and then the overhanging ground on the left edge of the main Diablo amphitheatre, using huge holds and massive pockets. The crux is at mid-height; above an easier diagonal feature and takes you rightwards to the top.
FSA. Mike Robertson 10.2001

❷ **Swing Both Ways** 6c *S1*
17m. A harder alternative to the above route, swinging right on to slightly more powerful ground in the bulging mid-section. Finish as for *The Italian Job*.
FSA. Neil Gresham 10.2001

❸ **Surfing Bird** 7b *S1/2*
17m. The first of local activist Miquel Riera's original lines. Take the leaning face and the cream/red streak, then boldly on into the top recess. Magnificent!
FSA. Miquel Riera, Pepino Lopez and Xisco Meca, late 1980's

❹ **Blue Tuna** . . . . 6c+ *S1/2*
17m. A great slice of climbing. Reach it either by a low, tricky traverse in from the left, or by dry-bagging into the cave. From the left edge of the low cave, climb powerfully through the roof (crux) and follow the biggest holds all the way to the top.
FSA. Julian Lines 9.2002

❺ **Microdot** 7b *S2/3*
10m. This extension to the lower routes gives some high and feisty moves, pulling through into the top recess. Spicy territory, and for the brave only.
FSA. Neil Gresham 9.2002

Surfing Bird Area — Cova del Diablo

6 Let's Have It! .... 7c+ S2
10m. This ace test-piece is just about horizontal. Start in the centre of the low/left sea level cave, from the very edge of the water itself, taking care with water depth early on. Climb up (out?) and continue to the big half-height recess, passing a crux slap for a two-finger pocket.
FSA. Klem Loskot 10.2001

7 Iguanodon 7b S1
12m. A mega-classic. Takes the silly-steep ground to the right of the last route, heading leftwards along a huge, juggy rail. As with *Let's Have It*, you're faced with a choice: either jump off, get involved with *Superwoman*, or have a go at one of the upper wall routes.
FSA. Neil Gresham 10.2001

8 Sunshine and Shadow
.... 8a+ S2/3
11m. The very steep upper rib is a sought-after prize. From the recess, step right and climb the right side of the rib to the top.
FSA. Klem Loskot 2002

9 Surfer Dead 7a S2
16m. A great route. Easy ground takes you up into a small, high cave. From here, an airy finale up the top face is your ticket to ride. The original, 1992 photograph of Miguel's ascent inspired the big 2001 foray to the island.
FSA. Miquel Riera late 1980's

10 Hip Hop .... 7b+ S2
16m. The streaked wall up and left of the big cave. Climb the left edge of the cave, and sprint to the top.
FSA. Miquel Riera 2002

11 Surfing in the Bar 6c+ S2
17m. Fantastic! Negotiates the right edge of the big central cave, thereafter firing rightwards up the very steep top face (tip: keep well right of the big, hanging tufa). Save some energy for the pumpy top crux, because there's not too many footholds.
FSA. Miquel Riera late 1980's

12 Sea Devil 7a S2
16m. The right side of the enticing orange streaks. Expect some high spice!
FSA. Grant Farquhar 2002

Diablo!
Mallorca's magnificent Diablo has now been a source of inspiration for some six years, and has officially passed into DWS-speak. When folk go abroad looking for fresh pastures, or imagine they're on the cusp of a major DWS discovery on some hitherto undeveloped Mediterranean isle, they'll use the word as a term of perfection. Thus we now hear, all too frequently (and mostly without much conviction!) the phrase: "Yeah, I'll be looking for a Diablo!"

Cova del Diablo — The Lobster Area

The Lobster Area

The central section of this fantastic wall gives more mega-quality routes, more buckets, and more utopia! Diablo holds the world crown for deep pockets.

Approach - Abseil to the base of *The Lobster*. You'll need to swing in a bit, and clip a thread with a 'biner on the way down (Tip: abseil in on a double rope, clip one in on the way down, and attach your harness to the loose half - then get your partner to haul both ropes out of the way). This allows you to reach routes from *The Lobster* through to *In the Night*...

For the next set of routes, from *Hair Bear* through to *Dogging Romp*, access is much simpler. They're all gained via the easy way down, and then the initial, rightmost section of *Superwoman*, which is the steadiest part of that route. For *First Impressions*, you'll only need to locate the way down.

Conditions and Tides - As with the left side, timing your visit to coincide with dry rock can pay dividends. The small tides are fairly immaterial. Pay close attention to the sea state, and avoid choppy seas.

Exit - Pay particular attention to your exit here. Your simplest swim is to the boulder beach, but your options to directly gain the rock are detailed on page 260.

❶ The Lobster . . . . **6c+** *S2*

16m. One of the best routes in Mallorca. Long, outrageously steep, and ludicrously juggy, with a relatively easy roof right at the top. Climbing just can't get much better than this! The crux is low; don't miss the sneaky lie-down rest at two-thirds height.
See photo on page 268.
FSA. Neil Gresham 10.2001

❷ Right Here, Right Now. . . . . **8a+** *S2*

16m. A proper blast. Sustained climbing takes you up to a powerful and fingery leftwards traverse below the final bulge.
FSA. Klem Loskot 2002

❸ Loskot and Two Smoking Barrels
. . . . **8a+** *S2*

16m. One of the most energetic deep water solos in Spain to date. Features a V10 boulder problem at 12m, which is essentially a gigantic dyno for a twin-barrel pocket. You have been warned!
FSA. Klem Loskot 10.2001

❹ Ejector Seat **7c** *S1*

16m. Another dash of utopia. Race up the leaning, pocketed face to a crux move for a tufa pinch, and then swing quickly right to easier ground. *See photo on page 260.*
FSA. Neil Gresham 10.2001. The first ascent photos featured on the cover of Climber magazine in 2002.

❺ In The Night, Every Cat Is Black
. . . . **8a** *S1*

16m. Immaculate climbing, and a perfect ground-up proposition for aspiring 8a DWS merchants. The centre of the brown streaks is climbed direct; save some energy for the rightwards move into the faint groove. The finish is much easier.
See photos on page 7 and 259.
FSA. Klem Loskot 10.2001

❻ Hair Bear. . . . . **7c+** *S1*

16m. Tackles the horrendously steep wall leftwards from the *Afroman* cave, to arrive at a complex sequence getting past a vertical slot. Thereafter trend right to enter the easier niche.
FSA. Ken Palmer 10.2001

The Lobster Area — Cova del Diablo

❼ Ronatron .... 7c+ S1
15m. A very steep line indeed. From the start of *Afroman*, swing leftwards and take the bulging wall on hidden pockets. The top section eases considerably.
FSA. Miquel Riera 2004

❽ Afroman .... 7b+ S1
15m. One of the best steep routes on the island! Exit the resting cave on brilliant, well-positioned pockets, to find yourself at a crux move gaining the horizontal seam. Further technical moves up and left gain the niche, and a well-deserved rest. Continue much more easily to the top. *See photo on page 261.*
FSA. Tim Emmett 10.2001

❾ Whiplash 7c S1
15m. A sequency, mega-steep route found immediately right of *Afroman*. From the centre of the small cave, pull out rightwards and dash through the roof. The top section is much easier.
FSA. Neil Gresham 10.2001

❿ Calamares 6c S1
17m. Great moves throughout. From the *Superwoman* traverse climb the long, faint groove diagonally leftwards, then take the bulging brown streak above, before trending right to finish.
FSA. Neil Gresham 10.2001

⓫ Dogging Romp .... 6a+ S1
16m. Steep and juggy, and at an amenable grade - a brilliant introduction to the crag. From the easy way down, head leftwards up an enticing diagonal feature. When the moves start to get tricky, take a look up, grasp big jugs, and finish straight up over the bulging roof.
FSA. Mike Robertson 10.2001

⓬ Superwoman .... 7a+ S0
100m+. Stunning climbing, weaving across the entire face of Diablo. This mini-expedition ventures to half-height in places, and could perhaps be better described as a girdle, with the preferred direction seemingly right to left (looking in). Because the line is such a lengthy outing, it naturally falls into four sections, with three excellent rests en-route. I'll split it up here:
1) 6b. Climb leftwards from the easy way down, to gain the rest in the *Afroman* start cave.
2) 7a+. The crux pitch. Traverse leftwards out of the cave, and finally embark on a lengthy and sustained down-climb to gain the low traverse across the centre of the crag. (An alternative has now been added, at the same grade: keep low onto a block feature, and make desperate moves off it to gain the original line.)
3) 7a. Climb gradually leftwards, gaining more and more height, until the big recess at the finish of *Iguanadon* is gained. A very steep and pumpy pitch, and not much easier than the second one.
4) 6b+. The final pitch is juggy and nicely sustained, heading across the steep wall to gain easier ground left of *The Italian Job*. Your choice is now to either finish for that route, or up the easier but less safe wall to the left. It's also possible to traverse all the way out, to reach the conglomerate bowl-cave to the south.
FSA. Ken Palmer, Grant Farquhar 10.2001

⓭ First Impressions 6a S1
12m. The first new route by the invading team of 2001. Slight but well-positioned, taking the colourful prow just to the right of the way down.
FSA. Mike Robertson 10.2001

Cova del Diablo — White Noise Area

White Noise Area

The grades found at this end of the crag take an abrupt dive, with the average grade here around 5+. You'll find the usual buckets and pockets, but with a sudden change in angle - it's a perfect place to get acquainted with Diablo. You'll notice some substantial gaps between routes here - this is due to the slabby nature of those unclimbed sections, which are not recommended for DWS.

Approach - To reach any of the routes here, you'll need to get yourself on the *White Noise* traverse, which is started from either end. From the left, use the easy way down, and from the right, walk around from the boulder beach and start climbing.

Conditions and Tides - The tides are not relevant. Climb when the sea is calm and make sure that you can swim and exit at the boulder beach, or rig the lower reef accordingly, below the way down (see page 260).

❶ White Noise . . . . . . 5+ *S0*
60m. Superb climbing across clean, pocketed rock, and above good water all the way. From the easy way down, traverse across steady ground, passing the start of *Slice of Heaven*. Drop down into the lower cave recess to a rest, and then make tricky moves on pockets to traverse the wall to the right. The crux is a technical sequence to pass the smooth grey streak right of *Bonobo*. Continue more easily to finish on the boulder beach.
FSA. Mike Robertson 10.2001

❷ Slice of Heaven 5 *S1*
15m. In a world with very few really brilliant easy DWS's, this one stands aloft! Start on the traverse of *White Noise*. Cross the next groove, and head on to the big, airy prow to the right. Holds simply cannot get any bigger than this! Finish up a slim, juggy layback groove on perfect rock. See photo on page 255.
FSA. Mike Robertson 10.2001. A Climb magazine cover shot in 2005.

❸ Eternal Flame . . . . 5+ *S1*
16m. All the pockets of the main Cove, but on vertical territory - wonderful! Drop into the big cave on *White Noise*, exit it, and then climb the wall on the right, grappling with more pockets than you can imagine.
FSA. Mike Robertson 10.2001

❹ Bonobo . . . . 5+ *S2*
16m. Follow *White Noise* to a bit of a rest on a slab underneath a curling, brown groovy feature. Take this feature on its steeper right rib - on jugs, of course, what else?
FSA. Mike Robertson 10.2001

The Voyage Area

The last two routes in the region are found on the two buttresses immediately north-east of the Diablo amphitheatre (see map on page 258). From the boulder beach, walk along the path for 100m to gain the next face - Big Bully takes the right side of this (looking in). To reach The Voyage, walk a further 100m to the next protruding buttress, and start from the far end.

❺ Big Bully . . . . 6a+ *S3*
18m. Spice and commitment! Ventures up the big, exposed face 100 metres to the north-east of the main crag, above a noticeable cut-out at the base of the cliff. Keep a steady eye on the protruding prow down to your right.
FSA. Mike Robertson 10.2001

❻ The Voyage 6a *S0*
50m. A super-safe journey, traversing the sort of ground Devon's *Magical Mystery Tour* might almost be jealous of. Start at the north-east end of the protruding buttress, and head back on the slightly overhanging wall, on the most gigantic holds known to man - jugs, pockets and threads. Finish up an easy groove, after about 50m of sheer paradise.
FSA. Mike Robertson 10.2001

Mike Robertson on the first ascent of *Feist Queen* (6c) - *page 269* -Tower of Falcons Area, Mallorca. Photo: Neil Gresham.

Cova del Diablo — Tower of Falcons

Gavin Symonds, and one of the best DWS's in Mallorca The Lobster (6c+) - *page 264* - Cova del Diablo, Mallorca. Photo: Mike Robertson.

Tower of Falcons

On the opposite edge of Porto Cristo is the Tower of Falcons: a big area, but with few established routes. The stunning cave below the Tower may one day host some absolute DWS masterpieces. *Morning Glory* provides your sunlit wake-up route!

Approach - Drive southwards out of Porto Cristo, up the hill from the small bridge, and make a left turn down a straight road to a circular car park at the end. Here you cannot miss the amazing stone Tower of Falcons, with its rather disturbing, eroded, inner staircase. You'll need your shoulders for an ascent (I jest you not!). The first route in the area is discovered by locating an easy way down, found about 200m west of the Tower. This is the start of *Shrek*, which is a fun 6a traverse useful for accessing *Feist Queen* and *Public Enema No.1*.

The Morning Glory traverse is found under the Tower. To reach it, walk along the cliff-top away from the Tower (north-east), and down to spacious sea level ledges.

Conditions and Tides - No tidal issues but pay close attention to the sea state. Avoid hot sun on *Morning Glory*.

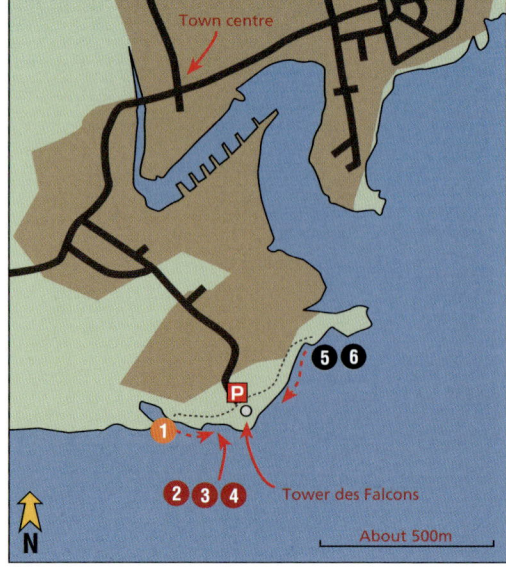

Tower of Falcons Cova del Diablo

Routes 1 to 4 200m

The first route on offer is the ubiquitous traverse, Shrek, which also provides delightful access to the next two routes described.

❶ Shrek 6a S0
140m. A long, supremely undercut traverse, starting from an easy way down some 200m west of the Tower. It finishes on the left edge of the striking *Feist Queen* face, where your easiest finish option is a swim, a reversal of the route, or a grade 3 climb (not DWS) up the spiky crag left of *Feist Queen*.
FSA. Gav Symonds 10.2001

❷ Shrek Extension ... 6c+ S0
15m. This tasty piece of climbing extends *Shrek* 15m past the *Feist Queen* face, to give a sturdier finishing grade of 6c+. Reverse, swim, or scramble out as detailed above.
FSA. Ken Palmer 10.2001

❸ Feist Queen 6c S3
18m. A feisty little number indeed. Approach it by way of *Shrek*, or by abseil. Attack the centre of the bulging face with commitment, above not quite enough water (around 2m deep). At the very top, take stock of your energy reserves, and get the crux done quickly! *See photo on page 267*.
FSA. Mike Robertson 10.2001

❹ Public Enema No.1 .... 6b S2
18m. The big line to the right of *Feist Queen*. Gradually escape rightwards up a groove, to a more amenable finish than its big sister.
FSA. Grant Farquhar 10.2001

The last routes in this region are found just right of the stunning cave below the Tower. As you'll see in the picture above, the cave is breathtaking, and holds DWS possibilities for the next generation and beyond. The cave provides some very atmospheric swimming and snorkelling, including a dive around/under a perfectly-formed underwater 'rock bridge'.
The *Morning Glory* traverse is lengthy and involved, and allows you to reach the project, which starts in the small cave that *Morning Glory* finishes in. To reach the traverse of *Morning Glory* from the tower, simply wander off leftwards (looking out), and drop down easy ledges until you gain the route's start.

❺ Morning Glory . 7a+ S1
160m. A long and highly involved traverse, taking full advantage of the early morning sun. It's found in the north (town) side of the huge cave lying underneath the Tower of Falcons. The phototopo should give all necessary info - basically, the line stays close to sea level, and finishes in a tiny cave on the edge of the massive cave. The crux is packed into the last 10m, and don't do it when it's hot - you'll fry! A small jump into the sea completes your ascent.
FSA. Mike Robertson 10.2001

❻ Project .... 8? S3
22m. This line has seen a number of attempts, all ending in the briny. The complex sequence on big slopers above the start cave needs a cold day. Expect steadier climbing above and a number of finishing options, including a possible fixed rope at the two-thirds ledge system.

Cala Barques

Discovered a year or so after the development of Cova del Diablo, Cala Barques offers a slightly less intimidating alternative to Diablo's taller cliffs. The rock is generally very solid and gives a variety of features, including stalactites, arches and some rather shapely caves. Most routes here were put up by Klem Loskot, along with the Salomon team, local enthusiast Miquel Riera and U.S. convert Chris Sharma.

There are four main areas at Barques. The first is known simply as 'Cova' - a stunning stalactite cave around fourteen metres high. Further along the cliff are two more caves known as the Metrosexual Area and the Snatch Area. Both of these crags are connected by a giant grotto which can be accessed from the top of the cliff. The final feature here is a little further around the headland and is known as the Tarantino Cave - this is the tallest cliff in the vicinity, and houses some of the hardest routes on the island.

Grades - Much of the information in this section was originally reported using the Spanish 'psicobloc' grading system, which deviates from the usual French grades, in that it has a very broad range for each grade. For the purpose of this guide, the psicobloc grades have been converted into the more usual and widely understood French grades - you may notice the odd random grade due to this recent conversion! It has been impossible to gain full First Solo Ascent information for Barques, due to the elusive nature of some of the protagonists!

Approach

Cala Barques is located just up the coast from the popular sport climbing crag of Cala Magraner. From Porto Cristo, follow the PMV401-4 southwards towards Porto Colom. After about 6km, pass a left turn to Cala Romantica, and negotiate a sharp right/left twist in the road. Continue on briefly to a left turn at a 'Coto Privado de Caza' sign (this is just before a right turn leading to Manacor which is probably the approach for people staying elsewhere on the island). Take this left turn and follow the amenable dirt track all the way to the end, to a large, chained iron gate. Park here, allowing room for the turning point in the road.

Squeeze through the gate and follow the path through the farmland and down the hill into the woods, thereafter reaching the beach. Follow the left side of the bay to reach the various areas.

Tides and Conditions

The Barques area enjoys good conditions, although the usual rules apply with steep rock and shade - a dry, cool day will give you your best chance. Pay the usual attention to the sea state, and sort out your exits before you set off - see the individual crag notes for these.

Bernard Exley on the upper half of *Big XXL* (7a) - *page 273* - on the Cova Area at Cala Barques. Photo: Daimon Beail

Cala Barques Cova Area

Cova Area

A delightful crag, with great rock and some amazing architecture. The crag is around 14m in height.

Approach - The left-hand routes, up to *Big XXL*, start from The Block, which is accessed by way of an abseil swing-in (tricky). The right-hand routes are reached by down-climbing the right side of the cave (6a) or by abseil down the same line. The descent to *The Barques Traverse* is a scramble but not above the water.

Conditions and Tides - A breezy, dry day will give the best conditions in the cave's darker regions.

Exit - There are two exit points. One is found 8m left of The Block, and the other is found just to the right of the start of *Mecca*.

❶ **Le Gashbomb** 7a *S1*
7m. This line was reported as being roughly 7a. It looks a lot harder than this grade though!

❷ **Funtlappen** 7a *S1*
8m. Start as for *Le Gashbomb* and move right just under the lip; it looks harder than the given grade.

❸ **Leistenmatz** . . . . 8a+ *S1*
7m. A desperate test-piece, tackling the smooth bulging wall.

❹ **Dachicas** 7a *S0*
9m. A popular line. From the block, launch up into the roof above. The crux is the upper wall.

❺ **Drop Shadow Diseases** . . . . 6c+ *S0*
11m. A popular link-up, and at a more realistic grade. Start as for *Dachicas* and follow the natural line rightwards to join the top half of *Transversal*.

❻ **Sixty's Silver Surfer** 7a *S0*
10m. Another popular link-up. Climb *Dachicas* into the traverse of *Drop Shadow Diseases* and finish up the remainder of *Klem's Erection*.

❼ **Klem's Erection** . . . . 7b+ *S0*
10m. From the block, reverse *The Might of the Stalactite*, then head up to a small roof. The top face is not as stiff.

❽ **Double Penetration** . . . . 7b+ *S0*
10m. An alternative start to *Klem's Erection* from the largest stalactite in Barques.

❾ **Transversal** 7a *S0*
10m. The most central line; independent and bold, and one of the classic Barques' routes.

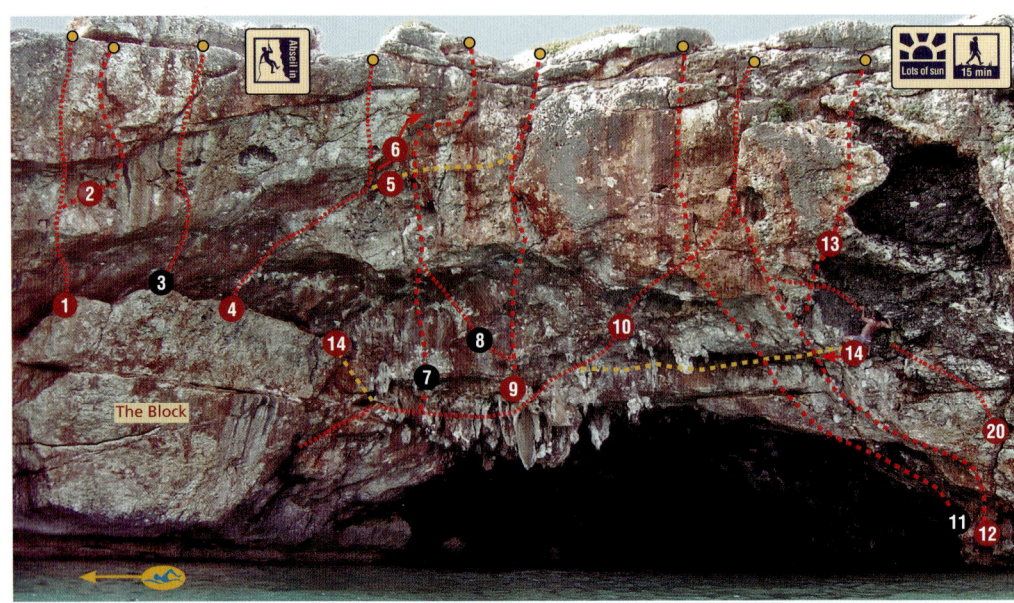

Cova Area Cala Barques 273

10 Big XXL 7a S0
18m. An absolute mega classic! Start from The Block and reverse *The Might of the Stalactite* until you begin to naturally elevate towards a small cave in the wall. Rest here before tackling the finale, which involves a pull over the roof to a good pocket, followed by a rising traverse to join *Mecca* at a large bucket hold. *See photo on page 271.*

11 Granaten-Einstiez .... 7b+ S0
18m. Often greasy at the start as well as being a little bit friable in places. Cutting out right onto the line of *Big XXL* reduces the grade to 7b.

12 Mecca .... 6c+ S0
18m. A parallel line to *Granaten-Einstiez*. The upper wall is much easier.

13 Genoveses 6b S0
12m. The line just left of the Darth Vader's helmet feature. Sometimes used as an alternative finish to *The Barques Traverse*.

14 The Might of the Stalactite .. 7a S0
15m. A right-to-left traverse over the lip of the cave. A 'must do' when visiting the Cova! *See photo on page 252.*

15 Golden Nase .... 7b+ S3
10m. This line is rarely climbed, on account of the jutting prow at its base.

16 Ralph Kaiser's Nehe Kleider's.. 7b+ S2
10m. A similar landing to *Golden Nase* - take care.

17 Goldie Hawn .... 7b+ S0
10m. Powerful and fingery climbing. A slight variation (*Kurt Husser* 7b+ S1) can be made by climbing *Goldie Hawn* to the final bulge near the top and moving left onto the finish of *Ralph Kaiser's Nehe Kleider's*.

18 Tower of Power ... 7a S0
11m. The most popular line on this section of the wall. After a juggy start, fingery climbing leads to a thin section under the lip. Climb the left side of the roof to the top.

19 Klem's Golden Shower . 7a+ S0
10m. A hard line up a vague prow.

20 The Barques Traverse 6b S2
90m. A long and fairly steady right-to-left traverse, usually finishing up the final section of *Mecca*. There are a few protruding ledges just below the water to look out for. A great Barques' warm-up.

Cala Barques — Metrosexual Area

❶ Bisexual .... 6c+ *S0*
12m. The most popular route on the wall, with great access from the top of the cliff. Swing out from the platform and tackle the smooth, steep wall above, past a deep pocket.
See photo on page 277.

❷ Metrosexual .... 7a+ *S0*
15m. This line can be approached from low down on friable rock or, for the shorter version, from the high platform. Either way, climb up to share holds with *Bisexual*, and move left on two pockets to finish on the upper prow.

❸ Transexual 7b *S0*
14m. From the platform, traverse right across the upper wall and onto the final section of *Bandito*.

❹ Solecito 7c *S0*
14m. Start on the right-hand platform and power your way across to join *Metrosexual*.

❺ Bandito .... 7c+ *S0*
11m. Start as for *Solecito* and about a third of the way across, head up for the recess just right of the large slot in the wall. Continue over the lip to finish.

❻ Homosexual .... 7b+ *S0*
9m. This is a rarely ascended line. Climb up the left side of the seeping cave, and continue up the bulging wall above.

Metrosexual Area

A great and well-positioned cave, with a handy entry point at half-height on the left. The routes are all S0's, and the climbing's all over at 12m above the sea.

Approach - Most of the routes on the left side are easily reached from the half-height platform, with the full-length *Metrosexual* starting from a sea level ledge. The right-hand routes are reached by a down-climb (6b) - not over water, or safer via a short abseil.

Conditions and Tides - The crag is generally sheltered. The rock can be greasy sometimes, but any dry, sunny day should give you plenty to do.

Exit - See the various exit points on the overview picture above.

Snatch Area — Cala Barques

Snatch Area
This cave is a terrific way to either fall off a lot or get very fit. It's full of grade 6's and 8's, and they're (almost) all at the magic grade of *S0*.

Approach - To reach the left-hand routes, use the down-climb (6a) - not over water, or safer via abseil. For the routes on the right side of the cave, use either the traverse of *Watch for the Jellies*, The Grotto's entry point scramble, or the easy down-climb over to the right of the cave.

Conditions and Tides - Usually sheltered. Take a dry breeze for the bigger grades!

Exit - Take care when exiting in the Grotto, as there are some deep holes dotted about underfoot.

7 Fortuna 6a *S0*
8m. An easy line up the left side of the cave.

8 Hercules .... 6c+ *S0*
10m. The line crossing the lip of the cave. The grade is uncertain and it could well be harder.

9 Snatch. 8b *S0*
9m. The first of three classics. It's unbelievably fingery and smooth.

10 Carlos Checa ..... 8a+ *S0*
9m. Follow the same line as *Snatch* and continue heading rightwards into the scoop.

11 Strangers In Paradise .. 7b+ *S1*
11m. Swing across the entrance of the Grotto and onto the adjacent wall - spotter advised. Move rightwards until you reach a series of ledges and pockets which help you attain a mega-pinch. Hold on! Continue making tricky moves up and right to finish. *See photo on page 256*.

12 Braune Gurken .... 6a+ *S0*
11m. A simple warm-up with smooth holds for your feet.

13 Watch for the Jellies .... 6c+ *S0*
8m. A tricky, central traverse that starts from the Grotto and traverses left around the scoop.

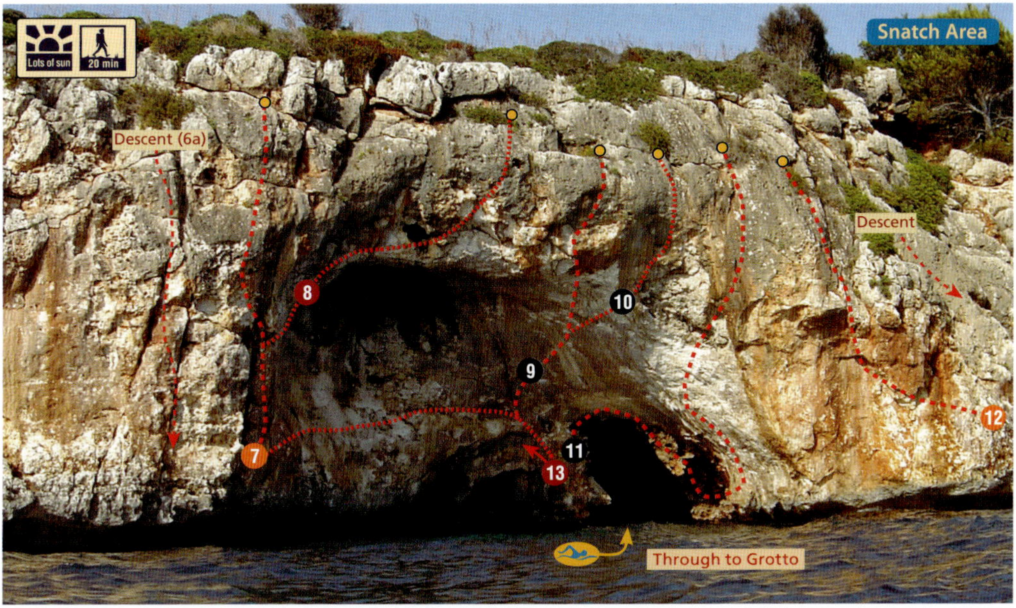

Cala Barques — Tarantino Cave

Tarantino Cave

This cave is full of big grades, and offers a high concentration of grade 7's and 8's. It's also tall, at roughly 22m, so if 'S0' is your preference, return immediately to the Snatch Area!

Approach - The crag is a late inclusion, and there's not a great deal of info available on approaches and exits. Take a rope and a dry-bag/kiddy boat, and use your loaf.

Conditions and Tides - This cave is exposed to the open sea, so the usual rules apply when soloing here. A balmy day will give best conditions.

❶ Big Mama . . . . 8c+ *S2*
26m. A desperate line, with the shallow start giving the *S2* grade. Cross the massive roof rightwards, and continue across the smooth wall above.
FSA. Chris Sharma 2006

❷ Mamasita . . . . 8a+ *S1*
22m. The little Mama. From a jug rail, head up and left for a rest and follow the remainder of *Big Mama* to the top.
FSA. Tony Lamprecht 2005

❸ O-Ren Lssii . . . . 8a+ *S1*
22m. From a jug-rail, move up and right to join *From Dusk 'Till Dawn*. Follow this over the lip, and then break out right to continue to the top.

❹ From Dusk 'Till Dawn . . 7b *S1*
18m. The most direct way up the wall. Start from the lower/right edge of the cave, and climb up to the overlap. After a quick rest, press on to the top.

❺ Kill Bill 1 . . . . 7c *S1*
19m. Follow *From Dusk 'Till Dawn* until you reach the overlap and a no-hands rest. Continue over the small lip and join *O-Ren Lssii* for the remainder of the route.

❻ Kill Bill 2 . . . . 7c+ *S0*
19m. The most famous of all the lines in the cave, with Sharma's bare-foot ascent topping it all. Climb *Kill Bill 1* to the overlap, then break out right to take on the steep upper wall.

❼ Raticida 6b *S2*
19m. An easier line just off the photo-topo. No further details are known.

Martin Putz on the final moves of *Bisexual* (6c+) - *page 274* - on the Metrosexual area of Cala Barques. Photo: Daimon Beail.

Cala Marçal

Cala Marçal is a terrific venue, home to a good variety of easy to mid-grade routes. Like Cova del Diablo, it's right by the road, with quick access. The crag, based around a headland, is split into two sections: the Cala Wall area offers a nice warm-up traverse, with the more extensive Main Cliff providing all the vertical challenges. The Main Cliff creeps up to about 16m high in places, but the climbing almost always eases off in the upper section.

Approach

Cala Marçal is just south of Porto Colom, some 20km south of Porto Cristo. From the PMV 401-2 coastal road, turn eastwards along the PM 401 to Porto Colom, then follow the signs south to Cala Marçal - a hotel at the beach with the words 'Cala Marçal' stamped on it will confirm your arrival!

From the beach, swing around the bay and drive up the hill. Keep going around to the left (miss a dead-end left turn here) and continue until you reach a roundabout. Go straight ahead and park at the end of the road, where the main crag is right beneath you.

Conditions and Tides

The Main Cliff is south-east facing, with shade later in the day. Mid-summer often finds it a bit greasy, but the vertical climbs here generally stay dry. The Cala Wall faces north-east, getting late afternoon sun only. Take the usual precautions when climbing close to a headland, and keep an eye open for possible currents.

Exits

Please note that exits here can prove tricky. It is possible to scramble out in one or two places, but you'll still be left with proper climbing to get back to the top of the crag. The best advice is to bring a knotted hemp rope/rope ladder along with you, and a little gear to fix it into place - this can be placed to line up with the easy way down.

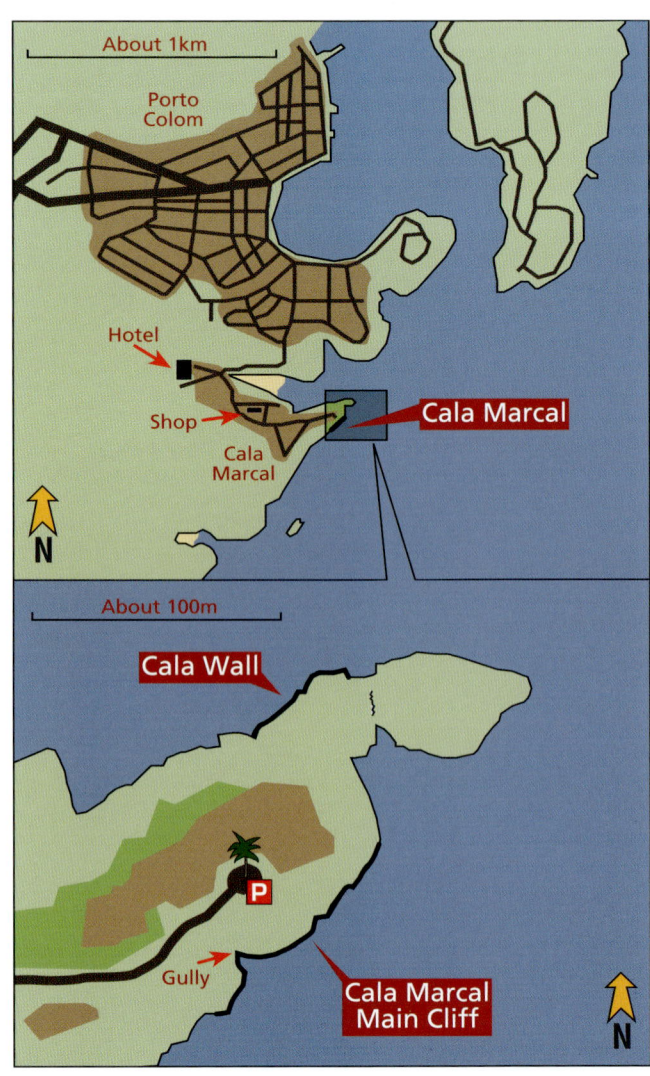

James Cole on *The Fat Crab* (6b+) - *page 280* - on the Main Cliff at Cala Marçal. Photo: Daimon Beail.

Cala Marçal — Cala Wall and Main Cliff

The Cala Wall
Expect a little 'S0' action here, with a good roof problem and a handy warm-up traverse.

Approach - Drop down to the cliff where the rock changes from sharp grey to orange and juggy - this will provide your entry point for both routes.

Conditions and Tides - Shady most of the day, so check for condensation when you venture in. Look out for currents around the headland.

Exit - You'll need to recce your exit from the water, which will usually be the ladder by the beach - that will give you a fairly lengthy swim of around 100m.

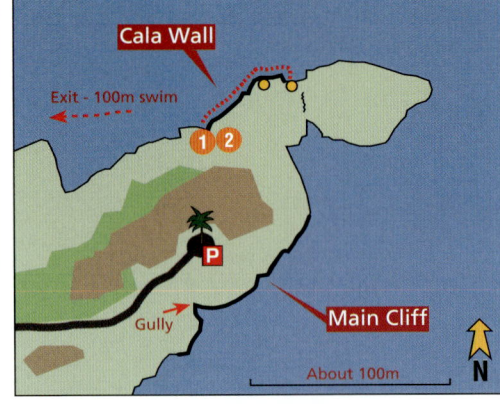

❶ The Marçal Traverse . . . . 5+ *S0*
20m. A steady warm-up. From the start of the juggy orange rock, traverse all the way to an exit platform, found on the edge of more grey rock.
FSA. J.Cole, S.Hazel, D.Beail, F.Fulcher 06.2005

❷ Rat Dog 6a *S0*
5m. Follow the traverse to the roof section and climb over it mostly on the right.
FSA. James Cole 06.2005

Main Cliff

❸ The Fat Crab . . . . 6b+ *S2*
15m. Traverse onto the main wall and climb the crack-line, which finishes at half-height below a slightly bulging wall. Make some moves out right to better holds, and up to the overlap. Traverse back left until you reach a gap in the lip. Pull onto a small shelf and reach for the top. Good Luck!
See photo on page 279.
FSA. James Cole 06.2005

Main Cliff
A nice clutch of juggy, solid routes in the mid-6's. This is the tallest section of the cliff, but the routes all ease off considerably in their upper bits. The exception is *The Fat Crab*, which requires a little more dedication! At the right-hand side of the cliff is a fun traverse and more great mid-grade routes.

Approach - The routes on the left-hand side are reached by way of an easy down-climb (4) and then traversing past the gully. On the right another easy descent (4) will get you to all the routes, along with the traverse of *The Odyssey*. These descents are not DWS climbing so abseil if you are unsure.

Conditions and Tides - The routes do sometimes get greasy early and late in the day, so time your visit for dry conditions, ideally with a cool breeze.

Exit - This needs a close inspection prior to your ascent. Your options are 1) a rope ladder at the Easy Way Down; tricky, sharp moves exiting around the gully area and a traverse leftwards from there; 2) a possible exit at the small cave just to the north-east. Decide before you climb.

Main Cliff Cala Marçal

④ ET v Predator 6b *S1*
14m. Traverse rightwards under *The Fat Crab*, and continue along to pass a sharp protruding fin. This leaves you under an overlapping wall. Climb the left side of this tiered wall to pass the right side of the cave, and continue much more easily to the top.
FSA. James Cole 06.2005

⑤ Mortal Combat .... 6b+ *S0*
14m. A great find, with good positions throughout. Attack the overlapping wall on good holds to the lip. Use two big pockets to pull over the lip, and trend left to find a large jug. Climb the rib from here, with much easier ground on the upper section.
FSA. Daimon Beail 06.2005

Another 20 metres right (looking in) from the gully is another easy way (grade 4) down which leads to the start of the next routes.

⑥ Canada 4 *S1*
10m. From the base of the easy way down, step up into the groove and follow the curving flake to its end. Easy climbing gains the top.
FSA. Daimon Beail 06.2005

⑦ The Odyssey 5 *S0*
36m. A nice traverse winding its way along the lower break, past a cave to the arete, where an easy-angled flake leads you to the top.
FSA. Daimon Beail 06.2005

⑧ Aquafresh 6c *S1*
11m. A tight bit of good wall climbing. Locate the two-finger pocket and climb the smooth wall above, mainly on crimps; the top-out is much easier.
FSA. Daimon Beail 06.2005

⑨ Lady Boys .... 5+ *S0*
11m. Excellent climbing. Find the large hold under the roof, and pull onto the slotted face above. The slot holds are all huge.
FSA. James Cole 06.2005

⑩ Higher than the Sun 6a *S0*
12m. A tricky start leads to excellent climbing, on good holds throughout.
FSA. James Cole 06.2005

⑪ Groove Rider .... 6a+ *S0*
12m. Brilliant! To the right of the small roof is a crack-line. Jamming and laybacking lead you to the top.
FSA. Daimon Beail 06.2005

⑫ Time 6a *S0*
13m. An alternative finish to *The Odyssey*. From the edge of the low cave, climb diagonally rightwards, to pull through the right edge of a roof section. Easier climbing awaits.
FSA. Daimon Beail 06.2005

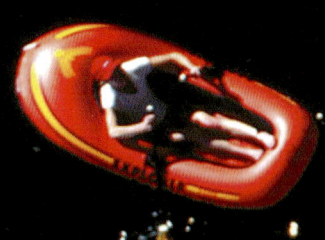

Rest of Europe

Steve McClure on his own route *Ring of Fire* (8b+) on the Holy Grail Wall, Mana Island, Croatia. Photo: Simon Carter.

Rest of Europe

The many countries and islands of Europe provide us with huge potential for deep water soloing, especially as so much of Europe's diverse coastline is limestone, which so often provides the soloist with all the necessary ingredients - steep, good holds, and usually plenty of variation in height. In Europe's south, the island-rich Mediterranean is home to huge amounts of limestone, the water is much warmer than we Brits have to put up with around our own shores, and the beer's often much cheaper!

For the keen new-router, there's mammoth amounts of exploring left out there, so no excuses! Go and find yourself some new crags, and make sure you tell this author about them.

This section contains some pointers to the remainder of Europe, including both the Mediterranean and other possibilities closer to home. The information varies from concise to vague, and you'll have to make much of it up as you go along. Many of these potential venues could be recced as part of a family holiday, or as an aside to a sport climbing trip.

One final point with regard to web-based coastal research - Google Earth, quite brilliant though it is, will unfortunately fail to spot any overhanging cliffs (think about it), so you'll have to read between the lines somewhat!

Katie Brown on *The March of the Jellyfish* (8a) near the Blue Lagoon, Isle of Camino, Malta. Photo: Paul Bride.

Ireland's West Coast

Ireland's West Coast is home to some very atmospheric sea cliffs, especially in the region of the Burren - and this includes the amazing Aran Islands chain. Will the area give the deep water soloist the right stuff? For now, you'll need to go and search it out. Bear in mind that the Atlantic swells have the potential to make your life tricky! Go there on a good, settled forecast - either fly over and hire a car, or take your car over on the Holyhead ferry.

Channel Islands

Jersey and Guernsey are already comparatively well-known for their stunning granite sea cliffs - both of these islands are pretty much just huge lumps of perfect rock. We know that granite often provides too much in the way of slabs (not so great for DWS), but do these islands offer the soloist any shorter, steeper walls? Time will tell.

North Spain

The Santander area of North Spain is known as the 'Green Coast' - this should give you an idea of the weather you're likely to encounter there; it's not unlike our own albeit warmer! This coast has an incredible amount of unclimbed limestone. There are about 4 Pembrokes' contained in the area (this is not an exaggeration), and the new-routing potential is absolutely vast. A kayaking/climbing foray in September 2006 revealed many future possibilities, but much of it seemed better suited to traditional and sport climbing. Is there a Diablo out there?... probably not.

Madrid Granite

There are rumours of river-side DWS bouldering on orange-pink granite boulders in the beautiful Pedriza National Park. This potential is likely to be found in the plunge pools of the Majadilla River. It's located some 50km north/north-west of Madrid, and sounds ace.

Italy

Island of Pantelleria - A search on the internet will provide the occasional shot of a feature known as the Elephant's Arch. It's found on the isle of Pantelleria, which is between Sicily and the north coast of Africa. Will this give us what we need? The ferry won't be super-cheap, as the island is some 160km to the south of Sicily's port of Trapani.

Island of Marrettimo - This island is about 40km west of Sicily. It has a remarkable feature known as the Blue Grotto which could offer some excellent DWS. The island is easily accessed by a ferry from the Sicilian port of Trapani.

Sicily

Home of the Mafia, endless coastline and perfect limestone. There are definitely more than just rumours about the island's DWS potential, and by the time this guide reaches the shops, exploratory visits will have been made! Sicily could well become the next Portugal, so expect to hear more about the Mediterranean's largest island in 2007. A further advantage is the chance of very competitive flights to Palermo airport, starting from £60 for a return trip. For now, here's some ideas:

Tonnara di Scopella Bay - This beautiful bay crops up time and again when searching for possible Sicilian DWS on the web, so take a look - it's quite stunning, with a series of limestone pinnacles and walls set in a serene, sheltered east-facing bay. Find it in the west side of the Castellammare Bay (Golfo di Castellammare), some 50km west of Palermo.

Zingaro Nature Reserve - 'Riserva Naturale dello Zingaro'. This is found just a little north of Scopello, in that same huge, sheltered bay. Various web-snaps indicate potential here too. There's no road negotiating this delicious, 10km slice of coast - kayaking or walking are the order of the day!

Mazzaro - This small sea cliff is found over on Sicily's east coast, near the town of Taormina. You'll find it in the Sicily sport climbing guide, and you'll notice the crag has a good amount of water underneath it! The bolted routes are reached by a short abseil, and the grades run from 6b+ to around 7c. Sicily's answer to Stair Hole?

William King on an attempt on *The Harbour Entrance* (7b+) Cassis, Calanques, France. Photo: Steve Taylor

France

Given the ridiculous amount of limestone the French have on their doorstep, it's somewhat surprising that DWS in France has yet to materialise, but the potential does exist. The Ardeche Gorge offers a number of possible venues, most famously the photogenic Pont d' Arc - the Ardeche's most impressive piece of architecture. But surely the most potential remaining in this huge and diverse country must be in the marvellous and shapely Calanques, found down in southern France, on the Mediterranean's northern shore. This eclectic and spidery section of coastline features an extended series of limestone inlets and headlands, with none more impressive than those found near the town of Cassis. The picture above shows a 120m traverse line, which is situated just off the eastern edge of Plage Bestouan - a small but stylish beach a few minutes walk from the town. The route has been dubbed 'The Harbour Entrance', and it weighs in at somewhere in the region of 7b+; it was first climbed by Neil Gresham in 1990.

Croatia

I drove the long and quite magical Croatian coast from Italy down to Dubrovnik some years ago, and failed to find any DWS potential. There is, however, much steep rock contained on Croatia's many islands, particularly in the region of Kornati. This region was explored by a British team in 2004, using boats; and the world's hardest deep water solo at that time (*see page 282*) was established by our own Steve McClure, with American Chris Sharma nipping in for the first repeat.

Croatian islands. Photo: Mike Robertson

There are two drawbacks to a visit to this amazing region. The first is that climbing is technically banned here (although it was when the team visited in September 2004, and they experienced no real difficulties with this), and the second is that, without an expensive boat, you're unlikely to see much action, as the climbing is really only accessible by way of the ocean.

Kalymnos

Kalymnos has had a number of forays by roving soloists, but not too much has been unearthed to date. There is, however, a great traverse to be found on the east coast. It's in Rina/Vathy Bay, and goes by the name of *Socratic Swimming Lessons*. The bay is also home to a good-sized cave, which is rumoured to harbour a number of realised and unrealised routes.

Malta

A number of soloists have touched rock in Malta and its smaller island neighbours Gozo and Camino. These include Crispin Waddy, who explored the region way back in the '90s. More recently a strong Canadian/US team have paid a visit, and the images from their trip are rather inspiring - hopefully more documentation on the three islands will come about in the next few years.

Bulgaria

The diverse and quite unique Black Sea region has been speculated about for years with DWS in mind, and we've now seen development in an area close to Tyulenova, on the east coast of Bulgaria. There have been video clips seen on the web, and the crags look somewhat reminiscent of Dorset's Stair Hole, with not too much height and lots of low-down burliness and cave action. 2007 will hopefully see further documentation of the area; I'm just firing the bike up now.

Crete

A search along part of Crete's south coast by Dave Pickford in 2006 uncovered some DWS potential. There's a number of interesting crags that would merit further attention, close to the small town of Loutro (not far east of the world-famous Samaria Gorge), which is accessible only by boat from the neighbouring port town of Hora Skafia.

The beautiful and barely-developed Marble Rocks, found just to the west of Loutro, provided the setting for the new route shown in the picture to the right. Elsewhere on the south coast there's likely to be further and more extensive DWS potential - consider a boat or kayak for further forays, as this will be a sure way of initially finding more crags, and may be essential for further visits. Hiring a small vessel for your adventure is not difficult or particularly expensive in Crete.

Dave Pickford on *The Cretan Runner* (6b+), Marble Bay, Crete. Photo: John Pickford

Turkey

This huge country just about slips into this European section of the guide, although it might seem like another world entirely! Turkey's south coast has almost definite DWS potential, as I've seen a number of snaps that can only mean one thing. This country is just ridiculously large, so any genuinely serious searches for DWS will inevitably take on mammoth proportions! I can tell you, however, that the region around Dalaman and Antalya will almost certainly provide some meat, and then there's that endless west-facing Turkish coastline, a little east of the Greek islands of Rhodes and Kalymnos.

Rest of Europe — Sardinia

The Italian island of Sardinia was perhaps once regarded as the future of deep water soloing in the Mediterranean, with its profusion of sea level limestone cliffs stretching along a massive portion of the east coast, to the south of the popular sport climbing area of Cala Gonone. This huge bay, known as the Golfo di Orosei, has long attracted climbers

Lots of potential

Tramariglio Bay. Photo: Mike Robertson.

in the search for the next 'Diablo', but, despite plenty of attention from a large number of boat-hiring DWS guns, the area has yet to find its true hub. Sardinia is essentially granite in the north (the sculpted, salmon-orange variety more usually associated with Corsica, its French neighbour), and limestone in the east and the north-west. Elsewhere you'll find a number of other possibilities lurking - maybe the next few years will bring some fresh discoveries - possibly in the south-west region. In the meantime, here's some flavour from the Mediterranean's second largest island, and some pointers for the future.

Getting there

There are various regular flights to Sardinia's airports, so shop around before you make your decision - the internet is your best choice here. Expect no problems acquiring a hire car out of season.

Accommodation

If you're planning a trip to Tramariglio Bay, there's a number of good, discreet possibilities to be had around the quiet Cala Galera headland, just a few kilometres out of the colourful little town of Fertilia. Follow your nose; there's a few dirt tracks to be negotiated. Investigate Fertilia or Alghero if you're seeking more luxury!

When to go

Your best timing for a visit is late season, when the prices are down and the sea is bath-like. Expect sea temperatures of around 25°C in September.

Sardinia Tramariglio Bay — Rest of Europe

Tramariglio Bay

This excellent venue has lots of potential, but only a handful of ascents to date. It was spotted by plane, just prior to a landing at Alghero airport! The bay is just one of a few possible venues in this area, so expect more to emerge over the next few years. A boat is highly recommended to explore the region properly. There are only three established routes so far. The remainder are likely to be in the hard bracket, and have been given possible grades after a swim-inspection. The rest of the crag, found to the left and not all pictured here, has stacks more potential.

Approach - The bay is 7 km from Sardinia's north-west airport, Alghero. From the airport drive, to the colourful coastal town of Fertilia, where a westwards tack provides way to the big, enclosed bay of Porto Conte. Drive down the 291 (signposted to the atmospheric caves of the Grotto ta di Nettuno), and park just east of the tiny village of Tramariglio. Skirting the hillside southwards for 10 minutes brings you to the eastern promontory of the bay, where you can see the crag. The routes are found by simply walking in that direction, then scrambling down a gully to gain the start of *Tramariglio Traverse*.

Conditions and Tides - The tides are minuscule. More important is the sea state - but the bay of Porto Conte is huge, so expect a degree of shelter, in general.

❶ **Project** .... ☐ 7b? *S2*
17m. The steepening wall to a steep slab.

❷ **Project** .... ☐ 7a+? *S2*
18m. Looks brilliant. Takes the enticing left edge of the steep slab.

❸ **Project** .... ☐ 7a? *S2*
20m. A stunning feature. The steep, juggy prow, gained from the easy lower crack.

❹ **Project** .... ☐ 8a? *S1*
16m. This appealing line one will one day take on the diagonal weakness.

❺ **Project** .... ☐ 8a+? *S1*
13m. The line between the two blue streaks looks ace.

❻ **Project** .... ☐ 7c+? *S1*
12m. The curling groove looks bloody fantastic.

❼ **Project** .... ☐ 7c? *S0*
21m. The sideways extension to *Tramariglio Traverse* looks hard, fingery and technical.

❽ **Project** .... ☐ 7a+? *S2*
19m. The high, stepped prow will one day be a great highball.

❾ **Harvey's Jaw** ....  6b *S1*
16m. From the end of *Tramariglio Traverse*, traverse the base of the narrow buttress, and climb the wide crack to a rest. Break out right and climb the tricky left edge of the prow. To exit, climb up into the tree-line and follow this down and right, back to sea level.
FSA. Mike Robertson 9.2003

❿ **Electrical Storm** .... ☐ 6a+ *S1*
15m. The centre of the appealing face. Step off the rest at the base of the buttress and climb the centre of the face to the top, on good pockets. Exit as above.
FSA. Mike Robertson 9.2003

⓫ **Tramariglio Traverse** ...... ☐ 6a+ *S0*
40m. The long and fun traverse in from the bottom of the start gully. It goes up and down a little, around all the mad architecture; follow your nose!
FSA. Mike Robertson 9.2003

Grotto del Bue Marino

This magnificent feature is found just a few minutes by boat to the south of Cala Gonone, and can also be reached by way of the coast, via the walkway/tunnel found inside it. The face to the right of the grotto harbours a number of possibilities; the need to stay as low as possible is of paramount importance. You'll probably need to climb at least 8b to have any chance of climbing out along the amazing tufa-clad hanging wall of the grotto, and the possible DWS lines are approximately marked on the shot. Expect good water below, and look for a way of reaching either the small cave or the right ledge system as your finishing point. Good luck!

Golfo di Orosei

This massive bay is found to the south of Cala Gonone, and is best explored with a hired boat. There are a number of hire companies in Cala Gonone's harbour, who all seem to offer medium-sized rigs, which are a little pricey. The breath-taking bay stretches all the way down to, and beyond, the amazing feature of Cala Luna and is one of the prettiest places in the Med. The shot here sums up the sort of architecture you'll find in the bay, although unfortunately much of the rock is poised above quite sizeable lower reefs - this is something of a bugger. So go and explore it, preferably with a decent GPS system!

Australia

by Mike Robertson, Anthony Alexander and Nick Hancock

Anthony Alexander and the sandstone of the Hawkesbury River, Sydney, New South Wales, Australia. Photo: Simon Carter.

Australia

It would be hard to imagine a continent the size of Australia with no rock poised above water. Yet this almost seems to be the case; in spite of a coastline of some 60,000 kilometres (an incredible distance; this figure includes all the islands), very few DWS crags have been unearthed. But there is some light at the end of the tunnel if your travels take you Down Under. Sydney's amazing river-side venue of Crafty's - an idyllic sandstone cliff on the Hawkesbury River - is a superb example of the genre, whilst down in Tasmania, the small dolerite and granite craglets of this diverse island offer some excellent sea-based adventure. If you seek to reclaim your tree-climbing childhood, a wander over to the west side of Tasmania gives you the striking dead-tree landscape of Lake Gordon.

Getting There

Both Crafty's Bay and the South Tasmania region are easily reached by way of international airports. A flight to Sydney, located in Australia's state of New South Wales, will get you to within striking distance of Crafty's Bay on the Hawkesbury River, which is found just north of the city. A flight to Tasmania's city of Hobart will usually fall into the category of an internal flight. From Hobart, all crags detailed in this guide are found within two and a half hours' drive.

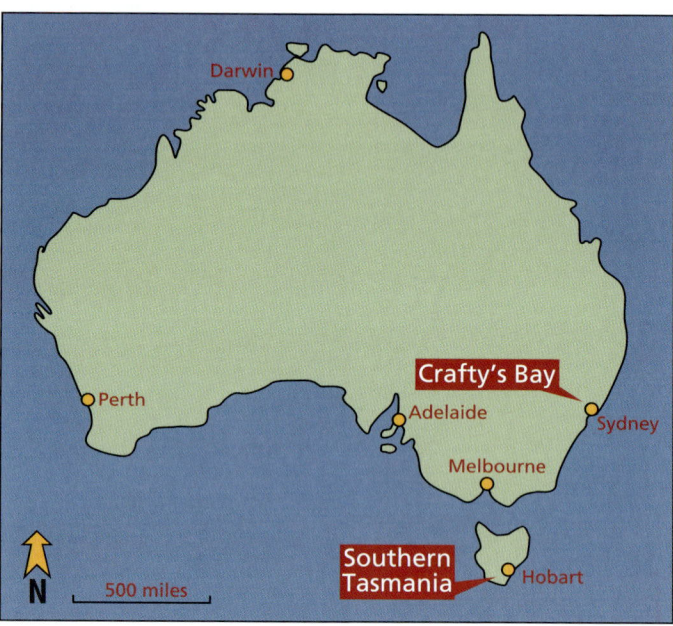

When to go

The best time to visit for DWS is certainly in the Australian summer, when the water is at its warmest. Crafty's is closer to the equator than Tasmania, so expect the river to offer a longer season for DWS visitors - probably from October to May. For a visit to the crags of Tasmania, you'll want to aim for December to March, when the sea is at its warmest.

Accommodation

Most folk visit Crafty's on day trips from Sydney, so if your travels result in a Sydney stay, you'll have Crafty's very close to hand - Sydney has a wealth of possible places to stay, including hostels, camping and motels. The gorgeous coastline found north of Sydney is also well-endowed with camping and motels. For Tasmania, your best option is a camper or a hire car/tent.

Ken Palmer on *Boatmen's Edge* (6c) Pinnacle Zawn, Blackman's Bay, Tasmania. Photo: Mike Robertson.

Crafty's Bay

Crafty's is a very striking riverside crag made of lovely hard, fine grain sandstone, and is around 16m high. It's tucked away in Joe Crafty's Bay and offers shade for most of the day - ideal for those steamy summer days. The cliff is often stepped in nature, which tends to provide good rests in-between the harder moves.

The cliff was discovered in 2003 by Anthony Alexander, who did a little cleaning and tried a few problems. It then lay dormant until late 2005, when Jason Piper and Anthony hired a house boat from Brooklyn and headed up river with a crew of soloists to siege the cliff. Their first day at the crag saw ascents of *Aquarius* (6b+), and the lower traverse of *Cronulla Karma* (7a+) - probably the most popular routes on the crag. Many trips soon followed in hired 'tinnies' from Berowra Waters, resulting in further classics, some big smiles, and a few bruises.

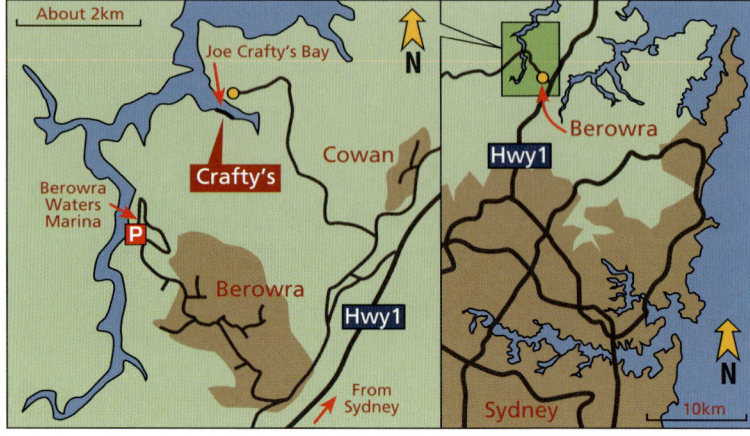

Approach

The cliff is only about 50km from the centre of Sydney. Drive along Highway 1 (the Pacific Highway) through Hornsby to Berowra, then head down the hill to Berowra Waters and the Ferry. Park there - don't go over the river on the Ferry! Walk 100m along river to Berowra Waters Marina (029456200) to hire yourself a small outboard.

Boat ('tinnies') cost around $110 per day (c£50 UK equivanet) 8am - 4pm with a $50 deposit; this can be split between 6 people maximum. You can also hire BBQ boats that carry 12 people.

Conditions

Sea-water devotees bear in mind you'll have less buoyancy in fresh water - expect to sink noticeably quicker! Stay in the shade for your summer ascents, and take sunscreen for the boat.

There are other things to worry about when deep water soloing in Australia! Photo: Mike Robertson.

Jason Piper and the chance of *Not Waving, Drowning* (6c+) - *page 300* - Crafty's, Hawkesbury River, near Sydney, NSW, Australia. Photo: Simon Carter.

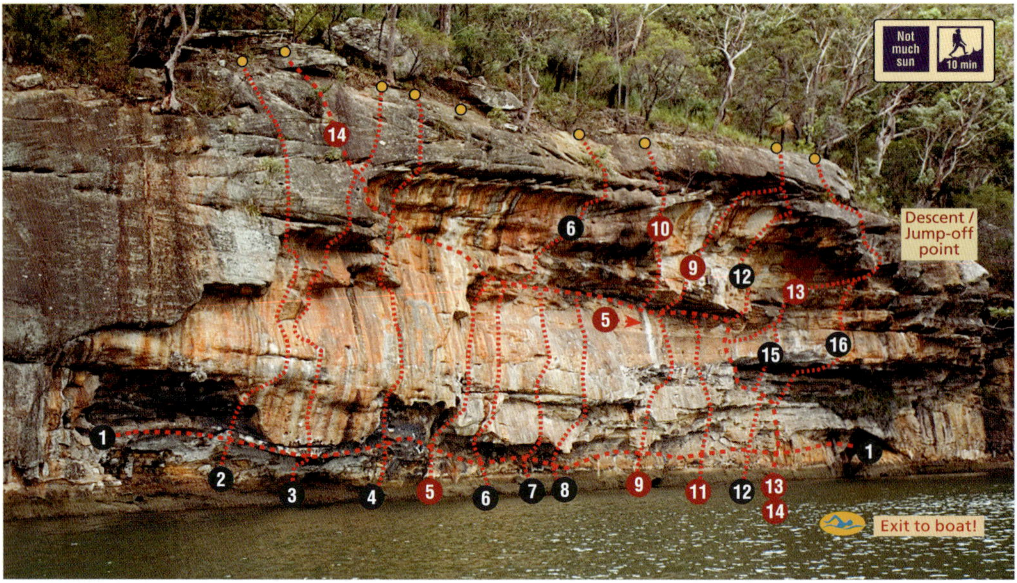

1 Cronulla Karma .... 3 stars 7a+ S0
30m. The low traverse is brilliant; one of the crag's best routes. It can be tackled in either direction.
FSA. Tim Hasnoot 12.2005

2 Munchhausen Syndrome ... 1 star 7a+ S2
15m. The orange scoop is followed by the darker slab above.
FSA. Anthony Alexander 12.2005

3 Fish Sphincters .... 3 stars 7b S0
16m. Ace! Climb up the orange wall, then break out onto the prow.
FSA. Anthony Alexander 2.2006

4 Blowing Bubbles .... 3 stars 7c S1
15m. A classic, taking the left edge of the orange scoop.
FSA. Monique Forestier 3.2006

The gap to the right of Blowing Bubbles has been attempted, but the slab below catches the unwary - best avoided.

5 The Fishing Line .... 1 star 6b S1
24m. The crag's rightwards girdle. Climb up into the recess, then traverse rightwards across the recess, to finish back down on *Cronulla Karma*.
FSA. Anthony Alexander 1.2006

6 Brackish .... 2 stars 7b+ S2
17m. Exciting stuff! Follow the last route, then break out right to tackle the stepped roofs.
FSA. Jason Piper 3.2006

7 Glassy .... 1 star 7a+ S0
8m. To half-height only, with a number of finishing options.
FSA. Jason Piper 4.2006

8 Bung Plug .... 1 star 7b S0
8m. Also to half-height.
FSA. Anthony Alexander 4.2006

9 Not Waving, Drowning .... 3 stars 6c+ S1
17m. A stunning line, diving right through the upper scoop.
See photo on page 299.
FSA. Anthony Alexander 2.2006

10 Surface Tension .... 3 stars 7a S1
16m. Beautifully-positioned climbing. Start up the last route, then move left to climb the very edge of the upper scoop.
FSA. Anthony Alexander 4.2006

11 Fish Lip .... 1 star 6c S0
8m. A short trip to the half-height recess.
FSA. Anthony Alexander 4.2006

12 River Rage .... 3 stars 7c S1
17m. Wild climbing with an amazing finale, climbing the steep right edge of the upper scoop.
FSA. Jason Piper 2.2006

13 Aquarius .... 3 stars 6b+ S0
17m. A great excursion, and a terrific intro to Crafty's. From the rest under the roof, traverse right to swing around the right edge of the crag.
FSA. Anthony Alexander 12.20055

14 Pician Passage .... 3 stars 6b S1
28m. An excellent voyage, taking a rising right-to-left line across the crag.
FSA. Monique Forestier 2.2006

15 The Fraser's Edge .... 1 star 7a+ S0
7m. The left side of the lower roof.
FSA. Brendon Fraser 11.2006

16 Atkin's Roof .... 1 star 7c+ S0
9m. A burly number through the lower roof.
FSA. Mr Atkins 12.2006

The Blue Mountains

Elsewhere in Australia, there's potential for some added freshwater action. The picture shows the middle section of the Wollongambee Canyon, which is found west of Sydney, in the idyllic Blue Mountains. Its sandstone walls kinda look ideal, don't they?
Photo: Joff Cook.

Tasmania

Nick Hancock on the first ascent of *Hippy Chicks in the Styx* (6a+) Stand Up Point, Tasmania. Photo: Mike Robertson.

Australia's big southerly island has long been known for its wilderness walking, its emptiness, and its perhaps best-known climbing landmark, the towering dolerite column known as the Totem Pole, which has featured in the climbing press on numerous occasions. Less known are the dotted-about, much smaller dolerite coastal crags. These offer the soloist short, clean possibilities more in keeping with the DWS genre, although they are sometimes tricky to find without a boat of some sort. The dolerite is supplemented by the perfect granite found on the east coast, in the Coles Bay region - part of the stunning Freycinet National Park.

This chapter has only basic introductory information, but hopefully it will inspire some to further develop Tasmania's south and east. For up to date information or climbing/kayaking guiding in the region, contact local DWS expert (and ex-Devonian) Nick Hancock.

Getting There

Most soloists to date have investigated Tasmania's solo areas as part of a world trip. For whatever reason you find yourself there, it's likely that you'll land in Hobart's international airport. Car hire is pretty much like everywhere else so shop around for the best deals, and maybe think about getting a camper for maximum trip quality, if you can spare the pennies.

Approach

All the cliffs described here are found within two and a half hours' drive of Hobart. This small, easy-going city of about 200,000 people is a delightful and friendly base, and will provide you with just about anything you'll need for your Tazzy trip.

Tides and Conditions

Tasmania's tides are surprisingly small, about the same as Portugal's, so expect an average tidal variation of less than one metre. More important here is the sea state - choose your day carefully, especially when operating around the headlands. The water temperature is fairly accommodating in the Australian summer, which is around January.

Going back to your roots? Tasmania's wild and desolate Lake Gordon, and Nick Hancock in action. Photo: Mike Robertson.

Tasmania

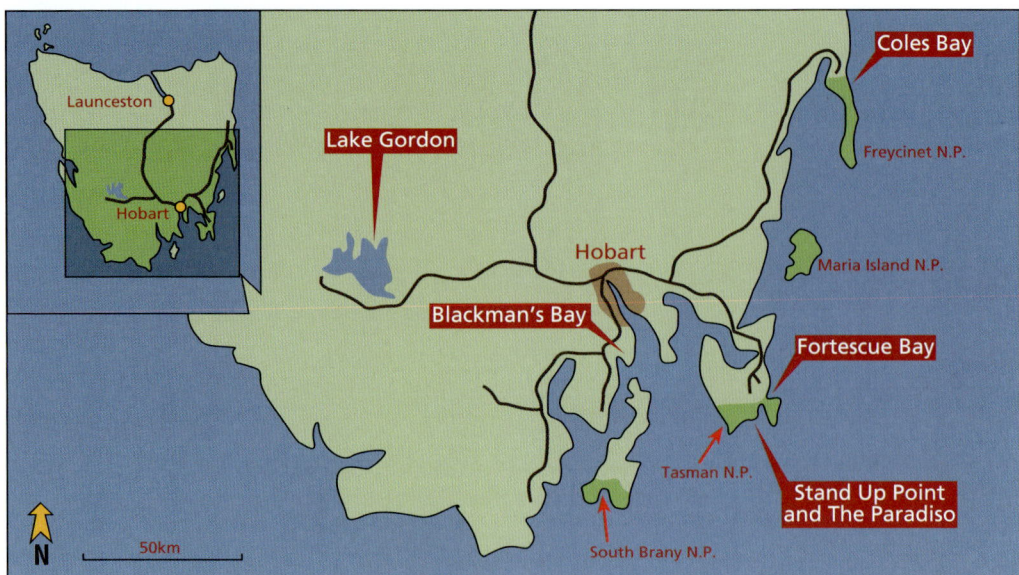

Blackman's Bay
This is the most developed DWS area just south of Hobart, with over 20 climbs at three nearby areas. Drive south 15km from Hobart to Blackman's Bay, where there's a beach, shops and plenty of parking.
Soldiers Rocks is reached by scrambling south along the coast from behind 63 Suncoast Drive. The crag features a sustained 30 metre 7a+ traverse of a south-facing zawn.
Pinnacle Zawn, the main area, with 16 climbs from grade 5+ to 7b+, is usually approached by kayak by paddling south from Blackman's Bay beach for 2km, where a square pinnacle in a deep zawn will be seen. It may be possible to approach on foot from Tinderbox Road East after asking permission from the landowner.
Double Zawn has five climbs from 5+ to 7b, and is approached by scrambling north from Fisherman's Haul Beach, opposite 267 Tinderbox Road East.

Coles Bay
Two and a half hours drive north-east of Hobart is one of Tasmania's major climbing areas, in the amazing granite wonderland of Freycinet National Park. There are excellent deep water solos from 6a+ to 7b: on the east side of the peninsula at **The Gonk**, a thirty minute kayak south from Sleepy Bay; towards **Carp Bay Point**, a ten minute kayak north from Sleepy Bay; and at **Deepwater Zawn**, a twenty minute drive north from Sleepy Bay.

Fortescue Bay
Fortescue Bay is an hour's drive east, then south, of Hobart on the Tasman Highway. Turn off the main highway just before the town of Oakwood.
The bay is home to the famous column known as the Totem Pole - the scene of Paul Pritchard's well-catalogued epic. This area has two deep water solos, and they tackle two prominent and striking aretes, with grades of 6a+ and 6c+. These are at the first cliffs reached on the walk to Cape Hauy, about five minutes from the car park. Scramble down the middle of the cliff and traverse left (facing in) to the aretes. The higher and harder left-hand arete needs an abseil approach down to its left.

Lake Gordon

This desolate region is some two hours' drive across Tasmania from Hobart on the main western highway. Shortly before you reach the termination of this road, you'll find Lake Gordon, which is huge, and well-marked on any Tasmania map. You'll need a kayak to go exploring, along with your camera! The region was dammed in the 1970's, and the trees here are all dead. This gives the lake a surreal, skeletal appearance - it's like nowhere else on earth.

Safety note: You need your wits about you at Lake Gordon regarding water depth. There are still sometimes smaller stumps in the water, and these can prove hazardous to your health! So check out your landing zone carefully before you set off.

Stand Up Point

There are two climbs in a box-shaped zawn graded at 6a+ and 6c+, and two on the point itself at grades of 6a and 6b. A 5km drive southwards from Oakwood on the Tasman highway takes you into the town of Port Arthur. From here, a short drive south brings you to Dog Bark Road, which is your turning for Crescent Bay. Walk to the bay itself (some amazing sand dune slides to be had) and then scramble north along to Stand Up Point.

The Paradiso

A couple of minutes' drive to the south of Crescent Bay brings you to the Remarkable Cave. From here, a walk east along the coast brings you to The Paradiso, a steep cliff riddled with bolts. The right extremity of the cliff is bounded by a big zawn. A long 6b traverse goes east from this zawn to the next major zawn, bounding a 200 metre unclimbed cliff.

Nick Hancock dry tooling over Lake Gordon, Tasmania. Photo: Mike Robertson.

Rest of the World

Neil Gresham on the first ascent of *Spiderman* (7c+) Chicken Island, Krabi Province, Thailand. Photo: Tim Emmett.

Rest of the World — South East Asia

Impressive rock in the Andaman Sea. Photo: Mike Robertson.

South-East Asia is about as eclectic as they come, and for the deep water soloist, there's some inspirational venues at hand. In Thailand, the gorgeous limestone crags of the vast Andaman Sea gives some prime action, with the tufa-laden crags around the Tonsai/Krabi region offering some well-catalogued lines. Whilst over in the mesmerising venue of Ha Long Bay in North Vietnam, the limestone islands and towers of the South China Sea are just inspirational.

Here's some images to inspire, along with some general information to match. In short, expect to go on a proper mini-expedition to delve into the amazing complexities of the idyllic Ha Long Bay area; whilst over in the sunny tourist haven of south-western Thailand, you can afford to be slightly less adventurous in the more user-friendly region of Tonsai Beach.

Thailand

The world-famous tufas of Thailand's Andaman Sea are a joy to behold, and rightly so. There's nothing quite like grappling with stalactites above a warm ocean, and the region is sure to attract deep water soloists for decades to come. Thailand's advantage over the equally stunning Ha Long Bay is the friendliness of the locals in their longtail boats, who are more than happy to drop you off, pick you up, and just about everything else in between! The region is still relatively cheap, and it's possible to organise decent ocean kayaks from Tonsai Beach - this is a major plus point when planning a long and complex winter break.

Guidebook - For Matt Maddaloni's guide to all Thailand has to offer the deep water soloist, go to **www.mattmaddaloni.com**. The PDF-download guide is in full colour, and covers over 100 routes in the area, with information on dozens of the area's islands. It costs $20.

If your plan is to be fully mobile, you might consider a kayak trip to explore the region. This is highly recommended as you'll get the chance to paddle calm, warm waters at your own pace. Go to **www.kayakthailand.com** for info on hiring a kayak from the very helpful ex-pat Jonny Greener, who's based at Tonsai Beach. He'll supply decent kayaks with dry hatches, and he'll add in camping gear, stove, dry-bags and suchlike.

A long-tail boat on the beautiful Andaman Sea. Photo: Mike Robertson.

Vietnam

Ha Long Bay is the place of dreams. Imagine a land where Deep Water enthusiasts finally come to rest, a sort of soloist's graveyard, where calmness and tranquility join hands with perfect rock and still, warm waters. You're imagining Ha Long Bay, a 60km wide stretch of coastline tucked away in the northern edge of the South China Sea. The region has become even more mysterious over the last few years, with some quite irrational extra rules and regulations governing the area. The 3,000 karst towers and islands are strictly protected (unless you happen to seek help from the right people, and line the correct pocket), and unaccompanied climbing missions are generally discouraged. (See **www.mattmaddaloni.com** for a great tale of Ha Long Bay derring-do!) So you'll need to have your wits about you, and have your adventurous (diplomatic?) head on!

Your journey will start with a flight to Hanoi, where a quite gripping bus ride may finally deliver you into the clutches of the crazy boatmen of Ha Long City (Bai Chay). From here, your best bet is to find someone who's prepared to take you out into the Bay for a little soloing, and is happy to offer an extended stay out there at sea. The Vietnamese chappie who agrees to this might prove somewhat elusive. Another option is to take your own vessel, but bear in mind that you'll need something that you can comfortably get out of, and onto the rock (although random boat trips are also discouraged). You'll have a wicked adventure, whatever happens. It might be worth applying that age-old adage - He Who Dares, Wins!

Cambodia

Cambodia's south coast is rich in karst formations and caves, and it does seem likely that there will be some DWS potential down there, along with friendly people, warm seas, and an inexpensive way of life. Watch your step when going off trail; the country is still littered with various munitions.

Burma/Myanmar

Any look at a map of Burma (now 'officially' known as Myanmar) will show that the west coast, just a couple of hundred kilometres north of Thailand's Krabi area, has more islands lying in the Andaman Sea than imaginable. There's almost certainly hundreds (or even thousands) of deep water solos possible in the region, but before you book your ticket, you'll need to be aware of how appalling Burma's current human rights record is. For an informative article on whether you should visit the country, go to **www.lonelyplanet.com**. All I can say is that if you can find a way of lessening the plight of the afflicted Burmese people, whose lives are made a misery by the ruling generals, then go there, and come back and write about it, but bear in mind that journalists of any description are not made welcome.

China

There's been many a tale about the acres of soloing above China's rivers, but after a visit in 2006, I found these wild claims might be a little off the mark. There is some great DWS near Yangshuo (south China's sport climbing paradise), but it is limited, and also dependent on the seasonal water levels. Watch out for the water buffalos! They're as friendly as can be, but sometimes found in your splashdown zone.

The Li River, Yangshuo, China
Photo: Mike Robertson.

Grant Farquhar on the classic *Ha Long Nights* (7a+), Ha Long Bay, Vietnam. Photo: Neil Gresham.

Bermuda

This beautiful Atlantic island is one of those annoying places: always sunny, the rain mostly falls at night, and the sea is always warm (I suppose it would be rather less annoying if you happened to live there). In short, bloody paradise.

The island, found in the middle of nowhere, some 1300km north-east of Miami, has seen some fairly keen DWS action in recent years, mostly due to

our very own Dr. Grant Farquhar spending some 'work time' there (you can always trust a shrink to sort things out for the rest of us). By far the best DWS venue in Bermuda is Clarence Cove, which is found near Spanish Point, up on the North shore. It has a selection of tasty little morsels, with one of the classics being *Atlantis* (6c+).

The routes are short in height but steep and intense, often involving a lot of traversing to gain access. The water is usually crystal clear and warm. For more information on Bermuda DWS, take a look at Grant's website, found at **www.evilpics.co.uk**.

Ward Byrum climbing the classic route *Atlantis* (6c+) Clarence Cove, Bermuda. Photo: Grant Farquhar.

Canada

Now you wouldn't think of Canada as somewhere you'd find deep water and soloing. You'd better think again: close to the world-famous town of Squamish (home to some massive granite multi-pitch routes) is the Lower Cheakamus River, which offers the soloist some right cheeky little solos.

USA

Odd that such a vast coastline offers so little DWS, but that's just how it is - America has legions of rock, but somehow it managed to put all its limestone up on Mount Charleston in Nevada, and over at Rifle, in Colorado. Damnit. So the freshwater venue of Summersville Lake seems to be where it's at. This mad venue is found in Virginia, and I'm reliably informed it offers some good solos, mostly on technical, vertical rock. Searches on the web will eventually guide you there, so off you go; please bring some decent action pictures back with you. Elsewhere in the States, you might well find some good sandstone DWS, probably in the region of Utah and Arizona, on either the Green River or the more famous Colorado River, home of the Grand Canyon. The shot, a self-portrait from 2002, was taken close to Moab, Utah.

Matt Maddaloni on the excellent *Fight or Flight* (7b+) Lower Cheakamus River, Squamish, Canada. Photo: Paul Bride.

Moab, Utah; the author, fresh sandstone, and the mighty Colorado River. This project is still unclimbed, and will probably go at about 7c+.
Photo: Mike Robertson (self-timer).

Rest of the World

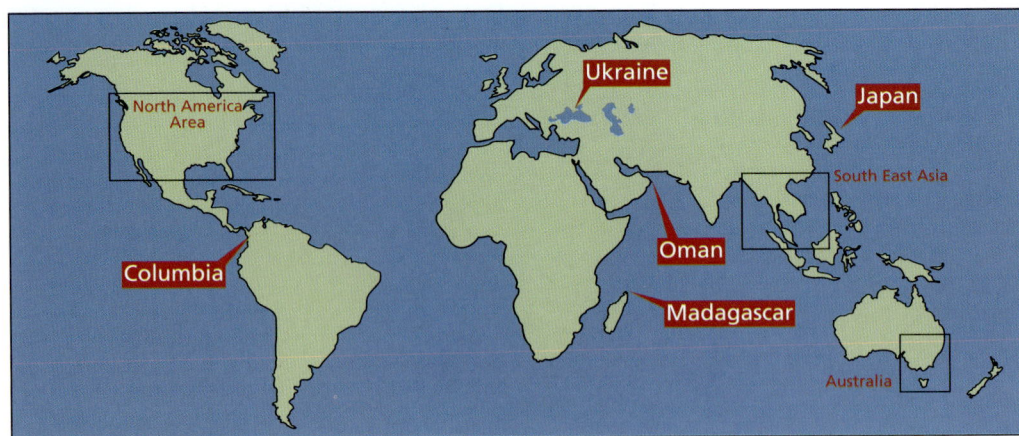

Oman - Musandam Peninsula
An immense wealth of as yet unexplored DWS exists on the cliffs of Oman's remote Musandam, which lies on the south-easterly apex of Arabia, guarding the Straits of Hormuz. It is separated from the rest of Oman and is in fact closer to Iran than its parent nation. Dave Pickford checked out the area in 2005 whilst on a working trip, and climbed a handful of new routes on the short cliffs below the road from the UAE border towards Khasab. The route in the photograph opposite lies on the short (10m) undercut wall directly below the Golden Tulip Hotel, which is found on the road towards Khasab.
The potential for further DWS exploration is almost immeasurably vast. Needless to say, a boat would be supremely useful in any serious DWS exploration. Various vessels may be chartered in Khasab. A basic knowledge of Arabic is very useful in Oman.

The Ukraine's Crimean Peninsula
This shapely chunk of land protrudes out into the Black Sea's northern extremity, and is home to inexpensive hotels and buses, a stunning mountain backdrop, and stacks of limestone sport climbing. Will that southern coastline offer us DWS? It's very possible; be the first to go and take a look.

Japan
There have long been questions asked about the possibility of DWS on Japan's coastline, but it's yet to be seriously looked at.

Madagascar
Most folk have only seen pictures of that huge granite dome in Madagascar's gigantic interior, but this African island's north coast is home to many limestone sea cliffs. There's yet to be a proper investigation of it all, but be warned, there are rumoured to be a fair old bunch of sharks hangin' around down there.

Colombia
Found over on the north-west edge of South America, and home to collections of granite boulders, limestone, and God knows what else. It's an exciting and absorbing country, but also a little quirky these days, so get away from the city as quick as you can, and find yourself some serene DWS action on the west coast somewhere. It does look like a crazy place to go and travel.

Dave Pickford on the first ascent of *The Preposterous Tulip* (6a), Oman. Photo: Andy Whittaker.

Route Index

Stars	Grade	Name	Photo	Page
★	7b+	9 ½ Weeks		162
★	6a	A Bridge Too Far		48
★★★	4+	A Girl's Best Friend		141
★	7a	A Thin Line		187
★★★	7a	Abduction		179
★★★	7b	Abyss, The		179
★★★	6b+	Acacia		199
★★★	8a+	Adrenochrome		67
★★★	6c	Aeronautics	97	105
★★★	7b+	Afroman	261	265
★	6a+	All Things Being Relative		81
★	6b	Allosaurus		42
★★★	6c	Amazonia		47
★★★	6c+	Amos		249
★★	6c	Amphibian		226
★★	7a	Anarchy Stampede		66
★	6a+	Anchana		231
★	6a+	And All Because		113
★★★	6c	And Captain Blood's Cavern		46
★★	7b+	Andy Pandy		89
★★	6c+	Andy Reid's Mystery Tour		218
★	6a	Angry Child		169
★★★	7a+	Animal Magnetism		62
★★★	6b+	Anthony Hopkins	210	230
★★★	7b	Anti Matterhorn, The		179
	6a	Aperitif		176
★	7a+	Appearing, The		49
★★★	6a+	Aqua Marina		125
★	6c	Aquafresh		281
★★	7a+	Aquamarina		85
★	5	Aquamarine		41
★	3+	Aquanaut, The		40
★★★	6b+	Aquarius		300
★★★	7a+	Arapiles, Oh Arapiles		130
★	7?	Arch Enemy		60
★	6a+	Arch Temptress		122
★	6a+	Arch Zawn Traverse, The		113
★★★	7b	Arcwelder		60
★	7a	Aristocrat		178
★★	5+	Astrid		51
★★	6b+	Atheist	117	121
★	7c+	Atkin's Roof		300
★	6c+	Audi, The		184
★	6a+	Austin's Powers		114
★★★	7b+	Bagheera		197
★★★	6c+	Bagpuss		181
★	7a	Baloo		197
	7c?	Bandito		274
★★★	7a+	Bare Reputation		90
★	4	Barefoot and the Hendersons		115
★	7a	Barkin' Mad		40
★	6c+	Barn Doors		124
★	6b	Barnacle Continuation Traverse		110
★	5	Barnacle Traverse		111
★★	6b	Barques Traverse, The		273
★★★	7c	Barrel Traverse		106
★★	6c	Barrel Traverse		152
★	6c	Barrel Traverse Extension		153
★★	7a	Bathtime		209
★	6b	Bathtubb		50
★	7a+	Bay of Peegs		93
★	6c+	Bay of Rainbows		93
★	6a+	Belly Button Traverse		93
★	6b	Benidorm Bender		250
★	6c	Bent Pigeon		80
★★★	7a	Best Seller		227
★★★	6c	Between the Devil and the Deep Blue Sea		195
★★	6b+	Big Blue, The		145
	7a	Big Boss		83
★	6c	Big Boss, The		244
★	6a+	Big Bully		266
★	5	Big Easy Arete		85
★★★	6a+	Big Easy, The		85
★	7a+	Big Hair		165
★	8c+	Big Mama		276
★	4+	Big Screen		174
★★★	7a	Big XXL		273
★★	7b+	Bill Peascod		227
★★	7a	Bingo Master's Breakout		158
★	5+	Bird's Nest Arete		50
★	6c+	Bisexual		274
	5	Bishop's Finger		143
★	6c+	Black Traverse, The	134	144
★	6a	Blackboard Wall		184
	5	Blackie Collins		246
	4+	Bleating Nincompoops		80
★	7a	Blind Man's Traverse, The		178
★★★	7c	Blowing Bubbles		300
★	6c	Blue Mood		169
★★	7b+	Blue Planet	133	132
★★	6c+	Blue Tuna		262
★	6c	Boat People		249
★	5+	Bolshy Bridesmaid		221
★★	5+	Bonobo		266
★	5	Bonobo Arete		165
	6c	Book of Laughter, The		131
★	6b	Boomerang		179
★	7b+	Brachiosaurus		43
★★	7b+	Brackish		300
★	6b	Brahma		143
	6a+	Braune Gurken		275
★★	7a	Breathless		112
	5+	Bridie Girl		169
★★★	6b	Brine Shrine		201
★	6a+	Bristol Biters		223
★	7a	Broadhaven Cove Traverse		167
★	6c	Brown Nose		228
★	6a+	Brown Paper		115
★	7a	Brown Sugar		220
★	6a+	Bruce Lee		244
★	6a+	Brutus Stanton		246
★★	7c?	Brutus Traverse		130
★	7b	Buckyball		162
★	7b	Bung Plug		300
★	4+	Bungle, Zippy and George		93
★	6b+	Bunkhouse, The		239
★★★	7b	Cabelo Locko		226
★★★	7b	Cabelo Loco		226
★	6b+	Cafe Noir		144
★★★	6c	Calamares		265
★	5+	Calm		176
★★	6a+	Camel Filter		52
	4	Canada		281
★	6a+	Candy Trail		162
★★★	6c+	Captain Caveman		172
★	6b	Captain Haddock		88
★	6c	Carlo Varini		145
★★	8a+	Carlos Checa		275
★★★	7a	Caveman		101
★★	6c	Cavewoman		110
★	6b+	Ceaseless Tide, The		162
★	6a+	Cellar Deck		176
★★★	7b	Cereal Killer		156
★	6b	Cerveza, Por Favor		219
★	5	Charm		176
★	4+	Cheddar Direct	57	62
★★	7a+	Chicken Head		123
★★★	8a	Christine		132
★	6b	Circus Dog	23	246
★	6c	Clarence		80
★	6b+	Classical, The		166
★	6b+	Clean Ass		160
★	6a+	Cleanliness		160
★	6a	Clear Cut		219
★	6b+	Clockwork Orange		245
	5	Cocko		175
★	6b+	Cod Direct		111
★★★	7a+	Cod Tympani	3	107
★	5	Codfish		40
★	6b+	Coffee Anan		157
★	6a+	Cold Turkey		175
★	6b	Comeback Kid		108
★	6c+	Comedy of Errors		217
★	6b+	Confucius		166
★★★	6b	Conger, The		49
★	7a	Contortions		64
★	6a+	Cool Man Chu		174
★	5+	Coprolite		226
★	6b+	Cornflake Girl		93
★★★	6c	Crab Party	68	89
★★	7a+	Crazy Notion		62
★	4+	Crill Wars		175
★	6b	Crime Wave		48
★	4	Crispy Duck, No Noodles		123
★	7a+	Cronulla Ka Syndrome		300
★	6b+	Cruel Sea		229
★	4	Crunchie		114
	6b	Cryptoclidus		42
★★★	7a	Cult Classic		227
★★	6a	Curly Mick		153
★★	6b	Cut Diamond		140
★	6a+	Cutting Edge, The		169
★	6c	Cyber Pimp		199
	6a	Cyborg Crocker		105
★★	7a	Dachicas		272
★★	6c	Damocles		184
★	6c+	Dance on Dinkies		123
★	6c	Dave's Restaurant		230
★★★	6c+	Davy Jones' Lock-off		46
★★	7b	Dead In Europe		76
★	6a+	Deep House		114
★	6c	Deep Water Alien		179
★★	6a	Depth Charge	193	194
★★★	6b+	Depth Charge Direct		194
★★	6b	Desperado		84
★	7a	Despicable Terrier		66
	6c	Devolution		125
★	6a+	Diamond Traverse, The		140
	6b	Diana		40
	5	Dino		244
★	6b+	Disco Arete		249
	7a+	Disco Babes from Outer Space		114
★	7b	Disco Inferno		106
★	6a+	Disco Labrador		249
★	6a+	Disco Traverse		250
★	6b	Dog's Bollocks		249

Route Index 317

Stars	Grade	Route	Photo	Page
★★	6c	Dogfather, The		231
★★★	6a+	Dogging Romp		265
★★	6b+	Dolphins Always Make Me Cry		144
★	7a+	Don't Fear the Reef		122
★★	6a+	Donald, Where's Your Trousers?		47
★	6c	Dope on a Rope		209
★	4	Double Dragon		162
	7b+	Double Penetration		272
★★	6b+	Down and Out		184
★	6c	Down for an Hour		221
★	7a	Drake's Drum		153
★★★	7a	Dreamline		201
★★	6c+	Drill Sergeant, The		75
★★★	6b	Dromedario		217
★★	6c+	Drop Shadow Diseases		272
	5	Drop Squad		104
★★	7a	Drowning in Adrenaline		201
★★	7b+	Drowning Pool, The		49
	3+	Duck L'Orange	119	123
★	3+	Duckless in Torbay		123
	6b+	Dulux Start, The		115
★★	6b	Dynamite		172
★	4	Eastern Girdle		194
	5	Edge of Beyond		80
★	4	Edge of the Jungle		110
★	4+	Eight Ball		107
★	7a	Eight Inches		83
★★★	7c	Ejector Seat		264
★★	7c	El Diablo Suelto		64
★★★	7b+	El Guapo		64
★	6b+	El Lobo		178
★★	6a+	Electrical Storm		291
★	6b+	End of the Land		80
★★	6a+	Enter the Dragon		244
★	7a	Escobar		64
★	6b	ET v Predator		281
★★	5+	Eternal Flame		266
	6c	Eternal Golden Braid, The		153
★	3	Etna		92
★	7a+	Excession		159
	6a+	Extras		175
★★★	6b+	Exultation		160
★	6c	F.Y.B.		45
★	7b	Faceache		76
★★	6c	Falling into Fish		228
★★	7a+	Fancy Claps		177
★	6b+	Farewell Jim		223
	4+	Farewell Mrs L		245
★	7a	Faro Fawcett Finish		227
★	6b	Faroway Finish		229
	6b	Fashion Victims		220
★	6b+	Fat Crab, The		280
★★★	6b	Fathoms	37	47
★	7a	Fear of Flying		247
★	5+	February Wall		239
★★	6b	Feersum Endjin		159
★★	6c	Feist Queen	269	269
★	6a	Fifteen Minutes to Fame		93
★★	7b+	Fine Art of Surfacing, The		157
★★★	7a	Fireball XL5		180
★★	6b	Firestarter Traverse		242
★★★	6c	First Blood		230
★★	6a	First Impressions		265
★	6c	Fish Lip		300
★★★	7b	Fish Sphincters		300
★	6c	Fisheries of Fury		244
★★★	6b+	Fishing Line		229
★★★	6b	Fishing Line, The		300
★	6a	Five Star Traverse Part I		120
★	5+	Five Star Traverse Part II		120
★	6a	Flashing Eyebrows	149	161
★	6c	Flipper Force		88
	6b+	Flotsam		176
★	7a	Fooled by a Smile		169
★★	7b+	For Whom the Swell Tolls		47
★	6a	Fortuna		275
★	6a+	Foxy Chicks		85
★	7a+	Fraser's Edge, The		300
★	6a+	Freddy the Frog Hits Torquay		121
★★★	6c	Freeborn Man	2, 5	49
★	6c	French Kiss		122
	7b	From Dusk 'Till Dawn		276
★	6c+	Funhouse, The		246
	7a	Funtlappen		272
★	6b+	Furious Pig		48
	6b	G-String		90
★	6b+	Galileo's Balls		165
★	6b+	Ganges, The		199
★	7b	Gateaux Thief		160
★★★	7b+	Gates of Greyskull, The	54	63
	6b	Gav's Long Link-up		77
	6b+	Gemzone		41
	6b	Genoveses		273
★★	7a	Giant Farts		153
★	5	Gid's Landing		51
★	6b	Gill, The		104
★★	6c	Giraffes		184
★	7a+	Glassy		300
★★	7a	Gluteus Maximus		108
★	5	Goblets		158
★	6a	Godliness		160
★	6a+	Godzuki		83
	7b+	Golden Nase		273
	7b+	Goldie Hawn		273
★	4+	Gone in Twenty Seconds		221
★★	6c+	Gothic		112
	6a	Gourmet Shit Traverse		88
	7b+	Granaten-Einstiez		273
★★	6b+	Great Dane / Ringolino		157
★★	7a	Great Shark Hunt, The		48
★★	6c	Green Grotto Traverse		100
★	6a+	Groove Rider		281
★★	6c	Groovy Gang, The		110
★	7a	Gryposaurus		43
★	6c	Gyonyuru		93
	6c	Gyttja		93
★★	7c+	Hair Bear		264
★	5	Hairy Clamber		63
★★	6c	Hands Off Whizzy		104
★	6b	Harvey's Jaw		291
★	6c	Hash Brown	155	157
★★	5	Hate		187
	6a	Hazelnut Surprise		222
★★	6a+	Heaven Scent		230
★	6c+	Heckler, The		160
★	6c	Heimlich Manoeuvre		164
★	7a	Hell and High Water		195
	7a+	Herbert the Turbot		63
	6c+	Hercules		275
★	6b+	Here Comes the Hizbollah		45
★★	7b+	Herman Borg's Basic Pulley Slippage		49
★★★	7a+	Hidden Beach Traverse		248
★	6b	High Tide Running		105
★	6a	Higher than the Sun		281
★	7b+	Hip Hop		263
★	4+	Hippy		152
	7?	Hipster Extension		239
★	6c	Hipster, The	237	239
★	6b+	Hole in One		166
★★★	7a+	Hole in the Wall		197
	6a	Holes, The		106
★★	6b	Holes, The		246
	7b+	Homosexual		274
★	6c+	Honorary Society of Self-Publicising Water Rats		63
★★	6a+	Honour Bright		131
★★	6c	Honour Bright Arete		131
★★	6b	Hooked Like No Fish Before Me		
★★	7b+	Hornier than Thou		67
★★★	7a	Horny Lil' Devil	65	67
★★★	6c	Hot Lips		220
	6b	How About It?		223
★	7b	Howling, The		40
	7a+	Huge Reaches		86
★	6a+	Humanize		110
★	7b	Hump, The		52
★	6a+	Hung, Swung and Zawned Out		75
★	6c+	Hymenopteran Hippopotamus		111
★★★	6c+	Hyperspace		180
★	7a	Hysoscella Sideways		115
★	6b	I Love Eszter		66
★★	7b	I Ran the Bath		209
★	6a+	Icthyosaurus		42
★★	7b	Iguanodon		263
★	6a	Ilvico		219
★★	7b+	Imp of the Perverse		67
	4+	In the Flesh		217
★★	8a	In The Night, Every Cat Is Black		264
★	6c	In Too Deep		47
★	6b	Inimitable Toenails		105
★★★	7b	Instant Black		156
★	6a	Intimate Dancing		90
★	7b	Into the Fire		106
★★★	6c+	Iron Pirate		169
★★	7b	Isostacy		172
★	6b	Italian Job, The		262
★★★	6a	Ixtlan		86
★	6b	Jack Sprat		195
★	6a+	Jam-Master		125
★	6a+	Jargoniser		41
★★★	8a	Jaws	170	167
★	6a+	Jazz		249
★	7a	Jean Reno		145
★★	7b	Jehovah Kill		122
★	6b+	Jellied		49
★	5+	Jellystone	249	245
★	5+	Jessica Alba		141
★	6a	Jetsam		176
★	6b+	Jeux Sans Frontiers		194
★	6c+	Jose Sandeles		110
★	6c+	Just for a Day		77
★★★	6c	Just Klingon		181
★	6b	Karma		86
	6a	Kelpie Poodle		169
★★	7c	Kill Bill 1		276
★★★	7c+	Kill Bill 2		276

Route Index

Stars	Grade	Route	Photo	Page
★	7b	Killa Gorilla		101
	6c+	Killer Loop		92
★★★	7c	King of the Swingers		91
	7b+	Klem's Erection		272
	7a+	Klem's Golden Shower		273
★★	6a+	Koh-i-Nor		141
	4	Krakatoa		92
	4+	Labyrinth Pinnacle Traverse		115
	6b+	Labyrinth Variation Start		115
	7?	'Ladies Only' Tunnel		221
★	5+	Lady Boys		281
	4+	Lady's Ladder	240	247
★★★	6b	Land of Milk and Honey		199
★	6a+	Last Duck to Bombay		123
★★	7b	Last Great Innocent		51
★★	5	Last Season's Loozas		64
★★★	7c+	Laughing Hygena, The		181
★	7b+	Law of the Jungle		91
★	7b	Laws Direct Start		61
★★★	6b+	Laws Traverse, The		61
	6c	Laying Everybody Low		223
	7a	Le Gashbomb		272
★★★	6b+	Lean Meat		195
★★	6b+	Leap of Faith		48
	8a+	Leistenmatz		272
★★★	6b	Lemoria		144
★	4	Lens, The	53	40
★	7c	Let's Give It		229
★★	7c+	Let's Have It!		263
★★	6b+	Lick of the Cat		84
★★	6a+	Life		177
★★	7a+	Linesman, The		229
★	6a+	Little Hard, The		85
★★	6c+	Little Mac Traverse		238
★★★	7a	Liverpool Lady		231
★★	7b+	Living on Air		158
★	6a+	Llama Roundabout		52
★★★	6c+	Lobster, The		264
★★	5	Loftgroover		114
★★	7b	Long Dong Village		122
★★	4+	Long Traverse, The		130
★	6b	Look, Before You Leap		106
★★★	7c+	Losing my Religion		132
★★	8a+	Loskot and Two Smoking...		264
★★	4+	Lost in Time		40
★★	6b+	Lost Locals, The		105
★★★	7a+	Lotta		230
★	6a	Love	185	187
★	7a?	Love Action		169
★	6c+	Lower than Whale Shit		64
	6a+	Luc Besson		145
	6b+	Lucid		110
★★	6c	Lucretia, My Reflection		45
★	7a+	Lunge or Plunge		86
★	7a+	Luv-Groove-Dance-Party		121
★★	7a+	M.C. Navigator		114
★	6b	Mad About You		86
★	7a+	Mad Angus		184
★	6c	Mad Dogs and Englishwomen		223
★	5+	Mad Mei		153
★★	7a+	Mad World		187
★★	6a+	Magic Flute		183
★★	6a+	Magical Mystery Tour		100
★★	7c	Magnetic Gates		63
★★★	7b	Magnum		226
★	6a	Makin' Bacon		83
	8a+	Mamasita		276
★	6b+	Man in Black		112
★★	6b+	Manuka		199
	5+	Marçal Traverse, The		280
★	6b+	Marine Boy		83
★★	7a	Marine Life		231
★★★	7a+	Mariner's Graveyard		45
★★★	7c	Mark of the Beast	28	67
★★	6a+	Marvellous Maggs		41
	7b	Massive Amounts of Strength		86
★★★	7a+	Match of the Day		231
★	6b+	Matt Black		184
★	6a	Maypole, The		62
	6c+	Mecca		273
★	5+	Medic, The		172
★	6a	Memory Lane		83
★	7a+	Metrosexual		274
★	7b	Microdot		262
	6a+	Midget Gem		131
★★	7a	Might of the Stalactite, The		273
★	6c	Mike's Free Willy		84
	6a	Millie		247
★★	7a+	Mirthmaid		77
★	6b+	Miss Layton		250
★★	6a	Monkey Business		201
★★	7a+	Morning Glory		269
★★	6b+	Mortal Combat		281
★★★	6c	Mother Night		181
★	6b	Mouse Claws		153
★★	6c+	Mowgli		197
	4+	Mr. Fantastic		45
★★	7b+	Mucho Gusto!		45
★	7b	Muppet Splash		153
★★	6b+	Musketeer		169
★	6b	Musharagi Tree		49
	5	N'Butabit		160
★★★	7c+	Never Kneel to Skeletor		63
★	7a	Newton Traverse!, The		165
★	6b+	Nice but Dim		183
★	6b+	Night Shift		144
★	7c	Nightmirth		77
★	6a+	Nobody's Hero		172
★	5+	Nor' Wind Blows		107
★	6b	Not Now, Kato!		187
★★★	6c+	Not Waving, Drowning		300
★	7b	Nude Boy Slim		222
★	6b+	Numb Bum/Turkish Delight		52
	8a+	O-Ren Lssii		276
★	6a+	Oasis in Flames		243
★★★	6c	Octopuss Weed	19	92
★	5	Odyssey, The		281
★	6a+	Offshore Drift		176
	3+	Old Dog, New Tricks		245
★★★	6c+	Old Jock's Tunnel		143
	4+	Old Peculiar		143
	6a	Old Thumper		143
★★	7b+	Old Timer's Club		64
★	7b+	Once a Dogger	129	130
★	6c	One Cool Vibe		91
★★	7b	One Life		76
★★	7a	One-Eyed Man, The	151	178
★	7b+	Ong-Bak	137	145
	6b+	Ooh Lovely!		89
★	7b	Order of the Bath, The		209
	7a+	Out of Yer Shell		89
★★★	6c	Overexposed		158
★	7a+	Oviraptor		43
	6b+	Owen Meany		152
★★★	6b+	Oz Wall Traverse		110
★	6c	Paraphilias		75
★	4	Patch's Shorts		173
★	7a+	Peaked Tor Cove Traverse		120
★	6a+	Penny Lane		83
★	6b	Pepper Man, The		156
★	6a+	Perfect Pitch		177
★	6c	Piano, The		183
★★★	6b	Pician Passage		300
★	7a	Pick n' Mix		227
★	6a+	Pigeon Street		115
★★	6b+	Pink Bus		105
	4+	Pink Flamingos		223
★★★	7a	Pink Roadster		111
★	6a	Pirates of the Black Atlantic		85
★	5+	Planktonitis		174
	6b+	Please Rub Salt into my Wounds	188	201
★★	4	Plimsoll Line Traverse	127	126
★★	6b	Poet's Eye		245
★	6c	Pony, The		40
	6a+	Popacatapetl		93
★★	7a	Portugalz		228
★	6c	Portuge'E'zergood	225	230
	6a+	Portugeezers		228
	6a+	Previous Top-Rope Problem		92
★	5	Private Dancer		152
★★★	7b+	Privateer		46
★	7a	Prow, The		220
★	6a+	Psychoman		84
★	6b	Public Enema No.1		269
★★★	8a	Pump up the Beast		67
★★	7a+	Pump Will Tear Us Apart, The		45
★	7a+	Pumping Dancefloor Energy		121
★	6c+	Puzzle, The		50
★	6c+	Queen of Cool		219
★	6a+	Rags to Riches		239
★★★	7a+	Rainbow Bridge	Cover, 94, 109	102
★★★	6c	Rainbow Scoop		104
	7b+	Ralph Kaiser's Nehe Kleider's		273
★★	6a	Rangoon	139	141
★	6a	Rapture of the Deep		80
	6a	Rat Dog		280
	6b	Raticida		276
★★	6c	Raw Meat		195
★	7a+	Red Bully		49
★	5	Red Crane Traverse, The		81
	6a	Red Crane Wall		81
★	7a	Red Meat		195
★★★	7a	Reef Walker		173
★	6b+	Reel 'Em In		85
	6a+	Relativity		81
★★	7c	Renaissance		167
★★	6a+	Reso's Nose		174
★★	6b+	Restraint of Beasts		173
★★	7a	Rhythm of the Night		114
★★	6a+	Rich Tea Biscuits		238
★★★	7a+	Riding to Babylon		60
★★	8a+	Right Here, Right Now		264
★	6a+	Ring of Bright Water		201
★★★	7c	River Rage		300
★★	7a+	Roaring Forties		195
	6a	Robertson's Jar		90
★	6a	Rock Lobster		222

Route Index 319

Stars	Grade	Route	Photo	Page
★★	7b	Rocket USA	29	41
★	6a	Romeo & Juliet		222
★★	7c+	Ronatron		265
★	4	Rosen Traverse		143
★	6a	Route 66		64
★★★	6a+	Russian Roulette		86
★★	7b	Rusty Dog		187
★	7a+	Sad Young Biscuits		76
★★★	8a	San Simeon		157
★	7b	Sapphire		246
★★	6c+	Sardine Liberation Front		60
★	6b	Scarlett Tiger		221
★★	6b+	Scoop, The		183
★	7a	Scotch on the Rocks		172
★	6a+	Scotty Dog Traverse, The		51
	?	Sea Cat Direct Project		194
	?	Sea Cave Traverse		106
★	7a	Sea Devil		263
★	6a+	Sea Leg		172
★★	6c	Sea of Holes		230
	9a?	Secret Lagoon Traverse		243
★	6b	Seismosaurus		42
★★	6c	Semi-skimmed		199
★	5+	Sex-pack on the Beach		175
★★	7a	Shady Lane		115
★★★	7a	Shaft of Light	232	243
★★★	7c+	Shere Khan	196	197
★★★	7b+	Shield, The		159
	6b+	Shotgun, The		167
★	6a+	Show Goes On		105
★	6a	Shrek		269
★	6c+	Shrek Extension		269
★	7b	Silent Man, The		238
★★	7b	Sister of Night		77
★	7a	Sixty's Silver Surfer		272
★	6c+	Skeleton Surfers		92
	6b	Skelis		158
★★	6c+	Skin Trade, The		76
★	6a	Slap ya' Dromedary		52
★	5+	Sleek Pussy		246
★★★	5	Slice of Heaven	255	266
★	6c	Sliding Down the Banister		67
★	6a+	Smile Please!		90
★	6a+	Smile, The	215	220
★★★	6b	Smiley's People		220
★	6b+	Snake Pass		153
	6b+	Snap, Crackle and Plop		49
★★★	8b	Snatch		275
★	6a	Snobs		178
★★★	6c	Soap on a Rope		209
	7c	Solecito		274
★	4	Something Ducky		123
★	5	Soul to Soul		114
	6b+	Southern Rain		165
★	6b	Speleologist, The		227
★★	7b	Spitting Bullets	78	77
★	6a	Spittle and Spume		90
★	6b+	Splashdown		162
★★	6b+	Splendid Isolation		77
★★	7a	Stab in the Dark		218
★★	6b	Stage Divin'		66
★	6b	Stairs, The		187
★	5	Stegasaurus		42
	7c?	Stennis Traverse Extension		159
★	6c+	Stennis Traverse, The		159
★	6c	Sticky Vicky		250
★★	7a	Stingray		125
★	6a+	Stir Crazy		50
	6b	Stirling Bomber		195
★	6b+	Stone, The		141
★★★	7a	Strange Love		169
★★	6c	Strangeness		177
★★★	7b+	Strangers In Paradise		275
★★★	4	Street Serenade		223
★★	6a+	Striking it Rich		238
	6b	Stripper Robertson		105
★	6a	Stripper, The		217
	5	Student Grant		152
★★	6c	Su Doku		144
★	6c+	Submerged Man, The		231
★	7c	Sucked Away with the Scum		209
★★	7a+	Sugar Daddy		81
★	3+	Summer's Dying Days		40
★★	8a+	Sunshine and Shadow		263
★	7c	Super Bock	213	219
★	6a+	Super Galactic Hammy		157
★★	6c	Supersaurus		43
★★★	7a+	Superwoman		265
★	6c+	Surface Tension		85
★★★	7a	Surface Tension		300
★	7a	Surfer Dead		263
★★	7b	Surfing Bird		262
★	6c+	Surfing in the Bar		263
★	6c	Surrealist, The		165
★★★	7c	Sushi		195
★★	6b	Sweet Surrender		51
★	6c	Swing Both Ways		262
★★★	7b	Swingin' Nineties		91
★	6a	Swirling Pool		80
★★★	7a+	Swordfish Trombones		49
★	6c+	T-Minus Ten		115
★★	6c	Tarka	191	201
★	4+	Temporary Lifestyle		85
★★	7a+	Tentacle Master		92
★	4+	Terminal Slab		108
★★	6b+	Terminal Twelve		108
★	6b+	Terminal Viscosity		108
★★	7a+	Terrapigeon		153
★	6a+	That's Rich		239
★★	6b+	The Art of Reinvention		238
★	7b+	Thieving Gypsy		66
★★	6c	This is the Life		91
★★	6c	This Nation's Saving Grace		183
★	7a	Thoughtcrime		165
★	6b+	Three-legged Tufa		248
★★	7b	Tiger Tiger	181	181
★★	6a	Time		281
★	7a	Toffee Nose		178
★	6b+	Tombstonin'		80
★	6c+	Too Funky (For Me)		83
★★★	7a	Topology		177
★	7a	Tower of Power		273
★	6a+	Tramariglio Traverse		291
	7b	Transexual		274
★★★	7a	Transversal		272
	5	Trashy's Arete		61
★	6b	Trashy's Traverse		83
★★	6b+	Traverse Tea		157
★★	7b	Trench Warfare		227
★★	6b+	Triceratops		43
★	5	Troubled Waters	34	49
★★	6a	Trouser Snake		246
★★	6c+	Troy Tempest		124
★★	4+	True Blue	146	153
★★★	6c+	True Grit		227
★	6c+	Tsunami		48
★★	6c	Tulula		222
★	5	Twisting by the Pool		245
★★★	6c	Ultrasaurus		43
★★	7c	Unconscious		181
	6b+	Uncovered Rock		165
★★★	7b	Under-Bare		90
★★	7b+	Under-Bare Extension		90
★	6c+	Underwater Love		165
★	7a+	Until the End of Man		75
★	5	Upper East Girdle		194
★	6a	Vamos		172
★★★	7a+	Vanishing, The		49
★★★	6c	Variation / The Wave		107
★★	6b	Velcro Twins, The		246
★	6c+	Voyage of the Parrot Fish		153
★★★	6a	Voyage, The		266
★★	7c	Waiting for Charlie		132
★	6b+	Walking Dude, The		61
	6a	Wall of Squares		81
★★	7b	War Without Tears		194
★	6b	Warspite in Brief		104
	6c+	Watch for the Jellies		275
★	5	Watchtower Traverse, The		124
★★	7a+	Water Wings	27, 71	89
★★	7b+	Waterland		187
★	6c+	Watting Yer Ouzel		111
★★	7a	Wavewalker		112
★★	3+	Way out!		161
★	6b+	Welcome to Jamrock		153
★	6b+	Western Girdle		195
★★	6c	Wet Pussy		194
★	7a+	Wet T-Shirt Contest		167
★★	7c	Whiplash		265
★	6c+	Whistle Blower, The		218
★★★	7a+	White Dove		217
★★	6c	White Elephant		242
★	6b+	White Fang		178
★	5+	White Flag		51
★	7a	White Meat		104
★★	5+	White Noise		266
★	6a+	White Pocket Arete		221
★★★	7a+	White Rave		45
★	7a	White Rhino Tea		111
★	6b	White Rino		242
★	7a	White Teeth		220
★	6c	Whoomze Got der Keys to me Beema		111
★	6a	Wilma		244
★★	7b	Window of Opportunity		66
★★★	8b	Windows / Adrenochrome		67
★	7b	Wishing Well, The		209
★★★	8a	Wizard, The	28	186
	4	Woof Woof Splash		245
★★	6c+	World of Bonobos	163	164
★	6c	Wreck of the Hesperus		176
	6c+	Wreck of the Zephyr		153
★	7a+	X Factor		180
★	6b+	Yokel Hero		104
★	6a+	You and Me, Babe		222
★	7b	Z Cars		67
★	6a+	Zircon		41
★★	7a+	Zoony		181

General Index

Acknowledgments 31
Advertiser 30
Armchair Landing 22
Australia **295**
  Crafty's Bay 298
  Tasmania 302
Barnacle Line. 22
Bench Seat 18, 22
Boats 11, 22
Boots 20
Chalk Bag 18, 20
Chalking Stick 22
Contents 3
Cornwall **135**
  Nare Head 142
  The Lizard 138
Costa Blanca **232**
  Cala del Moraig . . . 240
  Cala Ximo 250
  Isla del Descobridor 249
  Moraira 236
Currents. 10
Devon **95**
  Babbacombe Area . 128
  Berry Head 98
  Berry Head Quarry . 112
  London Bridge Area 118
  Rainbow Bridge . . . 102
  The Old Redoubt . . 100
  Torquay. 116
Dry-bag 20, 22
Early Breakfast Venue. 22
Evolution of DWS 28
Exit 22
Flying Fish 24
Gear 18
Glossary 22
Grades. 14
Guidebook 6
High Water Mark 22
Introduction 4
Kiddy Boat. 11, 22
Lulworth **55**
  Durdle Door 60
  Stair Hole 66

Mallorca **252**
  Cala Barques 270
  Cala Marçal. 278
  Cova del Diablo . . 258
Pembroke **147**
  Barrel Zawn 152
  Broadhaven Beach. 166
  Lydstep Area 171
  Penally 182
  Range East 154
  Shrinkle Haven 168
Portland **68**
  Cave Hole 82
  Lighthouse Area . . . 79
  White Hole. 74
Portugal **211**
  Ingrina. 216
  Ponta Garcia. 224
Reefs 10
Rest of Europe **282**
  Bulgaria 288
  Channel Islands . . . 286
  Crete 289
  Croatia 288
  France. 287
  Ireland West Coast . 286
  Italy 286
  Kalymnos 288
  Madrid Granite . . . 286
  Malta 288
  North Spain. 286
  Sardinia. 290
  Sicily 286
  Turkey 289
Rest of the UK **202**
  Atlantic Coast 207
  South Coast 206
  Lundy 207
  North Pembroke . . . 207
  North Wales 207
  Scilly Isles. 206
  Scotland 207
  Vivian Quarry 208

Rest of the World . . . **306**
  Bermuda. 312
  Burma/Myanmar . . . 310
  Cambodia 310
  Canada 313
  China. 310
  Colombia. 314
  Japan 314
  Madagascar 314
  Oman 314
  Thailand 309
  Ukraine 314
  USA 313
  Vietnam 310
Rough Seas. 10
Route Index 316
'S' Grades 14, 22
Safety 10
Scotland **189**
  Baby Taipan Wall . . 198
  Craig Stirling 192
  Erraid 200
  The Red Tower . . . 196
Splashdowns 12
Sport Grades 14
Swanage **35**
  Conner Cove. 46
  Dancing Ledge 44
  Subluminal 50
Swimming 11
Symbol and Topo Key . 32
Tactics 18
Tape Harness 18, 22
Tides 16
Topo Key 32
Water Temperature . . . 10
Web Sites 6
Wet Suits 18